The Bible Speaks Today

Series editors: Alec Motyer (OT)
John Stott (NT)
Derek Tidball (Bible Themes)

The Message of
Love

The Message of Love

Love

The only thing that counts

Patrick Mitchel

Senior Lecturer at the
Irish Bible Institute, Dublin

Inter-Varsity Press

INTER-VARSITY PRESS
36 Causton Street, London SW1P 4ST, England
Email: ivp@ivpbooks.com
Website: www.ivpbooks.com

First published 2019

British Library Cataloguing-in-Publication Data
A catalogue record for this book is available from the British Library.

ISBN: 978–1–78359–591–4
eBook ISBN: 978–1–78359–592–1

Set in Stempel Garamond
Typeset in Great Britain by CRB Associates, Potterhanworth, Lincolnshire

*Inter-Varsity Press publishes Christian books that are true to the Bible and that
communicate the gospel, develop discipleship and strengthen the church for its
mission in the world.*

*IVP originated within the Inter-Varsity Fellowship, now the Universities and
Colleges Christian Fellowship, a student movement connecting Christian Unions
in universities and colleges throughout Great Britain, and a member movement
of the International Fellowship of Evangelical Students. Website: www.uccf.org.uk.
That historic association is maintained, and all senior IVP staff and committee
members subscribe to the UCCF Basis of Faith.*

For Tim and Ruth
Agapētoi

Contents

BST The Bible Speaks Today

GENERAL PREFACE

THE BIBLE SPEAKS TODAY describes three series of expositions, based on the books of the Old and New Testaments, and on Bible themes that run through the whole of Scripture. Each series is characterized by a threefold ideal:

- to expound the biblical text with accuracy
- to relate it to contemporary life, and
- to be readable.

These books are, therefore, not 'commentaries', for the commentary seeks rather to elucidate the text than to apply it, and tends to be a work rather of reference than of literature. Nor, on the other hand, do they contain the kinds of 'sermons' that attempt to be contemporary and readable without taking Scripture seriously enough. The contributors to The Bible Speaks Today series are all united in their convictions that God still speaks through what he has spoken, and that nothing is more necessary for the life, health and growth of Christians than that they should hear what the Spirit is saying to them through his ancient – yet ever modern – Word.

ALEC MOTYER
JOHN STOTT
DEREK TIDBALL
Series editors

Author's preface

Love requires relationship to exist and the same can be said of this book. It is a delight to write this preface, not only because of a satisfying sense of closure but, more importantly, because it is an opportunity to express my appreciation to many people without whom *The Message of Love* would simply not be.

It was in conversation with Derek Tidball some time ago that a seed was planted that eventually sprouted and grew into this book. Derek was my PhD supervisor and it has been a joy to work with him again. Thanks too to Phil Duce at Inter-Varsity Press for his experience, patience and always constructive suggestions for improvements. With two such good editors, this book is a good deal better than it would otherwise have been. At the copy-editing stage Eldo Barkhuizen did an outstanding job in knocking the manuscript into shape. Any errors, incoherence and waffle are solely my responsibility.

It can be a cliché to say, but I feel truly honoured to join the list of authors who have contributed to the BST series over the decades, not least John Stott, a particular hero of mine. As for countless others, its volumes have been hugely helpful in my own life.

I must mention some other people who have had particularly significant parts to play. To Grace Campbell my reader and colleague, thank you for your unwaning enthusiasm from day one combined with the ability to say critical things while living up to your name. Your insightful chapter by chapter feedback has meant more than you can know.

Who else but Warren Nelson could combine a love of the Bible, theological and linguistic expertise and mischievous humour to send back over twenty pages of handwritten notes on the draft manuscript that made me laugh out loud again and again while reading them? Many years ago it was Warren who first invited me to teach theology in a college setting. I am indebted to him in more ways than one.

Speaking of college, at the Irish Bible Institute in Dublin it is a privilege to work with colleagues who are also friends. It is special to be part of a team that cover for each other; to be prayed for and encouraged to write. Thank you to Steven, Liz, Sarah, Louise, Jonathan, Becky, Joan, Paul, Anna, Jacob, Ruth and Mimi and our adjunct teachers for your partnership in the gospel. I am grateful too to the Board who grant study weeks and value the importance of professional development and writing. But it is the students for whom a college exists. The theme of love has crept into a surprisingly wide variety of classes, so thank you both for being experimented on and for many of you who have been excited about the book and, in a reversal of roles, asking when the assignment will be finished!

Few have seen more clearly than Scot McKnight the importance of love within the life and mission of the church. His friendship and interest in the project from the outset has therefore been particularly significant. I am also deeply grateful to Craig Blomberg and Ben Witherington, scholars whose quality and quantity of work is really quite ridiculous, for generously commenting on the finished manuscript.

Much is said in this book about the church as a community of love and I am glad to report that it is not a fictional ideal. There are too many people in Maynooth to name, but thank you all for your prayers and interest – and for being guinea pigs for several sermons on love adapted from draft chapters. Our home group has a special gift for mocking one another (in love of course) – thank you Cathy, Denise, Jim and Breda, Kristen, Katie, Katherine, Ian, Martha and Jessica for your well-tuned pious claptrap radar and keeping things earthed. I am blessed to have friends like Andy and Lorraine, who throw a party to celebrate my pressing 'send'.

One theme that emerges from this book is that love needs constant attention and practice: a virtuous life of love flows from a Christ-formed character. So it is my very good fortune to be married to Ines, who demonstrates such love every day. She, more than anyone, has enabled this book to be written, not only in freeing me to disappear during weekends, evenings and holidays but in showing me what love is. To have someone orientated to your good without strings attached is a liberating and humbling thing for which I am indebted beyond measure. And she is a sharp theologian and editor as well.

Special gratitude has to be passed on to my other most favourite people in the world, Ciara and Catriona, for being massively and rightly unimpressed by all their father's talk of love. Although they know I am a bumbling amateur who fails most of the time they love me anyway.

This book is dedicated to my oldest and closest friend, Tim and his lovely wife Ruth, who is far too good for him. During the writing of this book they have had to walk a path no one would choose, but they have done so with faith and love. No one said faith working itself out in love is easy but they, more than anyone I have met, know it really is the only thing that counts.

Perhaps there was no BST volume on love because it is an act of either hubris or foolishness to write about such a magnificent yet daunting theme! While this book cannot begin to do it justice, my hope is that it will be helpful to preachers, teachers and anyone interested to grapple seriously with how the Bible Speaks Today on love. More personally, as I finish this final paragraph I am more convinced than ever of how love is both God's motive in redemption and his agenda for his people. I pray that as you read this book you will be inspired to love him more deeply and love your neighbour as yourself. It is in doing so that the Christian faith will be seen for what it truly is meant to be – a corporate life of human flourishing in the world that points to a more glorious life to come.

Patrick Mitchel

Abbreviations

1QS	Qumran Scrolls 1: Manual of Discipline
AOTC	Apollos Old Testament Commentary
ATJ	*Ashland Theological Journal*
AV	Authorized (King James) Version
BECNT	Baker Exegetical Commentary on the New Testament
BNTC	Black's New Testament Commentaries
BST	The Bible Speaks Today
BTNT	Biblical Theology of the New Testament
CC	*Christian Century*
ESVUK	English Standard Version: Anglicized
EvQ	*Evangelical Quarterly*
ICC	International Critical Commentary
JBL	*Journal of Biblical Literature*
JETS	*Journal of the Evangelical Theological Society*
lit.	literally
LXX	Septuagint: the Old Testament in Greek, third century BC
MT	Masoretic Text
NAC	New American Commentary
NCCS	New Covenant Commentary Series
NIBC	New International Biblical Commentary
NICNT	New International Commentary on the New Testament
NICOT	New International Commentary on the Old Testament
NIDNTT	*New International Dictionary of New Testament Theology*, ed. Colin Brown, 3 vols. (Grand Rapids: Zondervan, 1981)
NIGNTC	New International Greek New Testament Commentary
NIVAC	The NIV Application Commentary

NIVUK	New International Version: Anglicized (2011)
NRSVA	New Revised Standard Version: Anglicized (1995)
NT	New Testament
NTCS	New Testament Commentary Series
NTE	New Testament for Everyone
OT	Old Testament
OTT	Old Testament Theology
PCNT	Paideia Commentaries on the New Testament
PNTC	Pillar New Testament Commentary
QRT	*Quaker Religious Thought*
REB	Revised English Bible
SBL	Society of Biblical Literature
SGBC	Story of God Bible Commentary
STR	*Sewanee Theological Review*
TynB	*Tyndale Bulletin*
WBC	Word Biblical Commentary
ZECNT	Zondervan Exegetical Commentary on the New Testament

Select bibliography

Arnold, Clinton E., *Ephesians*, ZECNT (Grand Rapids: Zondervan, 2010).

Augustine, *The City of God*, tr. Henry Bettenson (London: Pelican, 1972).

———, *Confessions*, tr. Henry Chadwick (Oxford: Oxford University Press, 1992).

Bailey, Kenneth E., *Paul Through Mediterranean Eyes: Cultural Studies in 1 Corinthians* (London: SPCK, 2011).

———, *Poet and Peasant & Through Peasant Eyes: A Literary-Cultural Approach to the Parables in Luke*, combined edn (Grand Rapids: Eerdmans, 1983).

Barclay, John, *Paul and the Gift* (Grand Rapids: Eerdmans, 2015).

———, *Pauline Churches and Diaspora Jews* (Grand Rapids: Eerdmans, 2016; first published in Tübingen by Mohr Siebeck, 2011).

Barth, Karl, *The Word of God and the Word of Man*, tr. Douglas Horton (London: Hodder & Stoughton, 1928).

Bartholomew, Craig, and Thorsten Moritz, *Christ and Consumerism: A Critical Analysis of the Spirit of the Age* (Carlisle: Paternoster, 2000).

Bauckham, Richard, 'Monotheism and Christology in the Gospel of John', in Richard. N. Longenecker (ed.), *Contours of Christology in the New Testament* (Grand Rapids: Eerdmans, 2005), pp. 148–166.

Beasley-Murray, George R., *John* WBC, vol. 36 (Waco: Word, 1987).

Beck, Ulrich, and Elisabeth Beck-Gernsheim, *The Normal Chaos of Love*, tr. Mark Ritter and Jane Wiebel (Cambridge: Polity, 1995).

Beilby, James K., and Paul R. Eddy (eds.), *Justification: Five Views* (London: SPCK, 2012).

Bell, Daniel M., *Divinations: Theopolitics in an Age of Terror* (Eugene: Cascade, 2017).

————, *The Economy of Desire: Christianity and Capitalism in a Postmodern World* (Grand Rapids: Baker Academic, 2012).

Berkman J., and M Cartwright, (eds.), *Stanley Hauerwas: The Hauerwas Reader* (Durham, N.C.: Duke University Press, 2001).

Bird, Michael, *Romans*, SGBC (Grand Rapids: Zondervan, 2016).

Block, Peter, Walter Brueggemann and John McKnight, *An Other Kingdom: Departing the Consumer Culture* (Hoboken: Wiley, 2016).

Blomberg, Craig R., *Matthew*, NAC, vol. 22 (Nashville: Broadman, 1992).

————, *Neither Poverty Nor Riches: A Biblical Theology of Possessions* (Leicester: Apollos, 1999).

Bock, Darrell, *Luke 1:1–9:50*, BECNT (Grand Rapids: Baker Academic, 1994).

————, *Recovering the Real Lost Gospel: Reclaiming the Gospel as Good News* (Nashville: B&H, 2010).

————, *A Theology of Luke and Acts: God's Promised Program, Realized for All Nations*, BTNT (Grand Rapids: Zondervan, 2012).

Bonhoeffer, Dietrich, *The Cost of Discipleship* (New York: Simon & Schuster, 1995 [1937]).

Bonk, Jonathan, *Missions and Money: Affluence as a Missionary Problem Revisited*, American Society of Missiology Series 15 (Maryknoll: Orbis, 2006).

Bowler, Kate, *Blessed: A History of the American Prosperity Gospel* (Oxford: Oxford University Press, 2013).

Bray, Gerald, *God Is Love: A Biblical and Systematic Theology* (Wheaton: Crossway, 2012).

Brown, Colin (ed.), *NIDNTT*, vol. 2. (Grand Rapids: Zondervan, 1981).

Brown, Peter, *The Body and Society: Men, Women and Sexual Renunciation in Early Christianity* (London: Faber & Faber, 1989).

Brown, Raymond, *The Message of Deuteronomy*, BST (Leicester: Inter-Varsity Press, 1993).

Bruce, F. F., *The Epistles of John* (Grand Rapids: Eerdmans, 1970).

Brueggemann, Walter, *Money and Possessions* (Louisville: Westminster John Knox, 2016).

Brunner, Emil, *Dogmatics*, vol. 1: *The Christian Doctrine of God*, tr. Olive Wyon (London: Lutterworth, 1949).

Burge, Gary M., *John*, NIVAC (Grand Rapids: Zondervan, 2000).

Bushur, James G., *Irenaeus of Lyons and the Mosaic of Christ: Preaching Scripture in the Era of Martyrdom* (Abingdon: Routledge, 2017).

Carson, D. A., *The Difficult Doctrine of the Love of God* (Wheaton: Crossway; Leicester: Inter-Varsity Press, 2000).

Cavanaugh, William T., *Being Consumed: Economics and Christian Desire* (Grand Rapids: Eerdmans, 2008).

Christensen, Duane L., *Deuteronomy 1:1–21:9*, WBC, vol. 6A rev. (Nashville: Thomas Nelson, 2001).

Ciampa, Roy E. and Brian S. Rosner, *The First Letter to the Corinthians*, PNTC (Nottingham: Apollos, 2010).

Clark, Stephen B., *Men and Women in Christ: An Examination of the Roles of Men and Women in Light of Scripture and the Social Sciences* (Ann Arbor: Servant, 1980).

Cloud, Henry, and John Townsend, *Boundaries: When to Say Yes, When to Say No, to Take Control of Your Life* (Grand Rapids: Zondervan, 1992).

Cosgrove, C. H., 'A Woman's Unbound Hair in the Greco-Roman World, with Special Reference to the Story of the "Sinful Woman" in Luke 7:36–50', *JBL* 24.4 (2005), pp. 675–692.

Dennett, Daniel, *Breaking the Spell: Religion as a Natural Phenomenon* (New York: Penguin, 2006).

deSilva, David, *Honor, Patronage, Kinship & Purity: Unlocking New Testament Culture* (Downers Grove: IVP Academic, 2000).

Dodd, C. H., *The Epistle of Paul to the Romans*, 2nd edn (London: Collins, 1959).

Dunn, James D. G., *The Epistle to the Galatians*, BNTC (London: A&C Black, 1993).

Durham, John I., *Exodus*, WBC, vol. 3 (Waco: Word, 1987).

Dylan, Bob, 'The Disease of Conceit', *Oh Mercy* (Columbia Records: 1989).

Enns, Peter, *Exodus*, NIVAC (Grand Rapids: Zondervan, 2000).

Estes, Daniel J., *The Song of Songs*, AOTC, vol. 16 (Nottingham: Apollos, 2010).

Fee, Gordon, *1 and 2 Timothy, Titus*, NIBC (Peabody: Hendrickson; Carlisle: Paternoster, 1995).

———, 'The Cultural Context of Ephesians 5:18–6:9', *Priscilla Papers* 16.1 (winter 2002), pp. 3–8.

———, *The First Epistle to the Corinthians*, NICNT (Grand Rapids: Eerdmans, 1987).

———, *God's Empowering Presence: The Holy Spirit in the Letters of Paul* (Peabody: Hendrickson, 1994).

———, *Pauline Christology: An Exegetical-Theological Study* (Peabody: Hendrickson, 2007).

France, R. T., *The Gospel of Mark*, NIGTC (Carlisle: Paternoster, 2002).

———, *The Gospel of Matthew*, NICNT (Grand Rapids: Eerdmans, 2007).

———, *Matthew – Evangelist and Teacher* (Exeter: Paternoster, 1989).

Furnish, Victor, *The Love Command of the New Testament* (London: SCM, 1973).

Garland, David E., *1 Corinthians*, BECNT (Grand Rapids: Baker Academic, 2003).

Garrett, Duane, *Song of Songs*, WBC, vol. 23B (Nashville: Thomas Nelson, 2004).

Gifford, Paul, *African Christianity: Its Public Role* (London: Hurst, 1998).

Giles, Kevin, 'A Critique of the "Novel" Contemporary Interpretation of 1 Timothy 2:9–15 Given in the Book, *Women in the Church*. Part 1', *EvQ* 72.2 (2000), pp. 151–167.

Gledhill, Tom, *The Message of the Song of Songs: The Lyrics of Love*, BST (Leicester: Inter-Varsity Press, 1993).

Goldingay, John, *Biblical Theology: The God of the Christian Scriptures* (Downers Grove: IVP Academic, 2016).

———, *Israel's Faith*, OTT, vol. 2. (Downers Grove: InterVarsity Press, 2006).

———, *Israel's Life*, OTT, vol. 3. (Downers Grove: IVP Academic, 2009).

Gombis, Timothy G., 'Participation in the New Creation People of God in Christ by the Spirit', in Scot McKnight and Joe Modica (eds.), *The Apostle Paul and the Christian Life: Missional and Ecclesial Implications of the New Perspective* (Grand Rapids: Baker, 2016), pp. 103–124.

———, 'A Radically New Humanity: The Function of the *Haustafel* in Ephesians', *JETS* 48 (2005), pp. 317–330.

Gorman, Michael, *Inhabiting the Cruciform God: Kenosis, Justification, and Theosis in Paul's Narrative Soteriology* (Grand Rapids: Eerdmans, 2009).

Grant, Jonathan, *Divine Sex: A Compelling Vision for Christian Relationships in a Hypersexualized Age* (Grand Rapids: Baker, 2015).

Green, J. B., 'Death of Jesus', in J. B. Green, S. McKnight and I. H. Marshall (eds.), *Dictionary of Jesus and the Gospels* (Leicester: Inter-Varsity Press, 1992), pp. 146–163.

———, *The Gospel of Luke*, NICNT (Grand Rapids: Eerdmans, 1987).

Green, J. B., S. McKnight and I. H. Marshall (eds.), *Dictionary of Jesus and the Gospels* (Leicester: Inter-Varsity Press, 1992).

Hargaden, Kevin, *Theological Ethics in a Neoliberal Age: Confronting the Christian Problem with Wealth* (Eugene: Cascade, 2018).

Harris, Sam, *The Moral Landscape: How Science Can Determine Human Values* (New York: Free, 2011).

Hartmann, Laura, *The Christian Consumer: Living Faithfully in a Fragile World* (Oxford: Oxford University Press, 2011).

Hauerwas, Stanley, 'The End of War: Why Christian Realism Requires Nonviolence', <www.abc.net.au/religion/the-end-of-just-war-why-christian-realism-requires-nonviolence/10097052>, accessed 12 May 2019.

———, 'Faith Fires Back', <www.dukemagazine.duke.edu/article/faith-fires-back>, accessed 11 December 2017.

———, 'More or, a Taxonomy of Greed', in *Working with Words: On Learning to Speak Christian* (London: SCM, 2011), pp. 127–138.

———, *The Peaceable Kingdom: A Primer in Christian Ethics* (Notre Dame: University of Notre Dame Press, 1983).

———, 'Sex and Politics: Bertrand Russell and "Human Sexuality"', CC (19 April 1978), pp. 417–422.

Hauerwas, Stanley, and David Bourns, 'Marriage and the Family: An Open Dialogue Between Stanley Hauerwas and David Bourns', QRT 56.3 (January 1984), pp. 4–24.

Hays, Richard B., *The Moral Vision of the New Testament: Community, Cross, New Creation: A Contemporary Introduction to New Testament Ethics* (San Francisco: HarperSanFrancisco, 1996).

———, *Reading Backwards: Figural Christology and the Fourfold Gospel Witness* (London: SPCK, 2015).

Heil, John Paul, *Ephesians: Empowerment to Walk in Love for the Unity of All in Christ* (Atlanta: SBL, 2007).

Hick, John, 'Is Christianity the Only True Religion, or One Among Others?', <www.johnhick.org.uk/article2.html>, accessed 23 September 2016.

Hodge, Charles, *Commentary on the Epistle to the Ephesians* (Grand Rapids: Banner of Truth, 1964).

Hoehner, Harold W., *Ephesians: An Exegetical Commentary* (Grand Rapids: Baker, 2002).

Hoekema, David A., 'A Practical Christian Pacifism', CC (22 October 1986), pp. 917–919.

Holmes, Stephen, 'Late Modern Assumptions About Sexuality', in Thomas A. Noble, Sarah K. Whittle and Philip Johnston (eds.), *Marriage, Family and Relationships: Biblical, Doctrinal and Contemporary Perspectives* (London: Apollos, 2017), pp. 256–275.

Hurtado, Larry W., *A Destroyer of the Gods: Early Christian Distinctiveness in the Roman World* (Waco: Baylor, 2016).

———, *God in New Testament Theology* (Nashville: Abingdon, 2010).

———, *Mark*, NIBC (Carlisle: Paternoster; Peabody: Hendrickson, 1995).

Jeanrond, Werner G., *A Theology of Love* (London: T&T Clark, 2010).

Jenkins, Carrie, 'How a Hackneyed Romantic Ideal Is Used to Stigmatise Polyamory', *AEON Magazine*, <www.aeon.co/ideas/how-a-hackneyed-romantic-ideal-is-used-to-stigmatise-polyamory>, accessed 14 December 2018.

Jewett, R., *Romans: A Commentary*, Hermeneia (Minneapolis: Fortress, 2007).

Johnson, A. F., 'A Review of the Scholarly Debate on the Meaning of "Head" (*Kephale*) in Paul's Writings', *ATJ* (2009), pp. 35–57.

Johnston, Luke Timothy, *Letters to Paul's Delegates: 1 Timothy, 2 Timothy, Titus* (Harrisburg: Trinity Press International, 1996).

Keener, Craig S., *The Gospel of John: A Commentary*, vol. 2 (Peabody: Hendrickson, 2003).

———, *Paul, Women and Wives: Marriage and Women's Ministry in the Letters of Paul* (Peabody: Hendrickson, 1992).

———, *Romans*, NCCS (Eugene: Cascade, 2009).

Keller, Timothy, *Generous Justice: How God's Grace Makes Us Just* (London: Hodder & Stoughton, 2010).

Keller, Tim, with Kathy Keller, *The Meaning of Marriage: Facing the Complexities of Commitment with the Wisdom of God* (London: Hodder & Stoughton; New York: Dutton, 2011).

Kidner, Derek, *The Message of Hosea*, BST (Leicester: Inter-Varsity Press, 1981).

King, Don W., 'A Naked Tree: Joy Davidman's Love Poems to C. S. Lewis', *STR* 57.3 (2014), pp. 246–280.

———, *The Naked Tree: Love Sonnets to C. S. Lewis and Other Poems by Joy Davidman* (Grand Rapids: Eerdmans, 2015).

Köstenberger, Andreas J., *A Theology of John's Gospel and Letters*, BTNT (Grand Rapids: Zondervan, 2009).

Kruse, Colin G., *Paul's Letter to the Romans*, PNTC (Nottingham: Apollos; Grand Rapids: Eerdmans, 2012).

Lane, A. N. S., 'The Wrath of God as an Aspect of the Love of God', in Kevin J. Vanhoozer (ed.), *Nothing Greater, Nothing Better: Theological Essays on the Love of God* (Grand Rapids: Eerdmans, 2001), pp. 138–167.

Lane, William L., *The Gospel of Mark*, NICNT (Grand Rapids: Eerdmans, 1974).

Lausanne Movement, *The Cape Town Commitment: A Confession of Faith and a Call to Action* (n.p.: Lausanne Movement, 2011).

Levenson, Jon, *The Love of God: Divine Gift, Human Gratitude, and Mutual Faithfulness in Judaism* (Princeton: Princeton University Press, 2016).

Lewis, C. S., *The Four Loves* (London: Geoffrey Bles, 1960).

———, *A Grief Observed* (London: Faber & Faber, 1961).

———, *The Last Battle* (London: Puffin, 1964).

———, *Mere Christianity* (Glasgow: Fount, 1982).

———, *Surprised by Joy: The Shape of My Early Life* (New York: Harcourt, Brace, Jovanovich, 1966).

———, *The Weight of Glory and Other Addresses* (New York: HarperOne, 2001).

Liefeld, Walter L., *1 & 2 Timothy, Titus*, NIVAC (Grand Rapids: Zondervan, 1999).

Lincoln, Andrew T., *Ephesians*, WBC, vol. 42 (Dallas: Word, 1990).

Longenecker, Bruce W., 'Faith, Works and Worship: Torah Observance in Paul's Theological Perspective', in Scot McKnight and Joe Modica (eds.), *The Apostle Paul and the Christian Life: Missional and Ecclesial Implications of the New Perspective* (Grand Rapids: Baker, 2016), pp. 47–70.

———, *Remember the Poor: Paul, Poverty and the Greco-Roman World* (Grand Rapids: Eerdmans, 2010).

———, *The Triumph of Abraham's God: The Transformation of Identity in Galatians* (Edinburgh: T&T Clark, 1998).

——— (ed.), *Contours of Christology in the New Testament* (Grand Rapids: Eerdmans, 2005).

Longman III, Tremper, *The Song of Songs*, NICOT (Grand Rapids: Eerdmans, 2001).

McConville, J. G., *Deuteronomy*, AOTC (Leicester: Apollos, 2002).

McKnight, Scot, *Galatians*, NIVAC (Grand Rapids: Zondervan, 1995).

———, *The Jesus Creed: Loving God, Loving Others*, 10th anniversary edn (Brewster: Paraclete, 2014).

———, *Kingdom Conspiracy: Returning to the Radical Mission of the Local Church* (Grand Rapids: Brazos, 2014).

———, 'The New Perspective and the Christian Life: Ecclesial Life', in Scot McKnight and Joe Modica (eds.), *The Apostle Paul and the Christian Life: Missional and Ecclesial Implications of the New Perspective* (Grand Rapids: Baker, 2016), pp. 125–151.

McKnight, Scot, and Joe Modica (eds.), *The Apostle Paul and the Christian Life: Missional and Ecclesial Implications of the New Perspective* (Grand Rapids: Baker, 2016).

———, *Jesus Is Lord, Caesar Is Not: Evaluating Empire in New Testament Studies* (Downers Grove: IVP Academic, 2013).

Marshall, I. H., in collaboration with Philip H. Towner, *A Critical and Exegetical Commentary on the Pastoral Epistles*, ICC (Edinburgh: T&T Clark, 1999).

——, *The Epistles of John*, NICNT (Eerdmans: Grand Rapids, 1978).

——, *The Gospel of Luke*, NIGTC (Grand Rapids: Eerdmans, 1978).

——, 'Mutual Love and Submission in Marriage: Colossians 3:18–19 and Ephesians 5:21–33', in R. W. Pierce, R. M. Groothuis and G. D. Fee (eds.), *Discovering Biblical Equality: Complementarity Without Hierarchy* (Downers Grove: InterVarsity Press; Leicester: Apollos, 2005), pp. 186–204.

Matera, Frank, *Romans*, PCNT (Grand Rapids: Baker Academic, 2010).

May, Simon, *Love: A History* (London: Yale University Press, 2011).

——, 'Rethinking Our Fascination with Love', <www.yalebooksblog.co.uk/2011/04/27/author-article-by-simon-may-rethinking-our-fascination-with-love>, accessed 13 April 2017.

Millar, Vincent J., *Consuming Religion: Christian Faith and Practice in a Consumer Culture* (London: Continuum, 2003).

Mitchel, Patrick, 'The New Perspective and the Christian Life: *Solus Spiritus*', in Scot McKnight and Joe Modica (eds.), *The Apostle Paul and the Christian Life: Missional and Ecclesial Implications of the New Perspective* (Grand Rapids: Baker, 2016), pp. 71–102.

——, 'Sex, Truth and Tolerance: Some Theological Reflections on the Irish Civil Partnership Bill 2010 and Challenges Facing Christians in a Post-Christendom Culture', *EvQ* 84.2 (2012), pp. 155–173.

Moloney, Francis J., *Love in the Gospel of John: An Exegetical, Theological and Literary Study* (Grand Rapids: Baker Academic, 2012).

Moltmann, Jürgen, *The Crucified God: The Cross as the Foundation and Criticism of Christian Theology*, tr. R. A. Wilson and J. Bowden (London: SCM, 1974)

Morris, Leon, *Testaments of Love: A Study of Love in the Bible* (Grand Rapids: Eerdmans, 1981).

Niebuhr, H. Richard, *The Kingdom of God in America* (Middletown: Wesleyan University Press, 1988). First published by Harper & Row in 1937.

Nietzsche, Friedrich, *Beyond Good and Evil, Ecce Homo* and *On the Genealogy of Morals* in *The Basic Writings of Nietzsche*, tr. W. Kaufman (New York: Modern Library, 1967).

Noble, Thomas A., Sarah K. Whittle and Philip Johnston (eds.), *Marriage, Family and Relationships: Biblical, Doctrinal and Contemporary Perspectives* (London: Apollos, 2017).

Nolland, John, *Luke 9:21–18:34*, WBC, vol. 35b (Dallas: Word, 1993).

Nugent, John C., *Endangered Gospel: How Fixing the World Is Killing the Church* (Eugene: Cascade, 2016).

Nygren, Anders, *Agape and Eros: The Christian Idea of Love*, tr. Philip S. Watson (Chicago: University of Chicago Press, 1982 [1930–36]).

O'Donovan, Oliver, 'Flesh and Spirit', in Mark W. Elliott, Scott J. Hafemann, N. T. Wright and John Frederick (eds.), *Galatians and Christian Theology: Justification, the Gospel, and Ethics in Paul's Letter* (Grand Rapids: Baker Academic, 2014), pp. 271–284.

Oord, Thomas J., *Defining Love: A Philosophical, Scientific, and Theological Engagement* (Grand Rapids: Brazos, 2010).

———, *The Nature of Love: A Theology* (St. Louis: Chalice, 2010).

Osborne, Grant R., *Matthew*, ZECNT (Grand Rapids: Zondervan, 2010).

———, *Romans*, IVP NTCS (Leicester: Inter-Varsity Press, 2004).

Packer, J. I., *Concise Theology: A Guide to Historic Christian Beliefs* (Leicester: Inter-Varsity Press, 1994).

Padilla, Rene, 'What Is Integral Mission?', pp. 1–5, <www.tilz. tearfund.org/~/media/Files/TILZ/Churches/What%20is%20 Integral%20Mission.pdf>, accessed 29 April 2017.

Pierce, R. W., R. M. Groothuis and G. D. Fee (eds.), *Discovering Biblical Equality: Complementarity Without Hierarchy* (Downers Grove: InterVarsity Press; Leicester: Apollos, 2005).

Prior, David, *The Message of 1 Corinthians*, 2nd edn (Leicester: Inter-Varsity Press, 1993).

Ramachandra, Vinoth, and Howard Peskett, *The Message of Mission*, BST (Leicester: Inter-Varsity Press, 2003).

Ringrose, Jessica, Rosalind Gill, Sonia Livingstone and Laura Harvey, *A Qualitative Study of Children, Young People and 'Sexting': A Report Prepared for the NSPCC*, <www.nspcc.org. uk/services-and-resources/...and.../qualitative-study-sexting>, pp. 1–75, accessed 12 August 2017.

Routledge, Robin, 'Hosea's Marriage Reconsidered', *TynB* 69.1 (May 2018), pp. 25–43.

Rutledge, Fleming, *The Crucifixion: Understanding the Death of Jesus Christ* (Grand Rapids: Eerdmans, 2015).

Shaw, Perry, 'Towards a Multidimensional Approach to Theological Education', *International Congregational Journal* 6.1 (2006), pp. 53–63.

————, *Transforming Theological Education: A Practical Handbook for Integrative Learning* (Carlisle: Langham Global Library, 2014).

Sider, Ron, *The Early Church on Killing: A Comprehensive Sourcebook on War, Abortion, and Capital Punishment* (Grand Rapids: Baker Academic, 2012).

Smith, Emily Esfahani, 'Masters of Love', *Atlantic* (12 June 2014), <www.theatlantic.com/health/archive/2014/06/happily-ever-after/372573>, accessed 1 November 2018.

Smith, Gary, *Hosea, Amos, Micah*, NIVAC (Grand Rapids: Zondervan, 2001).

Smith, James K. A., *Desiring the Kingdom: Worship, Worldview and Cultural Formation*, Cultural Liturgies, vol. 1. (Grand Rapids: Baker Academic, 2009).

————, *You Are What You Love: The Spiritual Power of Habit* (Grand Rapids: Brazos, 2016).

Snodgrass, Klyne, *Ephesians*, NIVAC (Grand Rapids: Zondervan, 1996).

Sodha, Sonia, 'There's Love, You'll Say, but Is There Any Real Point in Getting Married These Days?', *Guardian*, 6 October 2018, <www.theguardian.com/commentisfree/2018/oct/06/theres-love-youll-say-but-is-there-any-point-in-getting-married-these-days>, accessed 14 December 2018.

Stein, Robert H., *Mark*, BECNT (Grand Rapids: Baker Academic, 2008).

Storkey, Alan, 'Postmodernism Is Consumption', in Craig Bartholomew and Thorsten Moritz (eds.), *Christ and Consumerism: A Critical Analysis of the Spirit of the Age* (Carlisle: Paternoster, 2000), pp. 100–117.

Storkey, Elaine, 'Shadows Across Gender Relations', in Thomas A. Noble, Sarah K. Whittle and Philip Johnston (eds.), *Marriage, Family and Relationships: Biblical, Doctrinal and Contemporary Perspectives* (London: Apollos, 2017), pp. 237–255.

Stott, John R. W., *Evangelical Truth: A Personal Plea for Unity, Integrity and Faithfulness* (Leicester: Inter-Varsity Press, 1999).

————, *The Message of 1 Timothy and Titus*, BST (Leicester: Inter-Varsity Press, 1996).

————, *The Message of Ephesians: God's New Society*, BST (Leicester: Inter-Varsity Press, 1984).

————, *The Message of Galatians*, BST (Leicester: Inter-Varsity Press, 1992).

————, *The Message of Romans*, BST (Leicester: Inter-Varsity Press, 1994).

————, *What Is an Evangelical?* (London: Church Pastoral Aid Society, 1977).

Stuart, Douglas, *Hosea–Jonah*, WBC, vol. 31 (Waco: Word, 1987).

Tan, Kim Huat, 'The Shema in Early Christianity', *TynB* 59.2 (2008), pp. 181–206.

Taylor, Charles, *A Secular Age* (Cambridge, Mass.: Belknap Press of Harvard University Press, 2007).

Thielman, Frank, *Ephesians*, BECNT (Grand Rapids: Baker Academic, 2010).

Thiselton, Anthony C., *The First Epistle to the Corinthians*, NIGTC (Grand Rapids: Eerdmans, 2000).

Thompson, James W., *Moral Formation According to Paul: The Context and Coherence of Pauline Ethics* (Grand Rapids: Baker Academic, 2011).

————, *Pastoral Ministry According to Paul: A Biblical Vision* (Grand Rapids: Baker Academic, 2006).

Tidball, Derek, *The Message of the Cross*, BST (Leicester: Inter-Varsity Press, 2001).

Tidball, Derek, and Dianne Tidball, *The Message of Women: Creation, Grace and Gender*, BST (Nottingham: Inter-Varsity Press, 2012).

Togarasei, Lovemore, 'The Pentecostal Gospel of Prosperity in African Contexts of Poverty: An Appraisal', *Exchange* 40 (2011), pp. 336–350.

Twenge, Jean, *Generation Me: Why Today's Young Americans Are More Confident, Assertive, Entitled – and More Miserable Than Ever Before* (New York: Atria, 2014).

Vanhoozer, Kevin J. (ed.), *Nothing Greater, Nothing Better: Theological Essays on the Love of God* (Grand Rapids: Eerdmans, 2001).

Volf, Miroslav, *Against the Tide: Love in a Time of Petty Dreams and Persisting Enmities* (Grand Rapids: Eerdmans, 2010).

————, *The End of Memory: Remembering Rightly in a Violent World* (Grand Rapids: Eerdmans, 2006).

————, *Free of Charge: Giving and Forgiving in a Culture Stripped of Grace* (Grand Rapids: Zondervan, 2005).

Volf, Miroslav, and Matthew Croasmun, *For the Life of the World: Theology That Makes a Difference* (Grand Rapids: Brazos, 2019).

Welby, Justin, *Dethroning Mammon: Making Money Serve Grace* (London: Bloomsbury, 2017).

Wells, David, *Above All Earthly Pow'rs: Christ in a Postmodern World* (Grand Rapids: Eerdmans; Leicester: Inter-Varsity Press, 2005).

Westfall, Cynthia Long, *Paul and Gender: Reclaiming the Apostle's Vision for Men and Women in Christ* (Grand Rapids: Baker Academic, 2016).

Wilkens, Michael J., *Matthew*, NIVAC (Grand Rapids: Zondervan, 2004).

Williams, Stephen, *The Limits of Hope and the Logic of Love: Essays on Eschatology and Social Action* (Vancouver: Regent, 2006).

Witherington, Ben, *Conflict and Community in Corinth: A Socio-Rhetorical Commentary on 1 and 2 Corinthians* (Grand Rapids: Eerdmans, 1995).

———, *The Gospel of Mark: A Socio-Rhetorical Commentary* (Grand Rapids: Eerdmans, 2001).

———, *Jesus and Money: A Guide for Times of Financial Crisis* (Grand Rapids: Brazos, 2010).

———, 'Jesus as the Alpha and Omega of New Testament Thought', in Richard. N. Longenecker (ed.), *Contours of Christology in the New Testament* (Grand Rapids: Eerdmans, 2005).

———, *Paul's Letter to the Romans: A Socio-Rhetorical Commentary* (Grand Rapids: Eerdmans, 2004).

———, *A Socio-Rhetorical Commentary on Titus, 1–2 Timothy and 1–3 John*, Letters and Homilies for Hellenized Christians, vol. 1 (Nottingham: Apollos; Grand Rapids: IVP Academic, 2006).

Wright, Christopher J. H., *Deuteronomy*, NIBC (Peabody: Hendrickson, 1996).

Wright, N. T., *How God Became King* (London: SPCK, 2012).

———, *Luke for Everyone*, NTE (London: SPCK, 2012).

———, *The Resurrection of the Son of God* (Minneapolis: Fortress, 2003).

———, 'Wouldn't You Love to Know? Towards a Christian View of Reality', <www.ntwrightpage.com/2016/09/05/wouldnt-you-love-to-know-towards-a-christian-view-of-reality>, accessed 12 April 2017.

Yancey, Philip, *What's So Amazing About Grace?* (Grand Rapids: Zondervan, 1997).

Yarbrough, Robert, *1–3 John*, BECNT (Grand Rapids: Baker Academic, 2008).

Introduction:
What is love?

The aim of The Bible Speaks Today series is to expound accurately the biblical text and in doing so connect it to the realities of our day-to-day life in order to help resource Christians to live faithful lives of discipleship to Jesus Christ. This volume is going to attempt to do that through focusing on the theme of love. Along the way we will discuss not only key texts on both the love of God and human love, but also what putting love into practice looks like. But before we 'dive in' to this great and profoundly important biblical theme, we need to try to clear some initial ground around the meaning of love. Perhaps no other word in the English language is as well known and yet there are all sorts of confusing and competing ideas about love swirling around within our contemporary culture. What is love? What are some general characteristics of love? What are some of those competing ideas about love popularly believed today?

1. What is love?

Love – such a deceptively simple and popular little word. There are few greater subjects in Christian theology – indeed in all of life – than love, yet it is a surprisingly complex and challenging concept to understand, let alone live by.

Rare is the person who does not want to love and be loved. Love appears to be intrinsic to our humanity. Sociologists may dissect behavioural mechanics behind the claims of love. Branches of medical research may explore the biochemistry of love. But, however explained, it is almost universally agreed that we need love in order to live and flourish as human beings. We are innately social beings and find identity, meaning, pleasure and joy in relationship with others. Love in this sense is powerful and personally transformative. Being loved in some way frees us to love others. Whether male or female right across generations and cultures, we are attracted to, and endlessly fascinated by, love. Music and film industries globally revolve around telling creative stories of love – whether unrequited, tragic, thwarted and then fulfilled or some other variation. Great literature through the ages and across national boundaries explores the complexities and paradoxes of love. We cannot, it seems, get enough of love.

What is it that is so universally powerful and attractive about love? James K. A. Smith has a persuasive and important answer. He builds on St Augustine of Hippo's (AD 354–430) insight that 'You have made us for yourself and our heart is restless until it rests in you.'[1] Our loves – what we desire and want and long for – are at the core of human identity; far more than what we say or know. Human beings, he proposes, are first and foremost *lovers*. We will commit and shape our lives around what we love. We are shaped by what we desire. It is the heart, not the head, that is at the seat of human identity. It is our loves that we orientate our lives around – that give us purpose. Or, as Smith puts it, we will worship what we love. 'So the question isn't *whether* you will love something as ultimate; the question is *what* you will love as ultimate. And you are what you love.'[2] This diagnosis of love is hugely helpful. While Smith writes as a Christian, it rings true for human beings, whether Christian or not. We love love itself because we are lovers. The great question of *what* we love will surface regularly in this book because it is a question that is consistently posed within Scripture, both Old and New Testaments.

While it may be difficult to put our finger on, we sense that we know healthy love when we see it and that it is always *good*. The idea of dispassionate or uncaring love feels like an oxymoron – a contradiction in terms. Love by definition involves an emotional attachment to that which we love, sometimes of profound joy as well as acute pain. Love is not coldly disinterested; it involves empathy for the other – whether rejoicing with their good news or mourning with their loss. In other words, love listens and love cares.

Authentic caring for the other involves a commitment that is determinedly orientated towards their well-being – whether spiritual, physical or emotional. In this sense, love is both an attitude (empathy, compassion, care) and action (responding to the needs of the other). While at times in the history of love within Christian theology, one 'side' of love might be emphasized more than the other,[3] they cannot be separated. How they relate to each other will

---

[1] James K. A. Smith, *You Are What You Love: The Spiritual Power of Habit* (Grand Rapids: Brazos, 2016), pp. 7–8. Quoting Augustine, *Confessions* 1.1.1, tr. Henry Chadwick (Oxford: Oxford University Press, 1992).

[2] Smith, *You Are What You Love*, p. 10. Emphases original.

[3] Werner G. Jeanrond, *A Theology of Love* (London: T&T Clark, 2010), p. 21.

be a recurring theme of this book as we discuss both the nature and praxis (practical outworking) of the love of God and human love.

Love reveals itself in a life orientated away from the self and towards the service of others: it is the antithesis of selfishness. It seeks the best for the other in a relationship that fosters life, growth, respect and human flourishing. Thomas Jay Oord, a theologian who has written much on love, defines it as 'acting intentionally, in sympathetic response to others . . . to promote overall well-being'.[4] What outward form love's relentless commitment to the other takes will vary depending on the relationship in question. For example, sometimes the commitment is made publicly within a formal and legal setting. In the Bible God's loving commitment to Israel takes the form of a binding covenant made after the giving of the law at Sinai (Exod. 20:6). In a traditional marriage ceremony a man and a woman make solemn vows to love each other before witnesses. Love for friends, family members, fellow Christians and others does not usually take a public and legal form, but generally love involves what has been called a 'rugged' commitment to stay with the other for their good whatever the changing circumstances of that relationship through time.[5] Rugged commitments, however, tend to be highly inconvenient as well as richly rewarding. In this sense, 'love costs'. It is a risky leap of faith to love the other. It may involve caring for a terminally ill spouse; pouring your life out in the service of the poor; or being heartbroken by having your love ignored, under-appreciated or rejected. This is why love does not make sense if the goal of a happy and fulfilled life is to prioritize the desires and needs of the self. From this perspective, to love your enemies, as Jesus commands, becomes almost incomprehensible nonsense. It is therefore no accident that love is often associated with altruism, where we put someone else's welfare before our own. The high cost of both divine and human love is another theme that will recur throughout the discussion in this book.

It may seem odd to say, but we need bodies in order to love. Put differently, we are embodied people living in a material world. For love to exist at all, one person has to love the 'other' – love cannot exist in isolation: it always has a focus. That 'other' is usually someone well known to us – whether parents, lover, friend, a child or colleague – and in this sense love is innately personal and

---

[4] Thomas Jay Oord, *Defining Love: A Philosophical, Scientific, and Theological Engagement* (Grand Rapids: Brazos, 2010), p. 173.
[5] Scot McKnight, 'The New Perspective and the Christian Life: Ecclesial Life', in Scot McKnight and Joe Modica (eds.), *The Apostle Paul and the Christian Life: Missional and Ecclesial Implications of the New Perspective* (Grand Rapids: Baker, 2016), p. 150.

relational. It is only in and through our bodies that we can experience and give love to other embodied people. It is possible to love people whom we have never met (a famous singer, an author or a globally beloved figure like Nelson Mandela, no longer alive), but such love is not of the same 'level' or 'intensity' as love for someone we know 'in the flesh'. Similarly we can even 'love' impersonal physical things (such as an Apple Mac, chocolate or a favourite place) as well as abstract concepts (like humility, courage, honesty, humour). But all of these sorts of loves can exist only within our material world. This means that there is something 'concrete' and 'physical' about love – it can find expression in virtually any aspect of life: a kind gesture, a text message, cooking a meal, a spoken word, a sexual embrace. The 'earthed' nature of love within a physical world will surface from time to time as our discussion of core biblical texts on love unfolds.

Love unites. For example, many people deeply love the country of which they are a citizen. A successful nationalism tells a compelling national story that gives citizens a collective identity and creates deep bonds of 'belonging' between them. In this way, a common love (in this case for nation) can bind strangers together. Love, in this perspective, creates a community consisting of individuals with a shared love. Their joint goal is to see the object of their love prosper. While not wanting to push this parallel too far (and it is a short step to where love of nation becomes all-consuming and destructive), comparisons to the church as a community of believers united within a shared experience of God's love (and their reciprocal love for God) are obvious. Love and unity within a shared identity is another theme that will emerge as we unpack biblical texts on love.

2. Love in the twenty-first century

All human love exists within a time and context. Ours is contemporary Western culture that has rapidly evolving understandings of what constitutes love.[6] When it comes to love, the past truly is another country.[7] It is important to appreciate that what seems 'normal' to us regarding what is love today is historically novel. 'Love' has come to mean all sorts of things and is used in all sorts of ways. The result is that it is a word which is at once ubiquitous and yet also so plastic as to be bent into virtually any shape we want. It

---

[6] While I am writing from within Western culture, I am aware that many readers will not necessarily share that context.

[7] To appreciate how love has been understood through the ages there is no better place to begin than Simon May, *Love: A History* (London: Yale University Press, 2011).

may be useful here briefly to sketch something of what 'love in the twenty-first century' looks like. This outline will not be comprehensive but it will help us to understand the context into which the Bible's teaching on love has to be applied if it is not to remain 'unearthed' in the ancient world.

a. From 'God is love' to 'love is God'

'In the wasteland of Western idols', says the philosopher Simon May, 'only love survives intact.'[8] We in the West live in an age that has (largely) lost faith in all the things that we once hoped could bring us meaning, value and even redemption itself. Faith in God is now very much a minority pursuit in a 'secular age'.[9] May argues that all other substitute objects of worship – reason, progress, the nation, the state, communism and 'the bevy of other idols and "isms" that were, and in one or two cases – like nationalism and art – still sporadically are, elevated to religions of salvation' have 'all failed to deliver the ultimate contentment or limitless promise expected of them'.[10] All, that is, except love.

A contemporary 'theology' of modern human love consists of such beliefs as love is unconditional, it is not based on any quality of the other, nor does it seek anything for the giver; love fully affirms the loved one, the 'bad' as well as the 'good' (it is non-judgmental); 'love is benevolent and harmonious – a haven of peace'; it is eternal – it, or its blessings, will never die; love is selfless, concerned for the flourishing of the other for their own sake; it alone can transport us to a state of purity and perfection 'beyond' the harsh and messy realities of this world; love can even redeem and deliver us from life's losses and sufferings. Beliefs of this sort saturate popular culture and profoundly shape our expectations of romantic love and of parents' love for their children.[11]

Today, it is love alone that is widely assumed to be what life is all about: our source of meaning and that which gives our lives purpose, joy and hope even in the face of stresses such as financial, political and job insecurity, terrorism, family breakdown as well as being faced with our own mortality through illness and bereavement. Even diehard atheists cling to love as the supreme universal virtue above all others.[12] Determinedly godless humanist funerals still seek

---

[8] Ibid., p. 4.
[9] For detailed discussion see Charles Taylor, *A Secular Age* (Cambridge, Mass.: Belknap Press of Harvard University Press, 2007).
[10] May, *Love: A History*, pp. 3–4.
[11] Ibid., p. 2.
[12] See below for the discussion of Daniel Dennett on love.

comfort in the love that 'survives' the deceased person – in her acts of love and in her being loved – giving her a measure of immortality that also lives on in the memories of her surviving loved ones. It is therefore hard to disagree with May when he concludes that love is the new god of our age: it is now the West's only generally accepted religion. The Bible's claim that 'God is love' has been subverted to become 'Love is God'.[13]

b. Romantic idealized love

Divorce rates in the West at least in part reflect our relentless pursuit of love with the 'right' person. The beauty industry tells us how to succeed in love: it can be ours if we have enough money to make ourselves lovable enough through fashion or surgery. The lovely and the attractive are celebrated, admired and envied; the 'unlovable' find themselves on the margins of popular culture. In this picture romantic idealized love is prized and pursued, umbilically linked to visions of happiness, sex, self-fulfilment, hope, self-esteem and cultural acceptance. Such love is ephemeral and dazzling, burning brightly but often dimming all too quickly as heightened emotions and intense feelings subside.

Such individualized love dominates our Western culture to such a degree that it becomes difficult to conceive of love in other terms – and Christians are not immune. This is a point that Stanley Hauerwas makes with typical bluntness and humour. He talks of ministers in pre-marriage counselling with a couple thinking it is

> interesting to ask if they love one another. What a stupid question! How would they know? A Christian marriage isn't about whether you're in love. Christian marriage is giving you the practice of fidelity over a lifetime in which you can look back upon the marriage and call it love. It is a hard discipline over many years.[14]

If what Hauerwas says sounds odd or surprising to us, perhaps it is a sign that we are far more influenced by our Western culture of individualism, eroticism and sentimentalized love than we imagine. This tension between a biblical theology of love and love within the contemporary world in which we live will be another recurring theme of this book.

---

[13] May, *Love: A History*, p. 1.
[14] Stanley Hauerwas, 'Faith Fires Back', <www.dukemagazine.duke.edu/article/faith-fires-back>, accessed 11 December 2017.

c. Hyper-sexualized love

Major corporations long ago took notice of the emotional and cultural power of love and sex in our Western individualized society.[15] In fact, you could say that the advertising industry has shown a better understanding of Augustine and human beings as lovers than has the church! Advertising has capitalized on the power of desire and that we are formed by what we love. Erotic sexualized love is now big business and endlessly marketable: products are sold to us on emotional terms, not because we need them but because we are persuaded to desire and want them – they give us identity and belonging and joy. So we are encouraged not only to acquire but to *love* the latest, sleekest, thinnest and fastest piece of computer technology or the most stylish car. It is not an accident therefore that love has become virtually synonymous with sex within consumerism. Sex is used to create desire and we are encouraged to desire – and therefore buy – everything from strawberries and cream, cars, clothes, holidays, soap, ice-cream and furniture. Such love is (mis) directed at created things rather than their creator; it also is focused on the self rather than other people. In this sense, love is pressed into the service of marketing strategies, a useful tool to boost sales. Various forms of misdirected love – what the Bible calls idolatry – will be identified and discussed as this book proceeds.

d. All-inclusive love

In the West we live in an increasingly post-Christian liberal secular democracy that prizes certain values – individual freedom, pluralism, tolerance and equality.[16] These values have not appeared out of thin air, but have developed over time. I can only touch on this here, but it is relevant for understanding modern ideas of love. Pluralism is linked to a deeply embedded fear of one group or faith having a dominant position. The role of the state is to make room for all and privilege none. Given Christianity's cultural and political dominance in the West for centuries, modern secular liberal democracy now wishes to constrain religion because it is seen as limiting individual freedom. For many, religion and religious beliefs are seen as either irrelevant or a malign influence in public life. Tolerance means all

[15] Alan Storkey, 'Postmodernism Is Consumption', in Craig Bartholomew and Thorsten Moritz (eds.), *Christ and Consumerism: A Critical Analysis of the Spirit of the Age* (Carlisle: Paternoster, 2000), pp. 100–117.

[16] Patrick Mitchel, 'Sex, Truth and Tolerance: Some Theological Reflections on the Irish Civil Partnership Bill 2010 and Challenges Facing Christians in a Post-Christendom Culture', *EvQ* 84.2 (April 2012), pp. 155–173.

beliefs and behaviours within the law should be endorsed and affirmed. Equality requires that by law all citizens must be treated equally, regardless of beliefs, sexual identity or lifestyles. The motivation behind these values is the belief that their political and social implementation will result in a fairer, more accepting and equal society than that of the past.

The reason for mentioning all of this is that these values are profoundly shaping contemporary perspectives on love and God. Love *is* individual freedom. Love *is* equality. Love *is* tolerance. Add these values together and you have a cultural context where it becomes unloving to make any sort of critical judgment on how people choose to live. When it comes to God, the idea of a loving deity can be welcomed and affirmed (after all, who is against love?), but only in so far as this God is not perceived as threatening the advances of secular liberal democracy. The result is a God who will be tolerated only if his love is affirming, inclusive and magnanimous – in other words a kindly God who can be left comfortably in the background, leaving us to get on with our lives.

e. Universal love

Another popular contemporary Western perspective on love is to see it as the essence of all religious expression. In other words, most of the world's major religions can be boiled down to having love at their core. John Hick proposed that salvation for all religions equates to being liberated to live a life of love and compassion for others and 'the call to self-transcending love and compassion comes to humanity through a number of channels', including Christianity, Judaism, Buddhism, Hinduism, Islam and others.[17] It is this basic moral code that is universal, not the laws and teaching that have evolved with each religion in particular historical contexts. These need to be adapted to facilitate love as cultures change.

But you do not have to be a religious person like John Hick to believe in the universal value of love. Cognitive scientist and well-known public atheist Daniel Dennett states:

> The fact that so many people love their religions as much as, or more than, anything else in their lives is a weighty fact indeed. I am inclined to think that nothing could matter more than what people love. At any rate, I can think of no value that I would place higher . . . I surmise that we almost all want a world in which love,

[17] John Hick, 'Is Christianity the Only True Religion, or One Among Others?', <www.johnhick.org.uk/article2.html>, accessed 23 September 2016.

justice, freedom, and peace are all present, as much as possible, but if we had to give up one of these, it wouldn't – and shouldn't – be love.[18]

Thus, both for religious pluralists like Hick and atheists like Dennett love is a universal human capacity to be valued and celebrated as giving meaning to life. They would agree, for different reasons, that there is nothing particularly *Christian* about love. If Hick and Dennett are representative of a significant number of people (and I think they are), then for many people Christians do not have some sort of monopoly on love. Love, they assert, can and does exist quite independently of any Christian truth claims. It is of course undeniable that many people that have no Christian affiliation do live lives of exemplary love and self-sacrifice.

f. Christians against love

A final popular attitude concerning love within our modern Western world is that religion and love do not mix. It is a sad fact that the Christian church, both global and local, has a history that all too often seems to pit the institution of the church *against* love. The church acts in its own self-interest rather than the interest of the weak, poor and marginalized – and particularly its victims. The church uses power, not to love, but to control behaviour. The church acts like a cold-hearted bureaucracy that functions by rules that oppress those that do not live by those rules. The church does not even love itself in the sense that it remains hopelessly divided. Jesus' command 'to love one another so that all men will know that you are my disciples'[19] is taken as an indictment that the church has failed to obey its Lord. Rigid church doctrine is also seen as antithetical to love – whether resistance to same-sex marriage, defending claims concerning the uniqueness of Jesus Christ as the one true Lord of all, or the notion of divine judgment – all contribute to a popular perception that the church and love are *opposed* to one another and that in terms of love, Christians are the problem rather than the answer.

3. Reasons for this book

Given the layers of meaning within the word 'love' and the myriad of conflicting love claims within our culture, it is clear that there are

---

[18] Daniel Dennett, *Breaking the Spell: Religion as a Natural Phenomeno*n (New York: Penguin, 2006), pp. 253–254.
[19] John 13:34–35.

at least two compelling reasons why we need to be reflecting clearly and biblically about love.

a. Authentic witness

As hinted at above, Christian love is increasingly at odds with contemporary romantic, sentimental and consumerist notions of love. Some reject that there is anything unique about Christian love. As our Western world becomes more and more disconnected from its Christendom roots, what Christians believe about love will sound increasingly 'out of sync', if not outrightly offensive to modern ears. In this sense, Don Carson is right to talk about the 'difficult doctrine of the love of God'.[20] There is nothing easy or soft about Christian love.

As Christians we need to be thinking about, and practising, love in winsome ways. Our task is not only to articulate what love is, but also to *show* to the world what countercultural Christian love looks like in practice. Gone are the days (if they ever existed) where it is enough to say 'This is what we believe. Now you may not see it embodied in our divided churches, but trust us: it's true. So believe it anyway.' Unless we are 'walking the walk' of Christian love as individual Christians and as local churches, our words will carry little weight in a post-Christendom world – nor should they. Love is inseparable from authentic witness; the apostle Paul can even say that 'The only thing that counts is faith expressing itself through love'.[21]

b. Reform and renewal within the church

My aim in writing this book is not to 'put the record straight' on what Christians believe about love. This book is written primarily for Christians, for it is not only those outside the church who struggle to hold together (for example) the love and judgment of God, what it means to love and follow Jesus in a consumer culture or what it means that Christian marriage is a covenant of love. As the comment by Stanley Hauerwas illustrates, we should not fool ourselves that we are somehow unaffected by sweeping cultural and philosophical changes. We live in, and are deeply shaped by, Western culture. There is therefore, I believe, no greater need for the renewal of the church than to grasp afresh the breadth, depth, scope and radically countercultural nature of the Bible's teaching on love. If

---

[20] Don Carson, *The Difficult Doctrine of the Love of God* (Wheaton: Crossway; Leicester: Inter-Varsity Press, 2000).

[21] Gal. 5:6. Love in Galatians is discussed in chapter 15.

we do not get our theology of love right, we will end up with a distorted view of God, his relationship with his people, the nature of the cross, the motivation for, and source of, the Christian life, the work of the Spirit, the dynamics of Christian worship, the purpose of the church and the nature of Christian hope! The message of love is crucial to the Christian faith.

I will unpack this message by concentrating on what the Bible itself teaches about love. One of the biggest challenges in planning this book was the amount of biblical material on love that could not be included. Part 1 begins with love in the Old Testament. At its centre is God himself. He enters into a covenant with Israel that is founded and sustained by love. That love even overflows to the weak, vulnerable and alien. We will explore how themes of judgment, restoration and love characterize God's relationship with his people throughout the story of the Old Testament as well as its celebration of human love in the Song of Songs. Part 2 focuses on how the love of God is supremely revealed in the mission and death of Jesus Christ; the love of Father for Son; the atoning love of God for the world; the love of God demonstrated at the cross; and the unbounded good news of Christ's self-giving love. Part 3 moves to the Gospels and love in the life and teaching of Jesus: his demand for wholehearted love; his kingdom-shaped teaching on loving neighbours and even enemies; his command to his followers to love one another; and the deep love and worship he inspired in return. Part 4 turns to only a small selection of the largest body of material in the Bible on love – that of the church called to be a community of radical love. Key issues chosen include Paul's famous teaching on love in 1 Corinthians 13; his consideration of the relationship between love, the Law (Torah) and the Spirit; and love within Christian marriage. A final chapter examines an example of misdirected love – the love of money.

Given the almost overwhelming volume of material in the Bible on love it is rather strange, is it not, that love tends not to be front and central in much Christian theology and praxis?[22] It is difficult to say why this is the case. I suspect that it is something to do with unspoken assumptions, that what really matters in Christian discipleship and teaching is 'knowing' the right things. 'I think therefore I am' said René Descartes and we have taken him at his word. Christian learning and spiritual formation, then, become about transmission of right information. Thinking the right things is what matters most.

---

[22] Of course this is a personal opinion, but it is supported from many discussions over years of ministry and teaching. It is also interesting that there were twenty previous IVP BST volumes before love was included!

Theological training has for centuries prioritized models of education that reflect this sort of Cartesian approach to learning and assumes that character formation somehow automatically follows.[23] We give prizes to those who can master complex information and who tend to work best alone with books and yet pay scant attention to character formation and how students love. Evangelical organizations often spend significant resources on statements of faith that define what they believe. Every word is carefully parsed and significant consequences can follow for an employee who can no longer sign that they affirm every detail. But it is extremely rare for such statements to be accompanied by equally important solemn and signed commitments to love God and one another.

I have been a Christian for several decades. I grew up in solid, orthodox, evangelical circles (for which I am grateful), have studied theology to PhD level and taught theology in a college setting for many years. But it has only been in more recent years that it has come home to me how love is the golden thread that ties the doctrine of God, the Trinity, the cross, the story of redemption, the work of the Spirit, holiness, the calling and mission of the church, the goal of the Christian life and believers' eschatological hope together. Researching a book chapter on Saint Paul and the Christian life a while ago, I was astonished at how pervasive love is within his letters; so much so that I now call him 'the apostle of love'. When I use this term people tend to look a bit puzzled – is not Paul the missionary to the Gentiles, the theologian of justification by faith alone, the stern defender of the gospel, the man of letters and ultimately a martyr? What, to paraphrase Tina Turner, has love got to do with him? Well, rather a lot – but that will emerge as you read this book.

Please do not misunderstand: I am not in turn proposing some form of anti-intellectual subjectivism where it only matters what we feel, not what we believe. I love theology. But I am suggesting that we need to be more biblical – in the sense of recognizing that the Bible has a holistic understanding of the human person, head (cognitive), hands (behaviour) and heart (affections). And that it is the heart (what we love) that is the most significant of these three in terms of shaping our lives and what we worship.

A disclaimer

Before proceeding any further, a disclaimer is required. While I am excited to write on such a wonderful theme, I am very conscious

---

[23] Perry Shaw, *Transforming Theological Education: A Practical Handbook for Integrative Learning* (Carlisle: Langham Global Library, 2014).

that it is not the 'church' that fails at love but individuals within the church. I fail to be loving every day. I fail to love God and I fail to love others. I am no expert in love and feel drastically unqualified to write a book about Christian love. But I would, in my best moments, like to love more. So I write this book for myself as well as for you. It is my hope that it will be a resource that will help us all develop our love lives and please God our Father in the process. This prayer seems an appropriate one with which to begin:

> O Lord, make us have perpetual love and reverence for your holy Name, for you never fail to help and govern those whom you have set upon the sure foundation of your lovingkindness; through Jesus Christ our Lord, who lives and reigns with you and the Holy Spirit, one God, for ever and ever. Amen.[24]

---

[24] *The Book of Common Prayer and Administration of the Sacraments and Other Rites and Ceremonies of the Church, Together with the Psalter or Psalms of David; According to the Use of the Episcopal Church* (New York: Church Hymnal Corporation and Seabury, 1977), p. 230.

Part 1
Love in the Old Testament

Exodus 34:6–7
1. Abounding in love, punishing the guilty

Exodus contains the first mentions of love in the Bible in the form of God's love for his covenant people. Our text is the third such occurrence[1] and states:

> *And he passed in front of Moses, proclaiming, 'The LORD, the LORD, the compassionate and gracious God, slow to anger, abounding in love and faithfulness, maintaining love to thousands, and forgiving wickedness, rebellion and sin. Yet he does not leave the guilty unpunished; he punishes the children and their children for the sin of the parents to the third and fourth generation.' (6–7)*

These verses belong towards the end of the dramatic and potentially devastating story of Israel's rebellion by their creation and worship of the golden calf told within chapters 32–34.[2] They raise all sorts of questions about love. What does it mean for God to *love* his own *apostate* people? What has love to do with punishment – are the two not mutually exclusive? How does divine love in Exodus 'collide head-on' with modern assumptions about love mentioned in the introduction – that true love is unconditional, non-judgmental, benevolent and harmonious? What picture of God emerges from this foundational story of the Old Testament?

1. The great apostasy (Exod. 32)

It is not my purpose here to work though chapters 32–34 step-by-exegetical step. Our focus is on the love of God, but to get at what

---

[1] Exod. 15:13 and 20:6 are the first two mentions of love. The word used is *ḥesed*, discussed further below.

[2] It is recommended to read Exod. 32 – 34 a couple of times before reading this book chapter.

this text is saying about God and love we need to locate 34:6–7 within the wider story and its aftermath – the overall flow of the golden calf account is one from apostasy[3] to intercession and eventually to re-establishment of the promise.

The golden calf incident, to our modern eyes, seems peculiar at a number of levels. Why the sudden rebellion? Why a golden calf? What was so serious about what the people did? Does Yahweh not massively overreact in his initial 'fierce anger' and intention of destruction? How is such a response 'loving'? A brief probing of these questions can help us appreciate what may be going on underneath the surface of the story.

Ultimately the people's actions are motivated by a deep failure to believe that Yahweh is going to keep his promise: they are on their own and need to act accordingly rather than wait in vain (1). Moses was the sole intermediary between the people and God. His unexpectedly long absence could have incited a panic[4] – what will be their fate now, abandoned in the wilderness? There is also a sense of distance from, and possibly anger and frustration at, *this fellow Moses* (1). Implicit in this language of disassociation lies an attempt to justify their decision to *make us gods who will go before us* (1). Even worse, credit is now given to these gods for the exodus (4). The contrast here with the announcement of God's ten great covenant commandments could not be sharper. Though the Decalogue is explicitly founded on the fact that 'I am the LORD your God, who brought you out of Egypt, out of the land of slavery'[5], Israel are now rewriting history and changing their allegiance in the process.[6] The past is being refashioned, as it often still is today, to fit the agendas of the present.

The choice of a calf was a common form for an idol in the ancient Near East. It is likely that the idol was not worshipped as a god per se but as a representation of a god. The idol, it is thought, was like a pedestal for the god, representing it in physical form.[7] The use of gold earrings was also significant. They had just been given detailed instructions on building the tabernacle which involved extensive use of gold, including within the building of the ark.[8] Earrings had pagan

[3] The golden calf incident is often called a rebellion but this does not capture the complete and intentional renunciation of faith in God by the people of Israel. See discussion below.

[4] See their earlier panic during the escape from Egypt (14:10–14); Peter Enns, *Exodus*, NIVAC (Grand Rapids: Zondervan, 2000), p. 569.

[5] Exod. 20:2.

[6] The plural 'gods' referring to the calf (singular) is intriguing and yet grammatically clear. See ibid., p. 570.

[7] Ibid., p. 569.

[8] See 25:10–22 for the ark. From chapters 25 to 31 gold is mentioned forty-seven times.

cultic associations (Gen. 35:4). All this meant that the golden calf was in effect a home-made representation of divine presence, like an alternative tabernacle or ark. Its purpose was to replace Yahweh with gods of their own making who could be relied upon to be present as required.

The depth of Israel's repudiation of Yahweh is almost impossible to overestimate. In one swift series of actions they have denied the foundation of their covenant relationship with their saving God and broken the first and second commandments (Exod. 20:2–4). In doing so they have reversed the entire history of the exodus and announced a sort of unilateral declaration of independence. They are intentionally recreating their own exodus narrative, complete with their own gods and pattern of worship that parodies the one that Yahweh had earlier revealed and commanded them to follow.[9] Fear of God has evaporated: they are acting as if he does not exist.

With these actions, Israel's apostasy is complete; it cannot get any more comprehensive in its scope and depth. This is Exodus's 'fall' narrative. Their rejection of God's saving work that has taken up the whole of Exodus 1 – 31, their abandonment of trust in his promise, their lack of confidence in his goodness and provision, their contempt for his commands, their celebration of false worship, and their hubristic arrogance that they can flourish with their own man-made gods combine to make the events at the foot of Mount Sinai Israel's first great 'original sin'. Their apostasy has effectively nullified the covenant. They have not only transgressed the covenant, but they have smashed it; and in this sense Moses' shattering of the two tablets (Exod. 32:19) is deeply symbolic of a spiritual reality. Tragically this infidelity would not be their last. The story of chapter 32 foreshadows an all-too-consistent pattern of faithlessness that reoccurs throughout the Old Testament.[10]

2. God's response to apostasy

The issue at stake from 32:7 on is whether Israel's apostasy marks the end of the new nation in the purposes of God. It is this question

[9] This mimicking of authentic worship is evidenced in three ways. First, Aaron's announcing of *a festival to the* LORD (32:5) celebrating the creation of their own 'liberating' gods parallels the original 'festival to the LORD' of the Passover and the Feast of Unleavened Bread (10:9; 12:14; 13:6). Second, the detail about 'rising early' to make burnt and fellowship offerings to the golden calf deliberately mirrors Moses' actions in 24:4–5 at the solemn ritual of covenant confirmation with Yahweh. Third, the eating and drinking (32:6) mimics the celebration of the leaders of Israel after glimpsing God himself in 24:11 ('they saw God, and they ate and drank').

[10] For a detailed account of Israel's 'Faithlessness' see John Goldingay, *Israel's Faith*, OTT, vol. 2 (Downers Grove: InterVarsity Press, 2006), pp. 254–349.

that is the subject of a series of four remarkable dialogues between God and Moses. In these dialogues we can trace God's response to his people's egregious sin that culminates in our key text of 34:6–7.

a. God and Moses' dialogues: a trajectory towards (God's) covenant renewal

These discussions are some of the most remarkable passages in the Bible. The text is unambiguous that Moses boldly persuades God to change his mind from his initial decision to deal with Israel as they deserve within the terms of covenant betrayal. This would have meant their utter destruction, marking termination of the promise and a plan to restart with Moses as a type of second Abraham (Exod. 32:10). In contrast, in the dialogues there is a trajectory in Yahweh's responses ranging from anger and threat of utter destruction (Exod. 32:10), to anger, interim judgment, repromising the land but withdrawal of the divine presence (Exod. 33:3), to a renewal of his presence and promise (Exod. 33:17) and a subsequent 'new' covenant agreement indicating God's acceptance of Moses' requests (Exod. 34:10–28).

I have space only to highlight three themes in the conversations that are particularly relevant to the question of God's love and judgment. We will return to these points in the final application section.

First, while the future of the people as a whole still hung in the balance, Moses climbed the mountain for a second dialogue with Yahweh, this time offering himself as an atoning sacrifice on behalf of the people – an offer that is refused (Exod. 32:30–32). No mere human could atone for the people's sin.

Second is the importance of the theme of God's presence. At one point, while God renews the promise of the land, he says, 'I will not go with you, because you are a stiff-necked people and I might destroy you on the way.'[11] This is devastating news, like an unfaithful partner in a marriage being told that, despite his hopes of reconciliation and a new beginning, the relationship is over – he is reaping what he sowed in being unfaithful. Trust has been irreparably broken, it cannot be reforged. All that remains is to work out the terms of the separation as the two parties go their own way. The people mourn (Exod. 33:4). In a very real sense, the withdrawal of God's presence would mark the end of the story of Israel.

However, Israel's mourning is not the last word. A further dialogue results in a second divine change of mind. Moses pleads with God to 'Remember that this nation is your people.'[12] His response is to

[11] Exod. 33:3.
[12] Exod. 33:13.

affirm Moses, not Israel – note the singular personal pronoun: 'My Presence will go with you, and I will give you rest.'[13] But Moses persists with his plural request: 'If your Presence does not go with us, do not send us up from here.'[14] It is the presence of God alone that marks out Israel, they will be nothing without their God. As Durham puts it, 'Without Yahweh's presence, in the dark and chaotic umbra of his Absence, Israel will cease to exist.'[15] With his reply in 33:17 we have the climax of a remarkable transition in God's response to Israel's apostasy, inspired at each stage by Moses, with whom God is pleased: 'I will do the very thing you have asked.'

Third, God's response is one of grace and compassion that leads to forgiveness and a new beginning. The dialogues lead to a formal and glorious ratification of a new covenant. Just as the giving of the Decalogue (Exod. 20:18–21) and the two stone tablets (Exod. 31:18) were accompanied by awesome signs of God's power and glory, so the 'regiving' of a 'renewed' covenant will be witnessed by Moses, a glorious manifestation of all the goodness of God (Exod. 33:19) and the subsequent remaking of the tablets (Exod. 34:1–4). In this mysterious encounter the name (the essential identity and being) of God will be proclaimed. Enns likens this to Moses' first commissioning by God through the revelation of God's name ('I am who I am') at the burning bush in Exodus 3.[16] Now here is a second commissioning, a second unveiling of God's name and a 'second' covenant with Israel. In both accounts God's decision to bestow his mercy and compassion on Israel is utterly undeserved: 'I will have mercy on whom I will have mercy, and I will have compassion on whom I will have compassion.'[17] Indeed we can even say that this 'second election' of Israel is even more gracious and compassionate for it leads to forgiveness in the face of intentional apostasy. No wonder that the dialogues conclude with a deepened relationship between Moses and Yahweh, the former bowing and worshipping, saying *Lord, if I have found favour in your eyes, then let the Lord go with us. Although this is a stiff-necked people, forgive our wickedness and our sin, and take us as your inheritance* (34:9).

b. 34:6–7: Abounding in love: punishing the guilty

And so we come to the momentous event of God's self-revelation to Moses of his divine name (Exod. 34:6–7). Just as God's love, grace

[13] Exod. 33:14.
[14] Exod. 33:15.
[15] John I. Durham, *Exodus*, WBC, vol. 3 (Waco: Word, 1987), p. 448.
[16] Enns, *Exodus*, p. 582.
[17] Exod. 33:19.

and compassion in forgiving Israel is even deeper in the light of their faithlessness, so Moses' experience of God's glory is even more exalted than at the burning bush. We are human and can comprehend human language only when it comes to thinking of God. Here God is described in human terms while his glory passes before Moses.[18] But the point is not some sort of literal description of God's 'standing' or of his 'back'; it is that Moses really does see and experience something of the mystery and glory of the presence of God himself. He witnesses something that he has never seen before and will never again in his lifetime – the 'maximum amount' of God's glory that any human can see without perishing. Verses 6–7 are the pinnacle of the entire golden calf episode and reveal the essential nature of Israel's God.

In verse 6 the repetition of LORD (Yahweh) emphasizes God's 'salvation name' as he recommits himself to saving Israel.[19] This is God's essential being, which results in loving actions – he abounds in love (in himself) and maintains love to thousands (to others). The Hebrew word used is *ḥesed*, one of the most significant words for 'love' in the Old Testament.[20] There is no simple equivalent in English. All Bible translations use a variety of words to render its meaning but by far the most common is 'love', either by itself or in some combination with kindness and loyalty words (like 'steadfast love').[21] *Ḥesed* conveys a sense of deep relationship, often covenant relationship (as in Exod. 34) – a covenant is durable only if both sides are committed to each other. But it is not necessarily restricted to covenant love. A relationship marked by *ḥesed* is one of love, goodwill, loyalty, affection and faithfulness. In 34:6 it is closely linked to compassion, graciousness, faithfulness. Yahweh's *ḥesed* means that he will be *slow to anger* – his essentially loving nature means that he is not irascible or unpredictable. While he still will become angry at the destructiveness of sin and act in judgment, it is almost a last resort, certainly anything but a joyful leap to wrath and destruction.

It is in this context that verse 7 follows. The *yet* at the beginning of the sentence shows awareness within the text itself of the potentially sharp disjuncture between the two clauses of verses 6–7 that describe the character of Yahweh. The idea of punishment, and especially that which is intergenerational, is jarring for our minds,

---

[18] Anthropomorphisms include Moses being covered by God's hand (33:22), God's standing with Moses (34:5) and Moses' seeing only God's back, not his face (33:20, 23).

[19] Enns, *Exodus*, p. 584.

[20] Leon Morris states that *ḥesed* is used 245 times in the Old Testament, *Testaments of Love: A Study of Love in the Bible* (Grand Rapids: Eerdmans, 1981), pp. 65–84.

[21] Ibid., p. 67.

which are used to *disassociating* love from anger and judgment. The Old Testament has no such qualms. However, God's anger is not arbitrary, nor does love mean that he ignores sin. Judgment here is rooted in the original penalty for breaking the second commandment (Exod. 20:5).[22] How are we to understand the apparent injustice of later generations being punished for the sins of their forebears? Perhaps what is in view here is not so much literal blood descendants being punished for the sins of their relatives, but a broader sense of Israel's corporate responsibility.[23] The people's obedience would bring blessing not only to the faithful generation but to their successors; likewise disobedience followed by God's judgment would have serious consequences, not only for the unfaithful practitioners but for following generations.[24]

c. Exodus 34:6 and Old Testament love

The wonder of the golden calf story is not God's anger, but how that anger and potentially devastating judgment were turned aside. It tells the good news of how Yahweh's *ḥesed* tempers his righteous judgment due to Moses' entreaties on behalf of Israel. Legitimate severe judgment (Israel's destruction) for covenant disloyalty has been put aside in favour of covenant renewal and forgiveness. *Ḥesed*, therefore, captures something of the Old Testament's sense of 1 John 4:8. Love is something God *does*, but his loving action flows out of who he *is*. His compassion and grace surpass the impact of Israel's apostasy and the very real potential for an ending of the covenant and all the implications that would have for the wider story of God's redemption of the world following Genesis 1 – 11.

It is therefore no accident that this great early statement about the abounding love, grace and compassion of God who is slow to anger is repeated in various forms throughout the Old Testament, often in response to Israel's unfaithfulness (Num. 14:18; 2 Chr. 30:9; Neh. 9:17; Pss 86:15; 103:8; 111:4; 112:4; 145:8; Joel 2:13; Jon. 4:2; Nah. 1:3). And yet these are only examples of where a specific form of words is used. There are hundreds of other texts using *ḥesed* and other Hebrew words for love that speak of God's acting in a loving and compassionate way not only to his people but also to those outside Israel. To these can be added the significant weight of Old

---

[22] Exod. 34:6–7 mirrors Exod. 20:5–6, with the latter structured by 'punishment–love' and the former 'love–punishment'.

[23] Enns, *Exodus*, pp. 416–417.

[24] E.g. Num. 14:28–35 recounts God's judgment that only Caleb and Joshua would enter the promised land and that the Israelites' children would suffer in the wilderness for forty years due to the previous generation's unfaithfulness.

Testament teaching that is virtually meaningless without the presupposition of love lying behind concepts like election, or father/son language, or God as shepherd of his flock or the vinedresser tending his vineyard, or the potter carefully and creatively shaping a pot.[25] All of this is to say that God's love forms the backbone of the Old Testament story. Here in Exodus it survives even the fiercest test: Yahweh's love is unceasing despite his having every reason to abandon Israel as a lost cause. In this light Simon May is right to conclude:

> The widespread belief that the Hebrew Bible is all about vengeance and 'an eye for an eye', while the Gospels supposedly invent love as an unconditional and universal value, must therefore count as one of the most extraordinary misunderstandings in all of Western history.[26]

3. Application: the love and judgment of God today

a. Love and worship

For Israel in Exodus 34, and repeatedly through the rest of the turbulent covenant relationship that we call the Old Testament, the love of God is life-giving good news. If all Israel had experienced of God was 34:7, there would have been no land, no covenant, no future and no hope. We can take this trajectory further to say that without 34:6 there would have been no kings, no temple, no prophets, no Messiah, no incarnation, no 'new exodus' liberation in and through the ministry of Jesus[27] and no atonement for sin at the cross. In other words, without divine love the story of God's redemptive mission through the story of Israel would have come to a cataclysmic end at the foot of Mount Sinai. Likewise, without love being essential to God's character, Israel's journey would have ended for good at numerous other points in their history, not least the trauma of the destruction of Jerusalem and the exile to Babylon.[28]

We can make these claims because judgment alone, however justifiable, leaves no room to deal with the reality of human failure and sin. Justice alone, without love and forgiveness, means the inevitable dissolution of any relationship, let alone that of a perfect, transcendent God and his imperfect, fallible people – just reflect for

---

[25] Morris, *Testaments of Love*, pp. 98–100.
[26] Simon May, *Love: A History* (London: Yale University Press, 2011), pp. 19–20.
[27] For discussion of how Jesus inaugurates a second exodus see chapter 6.
[28] E.g. the hope of restoration at the end of Jeremiah is based on Yahweh's previously declared love, 31:3; 33:11.

a moment on how long a marriage would survive if it were based purely on justice (both sides fulfilling the contractual obligations of husband and wife) and an absence of love. God's people then, and we as God's people today, depend utterly on the truth that the 'steadfast love of the LORD never ceases'.[29] Each of us, like Israel, has a 'fall narrative'. Like Moses, our only proper response to the love and forgiveness of God is to bow our heads and worship in thankfulness and awe (Exod. 34:8).

b. God's atoning, self-giving love

One of the most fascinating parts of the dialogues between God and Moses is when the latter offers his life as an atonement for the people's sins, an offer that is rejected by God since guilt and judgment will remain with those who rebelled (Exod. 32:30–33). Israel's first great 'fall' clearly raised the question of whether sin could in some way be atoned for. Clearly Moses' life was not a sufficient atonement, despite his being Israel's intercessor and the one who had a uniquely close relationship with Yahweh. Shortly afterwards would come the sacrificial system through which the reality of sin was graphically represented alongside the blessing of forgiveness for authentic repentance. Yet all of this only foreshadowed another prophet of Israel, greater than Moses (Heb. 3:3). While Yahweh is *pleased* with Moses (33:17), it is his own Son whom he loves and with whom is 'well pleased'[30] who becomes Israel's liberator. Jesus is the faithful Israelite who willingly takes the consequence for sin (death) upon himself, his life a perfect sacrificial atonement for sin (Heb. 10:14). But the glorious twist is that death does not have the last word: it is defeated in the resurrection of Jesus, the risen Lord. This is a theme to which we will return in this book – but it is important to say here that the abounding *ḥesed* of God shown in Exodus 34 leads to the supreme display of his love and compassion for his sinful people: the sending of one greater than Moses – a greater intercessor, a greater prophet and an infinitely greater atonement.

This means that as Christians today we need to read Exodus 32 – 34 through the lens of God's self-giving atonement, the resurrection, Pentecost and the widening of the covenant to include both Jews and Gentiles. What difference does this make? Well, on the one hand, God is unchanged. His response to the destructive power of sin is still anger and judgment (see next point). Yet, on the other

[29] Lam. 3:22, NRSVA.
[30] Matt. 3:17; 17:15; Mark 1:11; Luke 3:22.

hand, the good news of the gospel is that through faith in Christ there is forgiveness and new life in the Spirit. As Christians today therefore we do not live in fear of utter obliteration when we sin: we are not somehow to read ourselves back into the golden calf event in place of Israel. But we are certainly called to imitate Israel in humble repentance for sin and a turning daily to the love of God revealed at the cross, without which we would be lost and without hope.

c. Love versus judgment?

Let us read 34:6 through the modern understanding of 'love is God' that I outlined in the introduction. It is good to know, is it not, that God is abounding in love, compassion, graciousness, consistency (and therefore trustworthiness) as well as being forgiving and patient? Who could object to such a statement? Indeed who could object to such a God? For if God abounds in love, then that love will overflow to us. To love us will mean to accept us as we are, to enable us to live our lives to the fullest of our potential, to set us free to be ourselves and to find authenticity and joy in relationships of love – of whatever type of relationship they happen to be. A loving God will benignly endorse our pursuit of love since love itself is divine. Indeed such is the power of love, we need only invoke love's name in order to legitimate and sanctify our desires and behaviour. Few things can dare to stand in the way of love in modern Western culture. Including God.

The 'genius' of this theology is that, like most false teaching, it is half-right.[31] Verse 34:6 *is* one of the great love statements in Scripture. God *is*, as we have discussed, abounding in love. But modern Western and individualist thinking warps this to define love as uncritical tolerance, acceptance, affirmation and endorsement of our passions, longings, behaviours and desires. True love is non-judgmental. This is a type of 'creational-only' theology: a theology without the fall, without sin, and that assumes human beings as they are do not need to be transformed – they just need to be loved and liberated to be themselves.[32] But 34:6 is tied inextricably and without apology to 34:7; God's judgment is inseparable from his love. While this sounds like a contradiction in terms, two points can be made.

First, God's judgment is not his preferred course of action: it is always as a consequence of human sin, most often that of his people.

[31] Lit. in the case of 34:6–7.

[32] There are still some socially accepted boundaries to the liberation of human love in the West. The one almost universally abhorred form is paedophilia (literally 'love of a child'). In general, if love is consensual it should be affirmed.

God's judgment in Exodus 32 – 34 is on Israel for compromising their calling to be a people of love and justice in the world and imperilling God's bigger redemptive plan. In this vein Fleming Rutledge rightly says that 'the wrath of God is always exercised in the service of God's good purposes. It is the unconditional love of God manifested against anything that would frustrate or destroy the designs of his love.'[33] This is consistently the pattern in the rest of the OT. God is *slow to anger*. Despite Israel's intentional apostasy in Exodus 32, the outcome is limited judgment, renewal of the covenant and forgiveness. The story of Scripture is God's relentless love for his people, a love that culminates in Jesus the Messiah and continues today – and eternally into the future.

Second, and more broadly, God would not be loving if he were not also a judge. The more we love someone, the deeper the outrage and anger if someone else seriously harms the one we love. On a less personal level, we watch the news and see violence, injustice and hatred chart their destructive daily course and (in our more compassionate moments) we instinctively cry out for justice for the oppressed. Sometimes we are moved to pray, even to take up a cause, but we also know such is the scale of human sin that we are impotent to fix the world. If, as finite humans, we long for a world of justice and peace, how much more for the one who made the world 'very good'?[34] If God is not angry at the hatred, injustice, violence and misery that sin causes to people made in his image, he is not a loving God but an uncaring bystander. For God not to judge human sin and evil is to condone it. Ultimately the just judgment of God is intrinsic to the good news of his immeasurable love. Miroslav Volf captures this tension well as he reflects about war in his former homeland:

> I used to think that wrath was unworthy of God. Isn't God love? Shouldn't divine love be beyond wrath? God is love, and God loves every person and every creature. That's exactly why God is wrathful and against some of them. My last resistance to the idea of God's wrath was a casualty of the war in the former Yugoslavia, the region from which I come. According to some estimates, 200,000 people were killed and over 3 million displaced. My villages and cities were destroyed, my people shelled day in and day out, some of them were brutalised beyond imagination, and I could not imagine a God not being angry. Or think of

---

[33] Fleming Rutledge, *The Crucifixion: Understanding the Death of Jesus Christ* (Grand Rapids: Eerdmans, 2015), p. 323.
[34] Gen. 1:31.

Rwanda ... where 800,000 people were hacked to death in a hundred days ... Though I used to complain about the indecency of God's wrath, I came to think that I would have to rebel against a God who wasn't wrathful at the sight of the world's evil. God isn't wrathful in spite of being love. God is wrathful because God is love.[35]

d. Drawing close to the presence of God

Finally this story in Exodus reveals something remarkable – God not only listens to Moses' entreaties; he allows himself to change tack,[36] and in doing so responds to Moses' request to *teach me your ways* by revealing to Moses his identity, goodness, glory and presence – all captured in proclaiming his divine name (Exod. 33:12 – 34:8). As Durham puts it, the narrative is 'masterfully bold in its presentation of a Yahweh who is so secure that he does not mind being upstaged by his own servant Moses'.[37] A result is that Moses and Yahweh draw closer in their relationship: God is 'pleased' with Moses and promises to 'know you by name' – meaning his essential being (33:17), just as Moses would also know God by name. If we skip forward to the end of the golden calf section (34:29–35), Moses' face shines *because* of his unique fellowship with God himself and acts both as a sign of Moses' divine approval in re-establishing the covenant and also of God's renewed presence with his people through Moses. However we understand the veil of verses 33–35, the significant point is that Moses alone can enter the divine presence and *speak with the* LORD 'face to face' without a veil (35).

All of this is astonishing. So much so that Christians have often struggled to accept the very 'human' self-revelation of an almighty and sovereign God in these chapters. God cannot act in this way! But we should take the text as it is given to us. God is both all powerful (transcendent) and present with us (immanent).[38] He is both a righteous judge and abounding in love. His presence is both potentially fatal and a place of glorious acceptance. He has the complete freedom to act in weakness and constraint just as much as in power and glory. We see in the golden calf story not only his mercy,

---

[35] Miroslav Volf, *Free of Charge: Giving and Forgiving in a Culture Stripped of Grace* (Grand Rapids: Zondervan, 2005), pp. 138–139.

[36] This is what the text itself simply tells us. The question of whether God can be persuaded to change his mind or not is a theological issue beyond the text.

[37] Durham, *Exodus*, p. 448.

[38] Exod. 34:5: Yahweh comes down from the cloud (transcendence) and stands with Moses (immanence).

forgiveness and compassion, but how he chooses to work out his redemptive purpose in deep and even vulnerable relationship with the people he loves.

But this is not the end of the story. Paul in the New Testament picks up 34:29–35 as an analogy to make an even more astonishing claim: you and I can have a fuller and closer relationship with God than even Moses (2 Cor. 3:7–18). Moses, perhaps more than any other person in the long history of Old Testament Israel, knew and was known by God. As *one individual* he was tasked with mediating God's presence to others. Yet *all* those who are 'in Christ' have an even more glorious experience. 'We are not like Moses,' Paul says.[39] 'What was glorious has no glory now in comparison with the surpassing glory.'[40] What is this glory that outshines even that of Moses? It is the gift of the Spirit, the very presence of the Lord (2 Cor. 3:17).[41] Moses' glory faded, but Spirit-given glory never will. Indeed believers have the privilege and blessing of being continually in the presence of the Lord and are being transformed by the Spirit into the likeness of Jesus (2 Cor. 3:18). All this means that we are to be encouraged and not lose heart (2 Cor. 4:1, 16). We are to persevere when 'light and momentary troubles' inevitably come our way – for Paul this included being hard-pressed, perplexed, persecuted and struck down![42] It also means that we can face our own age and death with confidence: 'outwardly we are wasting away, yet inwardly we are being renewed day by day'.[43] Christians have a sure hope, based on Jesus' resurrection, that we will one day stand in the very presence of our loving God (2 Cor. 4:14).

---

[39] 2 Cor. 3:13.
[40] 2 Cor. 3:10.
[41] Paul twice says that the Lord (Jesus) is the Spirit, so closely are the two identified (17–18).
[42] 2 Cor. 4:8–9.
[43] 2 Cor. 4:16.

Deuteronomy 10:12–22
2. God's love for the outsider

As I write this, on the wall in front of me is a large map of the world. Apart from being a fascinating geography lesson, even a quick scan acts as a sobering reminder of how much of the world is suffering from political instability, war, ethnic cleansing, poverty, famine, dictatorships, terrorism and environmental destruction.[1] In this first quarter of the twenty-first century the scale of forced population movement has been unprecedented since the end of the Second World War. The implosion of an entire country like Syria, added to desperate crises in places like Myanmar, Iraq, Yemen, South Sudan, Somalia and Afghanistan, has led to millions of refugees forced to seek safety outside their home nations. The United Nations High Commissioner for Refugees (UNHCR) says that today there are about 68.5 million forcibly displaced people worldwide, including 25.4 million refugees.[2] The scale of the refugee crisis continues to precipitate political crises across Europe that will dominate politics in the region for the foreseeable future.

A refugee has been defined as a person who has fled his or her country because of a well-founded fear of persecution on one of five grounds: race, religion, nationality, membership of a particular social group or political opinion.[3] A refugee is typically in a highly vulnerable situation: often without official status; lack of access to basic resources; removed from networks of family, language and culture; and often deeply traumatized by violence or fear of violence. Over half of refugees globally are under 18 years old.

[1] For an interactive map of global conflict see <www.ucdp.uu.se>, provided by the Uppsala Data Conflict Programme, accessed 28 December 2016.
[2] Figures from UNHCR, <www.unhcr.org/figures-at-a-glance.html>, accessed 28 December 2018.
[3] A key document in international law is the United Nations 1951 Convention Relating to the Status of Refugees. Article 1(A)(2) defines refugee status.

Why begin this chapter writing about refugees? Because God's attitude – and that of his people – to the orphan, the widow and the forcibly displaced foreigner are central to our text of Deuteronomy 10:12–22. It has been described as one of the richest texts in the Hebrew Bible, intentionally summarizing core theological and ethical concerns of the book into a 'mini-symphony' packed with memorable phraseology.[4] Our particular focus within part 1 of this book is on *God's love* and this priority will be reflected in the exposition that follows. However, interwoven within what this passage says about God is also material concerning Israel's *response* to him and so the discussion and application will also consider how human love is to be shaped by God's prior love.

1. Israel's five obligations (10:12–13)

The title Deuteronomy means 'second law' and the book takes the form of a regiving of the law that was revealed to Moses on Mount Sinai. Now, at the end of his life, in preparation for Israel's finally entering the promised land and before Joshua is appointed as his successor, the great prophet once more represents the word of Yahweh to his people. This time the location is the plains of Moab and the people have already promised to listen and obey (Deut. 5:28–31).

The structure of the book is built around three sermons on covenant renewal (Deut. 1:1 – 4:43; 5:1 – 29:1; 29:2 – 30:20). Overall, the message of Deuteronomy can be summarized this way: God, out of electing love, has formed a covenant relationship with his chosen people and they are to remember him and obey his commands wholeheartedly.[5] The instruction to Israel to love their God (reiterated frequently throughout the book in 6:5; 10:12; 11:1, 13, 22; 19:9; 30:6, 16) is never divorced in Deuteronomy from the reality of God's judgment on his chosen people if they disobey their Lord. Love is no Cinderella theme in this final book of the Pentateuch; it lies at the core of the worship and identity of the people of God. Leon Morris in his classic book on biblical love reiterates this point: 'In Deuteronomy it is clear that God's love is the great, basic fact, and that that love awakens a response in those who accept it.'[6]

---

[4] Christopher J. H. Wright, *Deuteronomy*, NIBC (Peabody: Hendrickson, 1996), p. 144.

[5] For exposition and application of the whole book see Raymond Brown, *The Message of Deuteronomy*, BST (Leicester: Inter-Varsity Press, 1993).

[6] Leon Morris, *Testaments of Love: A Study of Love in the Bible* (Grand Rapids: Eerdmans, 1981), p. 41.

31

And now, Israel (12) links 10:12–22 with what has preceded it. In 9:7 – 10:11 Moses has just retold the sobering tale of Israel's repeated disobedience in the desert. In the light of this story and their future new life in Canaan, Moses lists five obligations that are to shape their life across the Jordan: *what does the LORD your God ask of you but to fear the LORD your God* (12), to *walk* in obedience (12), to *love* him (12), to *serve* him wholeheartedly (12) and to *observe* his commands (13). Keeping these obligations will be for their *own good* (13) – they will prosper and be blessed by God in their new home.

'Fear', 'walk', 'love', 'serve' and 'observe': this is what Deuteronomic faith is to look like in practice. Love is core to the five obligations and, given its prominence in the book as a whole, it is possible to see the other four as practical outworkings of what it means for Israel to love their God. There is no artificial compartmentalization at work here. Love means faithfulness in all areas of life. First, it is personal and emotional: Israel is both to fear and love God in gratitude and thankfulness. Second, they are also to imitate him: to walk in the ways of the one true God. This will involve an embodied love worked out in the world. Third, their love takes the form of a moral duty: to serve Yahweh wholeheartedly, without reservation, and therefore to obey his commands. Fourth, it will be for the Israelites' *own good* that they live this way. Deuteronomy is consistent that blessings follow obedience (Deut. 6:10–13).[7]

Long-established popular caricatures of Old Testament faith (from which Christians continue to be far from immune) depict it as a religion of works (in contrast to the New Testament's message of grace), as if Israel were desperately and continually having to obey the law in order to earn God's love and acceptance. Such a picture is a tragic distortion of the Old Testament in general and Deuteronomy in particular. Israel's love for God lies at the heart of obedience to his law. God's love for Israel lies at the heart of his choosing them to be his people. It is to God's love we now turn as our main focus in this chapter.

2. The impartial love of the Lord of Lords (10:14, 17a / 15, 17b–18)

In verses 14–22 the sermonic exhortation continues, but in verse 14 there is a switch of subject from Israel to Yahweh. *God himself* is the basis for their vocation to love well and live obediently. In other

---

[7] For general promises of prosperity, security and a good life in Canaan see 5:29, 33; 6:24; 30:15–20.

words, the five obligations of verses 10–12 are not arbitrary duties imposed by an inscrutable deity on an acquiescent and cowed people. Here in verses 14–22 they are unapologetically rooted in the nature of the God whom Israel are to worship.

Verses 14–16 and 17–19 are creatively structured in parallel, the second triplet reiterating and reinforcing the message of the first but with its own distinct content. Both sets of verses have three clauses. They begin with an outburst of praise concerning the exalted status, power and unique identity of Yahweh *the LORD your God* (vv. 14, 17a). A following clause then describes the actions and loving character of this almighty God (vv. 15, 17b–18). The concluding verse of each triplet applies the theological content of the previous two back to the sermonic purpose of Deuteronomy (vv. 16, 19). In both these concluding verses Israel is commanded to respond appropriately to God's remarkable love.

We are going to proceed with exposition of both triplets together, taking the first two clauses in turn (on God). The third pair of clauses will be considered in a separate section on Israel's response to God's love.

a. The unique status of Yahweh (vv. 14, 17a)

Verse 14 states, *To the LORD your God belong the heavens, even the highest heavens, the earth and everything in it*. It is difficult to think of much more exalted language than this. Everywhere and everything that exists belongs to God. The phrase *even the highest heavens* is a superlative way of emphasizing that God's ownership extends from the very highest place – in a sense beyond human imagination. This ownership extends all the way 'down' to the earth, but does not even stop there: it includes everything in the earth. This is language of universal cosmic rule of the one creator of all things that appears regularly within the Old and New Testaments. While not explicitly stated, the inevitable implication is that there can be no other God like this. Yahweh has no equals: his status is unique, and yet he is at the same time Israel's God (*your God*).

Verse 17a is a parallel outpouring of praise: *For the LORD your God is God of gods and LORD of lords, the great God, mighty and awesome*. This time the focus is not so much on God's universal ownership but on his supremacy and power over all other gods. *God of gods* and *LORD of lords* are superlatives, expressing and reinforcing the point that Yahweh alone is the incomparably *great God*. No one and nothing can rival his power and majesty. Again, while not explicit in the text, the implication is inevitable: Yahweh is the supreme God over all others. He is Israel's God and is no local deity.

33

He not only owns the world (v. 14) but runs it (v. 17).[8] This declaration of monotheism does two things at the same time: it reminds Israel first of the absolute, awe-inspiring authority and power of Yahweh, who, second, is astonishingly also their covenant God. This is the identity of the God whom they are to fear, imitate, love, serve and obey. This astonishing contrast of universal and local helps to set the scene for what sort of response is appropriate for Israel to demonstrate in clause three of the triad.

Verses 14 and 17 are powerful reminders that biblical love for God has a focus – the God of Israel. 'God' is neither some depersonalized abstract idea detached from the biblical narrative, nor is he one god of many equal options (such as the religious pluralism of John Hick mentioned in the introduction). Deuteronomy's claims about Yahweh stand in line with the Bible's consistent celebration of his unique identity as creator and ruler of all (see e.g. Isa. 40:12–31). In both Testaments God's people exist within polytheistic environments and yet are to demonstrate determined and consistent covenant love to the one God who is Lord over all.

b. God's electing, impartial and generous love (vv. 15, 17b–18)

Verses 15 and 17b–18 form the second clause of the two parallel triads. The focus moves from the glory of God to his character; more specifically to his loving actions in the world:

> Yet the LORD set his affection on your ancestors and loved them, and he chose you, their descendants, above all the nations – as it is today. (15)

> who shows no partiality and accepts no bribes. He defends the cause of the fatherless and the widow, and loves the foreigner residing among you, giving them food and clothing. (17b–18)

Yet (15) marks a stark contrast from verse 14, highlighting the sheer wonder and improbability that such a God as Yahweh would choose to set his affection on and love Israel in the past. This affection and love are unrelenting: he continues to hold this stance of grace towards Israel above all the nations. The subtext is that Yahweh's unimaginable greatness sits in sharp relief to Israel's smallness and vulnerability. These verses echo what is said in 7:6–9. It made no political or economic sense for God to have chosen Israel; rather it is the 'logic' of love at work. Israel are God's

[8] Wright, Deuteronomy, p. 148.

'treasured possession'.[9] He chose and rescued them from slavery simply because he loved them, not because of anything the Israelites had done or were in themselves. Love must always have an object, and Israel is the undeserving recipient of God's redeeming love. We have just discussed how Israel's love is to be directed towards Yahweh alone and nowhere else. But this love is simply in response to the prior decision of God to love Israel, and he keeps his 'covenant of love to a thousand generations'.[10] This electing love of God forms the backbone of the entire biblical narrative, Old Testament to New.

The second half of verse 17 is at first glance surprising. Why the sudden shift from God's absolute supremacy to a statement about partiality and bribery? It also seems to contradict verse 15 – is not election of one nation a rather big example of partiality in action?

Taking the second question first: partiality here is a corrupting ethos from the top down that leads to a destructive culture of bribery. Yahweh's election of Israel was explicitly not based on anything they could 'offer' to God. Even the gift of the land was not earned in any way; the nations of Canaan were dispossessed because of their wickedness, not Israel's righteousness (Deut. 9:1–6). And, as Israel are reminded throughout the Deuteronomic sermons (and later events of the destruction of Jerusalem and exile to Babylon give witness), they are not exempt from God's judgment for unrighteousness.

To return to the first question, Yahweh's impartiality reveals his moral superiority to the gods of the ancient Near East as well as his unassailable power (17a). Bribery was then, and continues to be today, a pervasive and corrupting practice. It favours the rich and powerful at the expense of those without access to the levers of power. Bribery is systemic and endemic in many countries, and Western democracies are by no means immune.

In this perspective the fact that Yahweh is incorruptible is startling good news for the poor and marginalized. But not only is God not favourably disposed towards the rich; he is actively on the side of the poor. Verse 18 is one of the most memorable and significant verses not only in Deuteronomy but in all of Scripture: *He defends the cause of the fatherless and the widow, and loves the foreigner residing among you, giving them food and clothing.* This is a revolutionary text, then and now. The gods of the ancient Near East were not exactly known for their love of humans.[11] The 'way of the

---

[9] Deut. 7:6.

[10] Deut. 7:9.

[11] E.g. in the Enuma Elish, the Babylonian creation epic, the god Marduk creates humans with a defeated rival's blood. Humans are created in violence and are little more than slaves.

(ancient) world' was power and violence (and it is little different today). The gods fought over it and human rulers claimed the backing of the gods to reinforce their own authority and status. This sort of power structure reinforced the status quo and utterly precluded any voice for those on the outside of the privileged ruling elites. From this perspective, verse 18 is like a grenade going off in the playground of the gods. The supreme Lord of all loves humans, but, even more, defends and loves the fatherless, widow and alien – categories of the most vulnerable and powerless people in the ancient world. There is no other god like this. This sort of love is impartiality in action and has radical social and political consequences that are worked out in the detailed social legislation of the law. Just as Yahweh has loved Israel by saving them from slavery and providing food and shelter for them in the wilderness, so he does likewise for the disenfranchised and even the non-Israelite. All this means that such impartial love is simply who God is: it reflects his nature. God is himself, as John would put it much later, love (1 John 4:8, 16).[12]

This dialectic between the covenant love of God for his people and his impartial, universal love is a dynamic tension that runs throughout the Bible – and will therefore recur throughout this book.

c. God and love in Old and New Testaments

The Old Testament, and its main character, gets a lot of bad press. This is nothing new: it was Marcion in the second century who drove a wedge between the harsh creator tribal god of the Old Testament (whom he called the Demiurge) and the loving and compassionate Supreme God of the New. There are many Christians who share this misunderstanding and, while not following Marcion all the way to rejecting the Old Testament (and quite a bit of the New), are semi-Marcionite in their virtual abandonment of reading and grappling with the Old Testament, and in attitudes that effectively recast God as little more than a special friend, whose unconditional love is always there when needed to help us get through life. Almost absent from such perceptions is the supreme 'otherness' of God, the immeasurable inequality of relationship between the Creator and his creatures, and how God's love for us is not 'unconditional' – as if nothing is required in return. As we have seen, our love for God is not incompatible with fear and complete obedience.

---

[12] See chapter 7 for discussion of this text.

3. A people of love and justice (10:16, 19, 20–22)

a. Israel's response to the love of God (vv. 16, 19)

If Yahweh's character is generous love directed in an unexpected direction, then his people are to reflect this countercultural, power-subverting, love for poor and marginalized. This is the point that the concluding clauses of each triad make without ambiguity, hesitation or apology. Such love is not some sort of nice 'optional add-on' to covenant obedience: it is an integral part of Israel's call to be a community of love and justice.

Verse 16 takes aim at Israel's hearts and necks: *Circumcise your hearts, therefore, and do not be stiff-necked any longer*. In the previous chapter they are reminded that they are a 'stiff-necked'[13] people – just as they were at the first giving of the law (Exod. 32 – 34). Loving as God loves does not come naturally. They need to *circumcise* their hearts – an evocative image that is picked up by Paul in the New Testament (Rom. 2:29). Here it refers to their need of repentance: to turn their hearts (the seat of identity and will) to God. It is only with such circumcision that they will be able to love (in 30:6 'heart circumcision' is an inner reality required 'so that you may love [God] with all your heart and with all your soul, and live'; see also Jer. 4:4).

Verse 19 complements verse 16 perfectly and provides the target that Israel is to love: *And you are to love those who are foreigners, for you yourselves were foreigners in Egypt*. Wright calls this the Deuteronomic version of the second greatest commandment, echoing Leviticus's commands to 'love your neighbour as yourself' and repeating exactly the command to love the foreigner.[14] This is an example of what it means to walk in the ways of Yahweh (Deut. 10:12). His way is the way of impartial, generous, redeeming, love that seeks justice for those forcibly displaced and in need. God's people, therefore, are to be a thankful community of practical love and justice, motivated to dispense the same mercy to others in need as they themselves have received from God.

In verses 20–22 the passage reaches its conclusion by reiterating the great truths just articulated. They are to fear God, praise, serve and hold fast to him alone. He has kept his promise to Abraham (v. 22; cf. Gen. 46:27) and delivered the Israelites from Egypt. They are 'not their own'; their identity is found in the Lord their God. Their mission is to be the people in the world whom God has called them to be by loving as he loves.

[13] Deut. 9:6.
[14] Lev. 19:18, 34. Wright, *Deuteronomy*, p. 150.

4. Concluding reflections: the motive and shape of Christian love today

In closing, I need to make two important points about the motive and 'shape' of Christian love in the world today. First, we are called to 'total obedient love' – but the motive for this love is not pragmatic or strategic. Israel are *not* told to love in order to create a more efficient, fair and just society – as if social cohesion is the motive for loving the marginalized. They are told to love *because of the character of their God.*

It is all too easy in Christian ministry to be motivated by pragmatic goals: we want to see a church grow, we have targets for evangelism, we wish to 'make a kingdom impact' within our community – we can even develop an eschatological framework for environmental concern since we believe God is going to renew all of creation one day. I want to tread carefully here since I am not disparaging such work. But the danger in all of these ambitions is that they are 'about us' and our agendas; what sound like pure goals can become little more than self-centred 'empire building'. Rather, I believe, all Christian ministry needs to flow out of the humbling and awe-inspiring truth that we worship a loving God who has first loved us. Ideally, then, we engage in mission and pastoral care and environmental work – indeed in all forms of ministry – primarily because we are to love people and God's creation. This is love for love's sake, not love subjugated to our own ends, however good they may seem.[15]

Second, the love of God explodes expected norms and turns ideas of divine power on their head. As Christians we have experienced the 'fruit' of God's impartial love in Christ. As a result, like Israel, it is our hearts that should be 'circumcised' by such love. In other words, *we are to love others as we ourselves have been loved.* If God loves and defends the cause of the vulnerable and forcibly displaced, then his people are to do likewise. Love for the poor and marginalized issues in a passion for justice. Justice is treating people justly, in line with their dignity as people made in the image of God.

This is no small theme in Scripture: it is embedded in wisdom literature and the prophets and continues through into the New Testament. Later in Deuteronomy we find detailed provisions for the cancellation of debts and the freeing of servants after seven years.[16]

---

[15] For theological discussion of this point see Stephen Williams, *The Limits of Hope and the Logic of Love: Essays on Eschatology and Social Action* (Vancouver: Regent, 2006).

[16] Deut. 15:1–18 is worth noting: the freed servant is to be generously blessed on leaving service: 'Give to him as the Lord your God has blessed you.' Human generosity is rooted in God's prior blessing.

The purpose of such commands is that 'There should be no poor among you' within the land gifted by God.[17] Deuteronomy 23:15 is remarkable: 'If a slave has taken refuge with you, do not hand them over to their master. Let them live among you wherever they like and in whatever town they choose. Do not oppress them.' This is a radical command. Instead of hard borders and forced repatriation, refugees fleeing from slavery are to be given shelter. Instead of oppression, they are to be given freedom, safety and a new start in life. *This is exactly what refugees today long for* (if they cannot go home). Proverbs 31:8 states:

> Speak up for those who cannot speak for themselves,
> for the rights of all who are destitute.

Micah 6:8 is well known:

> He has shown you, O mortal, what is good.
> And what does the LORD require of you?
> To act justly and to love mercy
> and to walk humbly with your God.

Laws of gleaning were designed to provide for the poor, widow and the foreigner, who did not have access to their own land (see Exod. 22:21–27; Lev. 19:9–10; Deut. 24:19–21; Ruth 2:17–23). Job is considered righteous because of his just treatment of the poor. Isaiah records Yahweh as saying:

> Is not this the kind of fasting I have chosen:
> to loose the chains of injustice
> and untie the cords of the yoke,
> to set the oppressed free
> and break every yoke?
> Is it not to share your food with the hungry
> and to provide the poor wanderer with shelter –
> when you see the naked, to clothe them,
> and not to turn away from your own flesh and blood?[18]

In the New Testament Jesus the Messiah comes announcing the kingdom of God and preaching 'good news to the poor' in fulfilment of Isaiah's promise (Luke 4:18–19, quoting Isa. 61:1–2). Jesus affirms the Old Testament pattern that giving to the poor is an act

[17] Deut. 15:4.
[18] Isa. 58:6–7.

of righteousness (Matt. 6:1–2). Similarly regarding Paul, Bruce Longenecker, in a ground-breaking study, has demonstrated that while economic assistance of the poor was not exhaustive in his Gospel:

> neither was it supplemental or peripheral to that good news. Instead, falling within the essentials of the good news, care for the poor was thought by Paul to be a *necessary* hallmark of the corporate life of Jesus-followers who lived in conformity with the good news of the early Jesus-movement.[19]

Paul's command in Galatians to 'Remember the poor' is symptomatic of how integral concern for the poor was in his ministry and teaching (Gal. 2:10). This priority cost him dearly, both economically and ultimately his life.[20] In other words, Paul put his money where his mouth was in regard to justice for the poor.

Yet in the church today those who do pour out their lives in service to the poor tend to be seen as admirable but *extraordinary*. When this sort of attitude is combined with a Western tendency to individualize the gospel in terms of personal salvation, the result is that *within most churches in the West direct engagement with the poor and marginalized is itself a marginal activity*. This is not to minimize the immense contribution that many churches make to alleviate poverty,[21] but it is significant that it has been non-Western evangelical Christians, most familiar with deep societal inequalities and the explosive growth of the predominately poor global church, who have done much to challenge this sort of myopic dualism. People like René Padilla (Ecuador), Samuel Escobar (Peru) and Vinoth Ramachandra (Sri Lanka),[22] among others, have been champions of an integral form of mission that 'is called to demonstrate the reality of the Kingdom of God among the kingdoms of this world, not only by what it says, but also by what it is and by what it does in response to human needs on every side'.[23] Organizations

---

[19] Bruce W. Longenecker, *Remember the Poor: Paul, Poverty and the Greco-Roman World* (Grand Rapids: Eerdmans, 2010), p. 1. My emphasis.

[20] Paul's visit to Jerusalem primarily for relief of the poor was dangerous and ultimately led to his execution. Longenecker, *Remember the Poor*, p. 316.

[21] Two examples come to mind: one is the huge contribution churches make to food banks across the UK; the other is the significant impact of Christians Against Poverty (CAP, <www.capuk.org>).

[22] See Vinoth Ramachandra and Howard Peskett, *The Message of Mission*, BST (Leicester: Inter-Varsity Press, 2003).

[23] René Padilla, 'What is Integral Mission?', pp. 1–5, <www.tilz.tearfund.org/~/media/Files/TILZ/Churches/What%20is%20Integral%20Mission.pdf>, accessed 29 April 2017.

like the Micah Network,[24] Tearfund,[25] the Lausanne Congress for World Evangelisation and others are now formally committed to this vision of mission. It is rooted in the belief that love for the poor flows from the character of God himself and is therefore to be an integral part of Christian life and ministry. Tim Keller captures the thrust of this truth in his excellent book *Generous Justice*:

> Before you can give this neighbour-love you need to receive it. Only if you see that you have been saved graciously by someone who owes you the opposite, will you go out into the world looking to help absolutely anyone in need. Once we receive this ultimate radical neighbour-love through Jesus, we can start to be the neighbours that the Bible calls us to be.[26]

This is where love can become costly (literally and metaphorically) and inconvenient to nicely ordered lives. In reviewing our own priorities, and those of our churches in an era of a global refugee crisis, we should therefore be asking ourselves are we marked by a radical, countercultural generosity to those in need that turns the power structures of the world on their head? One thing is sure: our hard-edged capitalist culture has no room for those who are not contributing to its ruthless system of acquisition and consumption. The church's vocation is to provide, with generosity and love, that room for those forcibly displaced.

[24] A global coalition of Christian agencies committed to an integral form of mission, <www.micahnetwork.org>, accessed 28 December 2016.

[25] Tearfund defines integral mission as 'the work of the church in contributing to the positive physical, spiritual, economic, psychological and social transformation of people', <www.tilz.tearfund.org/~/media/Files/TILZ/Churches/041%20 Tearfunds%20definition%20of%20integral%20mission.pdf>, accessed 28 April 2017.

[26] Tim Keller, *Generous Justice: How God's Grace Makes Us Just* (London: Hodder & Stoughton, 2010), p. 77.

Hosea 1 – 3
3. God the betrayed, yet persistent, lover

We live in a world full of conflicting ideas about God. For some he is a projection of a human search for meaning. For others he is a malicious force, inscrutably watching us struggle, suffer and die. Others go as far as theism: a God exists who made an ordered universe, but his identity is unknowable. At the other end of the spectrum some imagine God as synonymous with human love or like a supportive friend there to help us in our pursuit of happiness. For believers, perhaps words like 'creator', 'holy', 'Father' and 'sovereign' come to mind. But rarely, if ever, do you hear someone describing God as a 'betrayed lover'.

It is this stunning image of God that we are confronted with in Hosea: an erotic image of a loving husband and his faithless wife.

Earlier we discussed *ḥesed*, the Hebrew word for covenant love and loyalty. Another important Hebrew term, used by Hosea, is *'āhab*. Words from the *'hb* word group usually refer to sexual love between a man and woman committed to each other's well-being.[1] Other prophets, such as Jeremiah (e.g. Jer. 2:2, 25) and Ezekiel,[2] use this same imagery in the context of God's love being rejected for false gods. But Hosea's story *embodies* such love in his marriage to Gomer. Unparalleled in the rest of the Bible, it is a unique portrayal of the passionate love of God for his (unfaithful) people. God's love is no abstract idea: he gets deeply *involved* in the world. Hosea shows us afresh how God's redemptive commitment to Israel is far more than a covenant treaty – it is also a passionate union of tender love.

---

[1] Leon Morris, *Testaments of Love: A Study of Love in the Bible* (Grand Rapids: Eerdmans, 1981), p. 14.

[2] Ezek. 16 describes Israel as an adulterous wife. In the X-rated ch. 23, the sinning sisters of Judah (Oholibah) and Samaria (Oholah) are compared in highly explicit terms to rampant promiscuous lovers (Judah the worst), whose end will be destruction.

Love is risky. While love can be commanded and promised, it cannot be enforced. Loving someone else opens you up to the possibility of rejection and the enduring pain of a once joyful but now broken relationship. The message of Hosea is that even God allows himself to enter a relationship in which he becomes vulnerable to betrayal.[3] Yet God is not in Hosea (or anywhere else in the Bible) the heartbroken, helpless lover, distraught at the shock of his partner's rejection. God responds to Israel's unfaithfulness with both terrifying judgment[4] and surprising, determined love.

All this means that if we want to understand who God is and what his love looks like in practice, we need to read Hosea.

The setting is the late eighth century BC in the northern kingdom of Israel during the rule of Jeroboam II (793–753 BC) and beyond.[5] It was a time of prosperity and security. However, religious syncretism with Canaanite Baal worship meant that Israel had 'prostituted' herself by worship of other gods.[6] Baal worship meant participation in pagan fertility festivals with associated temple sacrifice (Hos. 2:13; 4:11–14; 11:2; 13:2). This religious crisis would overlap with a political one: the rising threat of the fearsome and militaristic Assyrian Empire would eventually overwhelm the northern kingdom, culminating in its invasion, the destruction of the capital Samaria and the deportation of much of the population in 722 BC.

Hosea's unenviable task was much the same as any other biblical prophet – to call the people of God back to covenant faithfulness, and to warn of impending judgment if they did not heed the words of the Lord.[7] As a result, most of the book consists of gloomy oracles of doom, but there remains an unbreakable thread of God's persistent love.

---

[3] See Gerald Bray, *God Is Love: A Biblical and Systematic Theology* (Wheaton: Crossway, 2012), in which he discusses the rejection of God's love within various belief systems and within the Bible, pp. 345–472.

[4] W. Eichrodt comments that 'Hosea is outdone by hardly any other prophet in the ferocity of his [God's] threats and the savagery of his proclamation of punishment,' *Theology of the Old Testament* (London: SCM, 1961), p. 252; quoted in Morris, *Testaments of Love*, pp. 18–19.

[5] While only Jeroboam of Israel is mentioned, the list of Judah's kings in Hos. 1:1 takes Hosea's period of ministry beyond Jeroboam, probably right up to the end of Israel in 722 BC. Gary Smith, *Hosea, Amos, Micah*, NIVAC (Grand Rapids: Zondervan, 2001), pp. 24–25.

[6] It seems that it had gone as far as some Israelites thinking that Yahweh and Baal were names for the same God, Hos. 2:16. Golden calves were located within the Israelite temples at Bethel and Dan. See Hos. 8:5–6; 10:5.

[7] Hosea's ministry in the northern kingdom probably followed that of Amos and overlapped with Isaiah's and Micah's ministries in Judah. Smith, *Hosea, Amos, Micah*, p. 24.

Since chapters 1–3 form a distinct literary unit and contain themes that resurface in the rest of the book, our approach will concentrate here. The questions Hosea's prophetic word to Israel raise are ancient ones but are as pressing as ever for us today: Who is the God we worship? How does God love? How is divine love compatible with divine judgment? Are there limits to God's love? What does it mean to love God faithfully today?

1. A symbolically dysfunctional family (1:2–9)

a. Gomer the adulterous wife (1:2–3)

Has someone in authority ever told you to do something that seems completely crazy? However you tried to understand the reasoning behind the order, it did not make any sense at all? But you followed the instructions, hoping and trusting that your boss knew what he or she was doing? This is what we can imagine Hosea feeling as the book opens.

I say 'imagine' because in many ways Hosea is a mysterious book. It begins abruptly with a shocking assignment for the prophet from God himself to *Go, marry a promiscuous woman and have children with her, for like an adulterous wife this land is guilty of unfaithfulness to the* LORD (2). While we can guess what he felt when he heard this divine command, there is no point trying to psychoanalyse the prophet, because we are told nothing about either his background or state of mind. Indeed we know virtually nothing about Hosea at all.[8] Remarkably for a book that bears his name, he is mentioned for the first time in 1:1, again in 1:2 and 1:4 and for the final time in 1:6! We are simply told that he did what the Lord commanded: *So he married Gomer daughter of Diblaim* (3).

Similarly for Gomer: little is known about her. In fact, how verse 2 is interpreted shapes the reader's understanding of the entire book.[9]

---

[8] It has been proposed that he was a young adult because of a relatively long prophetic career. But even this is speculation. Ibid., p. 27.

[9] The literal sense is 'wife of whoredom'. Does it mean Gomer *herself* is 'promiscuous', a 'whore' or a 'harlot'? Eugene Peterson's looser translation in *The Message* makes a judgment call: *Find a whore and marry her. Make this whore the mother of your children.* In this view Gomer represents Israel by herself being a whore: *for like an adulterous wife this land is guilty of unfaithfulness to the* LORD (2). However, some suggest the text means Gomer represents Israel spiritually rather than literally. Chapter 1 does not tell us that Gomer was unfaithful to Hosea, nor does it say she was a prostitute. It simply tells us that she bore Hosea three children who were named to reflect Israel's covenant infidelity. Is she therefore like any other Israelite woman among a nation that was, as a whole, guilty of 'spiritual prostitution'? A key strand to this view is that in ch. 3 the wife that Hosea buys back and marries

After consideration of the options, we are going to proceed on the basis that Hosea and Gomer's marriage was a real one, that Gomer was unfaithful to Hosea, that she was likely a promiscuous woman before her marriage,[10] and that it is Gomer that Hosea 'remarries' in chapter 3. The key image to keep in focus is that Hosea is commanded to participate in an extraordinary prophetic 'sign-act' in which he is literally to act out the word of the Lord to Israel in a way that will be guaranteed to get attention.[11] That word is one of both severe judgment and astonishing love.

b. Children of doom (1:4–9)

The names of the children of this unlikely marriage are to reflect the consequences of their mother's faithlessness. Rather than representing the usual joyful celebration of new life, each birth tragically adds to a gathering sense of doom.

Gomer *bore him a son* (3) who is to be named *Jezreel* (4). It is an ominous name, inextricably linked to death and violence. It was in the Valley of Jezreel that king Jehu had shed blood in a ruthless uprising to solidify political power (2 Kgs 9). Now God announces that *I will soon punish the house of Jehu for the massacre at Jezreel, and I will put an end to the kingdom of Israel. In that day I will break Israel's bow in the Valley of Jezreel* (4–5). The reigning king of Israel at the time of this prophecy was Jeroboam II. His son Zechariah, the last king of the House of Jehu, was later assassinated after six months in power (2 Kgs 15:8). Soon afterwards Israel's 'bow' was indeed broken with conquest and exile by the Assyrians.

The names of the other two children speak more explicitly of the brokenness of the relationship between God and his people. Unlike Jezreel, neither is specifically attributed to Hosea. We cannot be sure

is *not* Gomer, but a second woman. This marriage, unlike the first, is unconsummated; again, like the first, it symbolically represents God's relationship with Israel. Douglas Stuart, *Hosea–Jonah*, WBC, vol. 31 (Waco: Word, 1987), pp. 11–12. Robin Routledge has recently defended the traditional interpretation – Gomer is unfaithful and 3:1–5 depicts the restoration of their earlier relationship, 'Hosea's Marriage Reconsidered', *TynB* 69.1 (May 2018), pp. 25–43.

[10] While it is not certain that Gomer was a prostitute before marrying Hosea, such a reality fits the message of the book. Hosea marries an already faithless woman to symbolize Israel's already broken relationship with God. Or some suggest that Gomer was pure at the time of her marriage and Hosea writes looking back in the light of her unfaithfulness after their wedding. This is also possible and is argued by Routledge, ibid.

[11] Another prophetic sign-act, in Isa. 20, is Isaiah's going naked and barefoot for three years.

but perhaps Gomer is paralleling Israel's unfaithfulness in marriage to Yahweh by her own unfaithfulness to Hosea. Few names could be more awful than that of the daughter *Lo-Ruhamah* (6). It means 'unloved' or 'no compassion'. God is announcing symbolically the terrible verdict that *I will no longer show love to Israel, that I should at all forgive them* (6). God's love for Israel is at an end. After pursuing love in many directions, the terrible irony is now that they themselves have become 'Unloved'.

The third child's name, a son, is *Lo-Ammi* and is defined by verse 9 as *not my people*. The name is a logical and dreadful climax to the opening section of the book. Due to Israel's continual betrayal, the covenant, in effect, is cancelled. In total contrast to Yahweh's initial covenant announcement that 'I will take you as my own people, and I will be your God,'[12] there are now only stark words of disassociation: *I am not your God* (9).

Imagine transposing this description of complete relational breakdown to a husband and wife today. The husband has found out that his wife has been having multiple affairs over a long period of time. He is completely betrayed. He has kept his side of the marriage vows but his wife's actions have made a mockery of his loyalty. The result will almost inevitably be our default modern solution – divorce.[13] Love has died. Trust is shattered. Grief consumes the deceived lover. All that remains from this wreckage is for two autonomous individuals to go their separate ways.

And yet, and yet, this is *not* what happens in Hosea. Jon Levenson, a Jewish scholar, suggests reasons why the option of divorce in ancient Israel was no easy matter. To begin with, in Israelite society the wife was a member of the husband's household. Divorce was not her choice but her husband's. But even justified divorce could not easily resolve two major issues. The first is the profound sin of the unfaithful partner. Second, within a covenantal relationship, permanent separation of the partners is not a default option. As we saw in chapter 1 with Israel's first great 'fall' in Exodus 32, the covenant between God and his chosen nation Israel involves his deep commitment to permanence and unconditionality. For this reason 'the rejection and punishment of the faithless vassal for violation of the conditions are not the end of the story, though it often seems that they surely will be'.[14]

---

[12] Exod. 6:7.

[13] According to the UK office for National Statistics, about 45% of marriages end in divorce in the UK.

[14] Jon Levenson, *The Love of God: Divine Gift, Human Gratitude, and Mutual Faithfulness in Judaism* (Princeton: Princeton University Press, 2016), p. 96.

So while some see 1:10 – 2:1 as a later insertion incompatible with the grim scenario of 1:2–9, what Levenson says makes much better sense of the unexpectedly wonderful verses that come next.

2. Breath-taking hope (1:10 – 2:1)

Dramatically, the pronouncement of doom is followed by an oracle of astonishing blessing: not only will Israel have a future after all, but it will be the one promised by God to Abraham, *Yet the Israelites will be like the sand on the seashore, which cannot be measured or counted* (10a; Gen. 13:16; 15:5; 22:17–18; 32:12). God will, despite their repeated betrayals, keep his covenant promise to his people. While now their name has become *You are not my people* in the future once again their name will be *children of the living God* (10b). Derek Kidner captures the sense of a prodigal nation being welcomed back, in a completely unexpected way, with open arms by their father: 'The mood is that of the great parable, as though to say, "These my sons were dead, and are alive again; they were lost, and are found." '[15] And not only this; also promised is a national reunion of the divided kingdoms: *The people of Judah and the people of Israel will come together* (11a). Gone will be the bitterness and suspicion dating back to the original division of the kingdom. A new united kingdom with a jointly appointed leader awaits (11b).[16] The declaration of 2:1 reverses that of 1:2–9. They will be *Ammi, My people* and *Ruhamah, My loved one*. The relationship of deep unbreakable covenant love of God for his people will be restored.

3. Wooing the heart of an adulteress (2:1–23)

These two themes – of devastating judgment juxtaposed with words of eschatological hope – continue throughout Hosea's word to Israel. In chapter 2:2 Israel/Gomer is to

> remove the adulterous look from her face
> and the unfaithfulness from between her breasts.

Without such repentance God says in verse 3:

> *I will strip her naked*
> *and make her as bare as on the day she was born;*

---

[15] Derek Kidner, *The Message of Hosea*, BST (Leicester: Inter-Varsity Press, 1981), p. 25.
[16] Hosea comes back to this idea in 2:22 and 3:5, and we will as well.

> *I will make her like a desert,*
> *turn her into a parched land,*
> *and slay her with thirst.*

Such words sound to us harsh, alien and incompatible with love. It is as if God is some sort of violent rejected lover, using his male power to threaten a wife who no longer wants anything to do with him. But this is to fail to appreciate the nature of the covenantal relationship to which Yahweh and Israel are bound by a solemn oath. It also misses the method through which God is communicating his message. It is through Hosea's visible sign-act of marriage to Gomer that Israel are confronted with their covenant obligation of obedience to, and love for, Yahweh, the one true God. As discussed in chapter 1, this is not a covenant of equals.[17] Hosea's marriage reminds Israel they are in a 'covenant of love' and their partner is deeply grieved by their faithlessness. God as a betrayed lover is a shocking idea – that is the very point of Hosea's commission. It is designed to strike at the *heart* of the people of Israel as they identify *themselves* with a whoring wife. God is going to extreme measures to 'win' Israel's love back, not by force but by doing all he possibly can to persuade them to repent and turn back to their first love.

This is why chapter 2 describes, in effect, a competition between two lovers (Yahweh and Baal) for Israel's heart. Because Israel *went after her lovers, but me she forgot* (13), God will *block her path* to her lovers so that

> *She will chase after her lovers but not catch them;*
> *she will look for them but not find them.*
> (6–7)

His desire is that they will say

> *I will go back to my husband as at first,*
> *for then I was better off than now.*
> (7)

They will remember his goodness to them: that

> *I was the one*
> *who gave her the grain, the new wine and oil,*

---

[17] While the marital relationship is a particularly striking metaphor for the relationship between God and his people, many other metaphors also capture its unequal nature: shepherd and flock, master and slave, king and servants, father and child. See Levenson, *Love of God*, p. 100.

> *who lavished on her the silver and gold –*
> *which they used for Baal.*
> (8)

By taking away their grain, wine, wool, linen, vines and fig trees
(9–12) their false trust in Baal's provision will be laid bare. What they
thought was *pay from her lovers* (12) will be shown to be idolatrous
worship of a false god who cannot deliver on his promises. Yahweh
is confronting and teaching his unfaithful wife in order to persuade
her to abandon Baal and be reconciled with him.

The rest of chapter 2 becomes a deeply moving account of the
wronged party wooing back his estranged lover. Now it is one thing
for an unfaithful partner to repent and seek forgiveness. Even with
remorse, grace and forgiveness cannot be demanded by the unfaithful
partner; they can only be hoped for. But here it is the faithful partner
who takes the initiative to *allure her*, *lead her into the wilderness* and
speak tenderly to her (14). This is a new-salvation narrative. Once
again Israel will emerge from the wilderness and into a promised
land of blessing. God will bless them by giving *back her vineyards*,
renewing their hope and giving them a reason to sing a song of
salvation once more *as in the day she came up out of Egypt* (15). The
images are beautiful ones of a rebirth of a relationship. This is a
picture of a lover winning back his bride. Once again they will call
God *my husband* (16) and will forsake the *Baals* (17).

All this echoes Yahweh's unmerited grace in Exodus 32 – 34. In
Hosea, once again, is a fresh beginning, a new exodus, a rekindled
romance between Lord and his people. Again, eschatological hope
exists only because of the forgiving love of God. The promise that
God will make a covenant with wild animals (18) is probably to
protect Israel from harm and reverse the curse of Leviticus 26:22.[18]
The Lord will also ensure their safety by abolishing *Bow and sword*
and battle (18), a promise that stands in stark opposition to the
ominous naming of Gomer's firstborn son (1:3–5).

The chapter closes with one of the great 'love passages' in the
Hebrew Scriptures. Instead of divorce and desolation God promises
his bride that

> *I will betroth you to me for ever;*
> *I will betroth you in righteousness and justice,*
> *in love and compassion.*
> *I will betroth you in faithfulness,*
> *and you will acknowledge the LORD.*

[18] Ibid., p. 103.

> *'In that day I will respond,'*
>   *declares the Lord –*
> *'I will respond to the skies,*
>   *and they will respond to the earth;*
> *and the earth will respond to the grain,*
>   *the new wine and the olive oil,*
>   *and they will respond to Jezreel.*
> *I will plant her for myself in the land;*
>   *I will show my love to the one I called*
>   *"Not my loved one".*
> *I will say to those called "Not my people",*
>   *"You are my people";*
>   *and they will say, "You are my God."'*
> (2:19–23)

The vision is breathtaking. The world itself will be caught up in the renewed love between Yahweh and his people. In a betrothal the groom would offer a payment to the bride's family. Here God (the groom) endows Israel with the gifts of *righteousness, justice, love, compassion* and *faithfulness* to enable them this time to fulfil their marital role of a faithful and loving spouse.[19] This marriage will not fail. In contrast to when *she decked herself with rings and jewellery, and went after her lovers* (13), now they will *acknowledge the Lord* (20). The NIVUK translation fails to do justice to the last clause. The sense in the Hebrew here is 'know' which carries deep resonances of the unique covenant relationship through which Yahweh knows Israel and they know him. To know also has a moral sense: to know God means to act accordingly.[20] Once again, we are reminded how biblical love is holistic. Israel's 'knowing' of the Lord involves their mind, heart and life within a restored marriage. They will now voluntarily experience sexual love within a marriage marked by righteousness, justice, goodness, mercy and faithfulness. The result will be a flourishing relationship of love where once there was no love and of mutual belonging where there was once estrangement. As Smith comments, this chapter closes with what sounds almost like a modern-day marriage covenant ceremony of 'I take you for my wife/husband.'[21] God joyfully proclaims *You are my people* and Israel gladly responds *You are my God* (23). This beautiful image of reconciliation is entirely due to the persistence and grace of Yahweh – the betrayed lover.

[19] Ibid., p. 105.
[20] Ibid., pp. 106–107.
[21] Smith, *Hosea, Amos, Micah*, p. 64.

4. Redemptive love (3:1–5)

This short narrative replays themes present within chapters 1 and 2, but in a different setting. Gomer is now estranged from her husband and with another lover. The text does not tell us the exact circumstances but it seems that she is in some way locked into a destructive relationship from which she cannot escape even if she wants to. Hosea's God-given task is to seek out his unfaithful wife and be reconciled to her (1–3). He is to *Love her as the* LORD *loves the Israelites* (1). This means showing 'illogical' and vulnerable love to someone who does not deserve it. Verse 3 gives us a startling new image of how Hosea effects Gomer's return: he buys her for *fifteen shekels of silver and about a homer and a lethek of barley* (2). This is a generous act of redemption, in some way releasing her from bondage – perhaps by paying off her debts, or perhaps it is the price to buy her freedom from effective slavery. The conditions for her release are faithfulness – *you must not be a prostitute or be intimate with any man* (3). The result will be that Hosea will once again be her husband – *I will behave the same way toward you* (3). Just as Gomer is to be faithful, so Israel will be required to forsake anything that has captured her heart and led her astray – whether *king or prince* (political leadership) or *sacrifice or sacred stones, without ephod or household gods* (worship practices) (4). God's pursuing love leads, as at the end of chapter 2, to a glorious eschatological future picture of the repentant, voluntary and free return of Israel to her husband. Not only are the Israelites freed from bondage; they will seek their messianic king of the line of David (5). The result will be a restored relationship of love, for God's endgame is ultimately blessing.

5. Application

We began this chapter by listing some of the big questions about God and love raised by Hosea's extraordinary mission. Let us try to answer them as we consider Hosea's message of love for us today.

a. Who is the God we worship?

Hosea shows us that God is primarily a lover. He is a loyal husband whose compassion saves his marriage from an ugly end. He goes to the brink of divorce but his covenant love draws him to win her heart back. God's love is the best news in the world: it means that he relates to sinful human beings with love *before* justice. In other words, he does not treat us as we deserve. Again and again, he takes the initiative to restore and redeem, against all the odds and at considerable cost to himself. If he enacted pure justice on Israel/Gomer there would be no future, no new covenant. If he related to us today only with justice, before him no one could stand (Rom. 3:9). The love of God makes forgiveness, reconciliation and hope possible. Love flows from the essential character of God, who embodies love in all that he does. This is the beautiful message of Hosea.

b. How does God love?

God's extraordinary campaign to 'win' his bride back shows us what love is better than any textbook ever could. He loves passionately, as a husband loves his wife. Yet his love is *unlike* any human love: it takes the form of an unrelenting covenant commitment to his unfaithful bride. In chapter 11 the image switches from husband to father and uses tender imagery:

> When Israel was a child, I loved him,
>   and out of Egypt I called my son.[22]

Despite their rebellion God says

> My heart is changed within me;
>   all my compassion is aroused.
> I will not carry out my fierce anger,
>   nor will I devastate Ephraim again.
> For I am God, and not a man –
>   the Holy One among you.[23]

Such stubborn love means that betrayal does not lead to withdrawal from Israel, nor from God's covenant promise of blessing to Abraham. He loves realistically, confronting the self-destructive idolatries of the human heart. He loves tenderly (see also Hos. 11:4), refusing to use his superior power to force reciprocal love. His love is costly, taking the initiative of grace to overcome sin and rebellion. Finally, God's love is, through Hosea, an *embodied* 'flesh and blood' love. Love leads God to involvement in the world. In this sense, Hosea foreshadows a later divine act of embodied love for rebellious humans, the incarnation of the Son. The motive is once again love, communicated this time not through a sign-act of a prophet, but

---

[22] Hos. 11:1.
[23] Hos. 11:8–9.

through God's *own embodied presence in the world*, the Word made flesh (John 1:14).

It is significant, then, that Hosea reappears in the New Testament within the context of the gracious love of God, not only for Israel but for the Gentiles as well. In Romans 9:25–26 Paul tells of how God's promises of blessing for Israel have, in Christ, been applied to pagan Gentiles. They were 'not my people', but now, due to God's long forbearance through which the promise of blessing has been kept alive, Gentiles can become 'children of the living God' and 'my loved one'.[24] Peter, likewise, writing to Jewish and Gentile Christians, encourages them in the words of Hosea that together they have been brought into God's promises of blessing and mercy to his people Israel (1 Peter 2:10). What were future promises of healing and unity have now been fulfilled through the love of God in his Messiah the king, the Son of David (Hos. 1:11; 3:5).

Jim Packer once wrote that 'Theology is for doxology and devotion – that is, the praise of God and the practice of godliness.'[25] As we reflect on the unwavering determination of God to love and bless Israel and, through her, the rest of humanity, the proper response is indeed doxology and devotion: to have hearts full of praise and to live lives shaped by a desire to please and honour the one who loves us with such immeasurable grace.

c. If he is a God of love, how is divine love compatible with divine judgment? Are there limits to God's love?

Yet Yahweh's love for Israel is not a form of cheap grace where there is forgiveness without the necessity of repentance and transformed behaviour. Israel 'owe' their covenant God wholehearted love and obedience. They are warned that terrifying judgment awaits unless they turn from their false lovers. And we should not forget that judgment did indeed fall in 722 BC with the annexation of the northern kingdom.

Hosea is therefore an inspiring book but also a sobering one. Oracle after oracle tells of the seriousness of sin and its consequences, both then and in the future. While God's love will not ultimately be thwarted, neither is sin condoned. In this sense, there are limits to the love of God. He is a lover, but is also a judge. Where there is pride, exploitation, injustice and arrogant human autonomy there will not be forgiveness and reconciliation. For God *not* to judge

---

[24] Hos. 1:10; 2:23.
[25] J. I. Packer, *Concise Theology: A Guide to Historic Christian Beliefs* (Leicester: Inter-Varsity Press, 1994), p. xii.

human sin and all the terrible damage it does would be a failure of both love and justice. From Hosea it is obvious that judgment is not God's 'heart's desire' – he goes to extraordinary lengths to make it *unnecessary*. Hosea's marriage is but a foretaste of the redemptive love of God poured out in the incarnation, life, death and resurrection of Jesus.[26] But where his costly love is rejected, people are in effect self-destructively choosing judgment rather than blessing. Such a tragic outcome grieves the heart of God. In speaking of the love of God, then, we must never set it in opposition to his judgment. To do so is to portray God in almost schizophrenic terms: his 'loving side' desperately trying to overcome his 'dark, judgmental' side. The Bible never gives a hint of such a dichotomy and neither should we.

d. Loving God in a world of competing loves

Hosea poses two challenges for Christian love today.

First, the book reminds us that faith in God is primarily a matter of the heart. Christian discipleship is not a matter of *if* we love, but more of *what* we love. In this sense, Israel's failure in Hosea stems from their misdirected desire. Their heart was restless. They desired what the Baals offered – fertility, wealth, power, autonomy – and went in pursuit of these 'other lovers' (idols) and their promise of a better life.

If Israel loved the wrong things, we are no different today. One of our greatest challenges is that we exist within a hyper-consumerist culture. Modern consumerism is an idol factory designed to manufacture and manipulate our desires and so shape our lives, priorities and buying habits. We are promised hundreds of times a day that the 'good life' – joy, pleasure, happiness, contentment, fulfilment, self-esteem and social worth – is instantly within our reach and control. We are tempted to love and pursue created things as the source of life rather than the creator. We are seduced to trust in technology, money and ourselves rather than the provision of God. As with Israel, we find out that those false promises do not deliver and we are locked in a spiral of vain pursuit. Like Israel, if we are to find our true joy and vocation, we need first to love God wholeheartedly and then changed behaviour will follow. As Jesus puts it, 'Seek first his kingdom and his righteousness, and all these things will be given to you as well.'[27]

---

[26] See part 2 of this book for more detailed exposition of key texts. It is at the cross that the love and judgment of God 'meet'.

[27] Matt. 6:33.

Second, Hosea shows us that biblical love is very different from modern notions of love. Our culture has optimistic, romanticized views of both love and human nature. Love is what each of us deserves, since human nature is essentially lovable. Love has become virtually a human right – no rules or beliefs should stand in its way. Love itself is pursued as the prime source of human happiness: it makes life worth living and lives on when we die.[28] Such is our obsession with love, it is not too much to say that it is a modern idol – something we pursue with all of our being. Yet in Hosea, love is obedience to God; it is corporate rather than individualistic, it is not about self-fulfilment but disciplined faithfulness. This means that we need to be clear-sighted in how we talk about love within the church. To say 'God loves you just as you are' or to sing worship songs framed in the romantic language of popular erotic love songs can all too easily be co-opted to feed voracious modern desires for self-affirmation. It runs the risk of collapsing the covenant love of God into the language of sentimental human romance. Without good teaching, divine love can be assumed simply to endorse behaviour and attitudes incompatible with authentic discipleship. Such therapeutic theology cuts off passion for spiritual transformation at its root because we have already 'arrived'. It can (mis)lead us comfortably to assume 'God loves me' and then get on with living life as if God does not exist.

The love of God is the greatest of all biblical themes. But Hosea warns us never to fall into the trap of equating God's love as a licence to pursue desires that take us far from his presence. We are not in a marriage of equals. God is not a slightly greater version of ourselves.[29] His love is a cause for wonder and joy; it is also a cause for humility, repentance, reverence and fear. It is this latter aspect that we Western Christians are in far more danger of forgetting. If God were to send us a shocking prophetic sign-act today, what do you think its target might be and would we get the message?

[28] For detailed discussion of the development of love from Plato to the modern day see Simon May, *Love: A History* (London: Yale University Press, 2011).

[29] This recalls Karl Barth's saying that 'One *cannot* speak *of God simply* by speaking of *man in a loud voice.*' *The Word of God and the Word of Man*, tr. Douglas Horton (London: Hodder & Stoughton, 1928), p. 195. Emphasis original.

Deuteronomy 6:4–25
4. Love the Lord your God

In this chapter we turn *from* the love of God *to* Israel's response to her Lord. There is no better place to begin than with one of Scripture's best-known statements, the Shema of Deuteronomy 6:4–5: *Hear, O Israel: the* Lord *our God, the* Lord *is one. Love the* Lord *your God with all your heart and with all your soul and with all your strength*. Significantly, this command to love God is reiterated by Jesus in the New Testament in Matthew 22:37, Mark 12:28–34 and Luke 10:27, and we will consider the Luke text in chapter 11.

The term Shema comes from the Hebrew word for 'hear'. Within first-century Judaism twice-daily reciting of the Shema had almost certainly become embedded within Jewish piety,[1] and has been ever since. If so, then Jesus and his disciples would also have followed this practice. It was then, and is now, one of the most familiar texts in all of Scripture to an observant Jew.[2] Today the Shema is said as a dying Jew's last words and the last thing a Jewish child utters before going to sleep at night.

The Shema's appearance in both Old and New Testaments is an obvious clue as to its special status. As we will see, this is a text of core significance concerning the message of love.[3]

Hear, O Israel is a phrase that occurs at various significant points in the book. Some see its appearance here as opening a major section that closes with another *Hear, O Israel* (as they are about to cross the Jordan in 9:1–29). In between are promises of blessing and warnings of disaster centred around the core imperative of 8:1,

[1] Kim Huat Tan, 'The Shema in Early Christianity', *TynB* 59.2 (2008), pp. 181–206.
[2] The complete form of the Shema in Jewish tradition includes Deut. 6:4–9; 11:13–21; Num. 15:37–41.
[3] For a brief introduction to the overall context and structure of Deuteronomy see chapter 2.

'Be careful to keep God's commandments'.⁴ In 5:1 'Hear, Israel' introduces a regiving of the ten commandments and now in 6:4 the phrase calls the people once more to pay close attention. What they are about to hear is of critical significance.

The exact wording of verse 4 is open to interpretation since Hebrew does not include the verb 'to be', but the NIVUK translation of *the* LORD *our God, the* LORD *is one* is probably the best reading.⁵ This combination of authoritative prophetic spoken words and need for open ears foreshadows a later and greater prophet than Moses who came speaking in parables (Luke 24:44; John 1:17; Heb. 3:3). The critical test in both cases is the same – would the people have 'ears to hear'?

1. Three-dimensional listening: cognitive love (6:4)

For Israel truly to 'hear' what it means to love God involves what we can call 'three-dimensional' listening across cognitive, affective and behavioural learning domains. The rest of this chapter is structured around unpacking these three dimensions.

First, they must *understand* factual truth – that the Lord their God is one. This sort of learning is *cognitive* – the act or process of knowing something in our minds. Verse 4 is essentially a propositional truth claim proclaimed before the gathered assembly for them to consider and accept. But what does it mean to say God is one?

There is more than one plausible reading of this verse. The emphasis on oneness acts to reinforce Israel's vocation only ever to worship the one true God who has delivered (Deut. 4:34–35) them from slavery: he alone is real, so it is by the Lord's name alone they are to swear (6:13). In other words, the oneness of God is linked directly to the exclusive relationship between Yahweh and his people.

The pronouncement of verse 4 also stresses the singularity of God. He is one, unlike the competing and warring false gods of the surrounding nations. 'Yahweh is not the brand name of a cosmic corporation. He is the one God, our God, and Yahweh is his personal name.'⁶ To worship something or someone else is to worship an idol (6:14). There is only one God and Israel's vocation is to be

⁴ Duane L. Christensen, *Deuteronomy 1:1–21:9*, WBC, vol. 6A rev. (Nashville: Thomas Nelson, 2001), p. 137.
⁵ Lit. the Hebrew reads, 'the LORD our God the LORD one'. The NIVUK footnote lists three other ways that this verse can be translated: *The* LORD *our God is one* LORD; or *The* LORD *is our God, the* LORD *is one*; or *The* LORD *is our God, the* LORD *alone*.
⁶ Christopher J. H. Wright, *Deuteronomy*, NIBC (Peabody: Hendrickson, 1996), p. 96.

his faithful people. Elsewhere in Scripture it is God alone who is the creator. The gods of the nations had a beginning; Yahweh does not (Isa. 43:10–13) and therefore he alone is God.

Oneness in verse 4, suggests John Goldingay, also alludes to the idea that God has an inner unity and consistency.[7] It is God alone who has chosen and redeemed Israel. He is the God of covenant love who will keep his promises and it is he alone who can be trusted to the uttermost. In this sense, Israel is being reminded of God's complete reliability.

It is not necessary to set any of these readings over against each other. The verse most explicitly supports God's singularity, but his uniqueness and covenant faithfulness are strongly supported by the wider context. Yahweh is one and this one true God is in covenant relationship with a particular people. That relationship is being worked out through all the messiness and contingencies of human history – the Shema after all is uttered on the cusp of a new chapter in that tumultuous journey. As they venture into the unknown promised land without their leader Moses the people of Israel are to hold tight to this astonishing revelation of who it is who goes before them.

2. Three-dimensional listening: affective love (6:5, 10–19)

But to 'hear' means more than cognitive understanding alone. A second dimension of listening that Israel must experience is *affective* – within the realm of emotions, feelings and attitudes – and this takes us right into verse 5. For Israel to 'hear' they are not only to understand but also to *love* the Lord their God with all their heart, soul and strength. This wonderful sentence reminds us that human beings are not brains who happen to have bodies, dispassionately processing information to make objective decisions. That is a modern Enlightenment idea that wrongly elevates the mind above the heart as the seat of who we really are as people. Descartes famously said, 'I think therefore I am,' and we have become dualists in prioritizing the head (thinking) above the heart. This move has had very unfortunate consequences for Christian teaching and discipleship. The 'love command' of Deuteronomy confronts us with the reality that the propositional truth of 'God is one' must be appropriated deep down personally in our hearts for it to be truly known.

To us, with our modern Western ideas of individualistic and free romantic love, it may seem very strange that love can be commanded,

---

[7] John Goldingay, *Israel's Faith*, OTT, vol. 2 (Downers Grove: InterVarsity Press, 2006), p. 38.

but that is certainly what is happening in Deuteronomy. However, while Israel is being instructed to 'love God', it is not in some sort of legalistic or robotic manner. Goldingay notes that the word for love used here (*'āhab*) has a broad sense, not altogether unlike the English word 'love'. It is the Old Testament's 'catch-all' word for affection, liking, passion, devotion, caring and dedication. For example, it is used of Isaac's love for Rebekah and Esau's love of stew (Gen. 24:67; 25:28; 27:4). In the Psalms it is used of love for violence, the temple, God's deliverance, and especially of loving God's commands (Ps. 119:47–48, 97, 113, 119, 159).[8]

Given this background, we can see how the love command to Israel gets beyond knowledge alone, to the affective domain. Israel's response of complete devotion is to be the antithesis of half-hearted obedience. They are to pour out *all of who they are* – heart, soul and strength – into honouring and obeying the God whom they love. God is speaking through Moses to the people he loves and calling them into a renewal of their covenant commitment. That renewal is not purely 'legal' but in a very real sense is sealed in love. Love is the language of relationship and knowing and pleasing the other person. This is why the command begins with focus on the heart. In the Bible the 'heart' (*lēbāb*) is the seat of the will, the essential core of our being. The people's wholehearted love for God will mean that they will live in grateful response to his love. In other words, Israel's love for God flows *from* God's prior love for his people and echoes the structure of the Decalogue in 5:6–21, which begins with who God is and moves to Israel's obedient response to that revelation. Leon Morris comments, 'love for God is clearly at the heart of religious life as it is envisaged in Deuteronomy'.[9]

The English translation to love with all your 'soul' can easily be misunderstood because of the popular Platonic idea of the soul as the disembodied essence of a human being.[10] The Hebrew word *nepeš* is quite different and refers to the life of each person – 'the whole inner self with all the emotions, desires and personal characteristics that make each person unique'.[11] To 'love with all your strength' in Hebrew literally means 'with all your much-muchness' – a very unusual use of the word as a noun here. Elsewhere it is used as an adverb like 'exceedingly' or 'greatly'.[12] The overall point is

---

[8] John Goldingay, *Israel's Life*, OTT, vol. 3. (Downers Grove: IVP Academic, 2009), p. 67.

[9] Leon Morris, *Testaments of Love: A Study of Love in the Bible* (Grand Rapids: Eerdmans, 1981), p. 40.

[10] For this reason Goldingay translates soul as 'spirit'. *Israel's Life*, p. 66.

[11] Wright, *Deuteronomy*, p. 99.

[12] Ibid.

unmistakable: these three terms together (heart, soul, strength) are commanding an extravagant, total, unhesitating and unrestrained love of God. All of God's people's energy and enthusiasm to be expended on loving him.

We should not miss how there is certainly a hierarchical or uneven relationship at play here: Yahweh and Israel are not equals within an egalitarian relationship. It is the Lord who is the one true God who is to be worshipped; he is their redeemer who has saved them from slavery; it is his covenant laws that they are to obey; it is his judgment that they will experience if they turn away. But there is no contradiction between one side of the covenant relationship being far superior to the other and its still being a covenant of love. God has pledged his complete loyalty and love to his chosen people; they are to do the same in return. God is the initiator of the covenant; Israel is the beneficial recipient, yet both sides are committed to love each other.

This context helps us to understand verses 10–19, which we will consider here since they are primarily about the heart – or, more precisely, about potential ways the heart can be misdirected from love of God. They contain a series of warnings about three future temptations the people will face in the promised land – wealth, worship (idolatry) and worry.

In verses 10–13 is a warning about the danger of their impending new-found life of ease. They will enjoy the land, given as a gift, flourishing cities they did not build, houses filled with good things, plentiful water, productive vineyards and olive groves. The result will be a life of satisfaction where they will 'eat and be satisfied'. All of this is a very long way from their previous homeless desert wanderings. The text shows no illusions: rest, pleasure, satisfaction and abundance can lead to complacency and forgetting the one who is the source of all blessing. They may also forget where they came from – the land of slavery (12). What is the protective 'solution' to this danger of forgetting? They are to *fear the* LORD and *serve him only* (13). There is a deliberate play on words in verse 13. The Hebrew for 'serve' shares the same root with 'slavery' – the people called out of slavery now must live as Yahweh's devoted slaves. Of course this sounds rather bizarre to our modern ears – how can love and 'slavery' coexist? This is where it helps to see the problem at issue as one of misdirected love rather than imposed law. The temptation of wealth and pleasure is not so much for things themselves but how they draw our hearts away from the creator of those good things. 'Heart, soul, strength' love is an utterly committed rightly directed love that resolutely refuses to be distracted by the temporary promises of wealth and pleasure. In a paradoxical way it is through such 'slavery' that the people of God find their true identity and freedom.

Similarly the second warning concerns false worship, this time of the specifically religious kind. They are not to let their hearts become captive to the gods of the surrounding Canaanite culture. To do so would be to deny the reality of Yahweh's presence with them and be a complete betrayal of covenant love. The consequences are fearful – they would experience Yahweh's consuming anger and severe judgment (15).

The third warning is brief but important. At Massah the people had rebelled at the lack of water in the desert (Exod. 17:1–17). Their grumbling was in effect 'putting the LORD to the test' as they worried that they would die in the heat, dust and sand of the wilderness. In a time of hardship they lost faith that God was with them and would keep his word. Again the underlying issue is affective – a lack of belief in the goodness and faithfulness of God when times get tough.

How are Israel to overcome these temptations of wealth, (false) worship and worry? By faithful obedience to God's commands. The land and all its blessings are going to be theirs by gift and fulfilled promise (18). Their obedient behaviour is not a means by which to gain the gift, but is to be a faithful expression of love, gratitude and rightly directed worship.

3. Three-dimensional listening: behavioural love (6:7–9, 20–25)

The third dimension of 'hearing' what it means to love God in this passage is *behavioural*. If the people of Israel are loving the one true God with their heart, soul and strength, they will be deeply committed to *act* in ways that honour God. What we love gives shape and practical organization to our lives. If Israel truly loves God, then they will orientate their entire life around their worship of him.

In his book *You Are What You Love: The Spiritual Power of Habit*, Jamie Smith makes a convincing case that love is a habit that can, and indeed must, be learned. This is because no culture is somehow 'neutral'. Our Western consumer one is constantly seeking to capture our hearts, our loves. It is what we orientate our lives around that will show what we truly love because, says Smith, we worship what we love. It is naive and reductionistic to believe that all we need to do is get our teaching right and 'know' the right doctrines in order to live well. This formula for discipleship simply misses how we are formed by all sorts of unconscious influences, desires and habits that dispose us to act in certain ways. Smith refers to modern psychology, which suggests that 95% of what we do in the world is unconscious habit ('second nature'), only 5% is the result of choices.[13] The challenge this poses for Christian discipleship is first for us to become aware of the importance of what we love (not just what we say or think we believe), and second then to build in good habits into our lives that help to 'train' and orientate and reinforce our love towards God.

I mention all this because it ties right in to what is going on in Deuteronomy 6. We need to relearn from the deep wisdom of Scripture what holistic love looks like in practice. Verse 6 is crucial. We might have expected the text to say, 'Keep these words that I am commanding you in your mind.' But the verse says *These commandments that I give you today are to be on your hearts.* It is our hearts that need to be trained in love. But how?

To begin to answer this question it is helpful to use an illustration from education and how people learn and then apply it to Deuteronomy. In respect to the role played by emotions, attitudes and motivations in learning, Perry Shaw describes a series of stages that lead to a full and transformative learning experience.[14] The first stage is 'receiving' – being willing to hear and consider a particular perspective. But passive receiving is a poor sort of learning. The next stage is 'responding', where the listeners do something with the material. For students in a class this can be entering into classroom discussion, asking intelligent questions or discussing key points with the instructor after class. A third stage is 'valuing', where the students have wrestled with a perspective and come to express a commitment to what view they prefer. But expression of preference is meaningful only when the fourth stage, 'organization', takes place. This is where students internalize the material and begin acting on it in practical ways. The final stage is 'characterization', where the student builds his or her life around the viewpoint and its value system.

It is remarkable how well this describes exactly the sort of learning that is going on in Deuteronomy 6. Israel has 'received' teaching from Moses. They are already committed to 'responding' to it in the light of failures and have promised obedience (Deut. 5:27) – a form of 'valuing'. As chapter 6 progresses we see practical 'organization' take place to embody and enact the command to *Love the LORD your God.* The whole goal of the chapter, and indeed the entire book, is 'characterization' – where Israel as a nation reorientates their

---

[13] James K. A. Smith, *You Are What You Love: The Spiritual Power of Habit* (Grand Rapids: Brazos, 2016), p. 33.

[14] Perry Shaw, 'Towards a Multidimensional Approach to Theological Education', *International Congregational Journal* 6.1 (2006), pp. 53–63.

entire life and worship around a deep-seated love for their God – heart, soul and strength.

We can see 'organization' and subsequent 'characterization' being implemented from verse 7 onwards. Israel are commanded to build in good behavioural habits in order to orientate and reinforce daily their love of God and his laws. This is in practice what it means for the people to incline their hearts to fear and obey God and so experience his blessing (Deut. 5:29).

> *Recite them to your children and talk about them when you are at home and when you are away, when you lie down and when you rise. Bind them as a sign on your hand, fix them as an emblem on your forehead, and write them on the doorposts of your house and on your gates.* (7–9, NRSVA)

This involves verbal repetition, memorization and physical reminders of God's laws, consciously and intentionally integrating them in everyday life at individual (hand, forehead, lie down, get up), family (recite to children, talk at home, doorposts) and public levels of life (when away, gates – the place of civic business).[15] These sorts of *embodied* habits or rituals will not only orientate and train the love of adults, but will cause children to ask their meaning (Deut. 6:20). Parents will be able to explain their significance in terms of the redeeming work of God, Israel's identity and belonging in the world as God's people and their vocation to live by the Torah in obedience to the living God (Deut. 6:21–25).

4. Concluding applications

The resounding theological claims of the Shema continue to reverberate today. There are at least five echoes that we need to hear afresh.

First, Deuteronomy 6 is a powerful example of a holistic and integrated understanding of love – cognitive, affective and behavioural. There is no artificial distinction here between thinking, feeling and acting in terms of what constitutes love. Neither is it a case of a nice linear one-, two-, three-stage process of getting our thinking right, which impacts our feelings and then changes our behaviour. What is going on is more simultaneously three-dimensional: what we think, what we feel and how we act constitute parts of what it means

---

[15] Scholars debate whether these commands were meant metaphorically or literally, but there is evidence that later Judaism did take them literally. The larger point is that there is harmony between the outward sign and inward reality. See J. G. McConville, *Deuteronomy*, AOTC (Leicester: Apollos, 2002), p. 142.

to love. All three are an integral part of what it means to 'Hear, O Israel'. Israel will not have 'heard' unless they do know, feel and also act on what they know and feel. This echoes what the American nineteenth-century pastor and theologian Horace Bushnell said: 'No truth is taught by words or learned by intellectual means. Truth must be lived into meaning before it can be truly known.'[16]

Evangelical Christians (of which I am one) need, I suspect, to learn afresh the holistic nature of Shema love. We are more shaped by Descartes than we might think (excuse the pun). With our love of objective doctrine and the Bible itself, combined with a suspicion of subjective emotionalism disconnected from solid truth, all too easily we equate knowing God with knowledge about God and prioritize the mind over the heart. Love, then, becomes a potential attitudinal add-on to an intellectually understood set of propositions about the gospel. Subsequent behaviour traditionally linked to holiness and sanctification within the church is also somehow less important than the individual assenting to the right beliefs.

Second, there is one aspect of this passage that is obvious but that we have only touched on and need to consider. That is, the Shema is given, not to isolated individuals each on his or her own journey to the promised land, but to the corporate nation of Israel. It is *together* that they know and love God and obey his commands. It is together that they are to *do what is right and good in the sight of the LORD* (Deut. 6:18, ESVUK). The plural language in 6:23–25 is worth noting because it is so striking:

> He brought *us* out from there in order to bring *us* in, to give *us* the land that he promised on oath to *our* ancestors. Then the LORD commanded *us* to observe all these statutes, to fear the LORD our God, for *our* lasting good, so as to keep *us* alive, as is now the case. If *we* diligently observe this entire commandment before the LORD *our* God, as he has commanded *us*, *we* will be in the right. (NRSVA)

Our Western ways of thinking about love as primarily an erotic and intense emotion that lone individuals can 'fall' in and out of, makes it difficult for us to see love in these more holistic and communal terms. Deuteronomy will have none of this. It calls each one of us into the discipline of the community of the people of God, for it is corporate worship that provides the God-given context for developing a right ordering of our loves.

Third, a text like Deuteronomy 6 challenges our fragmented thinking and practice about love. In particular it invites us to

---

[16] Quoted in Shaw, 'Theological Education', pp. 53–63.

consider how we might integrate daily routines into our lives that 'embody' countercultural messages of God's living and active presence, his measureless love and the call for each one of us to shape our lives wholeheartedly around loving him. One practical but possibly life-transforming idea is simply to recite the Shema first thing as you get up in the morning and last thing as you go to bed at night, reflecting and praying in the evening on the events of the day in the light of God's great command.[17]

Fourth, in the introduction to this book we touched on popular contemporary perceptions of love. One was 'universal love' – love as the essence of all religions or simply a virtue, chosen somewhat arbitrarily, that makes life in the absence of the divine worth living. Deuteronomy confronts any such dehistoricized, depersonalized and ill-defined notions about love and God. The Shema's declaration in verse 4 and command to love in verse 5 are specific and personal: it is Yahweh the God of the historic nation of Israel who is the one true God of all. The command to love in verse 5 is not an abstract call to love a vague idea of the divine at the centre of all reality. Nor is it a call to love love itself. Rather it is a command to love Yahweh in particular, for he is the one true God who alone is worthy of our complete devotion. The God who is the subject of our love has a name and a history. Chris Wright puts it well:

> the sharp precision of the Shema cannot be evaporated into a philosophical abstraction or relegated to a penultimate level of truth. Its majestic declaration of a monotheism defined by the history-laden, character-rich, covenant-related, dynamic personhood of 'Yahweh our God', shows that the abstract and definitionally undefinable 'being' of religious pluralism is really a monism without meaning or message.[18]

Fifth, the Shema should also cause us to reflect humbly and fearfully on the competing loves within our culture that seek relentlessly to capture our hearts and draw us away from the one true God. Idolatry is not simply an Old Testament problem that no longer applies in our modern world. We need to guard our hearts against false idols just as much as Israel needed to guard against the worship of false gods. For it is in wholehearted love for God that we find true purpose, identity and joy.

---

[17] This is a practice suggested by Scot McKnight in his book *The Jesus Creed: Loving God, Loving Others*, 10th anniversary edn (Brewster: Paraclete, 2014).
[18] Wright, *Deuteronomy*, p. 98.

Song of Songs 4 – 5
5. Erotic love

In the summer of 2010 a son discovered a large cache of his late mother's writings in an attic. Among hundreds of poems were forty-five sonnets written to the great love of her life, the son's stepfather. Most of the sonnets were penned between 1949 and 1954. The majority (seventeen to forty-five) tell of the woman's almost fanatical pursuit of her beloved and the anguish of unrequited love. The sonnets are not only beautifully written by a professional poet; they reveal with stunning honesty her fierce passion for him, her struggles with God as well as her loneliness and exasperation with the kind-hearted academic bachelor who was breaking her heart. I can give only a flavour here. In one she tells the story of her being awakened to vibrant life but her 'gardener' only wanting a platonic friendship:

> There was a man who found a naked tree
> Sleeping in winter woods, and brought her home.
> And tended her a month in charity
> Until she woke, and filled his quiet room
> With petals like a storm of silver light.
> Bursting, blazing, blended all of pearl
> And moonshine; he, in wonder and delight.
> Patted her magic boughs and said: Good girl.
> Thereafter, still obedient to the summer
> The tree worked at her trade, until behold
> A summer miracle of red and gold.
> Apples of the Hesperides upon her.
> Sweeter than Eden and its vanished bowers . . .
> He said: No, no, I only wanted flowers.

Another sonnet gives a flavour of her sexual frustration:

Do not be angry that I am a woman
And so have lips that want your kiss, and breasts
That want your fingers on them; being human
I need a heart on which my heart can rest;
Do not be angry that I cry your name
At the harsh night, or wear the darkness through
With blind arms groping for you in a dream
I was made flesh for this, and so were you.

The woman was Joy Davidman,[1] the man C. S. Lewis. The discovery
of Davidman's poems puts Lewis's *A Grief Observed* (in which he
called her H) in a new light. In a sense, here after her death, are the
man's written replies (if not in poetic form) to her earlier entreaties.
These are his words:

> For those few years H. and I feasted on love; every mode of it –
> solemn and merry, romantic and realistic, sometimes as dramatic
> as a thunderstorm, sometimes as comfortable and unemphatic as
> putting on your soft slippers. No cranny of heart or body
> remained unsatisfied.[2]
>
> There is one place where her absence comes locally home to me,
> and it is a place I can't avoid. I mean my own body. It had such a
> different importance while it was the body of H's lover. Now it's
> like an empty house.[3]

Davidman and Lewis's courageous honesty articulates for us how
erotic love is probably the most powerful expression of the universal
human need for intimacy. We are, after all, sexual beings, not disembodied minds. In this they mirror two other lovers to whom we
now turn.

1. Interpreting the Song of Songs

It would be deeply remiss, in a study on love in the Bible, to overlook
the book that speaks most of human sexual love – the Song of Songs.
It is a delightful collection of exchanges, primarily between two
lovers, expressing in poetry and song their love and erotic desire for

---

[1] The quotes above are from Don W. King, 'A Naked Tree: Joy Davidman's Love
Poems to C. S. Lewis', *STR* 57.3 (2014), pp. 246–280. Quotes from pp. 268–269 and
279 respectively © Estate of Helen Joy Davidman and used with permission. The full
set of sonnets is published in Don W. King, *The Naked Tree: Love Sonnets to C. S.
Lewis and Other Poems by Joy Davidman* (Grand Rapids: Eerdmans, 2015).

[2] C. S. Lewis, *A Grief Observed* (London: Faber & Faber, 1961), pp. 8–9.

[3] Ibid., p. 12.

each other. The form likely represents a series of songs, with main parts for a man and woman, interspersed with interjections by a female chorus (the daughters of Jerusalem). There is no clear narrative. Rather, together the songs combine to give us, within the Bible, a unique lyrical insight into the nature and joy of sexual love between a man and a woman. Some of the 117 verses that make up its eight short chapters contain unforgettable lines such as these:

> Place me like a seal over your heart,
>   like a seal on your arm;
> for love is as strong as death,
>   its jealousy unyielding as the grave.
> It burns like blazing fire,
>   like a mighty flame.
> Many waters cannot quench love;
>   rivers cannot sweep it away.[4]

These words are spoken by the woman, a Shulammite (6:13) who is the 'lead' character. It is she who most often takes the sexual initiative and who speaks most. She introduces herself as 'Dark, am I, yet lovely',[5] her skin darkened by manual work in the sun.[6] The book opens and closes with her passionate longing for her beloved:

> Let him kiss me with the kisses of his mouth –
>   for your love is more delightful than wine.[7]

And the book's final words:

> Come away, my beloved,
>   and be like a gazelle
> or like a young stag
>   on the spice-laden mountains.[8]

There are various uncertainties about the origin, structure and interpretation of the book. These need not delay us long here, save to outline our approach to the exegesis of the text. Our main focus is to explore this canonical text's 'message of love', which we will do by examining a representative dialogue between the woman and the man (ch. 4, the man; excerpts from ch. 5, the woman).

[4] Song 8:6–7a.
[5] Song 1:5.
[6] In contrast, fair skin for women was considered a sign of beauty and status.
[7] Song 1:2.
[8] Song 8:14.

The date of composition is debated. Seven mentions of Solomon, not least in verse 1:1, suggest a pre-exilic date during his reign (Song 1:1, 5; 3:7, 9, 11; 8:11–12),[9] but many scholars opt for a post-exilic date. Some see two men involved, one a humble shepherd (Song 1:7–8), the other the great king wooing the first's true love and trying to take her away for himself. A similar question exists around the identity of the woman. She appears to be a beautiful country girl, yet also is known in the royal courts where 'queens and concubines praised her'.[10] We will follow Jon Levenson's proposal that these descriptions of the main protagonists are most likely 'a literary device that advances a key theme of the whole book – the transience of the lovers' availability to each other'.[11] The poems are mostly the imaginative desires of two people longing to be together. For example, in 1:6–7 she has been made by her brothers to tend vineyards in the sun while her own 'vineyard' (her body, her deepest desires) is neglected. So she seeks her lover where he grazes his flock. Chapter 3 begins:

> all night long on my bed
> I looked for the one my heart loves.[12]

Not finding him, she searches for him in the city. In chapter 5:2–8 there is a curious story (or dream) of her sleeping and his leaving. In her vain seeking for him she is beaten by the watchmen who steal her cloak (why is unclear). In chapter 7 she longs to get away with him to the countryside and its village vineyards, where 'there I will give you my love'.[13] In chapter 8 she wishes he were her brother that she could 'kiss you, and no one would despise me'.[14] All this suggests that as a result of some sort of social opposition the lovers desperately imagine scenes where they can delight in each other in uninterrupted peaceful seclusion. So when she finds 'the one my heart loves, I held him and would not let him go' and takes him to the privacy of a room in her mother's house.[15] Other images of peace and solitude include a garden (Song 6:2–3) or cleft of rock in the mountainside where he longs for her 'to show me your face, let me hear your sweet voice'.[16]

[9] For more detailed discussion, see Duane Garrett, *Song of Songs*, WBC, vol. 23B (Nashville: Thomas Nelson, 2004), pp. 47–57.

[10] Song 6:9.

[11] Jon Levenson, *The Love of God: Divine Gift, Human Gratitude, and Mutual Faithfulness in Judaism* (Princeton: Princeton University Press, 2016), p. 128.

[12] Song 3:1.

[13] Song 7:12.

[14] Song 8:1.

[15] Song 3:4. This image of bringing him to her mother's house is repeated in 8:2.

[16] Song 2:14.

This is 'young love', reflecting the intense physical attraction of two lovers intoxicated with each other's bodies and the thrill of the adventure of a future life together. It is also 'married love'.[17] The book does not tell us the lovers' identities or details of their lives. We can only speculate, but perhaps the songs are compiled by the author to represent the joys and longings of a young couple passionately in love, getting married probably by arrangement between their families, wrestling with obstacles that are combining to keep them apart. It seems that the marriage is not yet consummated (Song 4:12) and all they want to do is to escape to be with each other. Perhaps the poet based his work on observations of a couple he knew, or perhaps he wrote out of his own experience of love, or perhaps it is all a work of creative imagination. The poetic form suggests that such questions are largely irrelevant; ultimately 'all we have is an idealized portrait of love'.[18] This means that the book tells us little about marriage itself[19] and it is anachronistic to read it as some sort of ancient sex manual. Rather, our approach will be to read the songs at face value – as an artistic form celebrating the joys and beauty of erotic love between a man and a woman. The lovers in this sense are archetypal characters rather than historical people. In the exegesis below, therefore, the questions we will be asking revolve around the poetic meaning of images and metaphors rather than any other 'hidden' levels of significance implied by the text.

This approach means that we are rejecting reading more into the Song of Songs than is in the text. In my view few other books of the Bible, apart from perhaps Revelation, have suffered more from eisegesis (reading external meanings into the text). Famously, strands in both Jewish[20] and Christian (early church, Catholic and Protestant) interpretation over the centuries have seen in the lovers' relationship an allegory of God's love for Israel or Christ's love for the church / pious soul respectively.[21] But the fatal problem of allegorical interpretations is that they effectively silence the text and replace its plain meaning with one invented by the allegorizer. While there is a spectrum of modern feminist interpretations of the book, they too tend to see levels of meaning in the text that are highly

[17] He calls her his 'bride' six times in 4:8 – 5:1.

[18] Garrett, *Song of Songs*, p. 91.

[19] The theme of love and Christian marriage is discussed in chapter 16.

[20] For a recent example of a Jewish reading of the book within the wider story of Israel, see Levenson, *Love of God*, pp. 131–142.

[21] There is a bewildering variety of allegorical interpretations of specific metaphors but these are the main themes. For an entertaining tour of imaginative allegories over the centuries see Garrett, *Song of Songs*, pp. 59–76. He makes a telling point that once the church embraced celibacy and sexual renunciation as a spiritual ideal, an allegorizing approach to the Song of Songs was inevitable (p. 69).

debatable – the most common being that the poem is deliberately subversive to ancient Israelite patriarchy.[22] Yet is it highly unlikely that this is the intent of the poet.

2. The man's love for his beautiful bride (4:1–15)

a. An adoring male gaze (1–7)

We join the lyrical dialogues with the man's voice. Verses 1–5 are highly visual, one metaphor tumbling over another in describing her eyes, hair, teeth, lips, mouth, temples, neck and breasts (Song 4:1–5).[23] The metaphors he uses are alien to us, but the overall tone is clear – she is, to use a modern phrase, 'drop dead gorgeous' in his eyes. She is his *darling* (beloved companion). Many commentators discuss potential sources of meaning of *eyes behind your veil are doves* (1) but without much certainty beyond that her eyes are very attractive. Her hair is perhaps thick, dark and wavy (*like a flock of goats*, 1). She has a full set of white teeth (2) – a striking feature in the ancient world centuries before the development of modern dentistry. That *her lips are like a scarlet ribbon* (3) speaks primarily of the colour red, considered an attractive feature then and today (her look imitated by countless women today via red lipstick). The phrase *your mouth is lovely* (3) could mean her speech is pleasing but his focus is on her face, which he adores. Her temples probably refer to her cheekbones and side of her head, *like the halves of a pomegranate* most likely referring to their pink colour rather than the shape of a pomegranate per se. That a pomegranate is sweet to taste is also probably in the background. She is in vibrant health, striking in her beauty. Verse 4, *Your neck is like the tower of David*, built with stone and able to *hang a thousand shields*, is probably not recommended as a term of flattery today. We can make an educated guess as to what it meant then. The reference to Israel's great king combined with ideas of strength and military power suggests a woman who is self-assured and forceful. He evidently respects her as she respects herself. How her *breasts are like two fawns* (5) has been the source of much speculation! Gledhill's suggestion that they are 'graceful, sprightly and playful' may be on the mark.[24] They display her youth, femininity and sexual appeal. That he 'browses

---

[22] See ibid., pp. 84–90.

[23] Both this and her description of him in 5:10–16 (and 6:4–9; 7:1–8) are examples of a *wasf* – a love poem admiring the features of the beloved from the head downwards. Tom Gledhill, *The Message of the Song of Songs: The Lyrics of Love*, BST (Leicester: Inter-Varsity Press, 1993), p. 153.

[24] Ibid., p. 157.

among the lilies'[25] echoes how his lips are like fawns to her – together these verses invite an image of his kissing her breasts. Almost as if he cannot restrain himself anymore, he breaks from physical description into what he longs to do as he looks upon his perfect bride. *Until the day breaks and the shadows flee* (6) is a metaphor for the night. The *mountain of myrrh* and *the hill of incense* are obvious images for her breasts as places of sensual pleasure.[26] Quite bluntly, he is sexually aroused and desires to make love to her all night long. She could not be more perfect to him: *there is no flaw in you* (7).

It is worth pausing for a moment here to consider 'the male gaze'. The term originates in modern feminist cultural theory and refers to how women are pervasively objectified within contemporary Western culture as a source of male pleasure. It can be summarized as 'men do the looking; women are to be looked at'. Each time a man's gaze dwells on a woman's body, taking it in and greedily consuming her, he is objectifying her and using her for his own pleasure. It is this sort of selfish and lustful male gaze that Jesus condemns in Matthew 5:27–29 as equivalent to adultery. The day-to-day destructive impact of the male gaze on women is probably impossible to overestimate – especially if you are a man. It is the driving force behind the pornographic revolution of our Internet age – there would not be pornography without 'market demand'. But there is such a thing as a 'rightly directed' male gaze and it is described here in verses 1–7. By 'rightly directed' I mean that it is not sexual attraction of a man to a woman per se which is the problem; it is the *indiscriminate* gaze of male lust towards women that is destructive. What 4:1–7 describes is a celebration of sexual pleasure between two people in an exclusive marriage relationship. His (welcome) gaze is a passionate joyful expression of tender love and delight in the other.

b. How delightful is your love (8–11)

We noted earlier how a major theme in the book is the transience of the lovers' availability to each other. A sense of this appears in verse 8:

> Come from Lebanon, my bride,
> come from Lebanon.[27]

[25] Song 2:16.

[26] See 7:7–8 for an even more explicit image.

[27] The MT has 'Come with me'; but others support 'Come', which makes best sense here. The NIVUK has 'Come with me', which I have amended in the translation above.

> *Descend from the crest of Amana,*
> *from the top of Senir, the summit of Hermon,*
> *from the lions' dens*
> *and the mountain haunts of leopards.*

He calls her to him; she is utterly desirable but also remote and out of reach. The imagery is remarkable. He imagines her as a goddess in her mountain lair, dwelling with lions and leopards. Senir and Hermon are the same mountain, with Amana they represent the highest peaks in the region. Scholars point to multiple parallels in the ancient world of images of naked goddesses on a mountain top standing on or flanked by lions.[28] The point is that in her flawless beauty (7) she seems at once both powerful and remote – is it really possible, he wonders, if such a goddess could be his? There is veneration for her authority and autonomy here. The picture is a long way from the patriarchal male asserting his rights over the woman. She will only be his if she chooses to come to him freely.

His appeal to her is reinforced by his first use of the word 'bride', which is repeated in the next four verses as well as in 5:1 (the six occurrences of the word in the book). This 'burst' of bride language needs explanation. If newly married and not yet come together in union, it is as if he is using the word as a term of affection and intimacy, a reminder that she has entered into relationship with him. It is another form of invitation. Again this is far removed from a husband 'demanding' his rights for sex. He is wooing her with tender words, telling her of how she has captured his heart: she is everything to him. Verses 9–11 do not really need comment; they speak for themselves:

> *You have stolen my heart, my sister, my bride;*
> *you have stolen my heart*
> *with one glance of your eyes,*
> *with one jewel of your necklace.*
> *How delightful is your love, my sister, my bride!*
> *How much more pleasing is your love than wine,*
> *and the fragrance of your perfume*
> *more than any spice!*
> *Your lips drop sweetness as the honeycomb, my bride;*
> *milk and honey are under your tongue.*
> *The fragrance of your garments*
> *is like the fragrance of Lebanon.*

---

[28] Garrett, *Song of Songs*, p. 192.

c. A locked garden (12– 15)

The imagery changes in these verses. She is no longer a mountain goddess but an enclosed *garden*, *spring* or *fountain* (12). In the arid landscape of the ancient Near East gardens carried a special significance as places of life, beauty and pleasure (see Eccl. 2:4–6). The spring (or pool) and fountain (12, 15) likewise speak of life-giving water. The point though is that she is *locked up* and *enclosed* (12). Like the inaccessible goddess on the mountain top, she is beyond his reach. He is persuading her to open herself to him. Verse 13 is difficult to translate. The NIVUK probably rightly captures that *Your plants* (or 'your growth') refers to the plants in her 'garden'. The imagery is suggestive. The *choice fruits* along with *henna*, *nard*, *saffron*, *calamus* and *cinnamon*, combined with *incense, myrrh, aloes* and *all the finest spices*, speak of a sensual fertile paradise (which the NIVUK translates *orchard*). His point is that *she is that paradise* that he longs to enter.

Verses 8–15 are both beautiful and important in our pornographied sex-obsessed Western world, where girls and young women in particular are put under enormous pressure to comply with sexual demands from their male peers. This is a major and fast-changing problem that we can only touch on here, aware that current data will be out of date as soon as it is published. To take one example, a major piece of quantitative research in the UK into children, young people and 'sexting' was commissioned by the National Society for the Prevention of Cruelty to Children (NSPCC) to get beyond media headlines and popular stereotypes.[29] Among its conclusions were the following:[30] girls are having 'to manage daily barrages of verbal sexual harassment, including being asked at ever younger ages to perform sexual acts for boys like blow jobs'.[31] A girl saying 'Yes' was often captured electronically and posted on Facebook. Girls' bodies are monitored, judged and subject to unwanted 'touching up'. This includes 'daggering', a common practice 'where girls were aggressively thrust at by boys from behind and frequently pushed to the floor in corridors or the playground'.[32] The researchers found

---

[29] Jessica Ringrose, Rosalind Gill, Sonia Livingstone and Laura Harvey, *A Qualitative Study of Children, Young People and 'Sexting': A Report Prepared for the NSPCC*, <www.nspcc.org.uk/services-and-resources/. . .and. . ./qualitative-study-sexting>, pp. 1–75, accessed 12 August 2017.

[30] The following quotes are taken from ibid., pp. 54–55.

[31] The researchers reported that girls as young as 6 or 7 had received such requests.

[32] 'Upskirting' is a related trend, where a man uses a mobile phone secretly to photograph underneath her skirt and often then share online. See <www.bbc.com/news/magazine-40861875>, accessed 11 August 2017.

'the problematic assumption that boys should physically touch and grope girls until they were violently refuted'. They also 'explored pressures girls are under to send boys photos of themselves naked or nearly naked, typically of their breasts'. There was also pervasive use of pornography on phones and social networks with 'girls feeling discomfort around porn on boys' phones at school'. They found 'that attaining peer-produced images of naked girls was much more highly sought after' than use of professionally produced pornographic images. Collections of such photos functioned as one way through which boys gain status and respect among their friends.

However we extrapolate out from a study like this to wider UK and Western culture, it is difficult not to conclude that the picture is a depressing one. The NSPCC report developed many conclusions and practical recommendations for schools, parents, Internet service providers and child welfare professionals. But behind such behaviour lies a technological revolution where omnipresent pornography is having a profoundly dehumanizing impact on both genders. Behaviour will change only if there is a deep-seated respect for girls and women among boys and men. The man's lyrics to his beloved in the Song of Songs are thousands of years old. We desperately need to hear them afresh in our 'modern' and 'developed' technological age. Within the church, it is time to dust off the book, put it on our preaching rotas and allow it to speak its rich wisdom into our relationships. Sex is first the joining of two hearts and then two bodies. He speaks tenderly to her. He admires and woos her. He invites her rather than bullying, manipulating or coercing her. He refuses to claim any 'rights' or inherent 'gender roles' to get what he wants. He may be physically more powerful but he subordinates his passion to her free choice. In other words, the Songs shows us an attractive relationship of mutual respect.

3. The consummation of their love (4:16 – 5:1)

There is some uncertainty as to what order they speak in 4:16 – 5:1. We are going to follow the NIVUK. She replies in verse 16 to his words of devotion. The north and south *wind* (4:16) indicates a life-giving force that awakens the garden so its *fragrance* (4:16) bursts to life. Her passion is aroused. The reference to *garden* (4:16) is clear. She is offering herself to him: she is *his garden* (4:16), which her lover is welcome to enter and *taste its choice fruits* (4:16). This is an unambiguous image of a virgin responding to her beloved, offering herself to him to consummate their union. Garrett suggests that this moment of sexual intercourse is the structural centrepiece of the whole book.[33] The man's response in 5:1 echoes his description of her in 4:8–15, except now it is in the past tense. He has *come into* his garden; he has *gathered, eaten* and *drunk*. Note how *my* precedes the *myrrh, spice, honeycomb, honey, wine* and *milk* (5:1). She is no longer inaccessible: she is his. The voice changes at the end of the verse to the chorus who basically encourage the lovers to 'go for it'! *Drink your fill of love* (5:1) they exclaim; hold nothing back: enjoy yourselves! The verb for 'drink' here means to get drunk. They are to indulge to the fullest. A more positive, full-blooded view of sex and desire is hard to imagine.

4. The woman's voice: this is my beloved, this is my friend (5:9 – 6:3)

We are going to bypass 5:2–8 to move forward to hear the woman's voice talk of her beloved.[34]

5:9 – 6:3 is structured around two stanzas, each introduced by the chorus asking her a question. Chapter 5, verse 9 is a rhetorical device for the woman to explain *How is your beloved better than others?* It is a great question to ask any partner then or now! She has no problem thinking of what to say and launches into a joyful erotic declaration of his attributes. She begins with his skin, *radiant and ruddy* (5:10) – perhaps echoing the handsome King David, known for his healthy complexion (1 Sam. 16:12). He is one *among ten thousand* (5:10) – effectively there is no one really like him. She then works downwards, physically appreciating him from his head (5:11) to his legs (5:15). Again the metaphors are appropriate to ancient Israel. His *head* of *purest gold* (5:11) suggests that his face is pleasing to her eye and precious to her. His wavy black hair a sign of youth and vitality (5:11). His *eyes are like doves* (5:12) duplicates his description of her (Song 4:1). She adds that his eyes are *by the water streams, / washed in milk, / mounted like jewels* – all images for eyes that are sparkling. His cheeks *like beds of spice / yielding perfume* along with the image of *His lips are like lilies / dripping with myrrh* (5:13) combine typical images in the Song of Songs of sensual

---

[33] Garrett, *Song of Songs*, pp. 201–202. In this he is joined by Daniel J. Estes, *The Song of Songs*, AOTC, vol. 16 (Nottingham: Apollos, 2010), p. 262.

[34] This is for three reasons. First, the book is not clearly chronological and lacks a narrative structure. While some do see 5:2–8 following on from ch. 4, this is contested. Even if 5:2–8 does follow from 4:16, skipping forward to v. 9 does not lose the narrative thread, since whatever happened in 5:2–8 appears to be resolved. Second, 5:2–8 is a complex text with multiple interpretations: we simply do not have space to delve into it here. Third, examining 5:10 – 6:3 gives an appropriate balance to our discussion, since it contains the woman's confident rejoicing in her beloved's beauty, paralleling his rejoicing in her (4:1–15).

pleasure. She has already said that she delights to be kissed by those lips (Song 1:2). Arms like *rods of gold* set with precious stones speaks of strength and value, coloured by the sun (5:14). The phrase *His body* [*mēʿeh*; lit. 'loins'] *is like polished ivory / decorated with lapis lazuli* has caused much discussion. More literally it reads, 'His loins are a piece of ivory.'[35] How it is understood depends on how 'loins' and 'piece' are translated. Loins can mean internal organs or emotions but since it is a physical description, it is either his belly or genitals. The colour of ivory is pale, suggesting a part of the body hidden from the sun. Longman suggests that it is saying his penis is a 'tusk' of ivory.[36] If we are uncomfortable with this, the Song of Songs is hardly prudish. But whether it is or not, the bigger point is that her transparency simply mirrors his admiration of her body, including her breasts. She, like he, is taking pleasure in his body, including his sexual parts. She, like he, does not overly emphasize them: they are just like other parts of him also linked with precious metals and gems. All of her husband is beautiful and valuable to her, including his strong thighs of alabaster[37] *set on bases of pure gold* (5:15). Overall she summarizes his appearance as *like Lebanon* (5:15), whose cedars are strong and magnificent. He is *altogether lovely* (5:16). She cannot resist returning to the sweetness of his *mouth* (5:16), as if to connect his physical beauty with her experience of his intimacy. This is no imaginary statue or impressive stranger she has described: he is hers. Twice she emphasizes her exclusive 'ownership': *This is my beloved, this is my friend* (5:16).

The chorus ask their second rhetorical question

> *Where has your beloved gone . . .*
> *Which way did your beloved turn,*
>   *that we may look for him with you?*
> (6:1)

It is not that he has gone missing: the question simply invites her to complete her account of their relationship. She knows where he is – in *his garden* (6:2). The imagery is familiar from 4:16: she is the garden that belongs to him; *she* is the *beds of spices* (6:2) where he dallies among the *lilies* (6:3). The picture is of mutual belonging and pleasure of husband and wife. She is his; he is hers. He possesses her

---

[35] Garrett, *Song of Songs*, pp. 222–224.

[36] Tremper Longman III, *The Song of Songs*, NICOT (Grand Rapids: Eerdmans, 2001), p. 164.

[37] The NIVUK has 'his legs are pillars of marble'. The Hebrew *šôq* can be the leg or upper thigh. *Šēš* is more likely alabaster, not marble, and keeps the idea of a part of his body being hidden from the sun; hence 'thigh' is more likely than 'leg'.

and she possesses him: *I am my beloved's and my beloved is mine* (6:3). Their harmony is complete.

5. The Song of Songs today

In proposing some contemporary implications of chapters 4–5 the text needs to 'speak for itself', so I will not be alluding to allegorical interpretations of God's love in Christ for his bride (or the individual Christian). Indeed God is not mentioned at all in the Songs; nowhere do they explicitly say that love and sex are gifts from him. Yes, a compelling biblical theology for this view can be constructed, but its sources lie outside Song of Songs. So what are some of the key things that we need to hear from the two lovers today? This is an important question, because how we answer it will shape our spirituality of love, sex and the body – and that covers significant areas of human experience! It is a sad fact that the church has often got the answer to this question wrong. But in saying this we need to be humbly attuned to what C. S. Lewis called 'chronological snobbery'[38] – current Christian practice around sex and marriage also has much room for reformation.[39]

First has to be the beauty of sexual love in the form of a delightful erotic celebration of monogamous marital love between a man and a woman. The poetry is playful, indicating a relationship overflowing with pleasure. Sex is something to be enjoyed to the full, without guilt or fear. It belongs within an exclusive relationship, rooted in a passionate love and delight in the other. Such is the lovers' happiness that it is inconceivable that they would turn away to another.

The Songs's joyful affirmation of sexual union within marriage speaks a countercultural word today. We live in perhaps the most hypersexualized culture in human history. Pornography is produced on an industrial scale. We are jaded consumers, formed by a culture in countless ways to believe capitalist myths that happiness lies in satiating our restless desires – particularly of the sexual kind. True 'joy' lies around the corner in a never-quite-arrived at hope of something better. Monogamous marriage is a repressive institution limiting individual freedom. Sexual self-expression, of virtually whatever hue, is a human right. Sex has long been detached from love and marriage: it is a natural desire not to be thwarted. Those who claim otherwise (such as traditional Christians teaching on sex

---

[38] Lewis defined this as the 'uncritical acceptance of the intellectual climate common to our own age and the assumption that whatever has gone out of date is on that account discredited'. *Surprised by Joy: The Shape of My Early Life* (New York: Harcourt, Brace, Jovanovich, 1966), pp. 207–208.

[39] This claim will be further discussed in chapter 16, which is on Christian marriage.

within heterosexual marriage) are seen as bizarre relics of a past age, *opposed* to human flourishing. Celibacy is virtually inconceivable – equated with either childishness or stupidity.[40] Such beliefs have made deep inroads into the church as it loses touch with an authentically Christian, countercultural vision for human sexuality.[41] Perhaps due to increasing cultural marginalization it seems (to me at least) that churches have lost their voice when it comes to teaching a Christian theology of love and sex. When, I wonder, did you last hear a sermon on love and sex based on the Song of Songs? But silence is not an option. The poems are an invaluable resource here. Faithfulness and sex within marriage are not laws that can be enforced: they are a consequence of a joyful committed union where each partner can exclaim with utter trust that 'My beloved is mine, and I am her's/his.'

Second, the lovers' celebration of the physical challenges any form of Christian theology that views sex itself as tainted by sin. We are embodied sexual beings and it is in and through our bodies that we love. Love, in other words, is not an abstract feeling or emotion, but an embodied practice worked out in relationship with the other. I am painting with a necessarily broad brush here, but historically the church has had enormous problems with this notion of the goodness of the body and sex.[42] Whereas the Songs rejoice in the touch, sound, scent and taste of another's body without a hint of shame, from the early church fathers onwards sex and sexual desire have been inextricably connected with sin and a failure to live up to God's higher calling of celibacy. No one has been more influential in the development of this outlook within the Western church than Augustine, so it is worth dwelling with him very briefly. As we do so, we see that when it comes to sex the past truly is another country. Like many other church fathers, for Augustine celibacy was the spiritual ideal: holiness was linked to sexual asceticism. Of course there are good biblical reasons for this view – not least that Jesus and Paul were single! The resurrection and eschatological hope radically relativized the need for, and attraction of, marriage and sex – so much so that for many marriage was devalued. Augustine's great achievement was to affirm marriage, while retaining the ideal of

[40] Stephen Holmes, 'Late Modern Assumptions About Sexuality', in Thomas A. Noble, Sarah K. Whittle and Philip Johnston (eds.), *Marriage, Family and Relationships: Biblical, Doctrinal and Contemporary Perspectives* (London: Apollos, 2017), pp. 256–275, esp. p. 263.
[41] For an excellent discussion of these issues see Jonathan Grant, *Divine Sex: A Compelling Vision for Christian Relationships in a Hypersexualized Age* (Grand Rapids: Baker, 2015).
[42] The classic work is Peter Brown, *The Body and Society: Men, Women and Sexual Renunciation in Early Christianity* (London: Faber & Faber, 1989).

celibacy. Human sexuality is a good gift of God; marriage is the context for a right ordering of desire, and sex is 'by nature fitting and decent'.[43] But because sex after the fall could not occur without the sinful desire of concupiscence (lust) that acts against the 'restraining bridle of reason',[44] it is inevitably accompanied by 'a shame begetting penalty of sin'.[45] The only sin-free act of sexual intercourse was Adam and Eve copulating before their rebellion, in full control of their wills, above the dangerous passions of lust. Augustine imagines the first human sex scene this way:

> without the disease of lust . . . at the command of the will . . . without the seductive stimulus of passion; with calmness of mind and with no corrupting of the integrity of the body, the husband would lie upon the bosom of his wife.[46]

A bigger contrast to the Song of Songs is hard to imagine! So, while sex is essential for the good of procreation, its inextricable link with sin meant it should be used only for that purpose (the end justifies the means). Sex for pleasure was a venial sin since it was choosing to indulge in lust unnecessarily (sex as an end in itself). In short, we could summarize Augustine as 'the less sex the better'. Certainly all the fun, play and delight of the Song of Songs is off limits. Celibacy was preferable since the Christian's goal was to love God wholeheartedly and this could be done best by being freed from lower loves like lust. In addition, his doctrine of original sin located the transmission of Adam's sin in the act of intercourse. So it is not hard to see how this Neoplatonic fusion of 'desire', 'flesh', 'sex' and 'sin' became a fearful combination in subsequent church history. It was the body of a virgin or a celibate person that was seen as a 'pure' place for the Holy Spirit to dwell. Even *within* marriage sex was an obstacle to spirituality: the Spirit could not come upon a person in fullness who was sexually active. This attitude helps to explain the church's deeply ambivalent attitude to the Song of Songs and why the book's plain meaning has been allegorized to death. If the man and woman's poetic rhapsodies in chapters 4 and 5 teach us anything, it is that loving your beloved with your whole being – mind, body and heart – is an unambiguously *good* thing. The wider implication is that Christian spirituality is not some sort of Gnostic escape from the body and its tainted sexual desires. Rather, it leads to a

---

[43] Augustine, *The City of God*, tr. Henry Bettenson (London: Pelican, 1972), bk 14, para. 18.
[44] Ibid., para. 19.
[45] Ibid., para. 18.
[46] Ibid., para. 26.

redemption of our bodies because Christ has been bodily raised (1 Cor. 15:35–58).

Third, while the lovers' words are not meant to be copied as some form of sex manual, they do speak in ways from which we have much to learn. Zoning in more narrowly on the marital relationship, the man's respect for, and tender winning of, his beloved is deeply moving. Completely absent from the book is any hint of power, coercion or resort to hierarchical 'gender roles': they relate as equals. There is a remarkable mutuality about the lovers' descriptions of each other in chapter 4 and 5. He willingly *subordinates* his intense physical desire to the woman's assent. Sex is not a right, but first a joining of two hearts in intimacy and only then two bodies. If you are a husband reading this, perhaps it is worth considering how you can communicate afresh just why you love your wife. Similarly chapter 5 reveals a confident, sexually assured woman who freely compliments her beloved and shares her desire for him.[47] If you are a wife reading this, why not do the same for your husband? It is communication in a thousand ways, both verbal and non-verbal, of appreciation and respect that builds lasting marriages. Love delights in the other; it is in generous giving that it flourishes.

Fourth, the lovers' poetic descriptions express the truth that love is at the essence of what really matters in life. Our Western post-Christendom culture is increasingly bereft of belief in any truth that cannot be measured. Capitalists commit to a faceless and ruthless market by which all 'value' and 'progress' are judged. Atheists trust in philosophical naturalism – the belief that nature as understood by modern evolutionary science is all there is, all that is real. Logically, despite attempts to argue otherwise,[48] this means that there is nothing outside the realm of matter: neither the 'spiritual' or 'supernatural', nor concepts like 'love' or 'beauty'. They have no extrinsic reality in themselves. 'Love' is a mechanism of evolutionary success. In such a soulless environment we need the poetry of the two lovers. Their verses speak of what is really real and have no mention of the cold taskmasters of money and reason.

Fifth, as noted at the beginning, 'love is as strong as death':[49] the lovers long for each other amid the transience of life. As young lovers, they are 'frozen' in time, their bodies for ever perfect, their future lives together stretching ahead into eternity. Lewis's

---

[47] For further discussion see Derek and Dianne Tidball, *The Message of Women: Creation, Grace and Gender*, BST (Nottingham: Inter-Varsity Press, 2012), pp. 128–129.

[48] E.g. Sam Harris, *The Moral Landscape: How Science Can Determine Human Values* (New York: Free, 2011).

[49] Song 8:6.

'comfortable and unemphatic' love of older age was unimagined, death even more so. Yes, from our perspective it is difficult to read the Songs without a sharp awareness that youth is fleeting (Eccl. 11:9–11). They, Joy Davidman and C. S. Lewis and all lovers, live, love and die. Lewis wrote these poignant words at the end of his unexpected, dazzling and yet all too brief love affair:

> And then one or other dies. And we think of this as love cut short; like a dance stopped in mid career or a flower with its head unluckily snapped off – something truncated and therefore, lacking its due shape. I wonder. If, as I can't help suspecting, the dead also feel the pains of separation (and this may be one of their purgatorial sufferings), then for both lovers, and for all pairs of lovers without exception, bereavement is a universal and integral part of our experience of love.[50]

Leaving aside his musings on purgatory, his painfully earned insight speaks to the inseparable connection between love and death. Life is precious, and love gives it rich meaning and joy – so let us take every opportunity to love well in the time allotted to us.

Finally, without resorting to allegory or sacralizing sex,[51] the beauty of the two lovers' relationship gives us a glimpse of a deeper reality, a glimpse of transcendence, a glimpse of God. Lewis wrote much on love and heaven long before meeting Davidman. One of his enduring gifts in much of his fiction and theology is how brilliantly he evoked how this world, the 'shadowlands', is but a foretaste of the real one to come.[52] The lovers' love in the Songs is without blemish – no hint of selfishness, faithlessness or bitterness passes between them. Their love is unstained compared to our all too frequent failings. But as we read the Songs and enter their world, we are transported to a place of joy that speaks of the eternal reality of the one who is love itself. A world in which love will at last be 'really real'.

---

[50] Lewis, *Grief Observed*, p. 43.

[51] The Old Testament consistently resists surrounding pagan fertility myths and any divinization of sex. There is no hint that the Song of Songs is any different.

[52] E.g. in the final scenes of The Chronicles of Narnia, as the friends enter the new Narnia, Digory explains to Lucy that the old Narnia was 'only a shadow or a copy of the real Narnia'. In the final chapter, 'Farewell to the Shadowlands', Aslan explains that 'The dream has ended: this is the morning.' C. S. Lewis, *The Last Battle* (London: Puffin, 1964), pp. 153–165.

Interlude

1. Locating ourselves in the story

It should be clear by now that any sort of Marcionite division between an Old Testament God of wrath and vengeance versus a New Testament God of love and grace is completely misguided – Marcion was declared a heretic for good reason! The love of God is the 'backbone' of the Old Testament story; without it there would be no existence of Israel beyond their apostasy in the Sinai wilderness and no unfolding of God's saving grace in the New Testament. Israel is created in and through divine love. They are to be a community of love and justice flowing from their wholehearted responsive love for Yahweh. Despite repeated syncretism and disobedience, they are sustained, forgiven and reconciled only because of the stubborn covenant love of their God. In part 1 we have touched only on key highlights in this story, but the overall pattern is clear: Old Testament love speaks of God's *ḥesed* (faithful loving kindness) alongside his tender, passionate love (*'āhab*) for his people. This relentless love over against Israel's unfaithfulness ensures that God's redemptive action continues beyond the boundaries of the Old Testament narrative. But let us pause here for a moment to consider the broader theological picture before proceeding to part 2 and how God's love finds its expression in the sending of his Son.

In terms of a biblical theology of love, God's love for Israel is best understood within a wider, redemptive framework. Imagine four concentric circles.[1] Each circle represents a story. We will work from the outer to the inner. The largest circle sets the context for the three others, the second largest forms the context for the inner two, and so on. The stories interweave with one another; they are distinct

---

[1] The circles illustration is adapted from Ben Witherington, where he develops it in relation to Paul's Christology. 'Jesus as the Alpha and Omega of New Testament Thought', in Richard. N. Longenecker (ed.), *Contours of Christology in the New Testament* (Grand Rapids: Eerdmans, 2005), pp. 25–46.

but neither can they be understood properly in isolation from one another.

a. The story of God

The biggest circle embraces all the others. This is the story of the identity and character of God himself. The entire story of the Bible is utterly dependent on God's redemptive response to human sin and rebellion. God willingly enters into a solemn covenant commitment to restore blessing to his creation. How Father, Son and Spirit work together in love to do so results in the unlikely and remarkable stories of Israel and of Jesus. Divine love is not an abstract idea. If God is love, a consequence is that he will act in loving ways. This is what we see working out in the next three circles.

b. The story of a world gone wrong

The second circle is the story of a world gone wrong. From Genesis 3 onwards God's original good creation is disfigured by sin, death, violence, injustice, greed and grief.[2] It is a world in which the devil stalks and powers and principalities hold sway. All of creation is groaning for liberation from its bondage to decay (Rom. 8:21). This is our world: a theatre of joy and of despair; of beauty and of cruelty – one that we long to see transformed (Rom. 8:22–15). As we explored in part 1, the greatest news imaginable is God's loving response to human sin. Without it we would be lost and bereft of hope. God's ultimate purpose is to restore blessing to all of creation. Only because of his determination to bless do we have the privilege of living within the third and fourth circles – the story of God's redemptive work in the world.

c. The story of Israel

That redemptive work takes the form of the story of Israel. God chooses Abram and promises that he will be the father of a great nation and that

> all peoples on earth
> will be blessed through you.[3]

---

[2] Gen. 3 – 11 tells this story in microcosm. The chapters recount a descent into murder, misuse of power, growth of evil, arrogant human pride and awful divine judgment.

[3] Gen. 12:3.

He then establishes a covenant with the patriarch and promises that his descendants will be as numerous as the stars in the sky (Gen. 15:5). That solemn covenantal promise forms the bedrock of the rest of the biblical narrative. It holds through all the ambiguities, successes and failures of Israel, God's chosen nation. It continues forward from Old Testament to New, from ethnic Israel to the inclusion of the Gentiles within the people of God. It is *through Israel* that the love of God for the world comes to its astonishing climax – the long-awaited arrival of the Messiah.

d. The story of Jesus, the Messiah of Israel

The fourth, inner, circle then is the story of Jesus Christ. It is this narrative that is our focus in parts 2 and 3 of this book. Jesus is a Jewish Messiah who completes the story of Israel. He is unexpectedly also saviour of the world. The astonishing paradigm shift from Old to New Testaments is that now both Jews and Gentiles can enter into God's redemptive story through faith in the Son. It is through the Son that the second story is decisively addressed: sin and death are confronted and defeated through the cross and resurrection of Jesus. This is the victory of God, the good news (gospel) to be proclaimed to the whole world.

However, most amazingly of all, this inner story connects in an unforeseen way to the outer circle. A Galilean peasant, carpenter by trade (Mark 6:3), of dubious parentage, rejected by his immediate village community and ultimately by his people as a whole (Mark 6:33), is also, the New Testament writers tell us, God made man. Texts like Colossians 1:15–20 summarize the story. To paraphrase the text, Jesus exists *within* the story of God. He is the eternal Son, the one through whom all things, visible and invisible, are made. This Lord of creation enters the world he made as the image of the invisible God, a flesh-and-blood man (Col. 1:22). To see the human Jesus is to see God himself. He becomes the Lord of redemption through his death on the cross. The victory won there reconciles all things – all the corrosive effects of the world gone wrong are healed in and through the death of the Son.[4]

This fourfold narrative structure will be helpful to bear in mind for the rest of this book. In parts 2 and 3 our focus is primarily on the story of Jesus, yet this cannot be detached from the other stories. For example, in our next text within the Gospel of Mark all four circles overlap. Part 4 explores theological and ethical implications

---

[4] This includes human sin and spiritual powers and authorities opposed to God, Col. 2:15.

for God's people to live in the light of the full narrative, with each of its constituent stories now revealed.

2. New Testament use of *agapē* and *agapaō*

As we move our focus to the New Testament, it is also necessary to make some general comments about the Greek words used there for love, particularly the noun *agapē* and verb *agapaō*. In contrast to a wide variety of Hebrew words for love in the Old Testament, in the New Testament *agapē* language takes centre stage. Why is this the case and how significant is this development for understanding love in the New Testament?

The first mention of *agapē* is within the Septuagint (LXX), the Greek translation of the Old Testament dated between 300 and 200 BC that was used by Hellenistic Jews. The Septuagint also became an important source for New Testament writers, who quoted extensively from it. This suggests that the LXX was the Bible read by most early Christians. This makes perfect sense. Greek was the common language of the period and the LXX was therefore the most accessible form of Scripture available.

The translators of the LXX primarily chose the verb *agapaō* (to love) as the best equivalent for Hebrew words for God's love and for human love for God. Interestingly, considering its significance in the New Testament, *agapē* is of marginal importance in the LXX. It appears only twenty times and nowhere refers to God's love, and it most often relates to sexual love.[5] The other Greek word found in the LXX and the New Testament is *phileō* and its cognates. It appears much less frequently than *agapaō* and is most often connected with friendship love. It is never used to refer to divine love or human love for God.[6] It is, however, at times used interchangeably with *agapaō* and so caution needs to be exercised in assuming that the translators understood the two words to mean significantly different things.[7]

As we move to the New Testament, there are significant developments in the language of love. Hardly known beforehand, *agapē* now becomes the default New Testament word for love, virtually eclipsing all others. Morris gives some statistics. Strikingly,

[5] Leon Morris, *Testaments of Love: A Study of Love in the Bible* (Grand Rapids: Eerdmans, 1981), pp. 101–113.

[6] Ibid., p. 108.

[7] A famous example is the interchangeable use of *agapē* and *phileō* in Jesus' threefold exchange with Peter in John 21:15–17. Theories based on the contrast between 'divine' love (*agapē*) and 'human' love (*philia*) are speculative and without exegetical warrant. For John they seem to be interchangeable words for 'love'.

agapē appears 116 times and *philia* (friendship) just once. Of related words, *agapaō* occurs 143 times and *phileō* 25 times; adjectives *agapētos* (beloved) 61 times and *philos* (friend) 29 times. In total, *agapaō* words appear 320 times and *phileō* words 55 times.[8] Other Greek words for love like *storgē* (affection) and *eros* (passion) do not appear in the New Testament at all.[9]

Care is needed not to jump to conclusions from a summary of linguistic usage. Words must be interpreted in context by what their authors meant when they used them. The proliferation of *agapē* does not necessarily entail a negative attitude towards other Greek words not chosen by New Testament authors. For example, Anders Nygren's highly influential 1930s book *Agape and Eros: The Christian Idea of Love* has been extensively criticized for making far too sharp a contrast between *agapē* and *erōs*, the latter being seen in very negative terms.[10] His was an argument based on silence about how the first Christians thought of *erōs*.

But certainly the statistics strongly suggest that *agapē* and its cognates held a special significance for the writers of the New Testament. But what was it? Why develop what is essentially a new word for love?[11] Morris strikes a good balance here. It is not so much that *agapē* creates a new understanding of love, but that a deeper understanding of love leads to the use of *agapē*. Other older words for love were not used because they carried too much 'baggage', so the first Christians deliberately chose a new noun, free of established associations.[12] As noted above, the verb *agapaō* was well known. Morris suggests that the first readers of the New Testament would thus have had no problems associating *agapē* with some sort of love. As they read on they would come to appreciate the specific contours of *agapē* – a love seen most supremely in the self-giving love of Jesus at the cross, in the Father's sending of his beloved Son, and in the call of Christians to love one another as they have been loved by God. It is these sorts of themes that we will concentrate on in the remaining parts of this book.

---

[8] Morris, *Testaments of Love*, p. 125, n. 35.

[9] C. S. Lewis discusses these words in *The Four Loves* (London: Geoffrey Bles, 1960). The compound *astorgos* (without affection) appears in Rom. 1:31 and 2 Tim. 3:3, and *philostorgos* (loving dearly) in Rom. 12:10.

[10] Anders Nygren, *Agape and Eros: The Christian Idea of Love*, tr. Philip S. Watson (Chicago: University of Chicago Press, 1982 [1930–36]).

[11] *Agapē* is found only once outside the Bible, in the second century AD, referring to the goddess Isis. *NIDNTT*, vol. 2, p. 539.

[12] Morris, *Testaments of Love*, pp. 125–126.

Part 2
The love of God revealed in the mission and death of Jesus Christ

Mark 1:1–15
6. 'You are my Son, whom I love'

All of us have hopes and dreams. Take a moment – can you imagine a possible future reality, a vision of something better than your present experience that you hope one day will come to pass? Of course you cannot be sure that it will happen, but your dream is real nonetheless. It can motivate you now to work, long and pray for that dream to become a reality. When dreams fade, hope hibernates.

From the close of the Old Testament, Israel remained a nation with dreams aplenty, but hopes had fluctuated wildly. They still believed themselves to be God's loved and elect people, but the legacy of judgment, exile and centuries of continuous foreign invasion had taken a heavy toll. The promised land was not theirs. Since 63 BC, the brutal and oppressive pagan Roman Empire controlled virtually all aspects of their lives through puppet kings (like Herod the Great and his offspring) and Roman-appointed procurators like Pontius Pilate. Competing ideas of how to respond to their political and religious subjugation had resulted in deep internal divisions.[1] But many still dreamed of liberation from pagan rule and a return of God's kingdom, leading to periodic renewals of hope revolving around a Messiah figure. In Jesus' day these hopes were at fever pitch.

This background helps to explain why Matthew, Mark, Luke and John are called *Gospels*. The Greek word for 'gospel' (*euangelion*) means 'good news'. Each author is proclaiming, in distinct ways, the world-changing news that God has kept his promise of blessing to Abraham and Israel in a most unexpected and powerful way. They tell a story that no one saw coming – the story of Jesus Christ.

---

[1] Different Jewish groups with radically different understandings of how to embody national righteousness populate the Gospels: Sadducees, Pharisees, Scribes, Herodians and Zealots, plus other groups, like the Essenes, in the background.

All the Gospels are doing 'retrospective theology'. By this I mean that it is only *afterwards*, in the light of the cross, resurrection, ascension and Pentecost that the authors are enabled to interpret what God has been up to in sending a miracle-working prophet from an obscure backwater in Galilee who gets himself executed in Jerusalem. They now understand that God's anointed Messiah and king has arrived, bringing his kingdom with him in power. Evil, sin and death have been defeated. The risen Lord is reigning at God's right hand. Rather than the story of a crucified Messiah being catastrophic bad news, it is glorious good news. And if you have great news, what do you want to do with it? Tell everyone who will listen! Which is what each Gospel writer sets out to do.

Let us bear this background in mind as we turn to the prologue of Mark (which I take as extending to 1:15). The prologue is a self-contained unit that contains a rich array of themes that reappear throughout Mark's Gospel. My purpose is not to repeat verse by verse what many excellent commentaries say. It is rather to zone in on Jesus the beloved Son of God. Because the identity of the Son cannot be separated from the love of God, we will first reflect on how Mark's prologue answers the question 'Who is this Son so loved by the Father?' Second, we will then consider the unique relationship between the Father and his beloved Son.

1. Who is the Son? The 'story of Jesus' within the prologue of Mark (1:1–15)

The Gospels are essentially Christological but they do not offer us neatly packaged systematic theologies. What they do give us is *a narrative in which Jesus is the central figure*. Sometimes we tend to assume that real 'meaty' theology has to be framed in ordered theoretical systems. But a story can be packed full of meaning and the Gospels are outstanding examples. Each Gospel narrative is bursting with Christology (theology about Jesus): straining to tell its readers about the best news that has ever been heard in all of human history and cause them to respond in thanksgiving and faith.

a. The beginning of the gospel (1:1)

In typical style, Mark wastes no time getting started. From his very first sentence he lets his readers in on the 'secret' of Jesus' true identity. Verse 1 dramatically announces *The beginning of the gospel of Jesus Christ, the Son of God* (ESVUK). Immediately, three concerns are apparent, locating Jesus within the wider stories of Israel, the world gone wrong and of God himself.

First, the gospel is not an abstract theological formula to be believed: it is about a person – *Jesus Christ*. The name *Jesus* is the Greek form of Joshua, which means 'Yahweh saves' (see Matt. 1:21). This saviour is human, a real flesh-and-blood person. In Mark 6:1–3 he is described as Mary's son, brother of James, Joseph, Judas and Simon and a number of sisters.

Second, this man Jesus is the *Christ*, which is the Greek translation of the Hebrew for Messiah. This word identifies Jesus as God's long-awaited deliverer of Israel. In verse 15 we see Jesus the king, of the line of David, announcing the coming of his kingdom and preaching the astonishing good news. Blessing, liberation and spiritual renewal do come, but not in ways imagined within Jewish messianic expectation.

Third, Jesus is also the *Son of God*. This title is inextricably linked with Messiah and locates the Messiah within the 'story of God'. We will return to the unique relationship between the Son and Father in the discussion of 1:9–11.

b. Jesus, the fulfilment of Old Testament hopes (1:2–8, 12–13)

In verses 2–3 Mark quotes from the Old Testament.[2]

> *I will send my messenger ahead of you,*
> *who will prepare your way –*
> *a voice of one calling in the wilderness,*
> *'Prepare the way for the Lord,*
> *make straight paths for him.'*

This is retrospective theology in action. Imagine again our four concentric circles. Knowing the story of Jesus, Mark writes 'backwards' from that perspective, able to interpret the story of Israel afresh. Quoting Malachi, Isaiah and Exodus, Mark locates the arrival of John and Jesus as divinely ordered events within the bigger redemptive story of God.

Mark affirms John's special role; his focus however is more on John's *unequal* relationship to Jesus. If John preaches repentance and forgiveness of sins, in preparation for an imminent act of God in history,[3] Jesus is the one who can forgive sins (and outrage

[2] While Mark mentions only Isaiah, it is a composite quote of Mal. 3:1, Isa. 40:3 and Exod. 23:20a from the LXX. It seems these texts were associated with a future coming of an Elijah figure. Ben Witherington, *The Gospel of Mark: A Socio-Rhetorical Commentary* (Grand Rapids: Eerdmans, 2001), p. 71.

[3] Ibid., p. 72. The wilderness location has strong OT associations with repentance and a return to true sonship. William L. Lane, *The Gospel of Mark*, NICNT (Grand Rapids: Eerdmans, 1974), pp. 49–50.

people in the process; Mark 2:5). If John is a desert ascetic (Mark 1:6–7), Jesus is the one, like a new Moses figure, who has the miraculous ability to feed the people in the wilderness (Mark 6:30–44). John may be like a final Old Testament prophet, but he himself knows that *After me comes the one more powerful than I, the straps of whose sandals I am not worthy to stoop down and untie* (7). It is easy to miss the significance of this statement. A Jew was not to become a slave. But if he did, in later Jewish tradition one thing a Hebrew slave should never do was to untie the strap of his master's sandal in order to wash his feet. This was seen as too humiliating a task even for a slave.[4] So, even though he is a chosen Prophet of God foretold in the Scriptures, John knows he is unworthy even to serve the One to come in the lowest way imaginable. The difference between John and Jesus is not one of degree, they are in *two entirely different categories*. No one can compare to Jesus. If John baptizes with water, the Messiah will *baptize you in the Holy Spirit* (8). The arrival of the Spirit is the sign that God's power and presence have once more come to Israel, that God is now restoring his people and establishing his kingdom. John is powerless to effect this himself; he can only point to the One who has the unique authority and power to inaugurate a new era of the Spirit of God.

Staying with this theme of the Spirit and skipping on to verses 12–13, after his baptism Jesus is sent by the Spirit into the desert for forty days. There he *was tempted by Satan. He was with the wild animals and angels attended him* (13). This intense period of spiritual conflict immediately follows the public beginning of his redemptive mission. Here is another aspect of the Messiah: a 'spiritual warrior', accompanied by the Spirit of God, going into battle with the forces of evil. It sets the scene for multiple spiritual conflicts to follow in Mark (e.g. 1:24; 1:34).

It is hard to think of a more dramatic opening to the story of Jesus. There is a swirling mix of excitement, confusion, anger and fear revolving around the identity of this prophet and miracle worker. Evil spirits (1:24), the people (2:7),[5] scribes (2:16) and Pharisees (2:24) all wrestle with and try to make sense of this enigmatic figure. Who is this? Is he really the one we have been waiting for? By what authority did he do that? How can he say that? Is the mighty presence of God's Spirit once again present with his people? Are they at last going to be liberated and renewed?

---

[4] Darrell Bock, *Recovering the Real Lost Gospel: Reclaiming the Gospel as Good News* (Nashville: B&H , 2010), pp. 29–30.

[5] See esp. Mark 6:2, where the people are astonished at Jesus' wisdom and works.

Mark, the master storyteller, knows the answers to these questions. His prologue begins to draw readers into how the story of Jesus Christ reveals *the good news* [gospel] *of God* (14). How God keeps his promise of blessing to Israel takes the form of *far better news than anyone had ever dared to hope for.* The Messiah has indeed arrived. Of humble human origins, he is also the Son of God, who far surpasses any previous prophetic revelation of God. He is a saviour with divine authority to forgive sins. He is a royal King ushering in God's longed-for kingdom. He confronts sin and evil in the power of God's Spirit. But two things are most surprising of all. One is the shocking nature of Jesus' messianic task (Mark 8:27–33).[6] The second is the relationship of the Messiah with God himself, a theme to which we now turn.

2. Jesus, the beloved Son (1:9–11)

In his sparse prose Mark describes Jesus abruptly arriving from Nazareth and being baptized by John in the Jordan. But why was Jesus baptized? In 1:4 we are told that John's baptism is for the forgiveness of sins. In a parallel account, Matthew tells us of John's perplexity: 'I need to be baptized by you, and do you come to me?'[7] His question implies that Jesus needs no such forgiveness and John knows it. Jesus replies, 'Let it be so now; it is proper for us to do this to fulfil all righteousness.' While Mark does not spell this out, Jesus is acting in a representative role. In passively submitting to John's baptism, it seems that he is symbolically receiving the sign of repentance on behalf of Israel while simultaneously acknowledging God's judgment on his sinful people. 'Jesus comes to John as the true Israelite whose repentance is perfect. He is the beloved Son . . .'[8] In this sense, Jesus' baptism is an integral part of his obedience to his messianic task of suffering and death from which a new Israel will emerge. It marks the transition from the end of John's ministry to the public beginning of what will be a dramatic confrontation with evil, powerful religious opposition and the might of the Roman Empire itself. Jesus' baptism has the sense of 'now there is no going back; the die is cast', the Jordan reminiscent of another river, the Rubicon.[9]

---

[6] Peter's horror at Jesus' understanding of the Messiah's fate is a hinge point in all the Synoptic Gospels.

[7] Matt. 3:14–15.

[8] Lane, *Gospel of Mark*, p. 54.

[9] The phrase 'Crossing the Rubicon' refers to a river in northern Italy that Julius Caesar's forces crossed in 49 BC on the way to challenge the power of the Senate and Pompey in Rome. Julius is supposed to have cried out *Alea iacta est!* (The die is cast!) as they waded across.

Like Julius Caesar a few decades earlier, Jesus is now irrevocably committed to his course of action. Unlike Caesar, it would not be a violent military campaign for power and glory, but a campaign of an altogether more beautiful and peaceable kingdom.

As Jesus emerges from the water, Mark tells us that Jesus *saw heaven being torn open and the Spirit descending on him like a dove. And a voice came from heaven: 'You are my Son, whom I love; with you I am well pleased'* (10). At least two things are going on here, one visual and one oral, both acting to give divine affirmation and blessing upon the Son.

First, the visual. The Greek for being *torn open* is unusual and has the sense of splitting or being rent apart. It appears once more in Mark where the temple curtain is torn from top to bottom (Mark 15:38). These are eschatological images of the presence and glory of God being glimpsed at a deeply significant moment in human history (Ezek. 1:1; John 1:51; Acts 7:56; 10:11; Rev. 4:1; 19:11). God is about to act. The Spirit's descent like a dove on Jesus is described in all four Gospels. It is not clear exactly what the image of the dove represents and Mark does not elaborate. Perhaps it points to how Jesus' mission is one of peace and self-giving, not of violence or force. This would fit the 'upside down' nature of his kingdom, where the last are first and the first last (Mark 9:35; 10:31). But the real point is that Jesus is being anointed by the Holy Spirit of God.[10] He goes forward from the waters of the Jordan as the unique representative of a renewed Israel, empowered by God's blessing and presence for his redemptive mission.

Second, there is an oral affirmation unlike any in the rest of the Bible. While other figures receive, at various times and places, some form of divine affirmation, none comes close to paralleling this event in the Jordan. The splitting of the heavens, the anointing of the Spirit and the declarations of God's unqualified love reveal the cosmic significance of Jesus' identity and task. *Heaven* is the dwelling place of God. The divine affirmation does two things: it identifies Jesus as the Son of God and describes the Father's attitude towards his Son. We will look at these two aspects in turn.

a. You are my Son (1:11a)

In the Old Testament Israel are frequently called God's son (e.g. Exod. 4:22–23; Jer. 31:9; Hos. 11:1; and many other places). The

---

[10] In Acts 10:38 Peter summarizes the mission of Jesus thus: 'God anointed Jesus of Nazareth with the Holy Spirit and power, and how he went around doing good and healing all who were under the power of the devil, because God was with him.'

king, as God's chosen representative, is also called his son (2 Sam. 7:13–14). And in the Roman world the Roman emperor from Caesar Augustus (63 BC – AD 14) onwards was called 'Son of God' in divine terms.

Now in Mark (and the other Gospels) Jesus is revealed to be the beloved and only Son of God who fulfils both the vocation of Israel and their king. Verse 1 has already introduced Jesus as *the Son of God*. Here in verse 11 we see how Jesus' sonship takes the form of a unique, loving relationship with his Father. It probably links back to the royal Psalm 2:7, where the king is told, 'You are my son'; but it also clearly transcends human categories. *You are* (11) emphasizes that Jesus is already the Son; it is not a question of his somehow 'becoming' or being adopted as God's Son at his baptism.[11] This is consistent with the parallel declaration of sonship at Jesus' transfiguration in Mark 9:7, 'This is my Son, whom I love. Listen to him!' It is as if God is saying, 'Because you are my unique Son, I have chosen you for the task upon which you are about to enter.'[12]

I hinted earlier at how Jesus is a new Moses figure. He goes from his baptism into the wilderness. The forty days there are redolent of Israel's Sinai wanderings.[13] Matthew tells us that when tempted by Satan, Jesus quotes texts from Deuteronomy, originally given to Israel prior to their entering the promised land (Matt. 4:1–11). He succeeds where Israel failed. It is no coincidence that on passing through the test in the wilderness, Jesus immediately begins choosing twelve disciples, symbolic of a new Israel, a community of the kingdom being formed around the King (Mark 3:13–19). Here, in Jesus the Messiah, is embodied true sonship and true kingship.

All of this is amazing enough; but if we expand our focus to the rest of Mark, it is apparent that the rich Christology of the prologue keeps developing to a point where it is overwhelmingly clear that Jesus the Son is more than 'just' a messiah, king, healer, Spirit-bearer and man. Two brief examples from chapter 12 make this point.

First, in the parable of the tenants in the vineyard (Mark 12:1–12) Jesus explicitly identifies *himself* as the vineyard owner's loved Son. Jesus' quotation from the messianic Psalm 118 unlocks the shocking meaning of the story. He is God's Son and Israel's long-awaited Messiah, but rather than welcome and victory he will experience hostility and death.

---

[11] For further discussion see Robert H. Stein, *Mark*, BECNT (Grand Rapids: Baker Academic, 2008), pp. 58–59.

[12] Lane, *Gospel of Mark*, p. 58.

[13] Moses twice spent forty days and nights in the presence of the Lord on Mount Sinai (Exod. 24:18; 34:28).

Second, in Mark 11 at the triumphal entry, the people chant, 'Blessed is the coming kingdom of our father, David!' But in Mark 12:35–40 Jesus questions the meaning of this popular expectation by asking how the Davidic origins of the Messiah can be reconciled with the affirmation in Psalm 110 that the Messiah is David's Lord? In other words, in what way is the Messiah David's son? Jesus' point is Christological. If David himself distinguished between his earthly kingly role and the exalted kingly role of the coming Messiah, the Messiah is not only the 'Son of David' but his Lord. The Messiah's role is not to be 'just another David' with a job of re-establishing a political sovereign and independent Israel. No, he comes to establish a more exalted kingdom, ruled by a Messiah sitting at God's right hand. Jesus' proclamation about himself delights the crowd, who have this exalted Messiah sitting in front of them. Yet what no one has yet grasped is the most remarkable thing of all: the future exalted rule of the Messiah is about to be established through rejection, suffering, death, resurrection and ascension. This is the gospel! It is the good news of the crucified Messiah and Son of God, who is now the reigning and exalted Lord. Gordon Fee captures how

> the way the story turns out is a surprise to everyone: the messianic king of Israel, God's true Son, is not simply one more in the line of David; he turns out in fact to be the incarnate Son, who in his incarnation reveals true sonship and true kingship.[14]

Psalm 110 becomes one of the most quoted Old Testament scriptures in the New Testament to speak of Jesus. But its use originates in Jesus himself and his astonishing self-affirmation that turns the teachers of the law's understanding of the Messiah inside out and upside down. He does not point away from himself to God, but points to *himself as embodying the presence and action of God*.

N. T. Wright, describing the significance of the Son of God in the Gospels, says that

> in Jesus, Israel's God had become present, had become human, had come to live in the midst of his people, to set up his kingdom, to take upon himself the full horror of their plight, and to bring about his long-awaited new world. The phrase 'Son of God' was ready at hand to express that huge, evocative, frightening possibility, without leaving behind any of its other resonances.[15]

---

[14] Gordon Fee, *Pauline Christology: An Exegetical-Theological Study* (Peabody: Hendrickson, 2007), p. 543.

[15] N. T. Wright, *How God Became King* (London: SPCK, 2012), p. 95.

b. Whom I love; with you I am well pleased (11b)

God's statement *whom I love; with you I am well pleased* is like the Arkenstone in Tolkien's story *The Hobbit*: a jewel of dazzling beauty from the heart of the mountain that shines gloriously even in the midst of a vast treasure. The term *ho agapētos* is often translated 'the beloved', which can carry the sense of 'only' (the unique beloved Son).[16] The sense is of a dearly loved one; the object of special affection and of special relationship.

The second statement *with you I am well pleased* reveals the Father's delight and joy in his Son. Together these two clauses may allude to Genesis 22:2, where God commands Abraham to offer 'your only son Isaac, whom you love' and to Isaiah 42:1, where God's suffering servant is affirmed as 'my chosen one in whom I delight; I will put my Spirit on him, and he will bring justice to the nations'. Together they make clear that this beloved Son is the Messiah of Jewish hope, yet one who comes as a non-violent, suffering servant.[17] Since Mark does not tell us, we can only wonder what impact this had on Jesus himself, but can imagine that such a profound experience of divine love gave him a deep sense of confidence in his mission. In context, here and in Mark 9:7, the Father's pleasure is linked to key moments in the Son's faithfulness in carrying out that mission. Later, in Gethsemane, Jesus would call his Father *Abba*, an Aramaic word for Father that carried a sense of intimacy and familiarity appropriate only within families (Mark 14:36). Jesus' use of it for the holy creator God of Israel was unparalleled and gives us another insight into the unique relationship between God the Father and Jesus the Son, this time from the Son's perspective.[18]

The language of love and delight in Mark 1:11 reinforces the truth that God is not some kind of *Star Wars* impersonal force. While a fuller biblical theology of the triune God depends on the entire New Testament witness,[19] the relationship of love between Father and Son in Mark 1:11 clearly points to a deep joyful communion between distinct 'persons'.[20]

[16] This word is closely related to the Greek words for 'love' (*agapē*) and 'to love' (*agapaō*) that dominate the NT. See interlude between parts 1 and 2 for more discussion.

[17] Larry W. Hurtado, *Mark*, NIBC (Carlisle: Paternoster; Peabody: Hendrickson, 1995), p. 20. See also R. T. France, *The Gospel of Mark*, NIGTC (Carlisle: Paternoster, 2002), p. 82.

[18] The popular idea that *abba* can be translated as 'Daddy' is incorrect. See Stein, *Mark*, p. 662.

[19] For an excellent discussion of Father, Son and Spirit in the NT see Larry Hurtado, *God in New Testament Theology* (Nashville: Abingdon, 2010).

[20] There is no English word that easily describes how Father, Son and Spirit have distinct identities and roles and yet exist together as one God (monotheism).

Christians believe in the triune God of love. One of the most evocative ways to appreciate what this means is to understand God in social terms: a 'community of being' with each person indwelling the life of the other two in a trinitarian community of love. In this image, within the Godhead are a set of mutual and perfect inter-penetrating relationships between Father, Son and Holy Spirit, each member of the Trinity revolving around one another in an eternally revolving 'dance' of self-giving love, joy and delight.[21] For example, C. S. Lewis invites us to consider that 'the words "God is love" have no real meaning unless God contains at least two Persons. Love is something that one person has for another person. If God was a single person, then before the world was made, He was not love.'[22] He continues that a Christian understanding of the statement 'God is love' means that 'the living, dynamic activity of love has been going on in God forever and has created everything else'.[23] This belief means 'that in Christianity God is not a static thing – not even a person – but a dynamic, pulsating activity, a life, almost a kind of drama. Almost, if you will not think me irreverent, a kind of dance.'[24]

In Mark 1:10–11 we are given the privilege to glimpse this dance. It tells us that redemption is a work of mutual cooperation between Father, Son and Spirit: a harmony of salvation, each Person having distinct roles, motivated and energized by divine self-giving love. As one author puts it, 'it is God's very nature to go out from God's self in love'.[25] As we will explore more in this book, particularly in part 4, the wonder of the Christian faith is that believers are, in a sense, invited into this divine dance, to experience it for themselves and be transformed into people of love in the process. The goal of the Father, Son and Spirit is to remake us in the image of the Son as self-giving lovers of God and others. It is such love that fulfils the entire purpose of the law.[26] Love is the greatest calling, the goal of salvation and the truest sign of the presence of God's Spirit. But God's agenda is bigger even than this. Love and delight pulsate through divine relationships within the Godhead; the victory of God will see that love re-established at the centre of all reality, where

---

[21] This social model of the Trinity has been advanced recently in different ways by theologians like Miroslav Volf, Jürgen Moltmann and others. It is not without its critics, who caution against speculative attempts to use a model of the Trinity as a template for human relationships.

[22] C. S. Lewis, *Mere Christianity* (Glasgow: Fount, 1982), p. 148.

[23] Ibid., p. 148.

[24] Ibid. The Greek word most often used to describe this dance is *perichōrēsis*.

[25] Fleming Rutledge, *The Crucifixion: Understanding the Death of Jesus Christ* (Grand Rapids: Eerdmans, 2015), p. 297.

[26] E.g. in the Gospels see Matt. 22:37–40; Mark 12:28–34; Luke 10:27. In Paul see Rom. 13:8; Gal. 5:14.

there will be no room at all for any forces or people opposed to the God of love. God will, as Paul puts it, be 'all in all'.[27]

3. The gospel of God (1:14–15)

If the intratrinitarian love of God is a crucial theme within our text, we also need to draw together the wider themes related to the Messiah's mission discussed above and how they illuminate the love of God.

In verse 14 we are told Jesus *went into Galilee, proclaiming the good news* [gospel] *of God.* This wonderful phrase shows how Mark links *euangelion* interchangeably to God or Jesus Christ (v. 1). In other words, the story of Jesus described above is very good news about God. What is this good news? Perhaps I can explain it this way. There is a tension running through the prologue of Mark, and verse 11 in particular, between the transcendence and immanence of God. Transcendence means that God is utterly *distinct from* his creation. Immanence captures how God is near and present, intimately involved *within* the world. Both are, in different ways, sources of very good news.

First, transcendence. In verse 11 God is in heaven, his 'dwelling place': a different dimension of reality from the physical universe. It is only when heaven is 'split' open that the voice of God is heard. Mark's description gives readers a glimpse of the glorious 'otherness' of almighty God. In other words, 'behind the scenes' God is reigning. As the Son literally steps out of the Jordan in faith he is affirmed in his identity and mission. The Father is with him and anoints him with his Spirit. The presence of Father and Spirit remain with him in all the darkness to come.

If the transcendent love of the Father and the empowering of the Spirit are good news for Jesus, they are also good news for Christians today. Obviously the parallel is not exact: Jesus has a unique relationship with his Father. He alone is the anointed king and Messiah. But there is encouragement here for us nonetheless. Jesus announces that *The time has come . . . the kingdom of God has come near. Repent and believe the good news!* (15). As Acts later makes clear, God has now poured out his Spirit for all who respond in faith and repentance to the good news of the resurrected Son (e.g. Acts 2:38). Therefore, whatever trials we face in our daily lives, the 'otherness' of our transcendent God is a source of hope and comfort. Whether we are wrestling with cancer, broken relationships, grief, spiritual opposition, injustice or long-term unemployment, we can be

[27] 1 Cor. 15:28.

encouraged that this world is not all there is: it is the gospel of the transcendent God that will have the last word.

But God is also immanent (here with us). Many early church fathers so wanted to protect the transcendence of God from human categories of thought that they described him as 'apathetic' or 'impassible'. To explore exactly what they meant by those terms would need a book. The *Concise Oxford English Dictionary* defines 'Apathetic' as 'Not feeling emotion; uninterested' and 'Impassible' as 'Incapable of feeling or emotion. Incapable of suffering injury.' While the early church fathers had a much richer and more nuanced understanding of impassibility than this, they did, I believe, over-emphasize God's transcendence. The problem is that this too easily gives the impression that God is unfeeling and unapproachable: infinitely removed from 'lower order' human emotions.

But this is simply not the God who reveals himself to us in the Bible. As we have seen in part 1, God loves Israel passionately. He is also deeply angered by sin. Neither is he passive. In Mark the dramatic arrival of Israel's Messiah is God's (utterly unexpected) means by which to heal the story of our broken world. Mark's prologue is bursting to tell of the gospel of God's fulfilled promise to Israel, who is working *within* history to bring forgiveness and hope, a king establishing his kingdom *here on earth* and who is powerfully *present* in the world through his Spirit. Most astonishingly of all, through the *incarnation* and mission of his beloved Son, God shows us his utter commitment to this broken world. Jesus becomes vulnerable to hunger and temptation in the desert. Ultimately, as a human saviour, he allows himself to be vulnerable even to suffering and death. God has, in Christ, and through the Spirit, 'come down' to us. The Father is *well pleased* (11) to send his Son on such a mission because his endgame is blessing. Charles Wesley's great words capture perfectly this paradox of the limitless transcendent love of God being embodied in his Son:

> Love divine, all loves excelling,
> joy of heaven, to earth come down,
> fix in us thy humble dwelling,
> all thy faithful mercies crown.
> Jesus, thou art all compassion,
> pure, unbounded love thou art;
> visit us with thy salvation;
> enter every trembling heart.[28]

---

[28] Charles Wesley, 'Love Divine, All Loves Excelling' (1747).

All this tells us astonishing good news about the God we worship: Father, Son and Spirit. Mark, in his allusive and poetic style, does not spell this out, but invites his readers to think of 'God' through a new lens. He is at once totally 'other' and, at the same time, present in the beloved Son whose mission leads to the cross. Richard Hays suggests that 'if we have rightly followed Mark's narrative clues about the identity of the one on the cross', the most appropriate response is 'reticent fear and trembling' – where 'we stand before the mystery in silence, to acknowledge the limitation of our understanding, and to wonder'.[29] We would be wise to take his advice.

[29] Richard B. Hays, *Reading Backwards: Figural Christology and the Fourfold Gospel Witness* (London: SPCK, 2015), p. 32.

1 John 4:7–10
7. God is love

Situation

The church has existed for thirty years. At first it grew steadily. New people came to faith, often at great personal cost because the surrounding culture was at best indifferent and sometimes hostile. It was a dynamic community. Even outsiders noticed how deeply these Christians cared for one another and how they celebrated joyfully when they met in one another's homes. But gradually things started to go wrong. It was difficult to put a finger on exactly why. Some well-known members began insisting people follow them, but their ideas seemed different from what had always been taught. Relationships became strained and they left after a public row. Factions started appearing among those who stayed. The joy that had characterized the church ebbed away. In the town the church became known as a place of infighting and bitterness. Within the church, while many kept participating, there was little enthusiasm for prayer, Bible study and mission. Some knew that change was needed but disagreed on what was required. Some longed for a powerful leader to sort things out. Others lamented the church's lack of facilities, especially for children and young people and said that a new building was needed to attract families. Others said the problem was the lacklustre worship gatherings. Yet another group proposed that the church was out of date – it desperately needed to rebrand its image and embrace modern technology in order to reach a new generation.

Task

You are a regional leader of the network of which this church is a part. What would you say to such a church and why?

1. John: apostle of love

Our second text on the theme of God's love revealed in Jesus Christ takes us to the writings of John. While it is perfectly justifiable to call Paul an 'Apostle of Love',[1] even he cannot 'compete' with John when it comes to frequency of love language. Figure 1 is a graph of

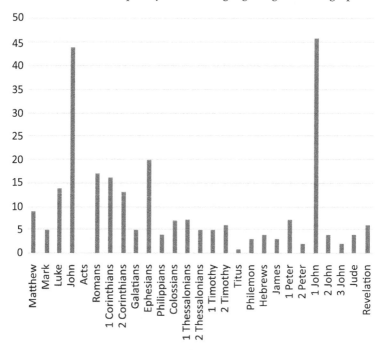

Figure 1: Occurrences of love language in the New Testament

occurrences of *agapē* (love) and *agapaō* (to love) within the New Testament.[2] It speaks for itself as you look at the figures for the Gospel of John and his letters.[3] Within 1 John, the use of love

---

[1] Patrick Mitchel, 'The New Perspective and the Christian Life: *Solus Spiritus*', in Scot McKnight and Joe Modica (eds.), *The Apostle Paul and the Christian Life: Missional and Ecclesial Implications of the New Perspective* (Grand Rapids: Baker, 2016), pp. 71–102, esp. 99–101.

[2] Robert Yarbrough, *1–3 John*, BECNT (Grand Rapids: Baker Academic, 2008), p. 174. The figures are for *agapē*. If *phileō* is included, this adds another 13 occurrences in John's Gospel.

[3] In 1 John there are 18.44 uses of love language per 1,000 words, 14.39 in 2 John and 7.87 in 3 John. The nearest other books are Philemon (7.77), Jude (7.53) and Ephesians (7.19). The Gospel of John scores 2.42. Yarbrough, *1–3 John*, p. 175.

language begins to intensify in chapter 3 (9 occurrences) but peaks within chapter 4 (27 occurrences). There are a remarkable 15 uses of the noun or verb for love in the eight verses of 1 John 4:7–14, making it the most 'love-saturated' text in the Bible. It is also the most theologically developed section on love within the letter.[4] Famously, of course, it contains the phrase *God is love* (8, repeated in 16). In a book on *The Message of Love* it is therefore an impossible text to ignore! It is located in part 2 of this book because the text, in good Johannine style, revolves around God: divine love leads to the sending of the Son. So while the text also has much to say about the interpersonal implications for those who know God's love first-hand, this is a secondary implication of who God is and what he has done in Christ.

John's other famous 'love text' is, of course, John 3:16. However, since there are very strong parallels between that verse and 1 John 4:9 we will link to theological themes contained within John 3:16 through the lens of 1 John.[5]

In what has already been said, certain positions that need to be made transparent are at play. Very briefly, in line with ancient church tradition and many scholars, I am taking it that Jesus' disciple John, Son of Zebedee, wrote the Fourth Gospel and the letters of 1–3 John.[6]

2. Rekindling love amid internal strain and external opposition

But what of John's reasons for writing so much about love within his epistles? This is not a straightforward question to answer since the letters do not identify the author, recipients or what has occasioned their compilation. However, there are substantial clues within 1 John that help explain his emphasis on love. He writes to believers who know God, have had sins forgiven and have been called into a new life of obedience (1 John 2:1–6). The tone is intimate: they are his 'dear children',[7] 'dear friends'[8] and

---

[4] Ibid., p. 235.

[5] The majority of love language within John's Gospel appears in Jesus' farewell discourse in the upper room within teaching directed at his disciples. This is considered in chapter 13 below.

[6] Polycarp (c. AD 108), Ignatius (c. AD 110), Papias (c. AD 110), the *Epistula Apostolorum* (c. AD 140) and the Epistle to Diognetius (c. AD 125–150) all show appreciative awareness of the letters. Irenaeus (c. AD 180) makes mention of John as the author. For wider discussion see Andreas J. Köstenberger, *A Theology of John's Gospel and Letters*, BTNT (Grand Rapids: Zondervan, 2009), pp. 86–93.

[7] This phrase for 'dear' or 'little' children (*teknia*) occurs seven times in 1 John: 2:1, 12, 28; 3:7, 18; 4:4; 5:21.

[8] 'Dear friends' or 'dearly beloved' (*agapētoi*) occurs six times in 1 John: 2:7; 3:2, 21; 4:1, 7, 11.

'brothers'[9] with whom he is in joyful fellowship (1 John 1:3). John writes with apostolic authority, exhorting, teaching and warning these Christians to live lives consistent with their identity as those who have received the Word of life (1 John 1:1). The framework is strongly eschatological: they live in a time transitioning between passing darkness and 'the true light [that] is already shining'.[10] A life marked by light will be that which loves fellow believers. It will desire to do God's will as opposed to that of the world. The 'world' (*kosmos*) is one of John's favourite words. It occurs twenty-three times in 1 John alone and in his writings has a negative sense as a realm of sin (1 John 2:2) and destructive desires (1 John 2:26) that lies in the power of the evil one (1 John 5:19). Thus John writes, 'Do not be surprised, my brothers and sisters, if the world hates you.'[11] Like the darkness, the 'world and its desires' are also passing away;[12] they offer only death (1 John 3:14). In contrast, those who remain in the Son and the Father have eternal life (1 John 2:24–25). It is clear that John's warnings are not without cause. Some from among the community have abandoned their faith, led astray by false guides (1 John 2:26; 3:7).[13] Their departure has revealed that 'none of them belonged to us'[14] and they have denied 'that Jesus is the Christ' in the process.[15] In this context of external opposition and internal strain John encourages them to persevere until the coming of the Lord (1 John 2:28; 3:2–3). He reminds them of their identity as lavishly loved children of God (1 John 3:1) who are called to love one another (1 John 3:11, 14). This love will be patterned on the self-giving love of Jesus (1 John 3:16–18) and takes the form of obedience to God (1 John 3:21–24) empowered by the Spirit (1 John 3:24; 4:1–6).

Regarding the epistles' setting, strong tradition indicates that John was resident in Ephesus circa AD 70–100 and writing in that Greek context.[16] If this is so, it is, as Yarbrough says, 'not a world on all

---

[9] The singular 'brother' (*adelphos*) is mentioned twelve times, and the community as a whole addressed as 'brothers' three times (1 John 4:13–14, 16). The sense in all of these is of fellow believers regardless of gender.

[10] 1 John 2:8.

[11] 1 John 3:13.

[12] 1 John 2:15–17.

[13] John in 3 John 9 talks of Diotrephes, who is acting divisively.

[14] 1 John 2:19.

[15] 1 John 2:22.

[16] Polycrates, bishop of Ephesus, writing to Victor, bishop of Rome (c. AD 190), mentions 'great luminaries' buried in the region, including 'John who leaned on the Lord's breast', who 'sleeps in Ephesus'. Around the same time, Irenaeus of Lyons wrote that 'John the disciple of the Lord' published his Gospel while he lived in Ephesus. See F. F. Bruce, *The Epistles of John* (Grand Rapids: Eerdmans, 1970), pp. 14–15.

counts friendly to Christian presence and witness'.[17] John's response is to write a series of encouraging pastoral letters to relatively young, and in many ways precarious, Christian communities. In them, the wise old disciple of Jesus hones in on core issues in order to refresh their vision, relationships and eschatological hope – namely God's love, brotherly love, perseverance and doctrinal and ethical purity in a fallen world that is passing away. His priorities have much to teach us today.

This is where we come to the imaginary church situation outlined at the beginning. It is not meant to mirror Ephesus at the end of the first century, but there are intentional parallels. In such a situation it would be easy, would it not, to answer the hypothetical task by imagining that spiritual growth and renewal will happen if 'we' get 'externals' right – whether implementing cutting-edge worship, fun youth and children's programmes, dynamic and accessible preaching, moving to a new building, delivering outreach programmes, developing an excellent website, investing in sophisticated technology, restructuring home groups and investing in dynamic leadership? Now I am not saying these things are unimportant. But all of them represent, in different ways, trust in what 'we do' as the means to effect spiritual renewal. Yet trust in the 'mechanics' of religious organizational life misses, as John drives home again and again, that love for God and for one another are the heart of authentic Christian faith. There is no substitute: everything else is to flow from love. Imagining that we hold the power to control spiritual renewal makes hearing what God has to say to us almost impossible and repentance unnecessary. It precludes space for critical self-reflection in how *we* might be deeply compromised in our love lives – our love of the world and all it offers. This said, let us look at what John has to say about love in more detail.

3. Love because God is love (4:7–10)

Thus far in the letter love has been given a relatively limited theological foundation. We are going to zone in on 7–10, which is the first of two mini-exhortations to love one another.[18] Obviously these verses fit within a wider context and we could do an exegetical study of the whole section from 7–21. However, the rich theological content of 7–10 provides us with a lens through which to gain a broader appreciation of John's unique perspective on love.

---

[17] Yarbrough, *1–3 John*, p. 21.
[18] 1 John 4:7–10, 11–14 form parallel short exhortations to love one another.

a. An invitation to love (7–8)

Each mini-exhortation begins with a *Beloved* (*agapētoi*, ESVUK). As noted earlier, John uses this form of address only occasionally. In each case it functions as a personal and pastoral appeal to people he cares deeply about. Here it *invites* his readers into an exalted task – of loving one another. I say 'invites' because, uniquely in the New Testament, John uses the first person plural form *let us love* (*agapōmen*, 7, ESVUK) rather than the more usual second person plural imperative (e.g. 'love one another').[19] In other words, John humbly includes *himself* in the task of loving others. There is no hierarchy here – the revered apostle is under the call of love just as much as anyone under his authority.

The reason they are to love is that *love is from God* (7, ESVUK): he is the source of love. Love, in some sense, originates in the identity of God himself. As John makes clear a few words later, love is not just *from God* but in himself *God is love* (8, repeated in v. 16). This is the only time in the Bible that God is so described. But, as this entire BST volume is attempting to unpack, it is no isolated claim. While certainly a climactic moment, it stands in full continuity with the consistent witness of Scripture. It also stands in parallel with John's earlier declaration that 'God is light'[20]. It is not as though love stands above all other divine characteristics, but it is to say that *all* that God is and does is loving. Since love is intrinsically interpersonal, John's three-word statement is loaded with significance – God is ontologically relational. He is the only being who can possibly be called *love*. In our very best moments we may love well, but none of us can ever be described as love. *God is love* implicitly highlights the immense gulf between God and humanity.[21]

b. Whoever loves knows God (7–8)

The effect of God's love is that it is to be valued, pursued and practised by all who belong to God. It is the indispensable marker of authentic Christianity because *whoever loves has been born of God and knows God* (7, ESVUK). In other words, love is visible evidence of an invisible spiritual reality – of being 'born again' to use the language of John's Gospel.[22] Such is the defining importance

---

[19] There are eleven examples in the NT, all of them from 1 or 2 John.

[20] 1 John 1:5.

[21] I. H. Marshall, *The Epistles of John*, NICNT (Eerdmans: Grand Rapids, 1978), p. 213.

[22] See John 3:1–21 for parallel ideas of spiritual rebirth, eternal life and God's sending his beloved Son into the world.

of love, that anyone *who does not love does not know God* (8, ESVUK).
John does not hold back here; quite simply a lack of love reveals a
spurious faith (see 1 John 4:20). The word *to know* (*ginōskō*) is
repeated. To know God, to be in relationship with the God who
is love, means that someone will reflect the character of God. Not
to do so shows that there is no true relationship. The vertical shapes
the horizontal. John does not explain how this process works in
practice; he simply describes an apparently inevitable implication of
knowing the God who is love. But we are not left without resources
for understanding John's calm assurance. Within his writings, and
much biblical thought,[23] God's people are expected to exhibit the
character of the God they worship. John's imagery reminds us that
it is only a very modern idea that 'knowing' can be measured via a
mastery of abstract ideas disconnected from character and virtue.
For John, things work very differently: a virtuous life of love
flows from true knowledge of God. And this is not some vague
depersonalized sense of the divine; it is the God of Israel who loves
and whom we are to love in return. This is made crystal clear in the
next two magnificent verses.

c. God reveals his love (9)

Verse 9, *This is how God showed his love among us: he sent his one
and only Son into the world that we might live through him*, echoes
John's most famous statement, 'For God so loved the world that he
gave his one and only Son, that whoever believes in him shall not
perish but have eternal life.'[24] In both cases the sending of the
unique (*monogenēs*) Son[25] is *motivated* by God's love for a broken
and sinful world, and the *purpose* of the Son's arrival is new life in
those who believe in him.[26] John does not spell this out, but to
experience new life implies a doctrine of regeneration. As discussed
above, his diagnosis of the human condition is unsentimental. We
exist in a transient world of darkness, hatred, sin and death. It is only
the manifestation (*phaneroō*, 'to reveal') of the Son that can give
light and life.[27] That life, as the whole of 1 John makes clear, originates
in the love of God and takes the form of love for God and for others.

---

[23] E.g. 'Be holy as I am holy' is a core command in both Testaments.

[24] John 3:16.

[25] The NIVUK's translation 'one and only' captures well the sense of the unique Son,
who has an exclusive familial relationship with his Father.

[26] In John 3:16 eternal life is linked to faith (*pisteuō*, 'to believe'). 1 John is a little
less specific: *we might live through him* implies believing faith as the necessary
response to entering new life.

[27] Again John is allusive here. 'Showed' is shorthand for the incarnation, life and
ministry of Jesus.

We are in the realm of wonder and worship here. Divine love leads to self-giving redemptive action – there is no greater act of love in all of human history. Perhaps we can even say, in all of God's history. The 'sending' of the Son into the world is John's shorthand for the entire story of Jesus, which reveals the 'bigger' story of God – the story of his relentless love that releases his love and blessing within the world. Without God's love there would be no possibility of receiving the gift of eternal life: salvation rests *entirely* on God's initiative.

In the last verse of his mini-exhortation John strengthens his appeal by giving further theological underpinning to the nature of God's love. He makes two points. Both are extraordinarily important for us to hear afresh today and I will concentrate discussion here. The first is to do with the paradoxical relationship between divine and human love. The second concerns how God's love is made manifest most supremely at the cross.

d. The countercultural paradox of Christian love (10a)

Verse 10a, *This is love: not that we loved God, but that he loved us* (10), reiterates how love originates with God, not us. Before the love of God in the Son was made manifest, John's readers belonged to the world and were therefore in serious spiritual trouble. This means that it is *only* through God's love that they come to know God and are enabled to love. As Yarbrough says, the 'self must look beyond itself in order to access divine love'.[28]

John's words cut right to the marrow of human pride and self-sufficiency. It is not that John is saying humans are incapable of love, but that we can know the God who is love, and be transformed to live a life of love only by depending on what God has done for us in his Son. This is where a Christian theology of love confronts contemporary Western ideas about love head-on. Now that is a big claim – let me explain what I mean by discussing 10a while interacting with the wider section of 11–21.

There is a profound paradox in Johannine love. On the one hand is the glorious truth that ordinary men and women like you and me can know God, who is, in himself, love. The idea of 'abiding' or 'living' in God is repeated four times in four verses[29] and multiple times within the letter.[30] John's consistent emphasis is that there will be visible evidence if someone 'abides in' and thus knows God – that

[28] Yarbrough, *1–3 John*, p. 239.
[29] 1 John 4:12–14, 16.
[30] *Menō* means 'to live, dwell, abide, remain': to be in a state of ongoing relationship.

evidence is love. Conversely, 'whoever does not love their brother and sister, whom they have seen, cannot love God, whom they have not seen'.[31] A second tangible 'proof' that believers can be assured that we 'live in him and he in us: he has given us of his Spirit'.[32] It is the Spirit who makes known God's presence and love. Typically, John leaves the 'mechanics' of this statement unarticulated but the implications are clear. Salvation is entirely God's work, but living a life of love requires a human response of obedience to God's Spirit. As a result, Christians are expected and enabled to live radically attractive lives of love. This is an extraordinarily 'high' view of the significance of love. There is not a hint in John (or any NT writer for that matter) that knowing God is mere cognitive assent to the idea he exists. Knowing God *must* be transformative and for John that transformation means to love, at least to a limited degree, like God himself: 'God is love. Whoever lives in love lives in God, and God in them'.[33] What this looks like in practice could not be more exalted – 'in this world we are like Jesus'.[34] John does not unpack this, but it is likely he has in mind here something very much like Paul in Philippians 2:5–11. Christian love is not some abstract idea: it takes a specific form. To be like Jesus is to live a life of obedient self-giving love. Such a life will give John's readers a tangible basis for 'confidence on the day of judgment'.[35] Rather than fearing divine punishment, those who live in love live in God, are like Christ, have experienced forgiveness of sins through their saviour (1 John 4:14), and therefore have no reason to fear the future (1 John 4:18). It is hard to think of how the importance of love could be more elevated within Christian theology and experience, nor a more assured expectation that followers of Jesus will be communities of divinely inspired love.

Yet, on the other hand, to become such a lover requires humility – to acknowledge that we cannot love out of our own resources, as if love were an easy and natural instinct. As the second half of verse 10 makes clear (and is discussed more below), sins need to be atoned for if life and love are to flourish. We need God's presence and power in our lives: without the Spirit we cannot possibly obey the imperatives of verses 7, 11 and 21 to love one another. We need to *rely* (*pisteuō*, 'to believe' or 'trust in') 'on the love God has for us'[36] rather than trust in ourselves. Love, then, for John, is anything but

---

[31] 1 John 4:20b; see also 1 John 3:14, 17.
[32] 1 John 4:13.
[33] 1 John 4:16.
[34] 1 John 4:17.
[35] Ibid.
[36] 1 John 4:16a.

an innate human capacity, available 'on tap' to anyone, regardless of character and knowledge of God.

Johannine love, then, has within it a dialectical tension between exaltation and humility. In this it reflects the paradox of how God's love is most supremely revealed in the sacrificial death of his Son (10). But it is exactly here that it comes into sharp conflict with post-Enlightenment secular popular culture. We live in a period within 'the history of love' where, as Simon May has traced, the optimistic 'high' side of love has become detached from the need for humility and repentance. 'Without an all-powerful God to hold them together and serve as a standing reminder of how severely hard love is, as well as fundamentally beyond our control, they have simply gone their own separate ways . . .'[37]

At least two consequences follow. One is that today 'God is love' has been subverted to become 'love is God'.[38] We are daily surrounded by divine claims for this new god. Modern love is idolized and dreamed about – it gives our lives purpose; it is eternal, giving significance beyond death. We long for love as a source of security and happiness. So prized is true love that nothing has the right to stand in its way. Allow me an Irish illustration to explain what I mean.

At the top of Dublin's O'Connell Street, the city's main thoroughfare, is the Parnell Monument. On it is inscribed the words of Irish Nationalist leader Charles Stuart Parnell (1846–91): 'No man has a right to fix the boundary to the march of a nation.'[39] In Parnell's day the great 'unstoppable' force for good was nationalism. It had a life of its own; no one could, or should, obstruct its progress. It was an unmitigated blessing and those who believed in it dreamed of a future 'eschatological kingdom' (an Ireland liberated from British occupation) of justice and freedom. Over 100 years later, nationalism has lost its lustre, and not just in Ireland. Two global wars, the atomic bombing of civilian populations, the Holocaust and innumerable other national conflicts have rightly made many profoundly wary of nationalist utopias. Nationalism, along with other 'big stories' of our modern age, like reason, communism and capitalism have failed to deliver promised progress. Organized religion too is, in many places, in apparently terminal decline. As each has fallen, so love has risen to be the new god of our (Western)

[37] Simon May, *Love: A History* (London: Yale University Press, 2011), p. 93.
[38] For further discussion of this point, see the Introduction.
[39] The full text reads, 'No man has a right to fix the boundary to the march of a nation. No man has a right to say to his country, "Thus far shalt thou go and no further." We have never attempted to fix the ne-plus-ultra to the progress of Ireland's nationhood, and we never shall.'

age. Today it is trusted to bring blessing, justice and freedom. For example, the successful campaigns for the legalization of same-sex marriage in numerous Western nations have been, to a large part, driven by the perceived injustice of having legal barriers to true love. The gender of those in love is relatively unimportant – what matters is that love must be allowed to flourish. The right to marriage is therefore primarily about public legitimation of love. Marriage itself is redefined as being primarily an arena for love rather than a legal and covenantal relationship in which children are conceived and raised. Today, we might therefore paraphrase Parnell to say, 'No person has a right to fix a boundary on the onward march of love.'

A second consequence of love's ascent is a virtually unquestioned assumption that love is, unless resisted for some perverse reason, within instant reach of everyone – like an inherent human ability or human right. May provocatively challenges this conceit:

> Whereas becoming even a fairly competent artist or gardener or editor or plumber or banker or singer is dearly purchased with long effort and then only by the few with sufficient talent, love is a democracy of salvation open to all.[40]

He is on to something here: overconfident claims for modern love leave little or no need for humility, obedience or repentance. Largely absent is a critical self-awareness that love is difficult and demanding: that we need divine help to develop a character that is orientated outwards towards the good of others. As a result, much modern love tends to be superficial and overly optimistic; 'love' is a word that is at once ubiquitous, yet so elastic as to mean virtually anything.

e. The atoning sacrifice of the Son (10b)

The second half of verse 10 describes what God's love looks like in practice and is radically different from contemporary notions of love. Believers' capacity to love is grounded in the Son's *atoning sacrifice [hilasmos] for our sins*. As is his style, John does not go into detailed theological analysis of how this 'works'. The atoning sacrifice is clearly the death of Jesus, but what happened at the cross? *Hilasmos* is a rare word in the New Testament over which many pots of ink have been expended as to whether it should be interpreted 'expiation' or 'propitiation'. The former carries the sense of

---

[40] Simon May, 'Rethinking Our Fascination with Love', <www.yalebooksblog. co.uk/2011/04/27/author-article-by-simon-may-rethinking-our-fascination-with-love>, accessed 13 April 2017.

rescinding or waiving the penalty for sin. The latter includes this but within a wider meaning that involves a turning away of divine wrath against sin and sinners via an acceptable offering (the substitutionary death of the Son). We do not need to replay those debates here save to say that the evidence is in favour of propitiation.[41] While Jesus' death does 'wipe the slate clean', it also turns aside God's just punishment of sin and sinners. God's redeeming love does not exist in contradiction to his justice. The Son is sent into the world out of divine love (1 John 4:9), but there remains a day of judgment (1 John 4:17–18). The atoning sacrifice of the Son is God's supreme act of love that provides a means of forgiveness and eternal life right here and now to all who respond to the gospel. *Agapē*

> is not love given to the worthy: it is lavished on sinners. When we see man for what he is, the wrath of God for what it is, and the cross for what it is, then and only then do we see love for what it is.[42]

We can see how this collides with the hubristic optimism of modern love. The latter assumes we do not need to be forgiven; we do not need new life since we already have the inherent ability to be world-class lovers; the only thing we really need is the freedom to express our true identity.

The atoning death of the Son also, in some way, resources Christians in the task of loving. At the very least, there is an inspiring model to imitate. Verse 10 defines love in terms of God's action in sending his Son *for* a lost humanity. It complements 1 John 3:16, which also makes explicit a truly Christlike response to divine love: 'This is how we know what love is: Jesus Christ laid down his life for us. And we ought to lay down our lives for our brothers and sisters.' This is not to say we can love as God loves – that would be a colossal delusion. As finite created beings we can hardly begin to imagine the depth of divine love behind the Father's sending and the Son's voluntary atoning sacrifice. But we can, in our own small worlds, make daily decisions to act for the good of others, whatever the cost to ourselves. This, of course, is easier said than done! Rather than love being a universal 'right' through which we express ourselves, or a quality instantly and easily available to all, authentic

---

[41] This exact word is found elsewhere only in 1 John 2:2. The meaning of NT occurrences of the *hilas-* word group (Luke 18:13; Rom. 3:25; Heb. 2:17; 9:5) has long been contested. For further discussion, see Marshall, *Epistles of John*, pp. 117–120, 214–215. Also Yarbrough, *1–3 John*, pp. 77–81.

[42] Leon Morris, *Testaments of Love: A Study of Love in the Bible* (Grand Rapids: Eerdmans, 1981), p. 131.

Christian love will likely be enormously costly to the self – the cross is a stark reminder of that inconvenient truth.

4. Seven conclusions

John's writing is deceptive: it appears simple but his prose leads his readers, almost unwittingly, into deep, and refreshing, theological waters. Let us sum up some implications for how we think of God, love and discipleship. Seven conclusions can be made.

First, John takes as a given that his readers are first and foremost lovers. It is not a question of *whether* we will love; it is *what* we will love. John asks each one of us, 'How is your love life? Is your love for God as alive and vibrant as ever? Is it deepening and growing, or is it tired, disillusioned or misdirected?'

Second, he has important words for us about seeing the world through eschatological glasses. By this, I mean to appreciate John's perspective that we live in the overlap of the ages and that our loves need to ordered accordingly. We are not to love – and therefore give ourselves to – this transient fallen world, however tempting it may be. Christians need to see the world as both 'delicious and dangerous'.[43] Delicious, in that it is God's good world and is full of beauty, joy, relationships and pleasure. Dangerous, in that Western culture is not spiritually benign. Just as the early Christians in Ephesus lived in an inhospitable environment, so we in the West need to see clear-sightedly that our culture is laden with narratives of materialism, consumerism and selfism that seduce our hearts to love the world. Rather than pursuing its false promises, we are to love and give ourselves wholeheartedly to the God who is love.[44]

Third, we do not love alone. John is relentlessly corporate. Love can function only in relationship with others: we need one another in order to live the Christian life. No one in the community is exempt from the imperative to love. It is the fundamental requirement for all disciples, regardless of status, education, intellect and experience.

Fourth, John models truly Christian leadership. He writes authoritatively, but his epistles are suffused with a tender pastoral love for those in his care. He does not set himself up above his beloved brothers and sisters, but includes himself in the joint task of loving well.

Fifth, John knows nothing of 'cheap love', where we say we love God but do not act accordingly. Belief, behaviour and love are

---

[43] David Wells, *Above All Earthly Pow'rs: Christ in a Postmodern World* (Grand Rapids: Eerdmans; Leicester: Inter-Varsity Press, 2005), p. 16.
[44] We will return to this theme in more depth in chapter 17 (on the love of money).

inextricably linked. Johannine love is robust and practical: it gives concrete expression to the love of God in Christ. It takes tangible form as we lay down our lives for one another and live lives of obedience to God. Christ is our atoning sacrifice but he does not repent and believe for us. God has given us his Spirit, but he does not believe and obey for us. Salvation is entirely due to the love of God in sending his Son, but that divine initiative calls for a response of repentance, faith and costly obedience. In all these characteristics, authentic Christian love stands in sharp contrast to the optimistic divinization of modern human love.

Sixth, to know God is to love, and to love is to know God. We need to embrace and take John's teaching to heart here. A default assumption of our secular post-Enlightenment culture ever since Kant has been the splitting apart of objective and subjective knowledge. The objective is the realm of supposedly universally true facts that provide the only solid foundation for knowing. The subjective is the realm of unprovable feelings, dreams, beliefs and values that are of secondary value. But John will have none of this. He insists that God is truly known only in and through love. N. T. Wright is very Johannine here: 'If you want true knowledge you have to love. And to learn about true love you have to hear, to smell, to imagine the story of the crucified Nazarene.'[45] Wright is right and the implications for preaching, teaching and training are enormous – love needs to be front and centre of all ministry if it is to be authentically Christian. This is essentially John's 'strategy' for church renewal in Ephesus. He is unapologetically theological rather than pragmatic. He roots his reader's hopes and behaviour in the loving nature and self-giving actions of God rather than in their own resources and abilities. His is a theocentric theology, rejoicing in the good news that God is love and in the sending of the Spirit, rather than an androcentric theology, shaped by a naive optimism about our human capacity to love. In a technological age of relentless pragmatism (that I have tried to catch in the fictional scenario that began this chapter) where it is so easy to rely merely on ourselves, we need to learn afresh from John that it is through Christians loving one another that the world sees the love of God embodied in the world.

Lastly, and most importantly, John gives us a unique portrait of God himself. Derek Tidball writes in his significant book on the cross that 'More than any other New Testament writer, John associates the cross of Christ explicitly with the love of God, and so with

---

[45] N. T. Wright, 'Wouldn't You Love to Know? Towards a Christian View of Reality', <www.ntwrightpage.com/2016/09/05/wouldnt-you-love-to-know-towards-a-christian-view-of-reality>, accessed 12 April 2017.

the very nature of God himself.'[46] Twice John declares that *God is love*. We know this to be true because of the death of his Son *for us*. It is through him that we are given eternal life and enabled to love. There is no greater love in all of creation than this. We worship a God who is worthy beyond words of our complete allegiance and undying love. The 2010 Cape Town Commitment, a global evangelical affirmation of faith that is framed around the theme of love, puts it this way:

> The love of God is covenantally faithful, committed, self-giving, sacrificial, strong, and holy. Since God is love, love permeates God's whole being and all his actions, his justice as well as his compassion. God's love extends over all his creation. We are commanded to love in ways that reflect the love of God in all those same dimensions. That is what it means to walk in the way of the Lord.[47]

[46] Derek Tidball, *The Message of the Cross*, BST (Leicester: Inter-Varsity Press, 2001), p. 304.

[47] Lausanne Movement, *The Cape Town Commitment: A Confession of Faith and a Call to Action* (no publisher: Lausanne Movement, 2011), pp. 9–10.

Romans 5:1–11
8. Love and justification

Ask a hypothetical 'average Christian' words he or she associates with Paul and the reply might include mention of a Pharisee zealous for the law, Damascus road conversion, missionary to the Gentiles, justification by faith, theologian, letter writer, Roman citizen, shipwreck and martyrdom. I may be wrong, but for some reason it seems unlikely that 'apostle of love' would appear in any list. Yet love pervades his letters – in his theology, in his experience of God and in deep relationships forged in the heat of ministry. Paul uses *agapē* (love) 75 times, *agapaō* (to love) 34 times and *agapētos* (beloved) 27 times. This total of 136 occurrences of love language is 42.5% of the 320 uses in the New Testament as a whole.[1] Counting words is, of course, a fairly crude method of assessing someone's commitment to an idea, but in this case it is a clear indication of how pivotal love is to Paul's life and thought.[2] As Scot McKnight says, 'Over and over, Paul *explicitly claims* that love is the center of the whole Christian life.'[3] In this chapter we turn to our first of several Pauline 'love texts' and explore different aspects of love in Paul in several of the remaining chapters of this book.

In Romans, love appears at key junctures in Paul's complex explanation of God's saving action in the world. Our text is 5:1–11, where love first appears in Romans, and we will explore love's

[1] Leon Morris, *Testaments of Love: A Study of Love in the Bible* (Grand Rapids: Eerdmans, 1981), p. 138.
[2] For further discussion of specific examples see Patrick Mitchel, 'The New Perspective and the Christian Life: *Solus Spiritus*', in Scot McKnight and Joe Modica (eds.), *The Apostle Paul and the Christian Life: Missional and Ecclesial Implications of the New Perspective* (Grand Rapids: Baker, 2016), pp. 99–101.
[3] Scot McKnight, 'The New Perspective and the Christian Life: Ecclesial Life', in Scot McKnight and Joe Modica (eds.), *The Apostle Paul and the Christian Life: Missional and Ecclesial Implications of the New Perspective* (Grand Rapids: Baker, 2016), p. 149. Emphasis original.

relationship with the great doctrine of justification by faith. It is a particularly significant text in terms of understanding how God's love revealed in Jesus Christ 'works'. God's love is anything but an abstract idea. I will try to unpack what it looks like in practice.

Romans is perhaps the most influential letter ever written in human history. Every chapter resonates down the centuries of Christian theology. Frank Matera notes how 'there is hardly a chapter of Romans that has not played a vital role in the development of Christian doctrine'.[4] This means that it has also been the focus of a vast amount of research, debate and controversy, not least, of course, concerning justification by faith. From Martin Luther and the Reformation, through centuries of Catholic and Protestant polemics, down to modern ecumenical discussions and the development, since the late 1970s, of the New Perspective on Paul, justification has been a continuously 'live' theological issue for over 500 years! While aware of those debates and how they shape interpretation of the text, our focus will be on how justification helps to reveal God's love.

1. Context

To call Romans a 'letter' is to risk missing its main characteristic. While it includes personal and conversational elements, it is much more a form of theological *argumentation*, characteristic of the style of first-century rhetoric.[5] While theories vary, it is widely accepted that Jewish–Gentile tensions are a major reason why Paul writes. He does so from Corinth to a loose grouping of house churches throughout the city (Rom. 16:5)[6] that probably reflected a growth of Gentile converts and an increasingly Gentile-led Christianity.[7] There were likely conflicting expectations of what form Gentile obedience, belonging and holiness should take. As anyone involved in church life well knows, such competing ideas do not tend to remain abstract: they easily become personal and lead to rival factions with competing practices. Paul's response to this context is a magnificent and multilayered theological argument that sets the Jew–Gentile question within the fourfold framework of the story of God, the world, Israel and Jesus Christ while simultaneously

---

[4] Frank Matera, *Romans*, PCNT (Grand Rapids: Baker Academic, 2010), p. 3.

[5] Craig Keener, *Romans*, NCCS (Eugene: Cascade, 2009), pp. 2–4. See also Ben Witherington, *Paul's Letter to the Romans: A Socio-Rhetorical Commentary* (Grand Rapids: Eerdmans, 2004), pp. 16–22.

[6] See Michael Bird, *Romans*, SGBC (Grand Rapids: Zondervan, 2016), p. 3.

[7] Keener, *Romans*, p. 12.

providing a basis for love and unity within the body of Christ (e.g. Rom. 12:3–20).[8]

The apostle makes his objectives clear right from the beginning (Rom. 1:1–7). Quite simply, if Jesus is Israel's Messiah and risen Lord, he is Lord of all – of both Jews and Gentiles. Paul's understanding of his apostolic mission is of a God-given task to 'call all the Gentiles to the obedience that comes from faith'[9] in the one true Lord. He reminds the Gentiles in Rome that they are included in the calling 'to belong to Jesus Christ'[10] and 'to be his holy people'[11]. Much of the content of Romans is, then, explaining to and persuading his readers regarding what it means (and does *not* mean) in practice for formerly pagan Gentiles to be included in that calling.

Chapter 5 acts as a hinge between the soteriological exposition of justification (Rom. 1:16 – 4:25) and the present implications of justification worked out within life in the Spirit (Rom. 6:1 – 8:39).[12] The *Therefore* of 5:1 marks the transition from the previous section while linking to what follows.

2. Justification: past, present and future (5:1–11)

A while ago I did a multiday cross-country hike with my two daughters in Iceland. It was hard going. Each day, after some hours of walking, we took off our heavy packs, had a welcome rest and brewed a cup of coffee. Sipping it, we looked back with pleasure at the spectacular scenery and how far we had come. This achievement refreshed us and renewed our spirits in the present. But it also encouraged us to keep going for the remaining journey ahead. Likewise, in 5:1–11 it seems as if Paul is pausing within his overall argument to *look back* at the magnificent terrain of what God has done in Christ. He simultaneously relates the significance of justification to encourage his readers in the *present* while also exhorting them to *look ahead* in hope in the light of what has been accomplished by God *through our Lord Jesus Christ* (11).

Verses 1–11 are packed full of significant words: *justification, faith, peace, grace, boast, hope, love, wrath* and *reconciliation*. It would be easy to get lost within this theological forest. My purpose is neither to attempt to unpack the theology of each of these words

---

[8] For further discussion of the four stories see the interlude between parts 1 and 2 of this book.

[9] Rom. 1:5.

[10] Rom. 1:6.

[11] Rom. 1:7.

[12] Most scholars agree on this view. E.g. R. Jewett, *Romans: A Commentary*, Hermeneia (Minneapolis: Fortress, 2007), p. 346.

nor to do a detailed verse-by-verse commentary. Rather, I will focus on 'the message of love' in this text by using Paul's threefold past, present and future framework to bring out what the text is saying about love. The three are so closely connected it is not easy – and even somewhat artificial – to try to disentangle them. But doing so will help us to see how love is central to these great theological themes of Romans.

a. Looking back: God demonstrates his love

Do you notice how Paul predominantly uses the first person plural throughout verses 1–11? This 'we' language is significant. The truths and experiences described are universally available for *all* Christians – Jews (including the apostle himself) *and* Gentiles. Let us now focus on what he says has already happened in the lives of *all* the believers in Rome (and, by implication, in the lives of all believers since).

(i) Love the motive for justification

All people, of whatever background, who have turned to Christ in faith, *have been justified* (1). This is a completed act.[13] It is *through our Lord Jesus Christ* (1) that we *have gained access by faith into this grace* (2). The *grace* in question here is being justified, but also includes the present experience of having *peace with God* (1). In verse 9 the phrase *by his blood* is added to the fact that *we have now been justified. Blood* is simply a shorthand way of referring to the death of Christ on the cross. Justification is a consequence or blessing of the self-giving death of Jesus. To understand how justification 'works' is to turn to the cross and the atonement. This is made explicit in verses 6–8, which form the heart of section 5:1–11. They provide the explanatory basis for how justification became possible:

> You see, at just the right time, when we were still powerless, Christ died for the ungodly. Very rarely will anyone die for a righteous person, though for a good person someone might possibly dare to die. But God demonstrates his own love for us in this: while we were still sinners, Christ died for us.

This is one of the great 'love texts' in the Bible. God's love is the foundation for all the blessings of salvation available in Christ. This justifying love has at least three dimensions. First, this is not a vague

---

[13] Paul uses the nominative plural of the aorist passive participle, clearly emphasizing a past event. Ibid., p. 348.

impersonal love – it is love *for us* and is proved physically in the world through the death of the Messiah, God's Son. If love is acting selflessly for the good of others, no greater demonstration of love is possible to imagine. Second, that death is atoning and substitutionary – *for us* (*hyper*, 'on behalf of', appears in 6, 7 and 8) along with *by his blood* (9, mentioned above). The combination of his death for *sinners* (8) means that 'though the sins were ours and the death was his . . . he died as a sin offering, bearing in our place the penalty our sins deserved'.[14] It results in believers having unfettered *access* (2) into the holy presence of God himself. Third, Jesus' death is illogical, extravagant and utterly countercultural. Paul gives the analogy of what sort of person *someone* might *possibly dare to die* (7) for. It is unlikely to be a *righteous person* (7, probably a morally upright individual who engenders respect). It might be for a *good person* (7, someone whom we know personally who has done good to us; possibly a benefactor or relative).[15] What is inconceivable in the ancient world[16] – and our world today – is giving your life for someone who is completely undeserving of goodwill and is hostile towards you. But this is for whom Christ died. We are *powerless* (6), *ungodly* (6) and *sinners* (8). In verse 10 Paul adds that we were *God's enemies* and were facing his *wrath*. This is a devastating analysis of the human condition before God. Christ's death is redemptive, achieving what humans are unable to do themselves. Without it we would be lost.

(ii) The astonishing cost of divine love

But there is a further wondrous aspect of God's justifying love that we must not overlook. The depth of God's saving love can only begin to be fully appreciated when we consider *who it is who dies*.

The phrase *through our Lord Jesus Christ* acts as an inclusio in 5:1, 11: it begins and finishes the passage, leading to *peace* (1) and *reconciliation* (11). This repetition is no accident and indicates how important Jesus' identity is within Paul's doctrine of justification. Who Jesus is (Christology) is inseparable from what is achieved on the cross (justification).

In verses 1–11 Paul uses three terms to talk of Jesus: *Christ* (1, 6, 8, 11), God's *Son* (10) and reigning *Lord* (1, 11). Even in these few

---

[14] John R. W. Stott, *The Message of Romans*, BST (Leicester: Inter-Varsity Press, 1994), p. 144.

[15] Grant R. Osborne, *Romans*, IVP NTCS (Leicester: Inter-Varsity Press, 2004), p. 133.

[16] Sirach 12.1–7 advises, 'Give to the one who is good, but do not help the sinner' (NRSVA). Aristotle (*Nicomachean Ethics* 9.8.1169a) counsels doing good to one's friends. Witherington, *Paul's Letter to the Romans*, p. 137.

verses we get a glimpse of the rich Christology that pervades Paul's writings. We are into profound territory here and I will briefly summarize the significance of these three terms and how they shed light on the unimaginable depth of God's saving love.

Christ, Son and *Lord* all also appear right at the beginning of Romans (1:2–4) in Paul's dramatic Christological opening to the letter. It is a good lens through which to unpack their meaning. What is astonishing is how Paul clearly understands Jesus to be not only the Son of God in the sense of being God's chosen kingly Messiah and descendant of David but *also the pre-existing eternal Son*, sent by his Father into the world and whose resurrection reveals his true identity. *Appointed* in 1:4 does not mean Jesus only 'becomes' the Son of God after his resurrection (which would be an adoptionistic Christology completely at odds with the rest of Romans and all of Paul's other letters), but rather, as Gordon Fee puts it, refers to 'the Father's and Spirit's vindication of the eternal Son, who had previously been sent by the Father'.[17]

That Jesus is also the risen *Lord* (*kyrios*) takes us to the heart of Paul's exalted Christology. The apostle routinely uses *Lord* virtually like a name for Jesus, usually without explanation or justification. Literally hundreds of examples permeate his letters. Within Paul's writings the risen Lord shares every kind of divine prerogative with God the Father, yet he is not synonymous with the Father. This has led many scholars to conclude that for Paul and the first Jewish Christians something utterly astonishing had happened to their understanding of *God himself*.[18] Jesus is talked of in terms that include him in what God *does* and who he *is*. Yet they remain monotheists – believers in the one God. As 1:4 makes clear, the 'key' to this radical paradigm shift is the resurrection. The risen one comes to be understood not only as Messiah of Israel, but reigning Lord of all. He is 'the one who makes present and visible what the Old Testament said about YHWH himself'.[19]

In other words, *it is God himself who enters our world in Jesus*. It is God in the flesh who experiences what Fleming Rutledge calls the 'godlessness' of the cross where 'the wrath of God falls upon God himself, by God's own choice, out of God's own love'.[20] It is

[17] Gordon Fee, *Pauline Christology: An Exegetical-Theological Study* (Peabody: Hendrickson, 2007), p. 544.

[18] Examples include scholars like Howard Marshall, Richard Bauckham, Larry Hurtado, N. T. Wright, Ben Witherington and many others.

[19] N. T. Wright, *The Resurrection of the Son of God* (Minneapolis: Fortress, 2003), p. 577.

[20] Fleming Rutledge, *The Crucifixion: Understanding the Death of Jesus Christ* (Grand Rapids: Eerdmans, 2015), p. 143.

God himself who, out of love, atones for our sin and gives us new life and hope. The gospel is astonishing. It is not something that anyone would make up. The idea of an incarnate God was foolishness to Gentiles. The notion of a crucified Messiah was abhorrent to Jews. God's love takes scandalous form in the birth, life, death, resurrection and ascension of the man from Nazareth. If we find this gospel mundane, then it may be that we have never really grasped its revolutionary nature or truly experienced the depth of God's self-giving love.

b. Present experience: the Spirit and extravagant love

If justification is motivated by love, it also enables believers to *experience* God's love for themselves in at least two remarkable ways.

(i) Justification and relationship

First, justification is fundamentally a relational term. The *dikaioō* word group, often translated as 'justify' or 'justification', refers to righteousness. The English word 'justify' is often used because there is no English word to 'rightify'. In many ways this is unfortunate because 'justification' can carry an overly legal sense, as if it is primarily about a sort of abstract transaction whereby sinners' debts are resolved. A danger is that this can import impersonal notions of divine justice into our thinking about justification. Roman Catholic merit theology is one result. Another is how some popular evangelical presentations of the gospel give the impression it is primarily a mathematical resolution of my 'sin problem' that, once resolved, leaves little motive or theological necessity for a subsequent life of holiness and obedience. Paul, I imagine, would exclaim a loud 'No' to such theology! The whole purpose of his gospel and ministry is to see the moral transformation of believers under his pastoral care.[21] The real thrust of justification is God's *grace* (2) in effecting salvation through Christ by which sinners who were God's *enemies* (10) and under his *wrath* (9) can now enjoy a restored relationship with God. This is why *peace* (1) and *reconciliation* (10, 11) are key words in our passage and in Romans as a whole. They are words that speak of a healed relationship, where what had previously ruptured that relationship (sin) has been dealt with.

This is why the best way to understand justification, or righteousness, is in terms of union with Christ.[22] The idea at its core is simple.

---

[21] For more see James Thompson, *Moral Formation According to Paul: The Context and Coherence of Pauline Ethics* (Grand Rapids: Baker Academic, 2011).

[22] This theme comes to the fore in Rom. 6:1–14.

Irenaeus of Lyons captured its essence back in the second century, 'The Word of God, our Lord Jesus Christ . . . through his surpassing love became what we are that he might bring us to be what he himself is.'[23]

This language of union is everywhere in Paul. As we will see in a moment, it is made effective through the gift of the Spirit. The result is *all that is Christ's becomes ours by God's grace alone*: we share in his victory over sin and death and in God's declaration of righteousness concerning his Son.

(ii) God's love poured out through the Spirit

Second, this brings us to the other wonderful 'love text' within 5:1–11 and the connections between justification, love and the Spirit: *And hope does not put us to shame, because God's love has been poured out into our hearts through the Holy Spirit, who has been given to us* (5).

Justification, faith and the gift of the Spirit are inseparable in Paul and 5:1–11 is one example. For Paul, faith in Christ is intrinsically linked to an outpouring of divine love in the heart of the Christian through the Spirit, who is the very presence of God himself.[24] The Spirit is the one who brings life where before there was death (e.g. Rom. 8:6). *Heart* in Hebrew thought is the seat of our will and personality, the essence of who we are. To 'pour out' (*ekcheō*) carries the sense of extravagant provision reminiscent of Pentecost, where the same word is used of the Spirit's fulfilling Joel's prophecy (Acts 2:17–18, 33). But, as John Stott points out, technically it is God's love that is poured out by the Spirit. This is not a one-off temporary outpouring but the perfect tense indicates a 'permanent flood'. In his words, a crucial aspect of the Spirit's ministry is to make all Christians 'deeply and refreshingly aware that God loves us'.[25] This wonderful description captures how Paul is not talking of dry, abstract theory: he is talking of an extraordinary *experience* of divine love common to all believers. Love unites Jewish and Gentile believers. All Christians are simply beneficiaries of God's generous love. Robert Jewett links love to the theme of boasting and shame in verses 2, 5 and 11. Christians have nothing to boast about

---

[23] James G. Bushur, *Irenaeus of Lyons and the Mosaic of Christ: Preaching Scripture in the Era of Martyrdom* (Abingdon: Routledge, 2017), p. 159. Quoting Irenaeus, *Against Heresies* 5.

[24] There is some debate as to how this is best read. *God's love* can be translated 'love of God'. Is it an outpouring of our love for God or God's love for us? The latter seems most likely given 5:6–8 and 8:31–39. This does not, of course, preclude our subsequent response of love for God. Colin G. Kruse, *Paul's Letter to the Romans*, PNTC (Nottingham: Apollos; Grand Rapids: Eerdmans, 2012), pp. 231–232.

[25] Stott, *Romans*, pp. 142–143.

except 'the widely shared experience of the unconditional love of God that is conveyed by the gift of the Spirit'.[26] The Roman world of honour and shame has lost its power to put believers to shame because they are loved by God himself!

One last comment on this verse. The 'us' and 'our' language of verse 5 makes it very likely that Paul is speaking from experience of God's love here. In his letters there is a pervasive expectation that Christians will know and experience the Spirit in their lives and communities as a foretaste of the world to come here in the present.[27] It is this eschatological perspective through which we can interpret how Paul sees the future implications of justification and it is to this that we now turn.

c. Looking forward: justification, love and eschatological hope

We come now to the third dimension of justification – eschatological hope. Scattered throughout 5:1–11 are words and phrases like *the hope of the glory of God* (2); *we also glory in our sufferings, because we know that suffering produces perseverance; perseverance, character; and character, hope* (3–4); *how much more shall we be saved from God's wrath through him!* (9); *how much more, having been reconciled, shall we be saved through his life!* (10).

It is obvious that Paul has a tremendous sense of future confidence. But this is a long way from any form of human positive thinking. It is rooted in God's *past* love in sending his Son and in believers' *present* experience of God's love in and through the Spirit. So the apostle is able to encourage his readers in Rome (and us today) that, whatever happens in the present, hope will have the last word. God's love will indeed win. For those in Christ, salvation from judgment is assured. When suffering comes, as it certainly did soon enough for Paul and for the Christians in Rome, God's love remains the great irreducible reality that cannot be overwhelmed. This radically countercultural perspective means that, while still horribly real, suffering can be gloried in (Rom. 11:3), is 'not worth comparing' to future glory (Rom. 8:18) and can even be called our 'light and momentary troubles'.[28]

Later in Romans Paul returns to this theme of justification, love and hope in one of the most famous sections of the epistle (Rom. 8:31–39). It feels like the apostle simply cannot refrain from bursting

---

[26] Jewett, *Romans*, p. 357.

[27] Elsewhere Paul talks of the Spirit as the 'first instalment' or 'deposit' (*arrabōn*) of the age to come (2 Cor. 1:22; 5:5; Eph. 1:14).

[28] 2 Cor. 4:17.

into a doxology of worship at the unbreakable power of God's love in Christ:

> It is God who justifies. Who then is the one who condemns? No one. Christ Jesus who died – more than that, who was raised to life – is at the right hand of God and is also interceding for us. Who shall separate us from the love of Christ? Shall trouble or hardship or persecution or famine or nakedness or danger or sword? As it is written:
>
>> 'For your sake we face death all day long;
>> we are considered as sheep to be slaughtered.'
>
> No, in all these things we are more than conquerors through him who loved us. For I am convinced that neither death nor life, neither angels nor demons, neither the present nor the future, nor any powers, neither height nor depth, nor anything else in all creation, will be able to separate us from the love of God that is in Christ Jesus our Lord.[29]

3. Conclusion

It is time to pause and reflect on the breathtaking landscape that we have traversed. There is much beauty to take in and my concluding comments will necessarily be limited to some key messages of love emerging from our text.

a. God's love calls God's people to a life of love

First, the history of the doctrine of justification has been so complicated and political that it is easy to miss the wood for the trees. Divine love lies at the origin of justification; it takes the form of the self-giving incarnation and self-atoning death of the eternal Son; it results in believers being declared righteous and love being poured out in their hearts through the Spirit; and it offers a rock-solid hope that nothing, even suffering, can separate Christians from that love. It is intimately associated with all sorts of other blessings – God's grace offered to unworthy sinners, reconciliation, adoption into God's family, forgiveness of sin, deliverance from divine wrath, and the formation of a radically diverse people of God in a highly stratified ancient world. This constitutes a veritable tsunami of good news!

[29] Rom. 8:33b–39.

But Paul does not stop there and nor should we. Recall his 'mission statement' in 1:7 that he writes primarily to foster unity and to encourage 'all in Rome who are loved by God and *called to be his holy people*'.[30] In other words, his passion is for the great theological narrative of God's righteousness to have a transformative impact on his readers. The story of justification is not told in order to employ professional academics in complex debates! It is a doctrine that belongs to every Christian and it calls each of us to live in the light of the message of love that lies at its core. This is why, from chapter 12 on, Paul encourages Jewish and Gentile followers of Jesus with commands like these: 'Love must be sincere. Hate what is evil; cling to what is good'[31]; 'Love does no harm to a neighbour. Therefore love is the fulfilment of the law'[32]; 'If your brother or sister is distressed because of what you eat, you are no longer acting in love. Do not by your eating destroy someone for whom Christ died.'[33] To apply this to our world: it is a life of love lived within the diverse community of the church that tells the real story of whether we have grasped what justification and life in the Spirit are all about.

b. Love and suffering

Second, the message of God's love offers hope in a world that is full of suffering. Allow me to tell a personal story to illustrate. I went for a walk this week with a dear friend. It was a beautiful day. We walked by the sea shore, the water a shimmering blue and yachts with their billowing colourful spinnakers gliding gracefully over its surface. Yet, in the midst of this idyllic scene, he could only walk slowly, his kidneys working overtime to process toxic drugs given to shrink a tumour, his hair gone and energy levels wiped out. He knows what treatment lies ahead, having been there before in his life. He does not know if it will be successful this time. He does not know if he will be well enough ever to go back to work. And yet he still lives in hope. This is not an easy, superficial optimism that either ignores or dismisses the reality of suffering and death. He is wearily familiar with both and they are unwelcome, destructive intruders. He also has a wife and two boys he loves dearly and does not want to leave. But his is a hope that is rooted in his objective understanding of God's love in Christ (Rom. 5:8), that knows from subjective experience God's presence in and through suffering (Rom. 5:3–5), and that nothing ultimately can separate him from the love of God in Christ

[30] Rom. 1:7.
[31] Rom. 12:9.
[32] Rom. 13:10.
[33] Rom. 14:15.

Jesus his Lord (Rom. 8:39). He is the first to say that he is no 'hero': he is just a Christian who is holding on to the love of God when all else is uncertain. He knows first-hand what all Christians should know, that there is no innate conflict between suffering and the gift of the Spirit, who pours out God's love into our hearts. Indeed suffering should be expected and understood not as something that confounds God's love, but as something that is ultimately disempowered and transcended by Christian hope (Rom. 5:3–4, 11).

For black humour I sometimes say to students that experiencing suffering is only a matter of time. Every Christian should have his or her theology of God, love and suffering worked out in advance. Paul did for sure. We would be wise to do the same. Christians have overwhelming reasons to rejoice in the righteousness of God and be people of hope and gratitude – whatever the future may hold for each of us.

c. Love and judgment

As discussed in the introduction, love has become the 'god' of our Western age, the driving force of Western individualism and self-expression. Increasingly, even to question the absolute goodness of human free choice to 'be who we truly are' is to risk ridicule, hostility and cultural isolation. Read through postmodern eyes, Christian talk of sin is simply a vain attempt to maintain power by controlling and demeaning others. It is therefore a strong temptation for the church to try to live in a culturally acceptable comfort zone by proclaiming that God is loving while not talking about God's righteousness as that which saves sinners who are enemies of God, facing his wrath and utterly incapable of saving themselves. Such silence speaks a thousand words.[34] While not overtly denying texts like Romans 5:6–8, a one-sided emphasis on divine love effectively leads towards a type of theology that H. Richard Niebuhr warned against many years ago: 'A God without wrath brought men without sin into a Kingdom without judgment through the ministrations of a Christ without a Cross.'[35] Paul rejoices that our *hope does not put*

[34] For excellent discussion of the love and wrath of God see A. N. S. Lane, 'The Wrath of God as an Aspect of the Love of God', in Kevin J. Vanhoozer (ed.), *Nothing Greater, Nothing Better: Theological Essays on the Love of God* (Grand Rapids: Eerdmans, 2001), pp. 138–167. Lane identifies four ways that the wrath of God is suppressed today: (1) denial of the wrath of God; (2) a Marcionite contrast between the wrathful God of the OT and the loving God of the NT; (3) detaching God from wrath by viewing it as an impersonal cause-and-effect consequence of human action; (4) rarely, if ever, mentioning it in teaching and preaching (my point here).

[35] H. Richard Niebuhr, *The Kingdom of God in America* (Middletown: Wesleyan University Press, 1988), p. 193. First published by Harper & Row in 1937.

us to shame (5). May the church never be ashamed to tell the story of justification and its robust, realistic diagnosis of the human condition, along with the extraordinary story of the love of God in Christ to bring reconciliation, peace and hope while simultaneously delivering us from his just judgment.

Ephesians 2:1–10
9. God's great love

In the theological college where I work we have found that one of the most powerful skills a student can learn for Christian ministry is that of reflective practice. Basically this is an ability to consider – and answer well – a simple but searching question: 'Why?' Why questions get beyond the surface to deeper issues of motive and purpose. Reflective practice is learning to reflect critically on what we do (our ministry practice) by engaging in a cycle of reflective questions.

I mention this because our default is to tend 'to get on with things' as best we can without asking too many difficult 'Why?' questions. Church life is no different, and perhaps particularly evangelical church life. Evangelical Christians tend to be great activists. At our best we take the Bible seriously and the gospel seriously.[1] This commitment to biblical truth means that evangelicals tend to be very busy people engaged in preaching, teaching, training, writing, Bible studies, prayer meetings, mission, counselling, church development, social action, youth and children's programmes and so on. But this busyness, which is compounded by the increasing speed of the Internet age, can leave little space to ask, *Why are we doing what we do? What is the point of all this activity? What, indeed, is the purpose of the Christian life?*

Paul the pastor has a consistent and razor-sharp theological focus on *what really matters*. Ephesians is a magnificent example of the apostle as a big-picture strategist: encouraging his readers to understand God's 'Why?' and live in the light of it. So, while the letter covers a wide range of subjects,[2] behind them all stands the apostle's

[1] Many years ago John Stott defined evangelicals as essentially 'Bible people and Gospel people'. *What Is an Evangelical?* (London: Church Pastoral Aid Society, 1977).

[2] Arnold lists topics such as training new believers, divine sovereignty and human free will, spiritual warfare, worship, spiritual formation, marriage, racial reconciliation,

overarching concern for the moral transformation of those under his care. At the heart of that concern is love. Love in Ephesians is not only the origin of, but also that which gives purpose to, the Christian life.

Our primary focus here in part 2 is on God's love for us in Christ. Therefore I have selected a key text from Ephesians that speaks of this love.[3] We will explore the motive and content of God's love in this text and in closing reflect on some implications of divine love for the Christian life today.

1. Ephesians: love at the centre

John Paul Heil has made the most detailed case that love forms *the* central theme and overall purpose of the epistle.[4] Others agree that love is front and centre throughout the letter: 'The paramount virtue of the Christian life that Paul calls them to display is love'[5]; 'love is a theme of particular interest to Paul in this letter'[6]; 'The theme of "love" is dominant in Ephesians . . . This frequent use of love seems to furnish the key to the purpose of the book.'[7]

The verb *agapaō* occurs ten times (1:6; 2:4; 5:2, 25 [twice], 28 [thrice], 33; 6:24) as does the noun *agapē* (1:4, 15; 2:4; 3:17, 19; 4:2, 15, 16; 5:2; 6:23). Within the latter ten occurrences there are six instances of the significant phrase 'in love' (*en agapē*; 1:4; 3:17; 4:2, 15, 16; 5:2), which describes 'the dynamic domain or sphere of love' formed by God's love empowering human love for God and one another.[8]

In a sense, we are jumping into the middle of a conversation by beginning at 2:1, so it is worth first briefly asking our own 'Why?' question: 'Why is love so prominent in this letter?' At least one reason is the *spiritual authenticity* of the new church groupings in

---

ecumenical unity, living in a religiously pluralist culture, apostolic calling, prophecy, the role of Jewish law, mission, prayer, the nature of spiritual power, and the work of Satan and demons. Clinton E. Arnold, *Ephesians*, ZECNT (Grand Rapids: Zondervan, 2010), p. 22.

[3] Eph. 2:1–10. Eph. 1:3–10 is another text that unpacks God's saving love in Christ. I will refer to 1:3–10 at appropriate points where it helps to give a fuller picture of God's love.

[4] John Paul Heil, *Ephesians: Empowerment to Walk in Love for the Unity of All in Christ* (Atlanta: SBL, 2007), p. 1.

[5] Arnold, *Ephesians*, p. 501.

[6] Frank Thielman, *Ephesians*, BECNT (Grand Rapids: Baker Academic, 2010), p. 95.

[7] Harold W. Hoehner, *Ephesians: An Exegetical Commentary* (Grand Rapids: Baker, 2002), pp. 104–105.

[8] Heil, *Ephesians*, pp. 2–3.

Ephesus. If Paul[9] is writing to Gentile Christians (Eph. 2:11) from prison (Eph. 3:1, 13; 4:1; 6:20), this is most likely referring to his confinement in Rome (Acts 28:30–31). This scenario leads to a reading of Ephesians where Paul has been absent from the city for several years. In this context 'it is easy to imagine the Jewish and Christian communities in Ephesus drifting further apart' as the number of Jewish Christians dwindled and those of Gentiles rose.[10] In writing, Paul is therefore reminding the majority Gentile believers of their calling and identity: having been blessed to have joined Israel's story (Eph. 2:12) they should be committed to unity with the minority of Jewish believers (Eph. 2:14–22; 3:6). Both Jewish and Gentile believers are new creations (Eph. 4:22–24) who belong to another kingdom (Eph. 5:5; cf. 1 Cor. 6:9; Gal. 5:21); they are to live accordingly until their hope is one day fulfilled (Eph. 1:18; 2:12; 4:4). In other words, *love across Jew–Gentile boundaries is proof that God's eschatological new age has arrived.*

2. Because of his great love for us (2:1–10)

Our theme is the love of God revealed in Christ, so we are going to unpack these verses by following the 'logic of love' contained within them rather than a verse-by-verse analysis.[11]

a. Unworthy of love (2:1–3)

Since about the 1980s one of the most significant developments educationally in the Western world has been the self-esteem movement, now a multimillion-dollar industry. It developed in America out of a conviction that low esteem was the cause of a host of social crises (like teenage pregnancy, substance abuse, dropping out of school, etc.). Promoting self-esteem is now a virtually unquestioned tenet of Western primary and secondary school experience (whether it works or not is a whole other discussion). Children are told so often that they are special and that feeling good about yourself is a primary virtue that inflated understandings of the self are now deeply embedded in emerging generations'

---

[9] On authorship and destination of the letter, overall, I agree with Thielman that on balance the arguments favouring the originality of Pauline authorship and the city of Ephesus as the destination are stronger than those against it. Thielman, *Ephesians*, p. 15.

[10] Ibid., p. 26.

[11] For verse-by-verse exegesis and discussion it is hard to surpass John R. W. Stott, *The Message of Ephesians: God's New Society*, BST (Leicester: Inter-Varsity Press, 1984).

consciousness.[12] For example, below is a 'Student's Creed' that was recited at a secondary-school prayer service in Ireland at which I was present:

> **Today**, this new day, I am a successful student. Overnight my mind and body have produced thousands of new cells to give me the greatest advantages possible. I am born anew, revitalized, and full of energy.
>
> **I am** rare and valuable; unique in all the universe. I am nature's greatest miracle in action. I have unlimited potential. I believe in my abilities, attitudes, and goals. I am worthy of greatness because I am the most important person in my world.
>
> **Today** I push myself to new limits. I use my skills and knowledge every day. I begin the day with a success and end it with a success. My goals are being reached every day and I seek them eagerly.
>
> **I act** positively and happily, fully accepting myself and others. I live to the fullest by experiencing life without limits. I embrace life. I approach each class, each book, and each assignment with enthusiasm, happiness and joy. I thirst for knowledge. I look forward to reading and believing this creed each and every day.
>
> **I am** a positive and successful student. I know each step I must take to continue to be that way. I am clear on my goals and see myself reaching them. I now realize my infinite potential, thus, my burden lightens. I smile and laugh. I have become the greatest student in the world.

While a healthy self-image is important, this is the gospel of self-esteem on steroids! From this understanding of the self, virtually no room is left for imagining a need for forgiveness, grace or change outside the self. Sin, by the self or others (unless particularly heinous), becomes an almost incomprehensible concept.

The contrast with Paul's diagnosis of the human condition in 2:1–3 could not be starker. While addressing Gentile believers (*you*) in verses 1–2 and describing their pre-Christian status, his use of *all of us* (3) includes himself, and by implication all Jews as well as Gentiles. In other words, all humanity is *by nature deserving of wrath* (3).[13] *By nature* (*physei*) has the meaning of who we essentially are. While the text does not spell this out, the sense is of personal

---

[12] Jean Twenge, *Generation Me: Why Today's Young Americans Are More Confident, Assertive, Entitled – and More Miserable Than Ever Before* (New York: Atria, 2014).

[13] The Greek is literally 'by nature children of wrath', a term referring to all of humanity.

accountability, inevitably leading to just judgment. Actions have consequences. God will not overlook sin. Indeed it arouses his *wrath* (*orgē*) – his righteous hostility to sin and evil. While there is a sense here (and elsewhere in the New Testament) of wrath being almost an automatic consequence of sin, it is not convincing to argue it can be 'detached' from God's response to human disobedience.[14] God's wrath is intrinsically personal. As verse 4 will show, his love is inseparable from his anger at sin and what it does. 'God's love itself implies his wrath. Without his wrath God is simply not loving in the sense that the Bible portrays his love.'[15]

The Gentiles had *followed the ways of this world and of the ruler of the kingdom of the air* (2). The ruler is named as the devil elsewhere in the letter (Eph. 4:22; 6:11). The 'world' (*kosmos*), as in John's Gospel, carries a negative sense of being in opposition to the kingdom of God. The Greek word *kata* (according to) is linked to both the world and the devil. Living according to these two destructive forces results in *transgressions, sins* (1) and *disobedience* (2). Sin here is a consequence of living under malevolent and destructive powers, from which there is no escape. Those who live this way are *dead* (1). Future judgment will simply confirm this reality (cf. Rom. 6:23).

The image of human bondage switches in verse 3 from outer forces to the inner realm of desires. All humans, whether Jews with the Torah or Gentiles without it, are in a similar predicament, namely *gratifying the cravings of our flesh and following its desires and thoughts* (3). *Flesh* (*sarx*) in Paul is a theologically loaded term.[16] Here, and in most other places, it is best interpreted eschatologically as another type of power or realm from which humans are unable to free themselves. A life lived 'according to the flesh' (*kata sarka*) leads to death.[17] It reflects a life that belongs to this 'present evil age' that is passing away.[18] 'Desire' is another theologically significant word that we modern readers can easily skip over. The relationship between virtue and desire was much discussed in the ancient world. For example, for the Stoics, the 'passions' (*pathēmata*) – characteristics like desire, pleasure, love and grief – were obstacles to a moral life. The solution was their elimination through reason: 'a cure for

[14] A highly influential proposal along these lines was by C. H. Dodd, *The Epistle of Paul to the Romans*, 2nd edn (London: Collins, 1959), pp. 47–50.

[15] A. N. S. Lane, 'The Wrath of God as an Aspect of the Love of God', in Kevin J. Vanhoozer (ed.), *Nothing Greater, Nothing Better: Theological Essays on the Love of God* (Grand Rapids: Eerdmans, 2001), p. 139.

[16] It forms a major theme within Romans and Galatians in particular.

[17] Rom. 8:13. In Rom. 8 Paul uses 'according to the flesh' (*kata sarka*) to express the same idea as in Ephesians.

[18] Gal. 1:4.

the diseased soul and a path to virtue'.[19] For Jews the answer to misplaced desire was obedience to the Torah, the route to a holy life and the blessing of God. The radical and shocking implication in verses 1–3, made explicit elsewhere in Paul (Gal. 5:16, 24), is that neither human reason nor even the divine Torah can overcome the *cravings of our flesh* (3). Something more powerful yet is needed.

These three verses, then, deliver an uncompromising and matter of fact verdict: all of us are sinners, deserving of wrath, spiritually dead and utterly powerless to do anything to save ourselves. We are not living, *nor do we have the capacity to live*, virtuous lives pleasing to God. We have no grounds, therefore, for assuming that we should be loved and accepted by God simply on account of our innate lovability, high self-regard or bedazzling achievements. This, of course, is very difficult for us to hear, especially within a culture of uncritical self-esteem. As he so often does, Bob Dylan tells it as it is – conceit is a disease that deludes us into thinking that we are too good to die.[20]

b. Loved with a great love (2:4–10)

It is in response to this bleak diagnosis that the good news of God's saving love bursts forth from Paul's pen. It is solely *because of his great love for us* (4a) that God takes the initiative to redeem those who are dead, enslaved and condemned. 'Great' (*pollēn*) conveys a sense of scale, an extravagance that cannot be measured. We might say that God's love is 'off the charts'. Paul uses two associated ideas to communicate the nature and scope this immeasurable love.

(i) Rich in mercy (4)

The first is that God is *rich in mercy* (4). To be 'rich' (*plousios*) in something is to be abounding in that quality. The moral quality in question is 'mercy' (*eleos*). *Eleos* is the Septuagint's translation of the Old Testament's distinctive word for 'steadfast love' (*ḥesed*).[21] Together the phrase gives a picture of God's feeling compassion towards a lost and 'dead' humanity and then acting in kindness toward those in need.

---

[19] Patrick Mitchel, 'The New Perspective and the Christian Life: *Solus Spiritus*', in Scot McKnight and Joe Modica (eds.), *The Apostle Paul and the Christian Life: Missional and Ecclesial Implications of the New Perspective* (Grand Rapids: Baker, 2016), p. 97.

[20] Bob Dylan, 'The Disease of Conceit', *Oh Mercy* (Columbia Records: 1989).

[21] John Goldingay, *Biblical Theology: The God of the Christian Scriptures* (Downers Grove: IVP Academic, 2016), p. 21.

(ii) It is by grace you have been saved (5)

The second is that his saving actions are expressions of *grace* (*charis*, 'gift'). Twice Paul says that *it is by grace you have been saved* (5b, 8). Grace is often helpfully defined along the lines of 'unmerited favour': a gift given to someone with a focus on that person's benefit. This describes very well what is going on in Ephesians. In 8–9 Paul drives the point home that salvation is a gift of God appropriated by *faith* (*pistis*). The Ephesians are told that *this is not from yourselves* (8): they are unable to contribute to their own salvation and have no basis for 'boasting' in their own *works* (9).[22]

Now you are probably finding this quite familiar territory – after all the good news of God's grace is one of the most important and well-known themes in the New Testament. It also, of course, has immense significance within the history of Christian theology from Augustine, to Aquinas, to Luther, Calvin and the Reformation to the present day. While it refers more generally to salvation than justification, Ephesians 2:8–9 is a classic Protestant 'by grace alone through faith alone' text.

But let me suggest that our very familiarity of how grace, faith and works relate, can mask other important dimensions of this passage and how it sheds light on the love of God. Four dimensions come to mind.

First, the formula 'we are justified by grace alone through faith alone' can become just that – a formula marking out our Protestant and evangelical orthodoxy against any form of 'works-righteousness'. Please do not misunderstand me: I believe and am committed to the truth of this statement! But because *sola gratia* served such a crucial role in the Reformation, I wonder if the dominance of justification/ faith/grace within evangelical and Protestant theology and church life ever since has contributed to the curious marginalization of love discussed in the introduction. My point is that we must never lose sight of the fact that these truths are the fruits of God's prior *great love*.

Second, the text needs to be interpreted within the original missional context in which Paul writes. When we do this we begin to see afresh just how radical his notion of grace was in the ancient world (and still is today). Paul has deliberately emphasized that both Jews and Gentiles have no innate right to be loved and accepted by God. Indeed the only thing they have in common is the inevitability

[22] It is worth noting that Paul does not add his usual 'works of the law' here (as in Gal. 2:16; Rom. 3:20). It looks like he is deliberately speaking more generally to Jews and Gentiles that works of whatever hue cannot contribute to what is God's gift alone.

of God's wrath. The precious gift of Christ is given *despite* their unworthiness. As John Barclay has shown in his acclaimed book *Paul and the Gift*, there were different ideas of grace circulating in the ancient world.[23] Gifts were given within systems of patronage and relationship to worthy recipients. We do the same thing today in giving prizes to worthy winners and gifts of money to charities that reflect our values. What is so theologically shocking about 2:1–10 (and elsewhere in Paul) is that God's love and grace are extended with utter disregard to the recipients' worth. As Barclay puts it, 'It is because grace belongs to no one that it goes to everyone.'[24] This type of indiscriminate grace was unknown in Paul's world. It was revolutionary and dangerous, making God appear arbitrary and unfair and challenging the social status quo. It created communities of believers that crossed the great religious, ethnic, social, gender and cultural boundaries of the ancient world (Gal. 3:28; Col. 3:11). The ancient world, with its rigid structures of hierarchy, status, power and worth had never seen anything like this. The gift of Jesus Christ is 'the definitive enactment of God's love for the unlovely'.[25] Ephesians 2:11–20 unpacks the 'logic' of God's indiscriminate love and how it breaks down the 'dividing wall of hostility'[26] between Jews and Gentiles.

Third, Paul's theology of grace does not depend on some vague ideas about the character of God. He is specific: God's great love is relentlessly Christological (focused on Jesus). It takes the form of his making us *alive with Christ* (5); raising *us up with Christ* (6); seating *us with him in the heavenly realms in Christ Jesus* (6). This threefold action is surely a deliberate parallel to Christ's resurrection (death to life), his ascension (raising up) and current reign (enthroned at the right hand of God) that has already been summarized in Paul's prayer in 1:18–23. The point is remarkable – believers themselves share in Christ's resurrection, ascension and reign. This is what it means to be 'in' or united to Christ. The contrast with our previous status is impossible to exaggerate. There is wonder and glory here. The believer, once dead, powerless and condemned is now alive, exalted and enthroned.[27] We share in his power and victory over sin and any spiritual power, whether the world, the devil or the flesh. Because we are in Christ we can have a sure eschatological hope that

[23] John Barclay, *Paul and the Gift* (Grand Rapids: Eerdmans, 2015).
[24] Ibid., p. 572.
[25] Ibid., p. 565.
[26] Eph. 2:14.
[27] While not mentioned in this text, it is clear in Ephesians that it is the Spirit who plays the critical role in uniting believers to Christ and empowering them to live their new life in him.

in the coming ages he might show the incomparable riches of his grace, expressed in his kindness to us in Christ Jesus (7). The word for 'kindness' (*chrēstotēs*) refers to God's generous goodness. God cannot be more generous or good in giving us the gift of his Son.

Fourth, God's lavish grace requires a response. While we cannot contribute to our own salvation (Eph. 2:8–9), Paul has no problem at all in saying that God's love and saving grace will result in transformed lives: *For we are his workmanship, created in Christ Jesus for good works, which God prepared beforehand, that we should walk [peripateō] in them* (10, ESVUK). Believers owe their new existence in Christ to God. It is all his doing, planned long beforehand in love (Eph. 1:4–5). They have become his creative 'work of art' to do 'good works'. The 'works' are not specified here, but are obviously inseparable from God's saving grace (I will argue below that they constitute a life walking in love).

We need some clear thinking here. Ever since Luther in particular there has been an 'anxious Protestant principle' fearful of any sense of obligation or obedience in the believer's relationship with God.[28] The worry is that a requirement for a human response to divine grace will somehow import works back into salvation and introduce earning merit with God by the back door. While this concern is not without foundation, it has led to a destructive overreaction within much Protestant evangelicalism where 'good works' are viewed almost as a *threat* to grace, and faith is little more than a decision to believe. This is a bizarre situation. We see this thinking in popular talk of God's 'unconditional love' as if what the believer does in response is virtually irrelevant.[29] Philip Yancey's well-known phrase 'Grace means there is nothing I can do to make God love me more, and nothing I can do to make God love me less', while partially true, suggests that the believer's life of obedience is of little real significance.[30] The impression is that grace is not really grace if it requires anything from the recipient. The trouble with this is that it is not what Paul, or anyone else in the New Testament, teaches. In this vein John Barclay suggests it is better to say that God's love is unconditioned (not dependent on any prior condition), but not unconditional (it is conditional on a response of faith and obedience). What God has joined together (grace, faith and works) let no one separate! 'Faithfulness in Christian living is not an

---

[28] Luther was especially worried about any circularity of grace – that we give back to God so he in turn gives more to us.

[29] Comments in a public lecture, 'Grace as Free Gift: Freedom from What?', Irish Theological Association, 5 November 2016.

[30] Philip Yancey, *What's So Amazing About Grace?* (Grand Rapids: Zondervan, 1997), p. 71.

optional part of the faith.'[31] This confusion leads all too easily to what Dietrich Bonhoeffer called 'cheap grace', where a life of discipleship is an optional extra to saving faith and of no great importance:

> Grace is represented as the Church's inexhaustible treasury, from which she showers blessings with generous hands, without asking questions or fixing limits. Grace without price; grace without cost! The essence of grace, we suppose, is that the account has been paid in advance; and, because it has been paid, everything can be had for nothing.[32]

Bonhoeffer's warning, written many decades ago, is perhaps more relevant than ever. A lack of clarity about faith, grace and works within the church, combined with the gospel of self-esteem and our Western idolization of love as liberty and self-fulfilment, means that we need to grapple seriously with what is an authentically Christian response to God's extravagant love in Christ. It is to this question that we now turn.

3. Walking *en agapē* as the purpose of the Christian life

Recall John Paul Heil, mentioned earlier. The subtitle of his book captures well the purpose of Ephesians: *Empowerment to Walk in Love for the Unity of All in Christ.* 'Empowerment' is by the Spirit – a major theme of the letter. A key word used in Ephesians is 'walk' (*peripateō*), which is a common Jewish term for a way of life. Previous to their conversion the Ephesians walked as belonging to the world and its ruler (Eph. 2:2, ESVUK) and as pagan Gentiles walking 'in the futility of their minds'.[33] They were 'once in darkness'; now they are to 'walk as children of light'.[34] As Christians they are to walk in good works (Eph. 2:10, ESVUK) and walk 'in a manner worthy' of their calling.[35] They are to walk wisely, making the best use of their time according to the will of God (Eph. 5:15–33, ESVUK). The phrase 'walk in love' comes from 5:1–2, verses that perfectly capture the inseparable connection between the Christian life and divine love. It also combines two key ideas in the letter, *peripateō* and *en agapē*:

---

[31] Klyne Snodgrass, *Ephesians*, NIVAC (Grand Rapids: Zondervan, 1996), p. 115.
[32] Dietrich Bonhoeffer, *The Cost of Discipleship* (New York: Simon & Schuster, 1995), p. 44. First published in 1937.
[33] Eph. 4:17, ESVUK.
[34] Eph. 5:8, ESVUK.
[35] Eph. 4:1, ESVUK.

Therefore be imitators of God, as beloved [*agapēta*] children. And walk [*peripateite*] *in love* [*en agapē*], as Christ loved [*ēgapēsen*] us and gave himself up for us, a fragrant offering and sacrifice to God. (ESVUK)

These are wonderful verses. Together, they encapsulate the heart-beat of Ephesians as a whole. They bring us back to big overall 'Why?' questions of the Christian life. What is the purpose of God's saving love? What does faith look like in practice? What is the goal of Christian mission? What is the church for? Paul's answer is *walk in love*. There is a reciprocity to God's love and grace at work here. The Christian's walk is a form of imitation of divine love. God's grace brings us into relationship with him. We are beloved children, loved out of pure grace. We are to respond by loving God and loving others self-sacrificially, as Jesus loved us. To 'walk in love' embraces all of life and brings to mind Paul's short but stunning command to the Corinthians to 'Do everything in love.'[36]

This life of love is not an 'optional extra' to God's grace: it is the reason grace is given to us in the first place. These are the sorts of works *which God prepared in advance for us to do* (10b). The priority of love in Ephesians is reinforced throughout the letter. For example, note the closing greetings in the letter and its multiple emphases on love.

Peace be to the brothers, and love [*agapē*] with faith, from God the Father and the Lord Jesus Christ. Grace be with all who love [*agapōntōn*] our Lord Jesus Christ with love incorruptible.[37]

Heil's subtitle phrase 'for the unity of all in Christ' refers to how love in Ephesians is the essential 'ingredient' for unity to flourish. This is made explicit in Ephesians 4:

I . . . urge you to walk in a manner worthy of the calling to which you have been called, with all humility and gentleness, with patience, bearing with one another in love [*en agapē*], eager to maintain the unity of the Spirit in the bond of peace.[38]

---

[36] 1 Cor. 16:14.

[37] Eph. 6:23–24, ESVUK. While not in the Greek, most translations add a third 'love' to this sentence, namely 'love incorruptible' (ESVUK) or 'undying love' (NIVUK) in order to make grammatical sense of the final noun *aphtharsia* ('imperishability' or 'incorruptibility').

[38] Eph. 4:1–3.

Instead, speaking the truth *in love* [*en agapē*] we will grow to become in every respect the mature body of him who is the head, that is, Christ. From him the whole body, joined and held together by every supporting ligament, grows and builds itself up *in love* [*en agapē*], as each part does its work.[39]

Finally, Paul's magnificent prayer for the Ephesians in chapter 3 shows how passionately he hoped that they, as a community of believers formed as a result of God's saving love, would *experience* for themselves the reality of that love in Christ at a profound personal level:

> that . . . he may grant you to be strengthened with power through his Spirit in your inner being, so that Christ may dwell in your hearts through faith – that you, being rooted and grounded in love [*en agapē*], may have strength to comprehend with all the saints what is the breadth and length and height and depth, and to know the love [*agapēn*] of Christ that surpasses knowledge, that you may be filled with all the fullness of God.[40]

Lincoln comments on this text that

> Here in Ephesians love is the soil in which believers are to be rooted and grow, the foundation on which they are to be built . . . Love is the fundamental principle of the new age, of Christian existence in general and not just of Christian character.[41]

Scholars have different interpretations, but it is probably best to relate the four dimensions of verse 18 (breadth, length, height, depth) to the love of Christ in verse 19a. With typical insight, John Stott suggests that the

> love of Christ is 'broad' enough to encompass all mankind (especially Jews and Gentiles, the theme of these chapters), 'long' enough to last for eternity, 'deep' enough to reach the most degraded sinner, and 'high' enough to exalt him to heaven.[42]

This love is beyond measure and comprehension, so much so that believers need to be empowered by the Spirit to begin to grasp its

[39] Eph. 4:15–16.
[40] Eph. 3:16–19, ESVUK.
[41] Andrew T. Lincoln, *Ephesians*, WBC, vol. 42 (Dallas: Word, 1990), p. 207.
[42] Stott, *Message of Ephesians*, p. 137.

magnificent nature and so experience something of the fullness of God himself.

4. Conclusions

At least five applications to our lives and churches can be drawn from our discussion of love in Ephesians.

First, God's love is 'tough love'. Chapter 2:1–3, while not intended to be a complete doctrine of humanity in three verses, tells us essential truths about ourselves and our world. The gospel, and indeed the entire narrative of the Bible from Genesis to Revelation, hinges on the reality that this world, and more specifically humanity, is deeply broken. In a culture where love tends to be equated with uncritical acceptance, where our desires are to be pursued wherever they lead (unless harming others), and sin is merely a humorous marketing ploy to sell cream or perfume, the church needs to hold its nerve and speak about the realities of human sin and our desperate need for God's grace. Ultimately it is *not* loving to fail to act for the good of others in this way. Without God's taking the initiative to act for our good, we would have remained dead in our sins.

Second, Ephesians is a marvellous reminder that there are no limits to God's indiscriminate love and grace. God loves the unlovely, shamed, unimportant and despised as well as the rich, educated, successful and beautiful. His grace subverts all our notions of worth. It speaks good news to you and me that what matters to God is not what we have achieved (or not), but simply that we are loved and accepted in Christ. This is radically liberating and profoundly countercultural in a social-media-dominated world obsessed by status, Facebook 'friends', money, beauty and success, where those who do not fit in are shamed and excluded. Perhaps a way to test how deeply we have grasped this is to consider ageing and death. It is in old age that we lose friends, status, work, health, social mobility, and maybe even our minds. Yet God's love does not depend on any of these things.

Third, God's love creates communities of subversive love. Paul's vision for the churches in Ephesus was that they would be united communities of love that transcended all the great social, religious, political, cultural and gender hierarchies of the ancient world. No one is more important than anyone else, because all Christians are simply recipients of God's grace. We need to ask ourselves how our churches today are reflecting the radical social implications of such boundary-breaking love. What are the boundaries and hierarchies of the world around us that the church is called to subvert?

Fourth, God's love is powerful and transformative. His love is 'lavished' on us in order to form communities of moral virtue, empowered by the Spirit, united to Christ and walking in unity and love. This is no 'nice add-on' to the gospel: such works are the goal of God's great love. Love is the means by which the church makes advances spiritually in a world still under the power of the devil (Eph. 2:1; cf. 6:10–18). This challenges us to do an audit of our own lives and communities. Where is our faith little more than agreement with ideas rather than a way of life in Christ? Where are we divided and alienated from one another? Where are we failing to walk in love? What do we need to do to bring healing and reconciliation? Where do we need reform in order to 'walk in a manner worthy of the calling to which you have been called'?[43]

Fifth, Ephesians reveals to us the character of God himself. He demonstrates the *incomparable riches of his grace . . . in his kindness to us in Christ Jesus* (7). He is *rich in mercy* (4). Both his grace and mercy are constituents of his *great love* (4). This love not only gives us life, but the privilege of being seated with Christ *in the heavenly realms* (6) and the remarkable honour of being his *handiwork* (10). In other words, for no reason apart from love he gives us undeserving sinners both a glorious future and an exalted present vocation. Why does God act this way? It can only be because it is his essential nature to love: because he is love he acts in love. Emil Brunner has a helpful image here. A scientist might analyse radium: its properties, the compounds it forms and its atomic structure. But if the description omits to say that radium is by definition radioactive, it has missed its defining characteristic. It is the very nature of radium to radiate.[44] Similarly if we talk about God's holiness, goodness and sovereignty but omit to say that he is constantly giving himself in love, we have missed his essential nature. Quite simply, without love, God would not be God.[45]

---

[43] Eph. 4:1, ESVUK.

[44] Emil Brunner, *Dogmatics*, vol. 1: *The Christian Doctrine of God*, tr. Olive Wyon (London: Lutterworth, 1949), p. 192. Cited in Leon Morris, *Testaments of Love: A Study of Love in the Bible* (Grand Rapids: Eerdmans, 1981), pp. 143–144.

[45] Morris, *Testaments of Love*, p. 144.

Part 3
Love in the life and teaching of Jesus

We turn in part 3 to love in the life and teaching of Jesus. While Jesus talks of love much less than Paul, when he does so we need to listen well. This is not only because the Lord's words carry enormous weight, but also because love is theologically pivotal within his life and teaching. We will explore how wholehearted love is the only appropriate response of a disciple towards the Lord: how love for God and neighbour fulfils the entire purpose of the Torah, and how, in Jesus' life, love is no abstract theory but an orientation towards others expressed in deep and compassionate relationships.

Matthew 10:34–39
10. The cost of love

What, at a deep heart level, do you *long* for? What motivates you and gives you joy? Perhaps it is something you do that energizes and fills you with enthusiasm. Perhaps it is something or someone you are committed to regardless of any opposition that stands in your way. But whatever it is, it forms the core of your life: it gives you identity and shapes your priorities and behaviour. Life is virtually unimaginable without it.

These are searching and personal questions. How we answer them will in all likelihood reveal what we truly love. As Jesus says, 'where your treasure is, there your heart will be also'.[1] In context he is talking about money, but the principle holds for whatever is our beloved 'treasure'.

This deep connection between the heart and love brings us to Matthew 10:34–39, where we encounter an extraordinary statement of Jesus to his disciples about love, costly commitment and the purpose of life. What or whom do we love most? How does that love shape our priorities and behaviour? What is the cost of authentic Christian love? Where do we find significance in life? This chapter will reflect on how this text speaks to our lives today. To begin, I need to outline three interrelated themes of Matthew's Gospel.

1. Discipleship, mission and love

a. Discipleship

R. T. France argues that Matthew's narrative skill places him alongside the world's best novelists or dramatists. Both individual stories and his overall structure draw readers into his central concern – the

[1] Matt. 6:21.

149

significance of the birth, life, teaching, death and resurrection of Jesus, the Messiah of Israel.[2] In multiple ways Matthew reinforces how Jesus fulfils Old Testament Scripture. But this story is not presented simply as a dramatic tale to be observed: it calls us into a life of discipleship to the risen Lord.

The development of Matthew's story is marked by key phrases that act as structural markers. One such 'formula' of particular relevance to our text in chapter 10 is 'When Jesus had finished'. This phrase occurs at the close of each of five major discourses of Jesus' teaching (Matt. 7:28; 11:1; 13:53; 19:1; 26:1), all of which are focused on the call to discipleship (chs. 5–7, 10, 13, 18, 24–25).[3] Each discourse is woven into the larger unfolding story. Together they represent the most comprehensive compilation of Jesus' teaching among the four Gospels. It is therefore no accident that the early church used Matthew like a discipleship manual in teaching new believers what it meant to follow Jesus.

b. Mission

Matthew 10:34–39 is located within the second discourse and its focus is mission. Chapter 10 begins with Jesus' commissioning his disciples and commanding them not to go to the Gentiles or Samaritans but

> Go rather to the lost sheep of Israel. As you go, proclaim this message: 'The kingdom of heaven has come near.' Heal those who are ill, raise the dead, cleanse those who have leprosy, drive out demons. Freely you have received; freely give.[4]

The disciples are being given a mission that parallels that of Jesus himself. In doing so they are also warned to expect similar opposition. Jesus had cautioned them of this in the first discourse (the Sermon on the Mount, 5:10–12); now this theme comes to the fore in chapter 10. The level of hostility they are told to expect is sobering. He warns of flogging in the synagogues (Matt. 10:17), trials before Gentile rulers (Matt. 10:18), family betrayals (Matt. 10:21), being

[2] R. T. France, *Matthew – Evangelist and Teacher* (Exeter: Paternoster, 1989), p. 135. I was fortunate to be taught Matthew by the late Dick France. It is impossible to write this chapter without recalling his infectious enthusiasm, deep learning and heart for students – all aspects of his love for God. This chapter is dedicated to him.

[3] Wilkens labels each discourse with a discipleship theme: kingdom-life disciples (5–7), mission-driven disciples (10), clandestine-kingdom disciples (13), community-based disciples (18) and expectant-sojourner disciples (24–25). Michael J. Wilkens, *Matthew*, NIVAC (Grand Rapids: Zondervan, 2004), p. 32.

[4] Matt. 10:6–8.

universally hated (Matt. 10:22), persecution (Matt. 10:23) and being called followers of Beelzebul (Matt. 10:25b). Despite such a future, they are not to be 'afraid of those who kill the body but cannot kill the soul'.[5] Proclaiming the arrival of the Messiah and the kingdom of heaven is a dangerous business in a world opposed to his rule – a reality that continues to develop in intensity up to the Gospel's climactic events in Jerusalem.

c. Love

Love is a third prominent theme in Matthew. Jesus has earlier commanded his followers to 'love your enemies',[6] an apparently foolish act that forms the culmination of his teaching in 5:21–48 of what it means to be his disciple. Like the other Synoptics, Matthew also tells us of Jesus' summation of the law in terms of love for God and neighbour but uniquely adds, 'All the Law and the Prophets hang on these two commandments.'[7] A more pivotal role for love in the ethics of Jesus is impossible to imagine. Another unique Matthean addition is Jesus' description of the commandments to the rich enquirer, which finish with the words 'love your neighbour as yourself'.[8] While the 'golden rule' of 7:12 ('So in everything, do to others what you would have them do to you') does not mention love, like love it 'sums up the Law and the Prophets'. Overall, Matthew presents us with Jesus, who teaches about 'the broader principle of love which operates at the level of motives and relationships' rather than the detailed prescriptions of rabbinic Pharisaism.[9] Love lies at the core of a life of discipleship within the new community of the kingdom of heaven.

Given this broader context, let us turn to verses 34–39 and how they give us a unique perspective on love, mission and Christian discipleship.

2. Love of Jesus above all other loves – even family (10:34–37)

a. The coming of Jesus results in division (10:34–36)

Do not suppose that I have come to bring peace to the earth. I did not come to bring peace, but a sword (34) is one of Jesus' 'hard sayings'.

---

[5] Matt. 10:28.
[6] Matt. 5:44. Cf. Luke 6:27, 35. See chapter 11 for discussion of enemy love in Luke 6.
[7] Matt. 22:40; Mark 12:29–31; Luke 10:27.
[8] Matt. 19:19.
[9] France, *Matthew – Evangelist and Teacher*, p. 260.

Three times in verses 34–35 he uses the phrase 'I came to . . .' to refer to the purpose of his mission.[10] He seems to suggest that it is not *to bring peace to the earth* (34). Yet is not the mission of the Messiah precisely that (Isa. 9:6–7; Zech. 9:10)? The image of a *sword* speaks of violence and warfare, experiences all too real for those familiar with the brutality of Roman military occupation. If Rome wields the sword against Israel, Jesus' use of it is even more devastating. Rather than the division being that of empire against nation, the coming of Jesus leads to fragmentation of family ties:

> *a man against his father,*
>   *a daughter against her mother,*
> *a daughter-in-law against her mother-in-law.*
> (35)

Rather than enemies (*echthroi*, 'hostile adversaries') being hated external powers, now *a man's enemies will be the members of his own household* (36). Because of Jesus, 'enemies' are now 'within' the family – the very last place you would expect to find them.

What are we to make of such troubling imagery? Without doubt Jesus is being deliberately shocking. *Do not suppose* (34) flags how his mission does not fit with any preconceptions. As Matthew makes clear, the mission of the Messiah *does* bring peace.[11] But this peace is not achieved without conflict. It is vital we understand this. Many people today imagine Jesus as a man preaching a message of universal love and inclusion. While this idea may appeal to our modern notions of tolerance, it has little to do with the Jesus of the New Testament. It portrays him as little more than a comfortable talisman, safely relegated to the back of our minds as someone to turn to if we need encouragement or help. Absent is any sense of how Jesus confronts powerful political and spiritual forces 'head-on': a conflict that leads to trumped-up charges, an unjust trial and ruthless execution. In this sense, the 'sword' is not literal; indeed its use is expressly rejected by Jesus in Gethsemane (Matt. 26:51–52). It represents an inevitable consequence of faithful discipleship rather than aggression by the disciples. The source of violence comes not from the disciples but from those opposed to Jesus. In other words, the real issue here is antagonistic rejection of the personal authority

---

[10] This phrase also appears in 5:17; 9:13; 20:28. In each case it refers to the purpose of Jesus' mission.

[11] In 12:15–21 Jesus is identified with the suffering servant of Isa. 42:1–14. In Matt. 21:4–5 he is the messianic king who brings peace, and in chapters 26–27 he accepts unjust violence and death. In the Sermon on the Mount he teaches, 'Blessed are the peacemakers' (5:9).

of Jesus – and anyone who represents him must expect similar treatment.

The description of household division comes directly from Micah 7:6, which was popularly understood to refer to future woes of the messianic age.[12] Jesus' coming now fulfils Micah's words and expands on his earlier warnings in Matthew 10:21–22a that 'Brother will betray brother to death, and a father his child; children will rebel against their parents and have them put to death. You will be hated by everyone because of me.' It is not as if Jesus is extolling the virtues of family disunity! His words are simply predictive of what his disciples must expect. What this looks like in terms of competing loves is spelt out in the next verse.

b. Love of Jesus before family (10:37)

Verse 37 takes us into themes of desire, purpose and significance. *Anyone who loves their father or mother more than me is not worthy of me; anyone who loves their son or daughter more than me is not worthy of me.*[13] Jesus gets right to the point. *Christian discipleship ultimately is about who or what we love most dearly.*

We should not miss how this is primarily a Christocentric claim. By 'Christocentric' I mean it revolves around Jesus' own understanding of his identity, authority and mission. This text contributes to the overriding impression from the Gospels as a whole – that Jesus expects and commands love and loyalty that are appropriate only for God himself.[14]

It is because familial love is one of the most potent expressions of human commitment that Jesus chooses it as a foil for one of his most outrageous demands. In a culture where honour of parents and family was paramount, not even love of family can come before love for the Messiah.[15] Or, to put it more positively, our love for Jesus is to surpass the deepest and most devoted human love imaginable. To be *worthy of me* (twice in v. 37) is probably best understood as

[12] R. T. France, *The Gospel of Matthew*, NICNT (Grand Rapids: Eerdmans, 2007), pp. 408–409.

[13] It is worth noting that Matthew uses the Greek verb *phileō* here rather than *agapaō*.

[14] France concludes that relevant texts in Matthew 'assume, rather than state, some sort of "equivalence" between Jesus and God'. *Matthew – Evangelist and Teacher*, p. 309.

[15] This is consistent with teaching recorded elsewhere in the Gospels. A parallel text in Luke uses the shocking idea of a person 'hating' his or her own family and life (Luke 14:26). In Matt. 12:46–50 Jesus relativizes the importance of his own family compared to doing the will of his Father in heaven, and in 8:21–22 says that discipleship even takes precedence over burying one's father.

'having what it takes' to be a disciple of Jesus by loving him in this utterly committed way.[16]

But what does it mean to love Jesus before family? His words are extraordinarily subversive and are reinforced elsewhere in Matthew.[17] We need to hear them afresh as we try to navigate a Western culture in utter turmoil over 'family matters' – marriage, gender, sex and procreation. Contemporary attitudes to marriage and the family are complex and, at times, contradictory – what follows can only be a quick sketch. On the one hand, traditional notions of what constitutes the family are being deconstructed to accommodate an individualist concept of liberty and self-expression. The reshaping of marriage in the West has been about recognizing the rights of two individuals 'in love' – whether lesbian, gay, transsexual, bisexual or somewhere else on a 'spectrum' of human sexuality. Yet, on the other hand, the family is simultaneously idealized and romanticized as never before. Everywhere, in multiple ways, Western culture affirms that the path to individual fulfilment is through authentic romantic love. It is the 'Other' who meets our needs and us theirs. Never before in human history has happiness, meaning, fulfilment and purpose been so invested in one relationship. This is why the marriage industry is booming and vast sums of money are spent on the 'perfect wedding'.[18] Notions of the 'perfect family' are celebrated as the ideal, the be-all and end-all of our existence that gives our lives meaning. Within this vision of the family, children in particular become the ultimate source of fulfilment for parents. The pressure that these expectations place on the marriage relationship and between parents and children is intense – and statistics of divorce and familial breakdown show that tragically there are a lot of broken dreams out there.

Jesus' statement in verse 37 reminds us that an authentically Christian understanding of the family will form a radical challenge to both these cultural assumptions: Christians are neither to pursue the idol of the autonomous individual *nor are they to idolize the family*. To love Jesus above the family is not to dismiss its value, but it is to say that discipleship within the kingdom of heaven is a greater priority. Or, to put it differently, Christian marriage is never an end in itself: it is a vocation undertaken by disciples who belong to God's kingdom. Few Christian thinkers have understood the radically countercultural implications of Jesus' words for Christian

---

[16] France, *Gospel of Matthew*, p. 410.
[17] See Matt. 19:1–12 and 22:30 for two further examples.
[18] In Ireland, where I live, the *average* cost of a wedding in 2018 was €30,000.

discipleship concerning the family better than Stanley Hauerwas – below is a taste of what he has to say.

> For the Christian, marriage cannot and must not be seen as a necessary means for self-fulfillment. Christians are not called to marriage for 'fulfillment', but for the upbuilding of that community called church.[19]

And this means that the family and children need to be understood within a kingdom of God framework:

> For Christians do not place their hope in their children, but rather their children are a sign of their hope, in spite of the considerable evidence to the contrary, that God has not abandoned this world. Because we have confidence in God, we find the confidence in ourselves to bring new life into this world . . . From this perspective marriage (as well as the family) stands as one of the central institutions of the political reality of the church, for it is a sign of our faithfulness to God's kingdom.[20]

It is to this wider future-orientated vision of marriage and family that Jesus' words call us. As Hauerwas says, 'The church can never forget for long that marriage among Christians involves commitments not readily recognized by the world.'[21] This means that it is not the church's job to 'protect' or 'defend' the family as if it were our primary calling. Such activity for Hauerwas is nothing short of idolatrous and fails to realize that 'Christianity has been and will continue to be, if we are serious as Christians, a challenge to familial loyalties.'[22]

This is also why Christianity decisively breaks from Judaism in the former's affirmation of singleness as the *preferential* option for disciples. Christians, after all, follow a Lord who remained single and yet is the most fully human person who has ever lived. Paul, while affirming marriage as a valid calling, preferred celibacy because 'this world in its present form is passing away' and disciples need to keep focused on 'the Lord's affairs'.[23] Recall that the context of

---

[19] J. Berkman and M. Cartwright (eds.), 'The Radical Hope in the Annunciation: Why Both Single and Married Christians Welcome Children', in *Stanley Hauerwas: The Hauerwas Reader* (Durham, N.C.: Duke University Press, 2001), p. 512.

[20] J. Berkman and M. Cartwright (eds.), 'Sex in Public: How Adventuresome Christians Are Doing it', *Hauerwas Reader*, p. 499.

[21] Ibid., p. 502.

[22] Berkman and Cartwright, 'Radical Hope', p. 511.

[23] 1 Cor. 7:31–32.

Jesus' words in Matthew 10 is mission – the primary calling for disciples is to share the good news of the kingdom of heaven. The future of the church, in other words, depends not on marriage and procreation (biology) but on witness and conversion. And, as verses 38–39 will tell us, this means 'investing' wholeheartedly in the life to come (whatever the consequences) rather than determinedly giving our all to this life alone. Hauerwas again:

> The early church's legitimation of singleness as a form of life symbolized the necessity of the church to grow through witness and conversion. Singleness was legitimate, not because sex was thought to be a particularly questionable activity, but because the mission of the church was such that 'between the times' the church required those who were capable of complete service to the Kingdom. And we must remember that the 'sacrifice' made by the single is not of 'giving up sex' but the much more significant sacrifice of giving up heirs. There can be no more radical act than this, as it is the clearest institutional expression that one's future is not guaranteed by the family, but by the church. The church, the harbinger of the Kingdom of God, is now the source of our primary loyalty.[24]

This is wonderfully liberating for single Christians within an intensely sexualized modern culture. Within a church deeply impacted with Western romanticism singleness is often seen as some sort of failure, a cause for sadness and regret that is rarely talked about. Outside the church, celibacy is either weird, humorous or harmful. For example, in the 2005 film *The 40-Year-Old Virgin* Steve Carell's character is a buffoon, an immature idiot and source of comedy and pity, who must at all costs lose his virginity belatedly to enter adult life. Since sex is an essential part of our identity and self-expression, celibacy becomes virtually a form of self-harm. This is why in the movie Carell has to be rescued first from *himself*. In complete contrast, the radical implication of Jesus' words is that single disciples are freed from the cultural 'shame' of being unmarried and childless. As we will see in verses 38–39, true life, whether single or married, is found elsewhere.

---

[24] Berkman and Cartwright, 'Sex in Public', p. 498. In the light of v. 37 I would want to replace the word 'church' in the last line with 'Jesus'. A Christian's primary loyalty is to a person, not the church, even though the church is the body of Christ.

3. Love of Jesus means death (10:38–39)

Jesus continues to spell out the cost of authentic 'discipleship love'. To 'have what it takes' to be a faithful follower is now explained in the horrifying image of carrying a cross (see also 16:24). *Whoever does not take up their cross and follow me is not worthy of me* (38). As twenty-first-century Christians we are so used to the image and victorious theology of the cross (e.g. 1 Cor. 15:54–56) that it is very difficult to imagine the disciples' response to Jesus' words as people familiar with the carefully designed cruelties of Roman crucifixion. Ancient witnesses are united in their descriptions of crucifixion as the most terrible and savage form of death. It was reserved for the lower classes, not for free Roman citizens. Its victims included slaves, dangerous criminals and revolutionaries, killed slowly in a public place, the sufferer often naked, subject to ridicule and abuse and left to rot as a deterrent to any onlookers tempted to challenge the might of the empire. The process typically included the shameful experience of being forced to carry the heavy cross-piece in a public procession through the streets while enduring the mockery of the crowd.[25] The condemned was, to use a phrase from Death Row describing the journey from cell to execution room, a 'dead man walking'. For Jews it was especially shameful due to the link to Deuteronomy 21:22–23, where God's curse is associated with anyone executed and left hanging on a pole.

This, then, is the prospect that Jesus holds out for all those who would love him – a gruesome walk of public humiliation and then death! We miss the force of his words if we jump too quickly to metaphors like 'having a cross to bear'. The fate Jesus describes became his own, and almost certainly that of many of his disciples. Innumerable Christians through the centuries since have shared their experience of martyrdom and continue to do so today. At the very least, all disciples should understand and accept that 'discipleship love' means a willingness to die for Jesus and/or face social exclusion and hostility for 'carrying their cross'. As Western Christians living in cultures that prize security, comfort and pleasure we need to listen well to our Lord's sobering words. As Osborne puts it, 'true discipleship involves both a death to self and a willingness to die for Jesus'.[26] In contrast, often our response when opposition or pain comes our way is to ask, 'Where is God? How could he

---

[25] For more detailed description see J. B. Green, 'Death of Jesus', in J. B. Green, S. McKnight and I. H. Marshall (eds.), *Dictionary of Jesus and the Gospels* (Leicester: Inter-Varsity Press, 1992), pp. 146–163.

[26] Grant R. Osborne, *Matthew*, ZECNT (Grand Rapids: Zondervan, 2010), p. 406.

allow this to happen if he loves me?' Yet Matthew's perspective is more that if we are *not* suffering as faithful disciples we should be asking ourselves, 'What is wrong? Why are we living in a way that is not attracting the hostility of the world?'

Our text concludes with a famous and paradoxical aphorism, *Whoever finds their life will lose it, and whoever loses their life for my sake will find it* (39).[27] A key word in this verse is *psychē* ('life' or 'soul'), which is difficult to translate, depending on the context. 'Life' fits well here since *psychē* often carries a sense of the eternal or 'spiritual' life of a person as opposed to mere 'earthly' life. Both senses are in mind here within a very Jesus-like wordplay. Those who try to 'find' or hold on to 'earthly' life will lose real 'spiritual' life. France sums it up: 'If I value my life in this world more than I value Jesus and the life of the next world, I cannot be his disciple.'[28] Those who are willing to lose their 'earthly' life for Jesus' sake will find true 'spiritual' life.

This saying is easier to understand in theory than apply in day-to-day life. What does it mean to lose your 'earthly' life? Some Christians, like Augustine, have interpreted Christian discipleship in dualistic world-denying ways, where spirituality equates to an ascetic rejection of pleasure, and the overriding purpose of this 'lower' life is to escape to the next 'higher' life.[29] This sort of reasoning can creep into how many think of 'ordinary' life and work as somehow less 'spiritual' than Christian ministry: the secular–sacred divide, or a distorted piety that equates misery and joylessness with advanced godliness! But these are misreadings of Jesus' intent. From verse 37 'losing life' should primarily be interpreted literally. Thankfully, since this will not be the fate of most Christians, the 'loss' in mind most likely will involve a personal cost such as suffering, rejection and hardship. But Jesus' words also demand that we consider our priorities: what or whom do we love most? What or whom do we really live for? Do we shape our lives around the temporary things of this life that we love most (even good things like family) and thus lose real life? Or do we give our wholehearted love and allegiance to a crucified Messiah and so find lasting purpose and hope – in this life and the next?

---

[27] This is the most quoted saying of Jesus within the NT (cf. Matt. 16:25; Mark 8:35; Luke 9:24; 17:33; John 12:25). Craig R. Blomberg, *Matthew*, NAC, vol. 22 (Nashville: Broadman, 1992), p. 181.

[28] France, *Matthew – Evangelist and Teacher*, p. 210.

[29] See chapter 5 for how Augustine was heavily influenced by Platonism, a form of Greek dualism that meant he was overly negative concerning this material world (human love, the body, sexuality, etc.).

4. Discipleship as rightly directed love whatever the cost

While only six verses, this New Testament 'love text' is one of the most explosive in the whole of Scripture. Jesus' words cut like a scalpel to the core of Christian discipleship. The most important question of discipleship is indeed one of the heart – what or whom do we love most? At home we have a pasta-making machine; you put the pasta dough in one end, turn the handle and strips of pasta are rolled out from the other. I confess that I am frequently dismayed when reading Christian discipleship programmes that talk of discipleship in similar mechanical terms, as if people are like dough – put them through the right training programme and rightly shaped disciples will pop out at the end. The emphasis is on skills and behaviour, with little or no mention of love and the profound cost it involves. This is where we need to go back to Augustine, who has much to teach us about the heart of discipleship. While flawed (as mentioned above) Augustine's theology contains at least four brilliant insights into the nature of love that we have much to learn from today.

One insight is that the heart is the seat of our desires. Our behaviour reveals what is in our hearts and what we truly love. This is not a soft romantic view of the heart, but closer to the Bible's understanding of the heart as the core of our most fundamental being.[30] Augustine saw, in other words, that we are essentially lovers. It is not, therefore, a question of *if* we will love; the real issue is *what* we love.

The second insight leads on from the first: our heart 'aims' or 'orientates' our lives towards what we love. In theological language this means that we are teleological creatures. *Telos* means 'end' so the idea is that we are all seeking significance in something. We cannot *not* love, we cannot *not* be living for some end and we will inevitably shape our lives around that which we love most deeply. Or, to use Jesus' language again, the question is not whether we seek a kingdom; it is which kingdom we seek.

Third, Augustine perceived that since we are made by God we find purpose only in the love of God. Alternative loves will disappoint. His famous statement in his *Confessions* that 'You have made us for yourself, O Lord, and our hearts are restless until they find their rest in you'[31] flows from his own experience of a life of misdirected love before turning to God. Pursuit of other loves led

---

[30] See e.g. chapter 4 on Deut. 6:4–25.
[31] Augustine, *Confessions* 1.1.1.

only to sin, guilt and shame; it is only in the love of God that peace and happiness are ultimately found.[32]

Fourth, Augustine knew first-hand how difficult are the demands of love. Reflecting theologically on his pre-Christian life he concluded that he (like all of us) was utterly incapable of loving the right things because since the fall humanity is under the enslaving power of sin. Or, to put it another way, we are like addicts unable to liberate ourselves from that which is destroying us. Augustine says that our only hope is the grace of God. Only divine grace can set our wills free to love God. Our ability to love well, for Augustine, is therefore *not* a choice we simply decide to exercise one day: it is a gift from God we can receive only by faith.

Augustine's teaching echoes that of Jesus and vividly captures how Christian discipleship is not first a matter of behaviour (although it is not divorced from behaviour) *but principally concerns a wholehearted love for a person – Jesus Christ.* There is an inseparable link between love and loyalty. A life lived out of obedient love for Jesus will inevitably be profoundly countercultural to the values and loves of the world around us – with family and singleness one example. Yet it is in just such a radical path that true life is found. This path is anything but easy. Augustine knew well his own limitations when it came to loving God, but Jesus' commands go further than Augustine's often introspective struggles of personal spirituality. They assume that we his followers are constantly 'on mission' to make known the good news of the Messiah, and within that mission he forewarns us to expect hostility, opposition and even death as an intrinsic consequence of obedient witness. This is the costly way of discipleship love.

---

[32] For Augustine, complete happiness is not possible in this life. Even post-conversion life is marked by yielding to temptations to love things other than God. See e.g. book 10 of his *Confessions*.

Luke 6:27–36; 10:25–37
11. Enemy love

As a young girl, Chloe was sexually abused by her older brother.[1]
She told no one. As a young adult she committed her life to Jesus,
an event that had a profound impact on her deeply damaged self-
esteem and confidence. A powerful experience of the grace and
love of God within a welcoming church community began a slow
process of inner healing. She was in her thirties when what had been
hidden came to light. It was traumatic for her, for her parents and,
in a very different way, for her brother – from whom she had been
alienated for years. Chloe had buried memories of the past, long ago
concluding that no good would come from digging them up. Now
married with young children and a loving husband, she rarely
thought of her brother. Suddenly feelings of shame, anger and hatred
came flooding back into her mind. She was, once again, confronted
by what he had done and this time other people knew. How was she
going to navigate this unwelcome storm once again, this time as a
Christian? How on earth could she make sense of Jesus' command
to 'love your enemies'?

Enemies take many forms. An enemy is someone who acts in
ways hostile to our good. On a personal level it could be an abuser
like Chloe's brother or a bullying boss. On a communal level it
could be a terrorist organization, a rival tribe or an opposing nation
with malevolent intent. Few of us negotiate life without experiencing enemy animosity en route, and some of us find our whole
lives dominated by the consequences of what an enemy has done. I
am necessarily simplifying here, but in broad terms there are two
natural reactions to 'enemy action'. One is avoidance – as far as possible having nothing to do with those who seek to do us harm. This

---

[1] This account is based on a true story of a friend. Names and some details have
been changed.

strategy of self-protection makes perfect sense, particularly when the enemy is in a position of power over us.[2] The other is retaliation – taking on the enemy on their own terms: entering into a power struggle that, constructively, can confront and expose the enemy's behaviour but that, destructively, can lead to a spiral of hate, retribution and violence. In this chapter we are going to explore a radically different way of responding to enemies. It is the path that Jesus not only taught but also walked and one he *commands* his disciples to imitate. It is the apparently ridiculous calling of 'enemy-love'.

1. Jesus makes enemies and tells his disciples to expect the same (6:1–26)

We join the Gospel of Luke with Jesus' famous 'Sermon on the Plain', which has strong parallels with Matthew's 'Sermon on the Mount'.[3] The Sermon is one of the most influential portions of Jesus' teaching in the Gospels. It is therefore all the more significant that love forms its core theme. Darrell Bock comments, 'One often thinks of 1 Cor. 13 as the "love chapter" in the Bible, but Jesus' remarks on love in 6:27–36 form the center of his ethic and are even more profound.'[4]

These are the early stages of Jesus' Galilean ministry. In Luke 4 and 5 he has claimed to be God's anointed servant fulfilling Isaiah's prophecy (Luke 4:16–20; cf. Isa. 61:1–2), begun a powerful healing ministry, gathered disciples to follow him and started proclaiming 'the good news of the kingdom of God'[5] across the region. This has brought him into immediate conflict with people in his home town of Nazareth (Luke 4:23–30), impure spirits (Luke 4:31–36) and the Pharisees and teachers of the law (Luke 5:21–26, 30–31). It is the latter group who are in focus in Luke 6. He has just (outrageously) declared that he is the Son of Man who *is Lord of the Sabbath* (5).[6] Not only is this a claim of authority over God's holy day; it is also a messianic claim of a status greater than that of even King David

---

[2] A pattern replicated innumerable times in the experience of Rape Crisis and other counselling organizations is how abuse by a person in power is kept quiet by the person abused out of a mixture of shame, fear and powerlessness.

[3] The Sermon has three parts: blessings and woes (6:20–26), love of enemies (6:27–38) and righteous response (6:39–49). The relationship between the sermons in Matthew and Luke is complex and much debated. For detailed discussion see Darrell Bock, *Luke 1:1–9:50*, BECNT (Grand Rapids: Baker Academic, 1994), pp. 549–556.

[4] Ibid., p. 548.

[5] Luke 4:43.

[6] In the Gospels the title 'the Son of Man' is only ever uttered by Jesus about himself.

(3–4). In verses 6–10 he demonstrates this authority by deliberately performing a non-urgent miracle on the Sabbath (healing the man with a withered hand). The Greek is strong here: the watching Pharisees and teachers of the law are *filled with fury* (*eplēsthēsan anoias*, 11, ESVUK). It is clear that Jesus has already made some deadly enemies. This mounting sense of conflict is only exacerbated by what follows. He selects twelve apostles (13–16) and begins teaching them, a wider group of disciples *and a great number of people from all over Judea, from Jerusalem, and from the coastal region around Tyre and Sidon* (17), about life within the kingdom of God.

In a series of blessings and woes Jesus teaches about life in the new era of the kingdom. His focus is literally on the disciples: *Looking at his disciples, he said . . .* (20). Anyone who follows him must understand that the way of the kingdom *inverts* the way of the world at practically every point. Paradoxically, it is the poor, hungry and weeping who are *blessed* (*makarios*, 20–21). Also *makarios* are disciples

> *when people hate you,*
> *when they exclude you and insult you*
> *and reject your name as evil,*
> *because of the Son of Man.*
> (22)

These words aptly describe the Jewish leaders' furious opposition to Jesus, attitudes that would only intensify during Luke's Gospel and culminate in his arrest, trial and execution. His followers are now warned in advance to expect a similar experience. This is in complete contradistinction to normal expectations of divine blessing – being rich, well fed, happy and well respected (24–26). However, those who enjoy such a good life now should beware, for *that is how their ancestors treated the false prophets* (26). In other words, present physical and social blessings are *no guarantee at all* of God's blessing; indeed they are particularly dangerous because they can lull people into a false sense of security.

To use a contemporary image, if marketing is all about identifying and satisfying customer needs, Jesus does a terrible job at 'selling' a life of discipleship within the kingdom of God. He pulls no punches, sweetens no pill. Rather it seems as if he is trying to make it as difficult as possible for the listeners to follow him. They are promised little or no short-term gain in this life. Jesus' call to the upside-down values of 'kingdom life' hinges on trusting that God will one day act in justice to put all things right. So the poor are assured that in the present *yours is the kingdom of God* (20), but the 'proof' of this reality lies in the future. It is an act of faith to believe that they are *blessed* now and that one day they *will laugh* (21). On that day they will *Rejoice in that day and leap for joy, because great is your reward in heaven* (23a). But in the meantime those who follow *the Son of Man* (22) in the 'here and now' of everyday life are promised only difficulty, suffering, opposition and hatred. These warnings set the scene for how, in 6:27–36, Jesus explains what it means in practice to love enemies. He returns to this theme in 10:25–37 with the brilliant parable of the good Samaritan, which, as we will see, is really a story about enemy-love. We will now discuss each text in turn and reflect on what it means to love our enemies today.

2. Love your enemies (6:27–36)

The heart of the Sermon is a call to action – of what followers are to do as they navigate a hostile world populated with enemies. The overriding emphasis is that a disciple's love for others should be disarming and disconcerting, subverting normal expectations of love and pointing puzzled enemies to the eschatological future blessings of the kingdom of God. The verb *agapaō* appears six times in these verses. There are three exhortations to love in 6:27–28, 31, 35. Each one has a distinct emphasis; the first (27–28) includes three subsidiary exhortations detailing the nature of enemy-love. The first two exhortations are each followed by a set of examples: four are given in 6:29–30 and three in 6:32–34. The final exhortation of 6:35a is followed by a summative theological rationale for enemy-love, rooted in the character of God himself. The discussion below is structured around each exhortation.

a. Exhortation 1: three commands and four illustrations (6:27–30)

Jesus now turns from his woes of 6:24–26 back to his disciples. In verse 27 *But* marks the transition to *you who are listening. I say* bases the authority of the teaching that follows solely in Jesus himself rather than in the Torah or a body of rabbinic teaching – a move of remarkable chutzpah by this obscure Galilean upstart with messianic pretensions.[7] *Love your enemies* (27) is unparalleled – the closest the Old Testament comes is the Levitical command to love your neighbour (Lev. 19:18) and Deuteronomy's command to love

---

[7] This is a parallel to the six antitheses of the Sermon on the Mount. Each begins, 'But I tell you' (Matt. 5:22, 28, 32, 34, 39, 44) instead of appealing to authoritative biblical or rabbinic precedent. Jesus' frequent 'Amen' sayings ('Truly I say to you') and 'Let him who has ears, let him hear') function similarly.

the foreigner (Deut. 10:19).[8] But neither of these texts has overt enemies in mind. Leviticus refers to fellow Jews and Deuteronomy to those in need. To emphasize his point, Jesus adds a further three subsidiary exhortations to practical action. *Do good to those who hate you* (27b) gets right to the point. The command is utterly counterintuitive to natural human reactions of avoidance or retaliation. Love is to engage constructively with the enemy, not by returning hate[9] but by acting for his or her good. *Bless those who curse you* (28a) moves the focus to words. To bless is deeper than a modern secular 'good wishes': it is to ask God to direct his favour on their behalf. Blessing is the opposite of cursing – asking God to use his infinite power to harm or judge the enemy. Blessing enemies does not mean failing to challenge sinful actions or stating the truth of their standing before God,[10] but this sort of truth-telling is to be done out of love and not vindictiveness or some perverse rejoicing in their fate. The third subsidiary exhortation is to *pray for those who ill-treat you* (28b). Jesus' prayer on the cross 'Father, forgive them, for they do not know what they are doing'[11] embodies such love. It is extraordinary and difficult. Bock again:

> Such love is tough love, not because it requires harsh discipline against another as parental love might, but because it requires a sublimation of the self to such a great degree, a sublimation that is not normal for any human. It is a supernatural love, because doing it requires that one reverse all natural instincts. It is a love that can come only in light of a dependence on God.[12]

There is zero self-interest in such radical love! Disciples are called to this love simply because Jesus commands it and because of the nature of the God they worship (6:35–36).

Jesus' hard teaching on love continues with four challenging illustrations (6:29–30). The first is *If someone slaps you on one cheek, turn to them the other also* (29a). In Matthew 5:39 the right cheek is specified as the target, which suggests a contemptuous back-handed blow from a right-handed person. This would fit the wider context of physical and emotional ill-treatment well but, regardless, Jesus'

---

[8] See chapter 2 for discussion of Deut. 10.

[9] E.g. in the Dead Sea Scrolls of the Jewish Qumran community are multiple texts such as 'love the sons of light . . . and hate all the sons of darkness'. 1QS 1.9–10. John Nolland, *Luke 9:21–18:34*, WBC, vol. 35b (Dallas: Word, 1993), p. 584.

[10] Jesus of course has many harsh words of warning to Jewish leaders of his day. Paul opposes false teachers in Gal. 5:12 in very robust language!

[11] Luke 23:34.

[12] Bock, *Luke 1:1–9:50*, p. 590.

point is clear – disciples are to endure undeserved harm without resorting to retaliation. In doing so, they remain open to further wrongdoing. From 29b the focus shifts slightly to the use of possessions and money in the context of enemy misbehaviour. *If someone takes your coat* [*himation*, 'outer cloak'], *do not withhold your shirt* [*chitōn*, 'tunic'] *from them* (29b). The image is most probably that of robbery. The point is once again of non-retaliation that opens the disciple up to further maltreatment and even humiliation. A third, more general, illustration follows: *Give to everyone who asks you* (30a). This is likely a picture of borrowing (see 6:34–35) but is broad enough (*panti*, 'everyone') to include any requests for money or other possessions, including begging. The disciple is to be ready at all times to give generously; such open-handedness with possessions is a further way to love those who make demands on personal resources. The final example is closely linked, but pictures a situation where possessions are stolen: *and if anyone takes what belongs to you, do not demand it back* (30b). In such a scenario disciples are not to protect their own rights, but exercise generous self-denial as an expression of enemy-love.

b. Exhortation 2: the Golden Rule (6:31–34)

The sermon continues with a second, equally famous, exhortation that has become known as the 'Golden Rule': *Do to others as you would have them do to you* (31). The saying appears later in Matthew's Sermon on the Mount and is said there to sum up the Law and the Prophets, a phrase Luke omits.[13] While the closest biblical parallel is once again Leviticus 19:18, the Golden Rule is distinct in its positive command to treat others as you would wish to be treated.[14] Its motive is not pragmatic self-interest (treat others well so they will return the favour). The context and structure of the saying presumes a primary unconditional love and concern for others that leads to practical action for their benefit.

That such other-focused love will be untypical and costly is made clear in three short illustrations. Each one is structured with the rhetorical question *what credit is that to you?* (32–34). The answer obviously in each case being 'None.' To *love those who love you* (32),

[13] Bock notes that Luke consistently omits legal themes in his shortened version of the sermon. *Luke 1:1–9:50*, p. 595.
[14] Bock has a good discussion of other ancient parallels to the Golden Rule, including Rabbi Hillel ('What is hateful to you, do not do to your neighbour'), Seneca ('Let us give in the manner that would have been acceptable if we had been receiving') and Confucius ('What you do not want done to yourself, do not do to others'). Bock, *Luke 1:1–9:50*, p. 597.

to *do good to those who are good to you* (33) and to *lend to those from whom you expect repayment* (34) quite literally costs nothing. Such love is indistinguishable from how 'sinners' outside the kingdom of God act – *Even sinners love those who love them* (32), *Even sinners do good in return* (33) and *Even sinners lend to sinners, expecting to be repaid in full* (34). Jesus' point is that there is no 'credit' in loving only those 'like us'. To connect this to today's world, it is natural to spend time with people we like and who like us. They make us feel comfortable; they probably share our values, faith, sense of humour, and are probably of a similar age and socio-economic background. Jesus' words challenge his listeners, and us today, not to settle for the easy option of such mutually assured love. In contrast, there is 'credit' in loving people who are not only unlike us but who are our enemies – people opposed to us in some fundamental way. Such love makes no emotional, financial or rational sense because there is *no guarantee at all* that the second clause of the Golden Rule will be fulfilled.

In this vein, below are seven suggested principles for 'doing unto others' who are strongly opposed to us in some important way. They are offered as suggestions of how to put into practice Jesus' command today.

1 I do not want to be physically attacked, hurt or killed by my opponents. Therefore, I will not engage in violence against them.
2 I do not want people to dismiss what I believe as so obviously wrong that it is not worth a hearing. So I will take time to listen and to understand what my opponents are saying, even if I strongly disagree with them.
3 I do not want people to misrepresent or caricature what I write or say in order to win an argument. So I will state accurately and fairly what my opponents believe.
4 I do not want people to attack my character for being different from them. So I will not resort to character assassination in order to try to discredit my opponents.
5 I do not want people to assume that because I disagree with them I am motivated by selfishness or a desire for power. I will therefore not rush to judge the motives of my opponents.
6 I do not want people to try to silence me by threats, intimidation or coercion of any kind, or refuse to talk to me because I am morally obnoxious in their eyes. So I will treat my opponents with courtesy and respect.
7 I do not want people to be impervious to any damage their beliefs and attitudes are having on me or those I care about. Likewise, I will listen and be open to learn how my beliefs and attitudes may be injurious to others.

c. Exhortation 3 and the basis for enemy-love (6:35–36)

Verse 35a consists of a threefold summative exhortation that reiterates earlier themes. *But love your enemies* repeats verse 32, *do good to them* echoes verses 27b and 33, and *lend to them without expecting to get anything back* reasserts ideas in verses 30 and 34. This mini-summary of the Sermon's core section of verses 27–34 acts as a link to a marvellous concluding promise of hope: *Then your reward will be great, and you will be children of the Most High* (35b). Disciples who walk the costly path of enemy-love do not do so unnoticed. Their great reward is a blessing from God in response to their faithfulness. The reward itself is most likely God's favour and pleasure – a similar idea to the warm congratulations given to the good servant who earned ten minas in Luke 19:17. This is not merit for salvation[15] (as if they only then become children of God) but divine recognition for being a faithful son or daughter by daring to love enemies. Such love 'proves' their true identity as God's children *because he is kind [chrēstos] to the ungrateful and wicked* (35c).[16] Since enemy-love is intrinsic to God's nature, so it should characterize his children. This point is reaffirmed in verse 36 with another attribute of God: *Be merciful, just as your Father is merciful* (oiktirmōn, 'compassionate').[17] To display mercy is not to leap to judgment and certainly not to enter a spiral of violence and retribution with an enemy. Rather disciples are to love enemies in an extraordinary way because this is the character of the God they worship. In other words, *how you and I treat our enemies will reveal what sort of God we believe in*. Do we act as a mirror in which our enemies see reflected a God of harsh retribution, untempered by kindness or mercy? Or are we a window through which our enemies can, much to their astonishment, catch a glimpse of a beautiful alternative kingdom of love and forgiveness?

3. The parable of the Good Samaritan: neighbour-love redefined (10:25–37)

Later in his Gospel Luke includes a story of Jesus that perfectly illustrates his teaching in the Sermon on the Plain. Popularly known

---

[15] Ibid., p. 603.

[16] *Chrēstos* can also be translated 'gracious' or 'good'. It is used of God elsewhere in the NT in Rom. 2:4 and 1 Peter 2:3. In Matt. 11:30 Jesus' yoke is *chrēstos*. In the LXX, the Greek translation of the OT, the Father is frequently called *chrēstos*.

[17] Like *chrēstos*, God is often called merciful or compassionate in the OT. For an example see Exod. 34:6, discussed in chapter 1. In the NT *oiktirmōn* appears in Jas 5:11.

as the parable of the good Samaritan, it could be called 'How to love your enemies' or 'Neighbour-love redefined'. Samaritans and Jews had a long history of enmity well summarized in a Jewish saying that 'He that eats the bread of the Samaritans is like one that eats the flesh of swine.'[18] The story revolves around a double exchange of questions between Jesus and an expert in the law who wishes to test (and in some way expose) this messianic pretender. The first pair of questions revolves around inheriting eternal life. In response to Jesus' probing, the expert correctly summarizes how love of God and neighbour fulfils the law by quoting the Shema of Deuteronomy 6:5 combined with Leviticus 19:18: *Love the Lord your God with all your heart and with all your soul and with all your strength and with all your mind* and *Love your neighbour as yourself* (27).[19] The second pair of questions then zones in on what 'neighbour-love' means. So, while the expert's supplementary question is *And who is my neighbour?* (29), Jesus' storied answer of a Samaritan's practical love for a Jewish enemy,[20] compared to the failure of a priest and Levite to show compassion, switches focus to the deeper issue of what *acting* like a neighbour means. This is made explicit in his question at the end of the parable, *Which of these three do you think was a neighbour to the man who fell into the hands of robbers?* (36). The expert cannot evade the obvious answer: *The one who had mercy [eleos] on him* (37). Jesus' command to *Go and do likewise* (37) summarizes what the expert must do to inherit eternal life – show mercy and love to anyone in need regardless of their identity. The Samaritan's actions perfectly fulfil the requirements of enemy-love described in the Sermon on the Plain and summarized in 6:35. He *had compassion* (33, ESVUK) for the beaten victim. He does good to him, gets his own hands 'dirty' in the process and, unlike the priest or Levite, puts his own needs second by taking the risk to help in an obviously dangerous situation.[21] He spends money generously on a man who has been robbed and cannot pay him back. And he does all this for someone very different from himself, bridging

---

[18] Nolland, *Luke 9:21–18:34*, p. 594.

[19] For discussion of Deut. 6:4–5 see chapter 1. Parallel appearances of this double OT love command appear in Matt. 22:37–40 and Mark 12:29–31. In both cases Jesus adds a clause emphasizing the significance of love: 'All the Law and the Prophets hang on these two commandments' (Matt. 22:40); 'There is no commandment greater than these' (Mark 12:31). Jas 2:8 references Lev. 19:18 in exhorting readers not to show favouritism.

[20] While not stated explicitly, it is very likely that the victim would have been understood by Jesus and his listeners as being Jewish.

[21] Speculation as to whether the priest and Levite were concerned over ritual uncleanliness is just that – speculation. The point is not their motive in failing to help, but the fact that they did not.

centuries of hatred, suspicion and alienation in the process. It is this sort of love that reveals the attitudes and behaviour characteristic of an authentic disciple. The story was undoubtedly deeply uncomfortable for the expert in the law, for it far extended traditional rabbinic understanding of the Torah as commanding neighbour-love only of a fellow Jew. The parable radically redefines neighbour-love as being synonymous with enemy-love. Such love does not pretend profound differences do not exist but rather, in the face of stark divisions, says *I love you as I would wish to be loved.*

4. Unworkable idealism? Loving our enemies today

We need to pause and ask just how realistic this command of enemy-love is. Jesus does indeed frequently use hyperbole to make a point – is his teaching here to be taken at face-value or is it an exaggerated ideal? Many have tried to soften these verses' literal meaning, but the arguments are not persuasive.[22] Perhaps the most influential modern theological attempt is Reinhold Niebuhr's theory of Christian Realism. Niebuhr, a twentieth-century American theologian, had been a pacifist but, faced with the violent horrors of Hitler and Stalin, rejected it as an unrealistic ideal of absolute love in a world dominated by sin and power. Since, even after Christ, war remains intrinsic to human nature, Christians cannot afford to be perfectionists. For civil society to survive, he argued, the realistic necessity of just war must take priority over the unrealistic ideal of love. But great caution is needed here. The main thrust of our texts in Luke 6 and 10 is an astonishing *contrast* between reactions to enemies from those within the kingdom of God compared to those outside it. Such is the power of Jesus' discomforting words that those of us claiming to be his disciples need to feel their full force. Within the Sermon on the Plain Jesus' ethic of enemy-love is *the* distinctive marker of authentic kingdom life. We cannot evade the challenge that we are to exhibit such an extraordinary quality of love that it appears 'off the charts' compared to typical human responses to enemies. N. T. Wright captures this well:

> The kingdom that Jesus preached and lived was all about a glorious, uproarious, absurd generosity. Think of the best thing you can do for the worst person, and go ahead and do it. Think of what you'd really like someone to do for you, and do it for

[22] Richard Hays lists six of the most common attempts (regarding Matt. 5). After an outstanding discussion he rejects them all. Richard B. Hays, *The Moral Vision of the New Testament: Community, Cross, New Creation: A Contemporary Introduction to New Testament Ethics* (San Francisco: HarperSanFrancisco, 1996), pp. 317–346.

them. Think of the people to whom you are tempted to be nasty, and lavish generosity on them instead.[23]

While there are some oft-quoted inspiring examples of Christian enemy-love, their very ubiquity suggests that they are the exception rather than the rule.[24] But what if Christians *typically* lived like this? Would not the church – and even world history – be very different? Let us imagine some implications if Christians allow Jesus' words to speak today.

First, the church itself. While Jesus' teaching is aimed at how disciples respond to enemies *outside* the kingdom, the principle of enemy-love applies *within* it as well. John Stott, in one of his later books written after nearly sixty years in ministry, lamented that 'many of us evangelical Christians acquiesce too quickly in our pathological tendency to fragment'.[25] Most of the time this fragmentation is not ultimately about orthodoxy versus heterodoxy, but a failure to love, do good, bless and pray for those with whom we differ. Rather than disagreeing well we insist on our way and respond in kind to those who act against us. We fail to trust that justice is in God's hands and take it into our own. Here is one sobering example from a strongly evangelical denomination that does not need to be named. It comes from an official report examining sixty cases of conflict that had been referred to a formal conciliation process within the church. Not one of these was found to be due to doctrinal matters: all of them revolved around a breakdown in relationships. Astonishingly, out of all the cases 'There were *no* positive experiences spoken of conflict being handled well, producing change, new growth, more real relationships, and a greater awareness of God's love and grace.'[26] The report concluded that 'It seems clear that we as a Church need to recapture the attitude and skills obvious in several Biblical models of talking, listening, searching for solutions, praying together, *and above all loving*, and the giving and receiving of forgiveness.'[27] The denomination in question is to be commended for making such findings public and taking steps to act on the report's recommendations. But sadly anyone involved in Christian ministry for any length of time knows that it is not exceptional. Within an age of social media there are countless examples on the

---

[23] N. T. Wright, *Luke for Everyone*, NTE (London: SPCK, 2012), p. 73.

[24] Corrie Ten Boom's forgiveness of her concentration camp guard is probably one of the most famous.

[25] John R. W. Stott, *Evangelical Truth: A Personal Plea for Unity, Integrity and Faithfulness* (Leicester: Inter-Varsity Press, 1999), p. 141.

[26] 2013 Report (full details withheld). Emphasis mine.

[27] Ibid. Emphasis mine.

Internet of Christian versus Christian invective and a rise of what can only be described as tribalism between different branches of global evangelicalism. Given the strength of Jesus' *command* to love enemies and reflect the character of God, such behaviour is simply scandalous. Our first response, then, to Jesus' teaching on enemy-love should, I suggest, be self-examination and repentance.

Second, despite arguments like Niebuhr's, it is difficult to evade the conclusion that the only option consistent with the Sermon on the Plain is the path of Christian non-violence. It is, to put it bluntly, difficult to love your enemies if you are trying to kill them – whether in war or at an individual level. But non-violence is grounded in Jesus' teaching at a deeper level. Enemy-love is rooted in faith that God's justice will one day prevail (6:22–23, 35). The resort to violence is to attempt to seize control of history and twist it for our own ends. It unmasks at least two things: that deep down we trust primarily in ourselves and the power we can exert, and how intensely we are committed to protecting and defending that which is most precious to us. Yet enemy-love commands disciples to trust in God, endure injustice and believe in love's subversion of violence. Along these lines, Stanley Hauerwas argues that 'God's kingdom, it seems, will not have peace through coercion. Peace will come only through the power of love, which the world can only perceive as weakness.'[28] This means:

> The task of the Christian people is not to seek to control history, but to be faithful to the mode of life of the peaceable kingdom. Such a people can never lose hope in the reality of that kingdom, but they must surely also learn to be patient. For they must often endure injustice that might appear to be quickly eliminated through violence.[29]

To love this way is to take the apparently crazy risk of living 'out of control'. Hauerwas adds, 'We thus live out of control in the sense that we must assume God will use our faithfulness to make his kingdom a reality in the world.'[30] While Christians should seek and work for justice, it will not, contrary to Niebuhr, be advanced through necessary use of power and violence, but through God's people living kingdom-shaped lives.

A common objection to the practice of such enemy-love is that it is naive, unrealistic and impractical. But this is the point. God's ways

---

[28] Stanley Hauerwas, *The Peaceable Kingdom: A Primer in Christian Ethics* (Notre Dame: University of Notre Dame Press, 1983), p. 79.

[29] Ibid., p. 106.

[30] Ibid., p. 105.

are not our ways. Disciples are *not commanded to love their enemies in order to 'win' a conflict or even to effect peace*. As noted earlier, 'doing unto others' carries with it no guarantee that your enemy will return the favour. Christians are simply to love enemies because such love is grounded in the compassionate character of God himself (6:35–36). Since disciples are beneficiaries of God's own practice of enemy-love they are to 'be' people of enemy-love in whatever circumstances they find themselves. So Hauerwas says:

> We discover that the patient hope that requires us to wait in the face of violence is not some means to a greater good, *but the good itself*. Such a patience is less something we do or accomplish than it is our recognition of what God has made possible in our lives.[31]

This means that Christian disciples are not faced with a choice of whether to engage in violence or not depending on circumstances. Rather *being non-violent* means you live and imagine life from that core identity and conviction without having constantly to question who you are. As Hauerwas says elsewhere, 'the church does not have an alternative to war. The church *is* the alternative to war.'[32]

Space precludes much further discussion, save to say that it is incontestable that the first Christians took Jesus' commands literally and at great personal cost. Stephen's prayer for his killers echoes Jesus' prayer of blessing for his executioners (Acts 7:60). Peter explicitly grounds his teaching on suffering and non-violence on Christ's example. As in Luke 6, disciples are to trust that final justice lies in the hands of God and are not to take it into their own hands:

> But if you suffer for doing good and you endure it, this is commendable before God. To this you were called, because Christ suffered for you, leaving you an example, that you should follow in his steps. 'He committed no sin, and no deceit was found in his mouth.' When they hurled their insults at him, he did not retaliate; when he suffered, he made no threats. Instead, he entrusted himself to him who judges justly.[33]

Often overlooked is how Paul also articulates and exemplifies a radical ethic of Christian non-violence, suffering and enemy-love. In an important book Michael Gorman notes how this was no

---

[31] Ibid., p. 146. Emphasis mine.

[32] Stanley Hauerwas, 'The End of War: Why Christian Realism Requires Non-violence', <https://www.abc.net.au/religion/the-end-of-just-war-why-christian-realism-requires-nonviolence/10097052>, accessed 12 May 2019. Emphasis original.

[33] 1 Peter 2:20b–23.

marginal tributary in Paul's theology but an intrinsic part of his new Christian identity:

> Seldom . . . is his turn from violence *qua* violence (as opposed to his turn from persecuting the early church to promoting the faith) seen as a constitutive part of his conversion and life, or as paradigmatic for, and therefore constitutive of, Christian conversion and therefore new life generally. If the conversion of Paul, grounded in the resurrection of Christ, is paradigmatic, it is paradigmatic in multiple ways, not least of which is his conversion from violence to non-violence.[34]

This is most powerfully captured in Romans 12:9–21. The parallels with Jesus' teaching are numerous and unmistakable:

> Love must be sincere . . .
> Bless those who persecute you; bless and do not curse . . .
> Do not repay anyone evil for evil. Be careful to do what is right in the eyes of everyone. If it is possible, as far as it depends on you, live at peace with everyone. Do not take revenge, my dear friends, but leave room for God's wrath, for it is written: 'It is mine to avenge; I will repay,' says the Lord. On the contrary:
>
> > 'If your enemy is hungry, feed him;
> > if he is thirsty, give him something to drink.
> > In doing this, you will heap burning coals on his head.'
>
> Do not be overcome by evil, but overcome evil with good.

Even from this brief survey it is clear that a life of enemy-love and non-violence is not just a personal ethical 'choice' for a Christian, but an intrinsic characteristic of life within the kingdom of God. It is significant that this vocation was universally understood in the early church. In a carefully researched book on all known sources in the pre-Constantinian church, Ron Sider has demonstrated that not one writer argues for justifiable killing (whether abortion, capital punishment or in war) or the legitimacy of joining the military. Some sources condemn baptized Christians joining the military and overall the evidence is compelling that early Christianity as a movement repudiated war and killing in all its forms.[35] Even Tertullian

---

[34] Michael Gorman, *Inhabiting the Cruciform God: Kenosis, Justification, and Theosis in Paul's Narrative Soteriology* (Grand Rapids: Eerdmans, 2009), pp. 158–159.

[35] Ron Sider, *The Early Church on Killing: A Comprehensive Sourcebook on War, Abortion, and Capital Punishment* (Grand Rapids: Baker Academic, 2012).

and Origen, who disagreed about many things and likely never met, both wrote treatises that Christians should refuse to join the military.[36]

While the story is complex and beyond our remit here, the church's subsequent legitimation of 'just violence' for the greater good can be seen as a tragic development that opened the door to the legitimation of coercion and often brutal violence to 'defend' and 'propagate' the Christian faith. It has caused – and continues to do so – deep damage to the integrity of the church's witness to her Lord, the Prince of Peace and crucified Messiah.

Third, the practice of enemy-love today is completely dependent on the hope of divine justice. Why endure unnecessary suffering and persecution in this life if justice is an illusion? Why not retaliate and fight your enemies to the death if all this life represents is a 'will to power'? In a very real sense, disciples today have *more* reason to take the risk of enemy-love than did Jesus' first hearers on the Plain. For, unlike them, Christians today know the full story of the gospel. We know that Jesus' teaching on enemy-love was far from an abstract theory: it found embodiment in the cruel nails of the cross, where he died for his enemies (Rom. 5:10). It was on that wood that forces of violence, sin, hate, injustice and malign powers appeared to have triumphed, but, to everyone's surprise (including the powers themselves, 1 Cor. 2:8) Jesus' resurrection was tangible proof of the victory of God's self-giving love over death. Because of this good news we can be assured that those who weep now will laugh (6:21) and those who suffer persecution will rejoice and leap for joy, for great will be their reward in heaven (6:23).

Fourth, and finally, Jesus' teaching is a reminder that love is far from a sentimental feeling – it involves costly action for the good of the Other. Such love is not passive or supine: it is a call to faith, obedience and courage. Recall Chloe at the beginning of this chapter. She was now a Christian, but to love or forgive her brother was the last thing she could contemplate doing. The best she could do was to begin, reluctantly, to pray for her enemy. The prayers released something deep down within her. She began to see that he too was also a prisoner of the past. To her surprise, she found that the hate and bitterness she had carried for so long melted away. She felt a powerful sense of liberation from the cycle of hate that had consumed her for decades. Today she can honestly say she loves him, even though he remains estranged. She recognizes that just as she could not control what happened in the past, she cannot control how

---

[36] David A. Hoekema, 'A Practical Christian Pacifism', *CC* (22 October 1986), pp. 917–919.

he reacts to her forgiveness in the present. She longs for him to know the freedom she has experienced in Christ and for his life to be healed. Chloe's story is by no means some sort of template for other victims of abuse – it is her particular experience. But it shows us that enemy-love, while costly and difficult, demonstrates something of the beauty and compassion of God himself. It is to this vocation that *all* disciples are commanded, not just the extraordinary few. It is only when we, and our churches, have a reputation *among our opponents* for inexplicable, reckless and generous love that we can even begin to feel that we may be on the right track in obeying our Lord's teaching to love our enemies.

Luke 7:36–50
12. A woman's great love

In this chapter we turn our attention to the extraordinary love of an anonymous woman. The scene is a meal in Simon the Pharisee's house. While Luke's account certainly has important teaching by Jesus, it is primarily a story of someone who has been *transformed from a sinner into a lover*. As such it links most closely with chapter 10 almost as a worked example of what it looks like in practice to love Jesus above all else. Other illustrations of loving relationships between Jesus and his followers could have been chosen,[1] but focusing on this one will allow us to unpack a remarkable story that has much to teach us about the message of love.[2]

While it is impossible to be certain, there are very good reasons to think that Luke's account is of a different event to that described in Matthew, Mark and John.[3] In terms of her reputation, Matthew and Mark tell of an unnamed woman who pours a jar of expensive perfume over Jesus' head shortly before his crucifixion. The implication is that she is an honourable Samuel-like character anointing the Messiah for his impending burial. Jesus himself defends her actions by saying, 'Truly I tell you, wherever the gospel is preached throughout the world, what she has done will also be

---

[1] Prominent examples include Jesus' love for Lazarus, Mary and Martha (John 11:5), his three questions to Peter 'Do you love me?' (John 21:15–17) and John's status as the disciple whom Jesus loved (John 13:23; 19:26; 20:2; 21:7; 21:20).

[2] For discussion of this passage in regard to Jesus and women see Derek Tidball and Dianne Tidball, *The Message of Women: Creation, Grace and Gender*, BST (Nottingham: Inter-Varsity Press, 2012), pp. 165–168.

[3] See Matt. 26:6–13; Mark 14:3–9; John 12:1–8. Bock summarizes the numerous differences and concludes that the evidence suggests that Matthew, Mark and John describe the same event, and Luke a different one. In Luke the event occurs early in Jesus' ministry in Galilee as opposed to the final days of Jesus' life. Darrell Bock, *Luke 1:1–9:50*, BECNT (Grand Rapids: Baker Academic, 1994), pp. 689–690.

told, in memory of her.'[4] In John it is Jesus' close friend Mary who anoints his feet in her brother Lazarus's house in Bethany – an action that is again linked with Jesus' burial (John 12:7). In both cases the only (rejected) criticism of the woman is of her extravagance. This is in contrast to Luke, where, uniquely, she is described as a sinner (37, 39), guilty of *many* sins (47), who anoints Jesus for a very different reason. Despite this being the sum total of what Luke says about her identity, the woman is routinely described as a prostitute who acts in a sexually shameless way by wiping Jesus' feet with her unbound hair.[5] This sensual interpretation has a questionable basis and has had unfortunate results in how Luke's unnamed woman has been portrayed throughout church history and in popular imagination.[6] Luke's restraint in downplaying the significance of her past has been undermined to a point where this tends to be the main image by which she is remembered.[7] This means, like Simon, we can be so blinded by her status as a 'sinner' that we fail to 'see' her properly (44). In the interpretation that follows it will be argued that we need to be cautious of unhelpful speculation that distracts from Luke's main emphasis – to celebrate and affirm the actions of a woman as a model of faithful discipleship from whom all believers can learn. Or, to put it more directly, to focus on her remarkable love, not her past sin.

1. The woman's great love (36–38)

The story begins with a dinner invitation (36) in an unnamed Galilean town by a Pharisee whom Jesus later calls *Simon* (40). While it later emerges that he could have been more hospitable (44–46), there is no sense of hostile intent in his invitation, as if he were trying to trap Jesus. He appears to be cautious but open to learn more of this man whom he calls *didaskale* (like 'Rabbi', a polite form of address indicating respect, 40). As was the custom at special banquets, Jesus *reclined at the table* (36), his feet pointing away from the table. Bock suggests that this helps to explain how the woman could join the meal party without it being noted as unusual – such

---

[4] Mark 14:9; cf. Matt. 26:13.

[5] E.g. see J. B. Green, *The Gospel of Luke*, NICNT (Grand Rapids: Eerdmans, 1987), pp. 309–310.

[6] There is a long tradition of equating Mary of Bethany with Mary Magdalene and conflating John's account with Luke 7. This confusion results in Mary Magdalene's being the repentant prostitute who anoints Jesus. This despite there being no hint of her being a prostitute in the four Gospels or that the two Marys are the same person!

[7] The passage heading in the NIVUK is typical: 'Jesus anointed by a sinful woman'.

banquets were often public so that uninvited guests could hear the conversation and perhaps share in leftovers.[8] What is of note is the fact that she is a 'sinner' (*hamartōlos*, 37). This word is repeated by Simon in verse 39. (The NIVUK's 'who lived a sinful life' is a less than helpful translation). As already noted, Luke tells us nothing more; probably for good reason. While her sin might have been sexual (prostitution or adultery), it might also have been related to debt or her status as the wife of a man with a dishonourable occupation.[9] Regardless, Luke is not interested in the nature of her sin; he is much more concerned with what she, as a sinner, does next. The fact that she arrived prepared *with an alabaster jar of perfume* (37) suggests at least three possibilities. Perhaps she has already had a powerful liberating experience of Jesus' forgiveness and now seeks him out to show the depth of her gratitude. Or, a variation on this theme, perhaps she has had some initial contact with Jesus and, encouraged by that first meeting, is drawn to him in hope. Or perhaps this is the first time she has met Jesus in person. She knows of his attitudes to sinners like her by reputation and comes to Simon's house in desperate search of restoration and acceptance. All these options are compatible with the text, with the first the most likely given the parable Jesus tells implies that forgiveness has already been received (40–43). What is clear is that she has already decided to anoint Jesus with an expensive perfume, not just the olive oil normally used for such a purpose. Such a decision was not only sacrificial but also courageous. To go to the Pharisee's house was to risk his inevitable public scorn and, even more potentially devastating, to open herself to possible rejection by Jesus, in whom she was placing all her hopes.

Luke takes care to describe her every step in detail: *As she stood behind him at his feet weeping, she began to wet his feet with her tears. Then she wiped them with her hair, kissed them and poured perfume on them* (38). Jesus' feet would have been bare, his dusty sandals removed. She has evidently approached with the intention of anointing his feet but it seems as if she is unexpectedly overcome with emotion in doing so. Luke does not tell us why she cries. How we interpret her tears will, to a large degree, depend on which of the three options listed above we find most persuasive. If already forgiven, her tears are very probably of unrestrained joy and love. If approaching tentatively in hope, her emotion is perfectly understandable – her whole future is dependent on what happens next. One thing is clear: her weeping is unreserved and uncontrollable.

---

[8] Bock, *Luke 1:1–9:50*, pp. 694–695.
[9] Ibid., p. 695.

Her tears soak (*brechō*, 'to wet') his feet, a word that elsewhere in the NT is used to describe rain showers.[10] It seems as if it is only in response to this unplanned wetting of Jesus' feet that she uses her hair to wipe them.[11] Much has been made of this gesture, with many interpreters seeing it as immodest, if not outrightly erotic.[12] In almost every case this conclusion is linked to an assumption that she was a prostitute. While possible, this seems very unlikely for at least three reasons. First, this is no Graeco-Roman feast but a public Jewish banquet at a Pharisee's home. Second, and more significantly, her entire approach to Jesus is that of humble reverence: some sort of sexual expression would be completely inappropriate and is not hinted at in the text itself. Third, detailed research into the social symbolism of a woman's unbound hair in the ancient Mediterranean world has found a wide range of possible meanings of unbound hair, depending on the social context.[13] Extreme caution is therefore needed before leaping to a conclusion that unbound hair simply equates to some sort of brazen sexual act. Given the context of the story in Luke, Cosgrove concludes that 'the woman's gesture with her hair is not sexually provocative, indecent, or even a breach of etiquette'.[14] In context it is much more likely simply to be an impromptu gesture arising out of a mixture of necessity, love, devotion, gratefulness and hope. In similar vein, the kissing and anointing of Jesus' feet that follow the wiping with her hair, while definitely unusual in that it involved a woman touching a man in public, is not sexually charged behaviour. The verb used (*kataphileō*, 'to kiss') denotes deep reverence inspired by Jesus' gracious treatment of sinners like her. Consistent with this, a few verses later Jesus describes her actions positively as constituting *great love* (*ēgapēsen poly*, 47). Nowhere else in the New Testament is someone honoured with such a description by the Lord. Indeed the only other parallel is Ephesians 2:4, which talks of God's 'great love' (*pollēn agapēn*) for us.[15]

---

[10] Ibid., p. 696.

[11] I. H. Marshall, *The Gospel of Luke*, NIGTC (Grand Rapids: Eerdmans, 1978), pp. 308–309.

[12] Green, *Gospel of Luke*, p. 310; K. E. Bailey, *Poet and Peasant & Through Peasant Eyes: A Literary-Cultural Approach to the Parables in Luke*, combined edn, vol. 2 (Grand Rapids: Eerdmans, 1983), p. 9.

[13] C. H. Cosgrove, 'A Woman's Unbound Hair in the Greco-Roman World, with Special Reference to the Story of the "Sinful Woman" in Luke 7:36–50', *JBL* 24.4 (2005), pp. 675–692.

[14] Ibid., p. 691.

[15] See chapter 9 for further discussion of this text.

2. Simon's blindness to the woman's love (39)

Luke describes Simon's reaction to the woman's extraordinary behaviour: *When the Pharisee who had invited him saw this, he said to himself, 'If this man were a prophet, he would know who is touching him and what kind of woman she is – that she is a sinner'* (39). His shock is not necessarily caused by *how* she was touching him (this is reading into the text), but that she, a woman and an impure 'sinner', was touching him at all. The present tense *haptetai* (she is touching) suggests a prolonged scene that increasingly offends the Pharisee. This supposed prophet of God, presumably blessed with the Holy Spirit of God and claiming to speak with the authority of God, is allowing himself to be made ritually unclean.[16] We can imagine Jesus' probable acknowledgment to the woman and his calm lack of concern for what is going on down at his feet in contrast to Simon's increasing indignation. The conclusion of Simon's internal dialogue is inevitable – this man cannot be a prophet since he does not know what sort of woman is touching him. If the purpose of the dinner party was in Simon's mind to provide an answer to Jesus' true identity, Simon now knows the answer. *Completely absent from Simon's thinking is any consideration of the woman in her own right.* Why had she come to his house? Why was she so visibly upset? Why was she anointing Jesus' feet? In his eyes she was a sinner and that was all he needed to know. Her love and humanity were irrelevant within his theological framework of pure insiders and impure outsiders.

3. Jesus' defence of the woman's love (40–50)

The rest of the story forms a contrast between Simon's and Jesus' interpretations of the woman's behaviour. A gulf in conflicting perceptions becomes evident. Jesus defends and explains the woman's actions to Simon and the listening bystanders first through a parable (40–43) and then by contrasting her behaviour with that of Simon (44–47). The section closes with Jesus' finally addressing the woman directly (48–50).

a. A parable on love and forgiveness (40–43)

In true rabbinic style Jesus invites Simon into a theological conversation (40), which proceeds via a simple parable. *Two people owed money to a certain money-lender. One owed him five hundred*

---

[16] Marshall, *Gospel of Luke*, p. 309.

denarii, and the other fifty. Neither of them had the money to pay him back, so he forgave the debts of both (41–42). A denarius was a soldier's or labourer's daily wage. The surprise in the story – both then and now – is that the money-lender decides to forgive both people their unpayable debt. This is not by definition what money-lenders tend to do, regardless of whether debtors have the ability to repay or not! It is therefore an unexpected action of unmerited generosity. The question that Jesus asks Simon is fascinating. It links gratitude for forgiven debt with love (*agapaō*, 'to love'). *Now which of them will love him more?* (42b). Simon has no option but to reply *I suppose the one who had the bigger debt forgiven* (43).

At least two things are going on here. At one level it is as though Jesus, through a story, is educating Simon of the need to treat people with compassion and as individuals. The Pharisee's theological assumptions blind him to what is really happening before his eyes. His category of 'sinner' has dehumanized the woman: she simply represents a group that is to be avoided. He, and the Pharisees in general, in effect had no gospel of good news to such sinners. His heart was untouched with compassion for her need; she was merely a potential source of impurity. As a result, her love, her tears, her humility and her courage were invisible to him. *But they were not to Jesus* (as vv. 44–47 make crystal clear). His response to her is as extraordinarily important today as it was then. Our world remains riven with all sorts of group conflicts, where the 'Other' is dehumanized, ignored, excluded or violently rejected. Human nature seems intrinsically tribal – whether in the form of colonialism, ethnocentric conflicts, nationalist politics, religious terrorism or multiple other forms of group competition for 'authenticity' and power. Christians are far from exempt from such politics of exclusion. For example, there is something scandalous, is there not, that Martin Luther King's words still ring true today?

> We must face the fact that in America, the church is still the most segregated major institution . . . At 11:00 on Sunday morning when we stand and sing and Christ has no east or west, we stand at the most segregated hour in this nation.[17]

The situation in the UK is only slightly better. In 2016 the Archbishop of Canterbury, Justin Welby, said that racial segregation

---

[17] Words spoken on 18 December 1963 at Western Michigan University in Kalamazoo. One study has estimated that about 87% of churches in America are either all White or all African-American in membership.

was 'the single biggest failure of the Church of England over the last 40 or 50 years'.[18] Like Simon, we can construct theologies that exclude and ignore. Jesus shows us another way in this story.

At another level, Simon also needs to understand the theological point that Jesus makes about God, forgiveness, himself and the woman. The money-lender is obviously God, the great debtor represents sinners like the woman, the minor debtor those like Simon who are still sinners but have not been socially stigmatized as such. The implications for Simon's doctrine of God are radical. Rather than a God who excludes the impure, here is a God who freely and generously forgives sinners regardless of the level of their debt. This is why Jesus' ministry is to sinners. Those who have experienced such forgiveness will be transformed from people without hope to grateful lovers of God. Where Simon saw only a disgraced sinner, Jesus looked on the woman and saw someone who could be set free from social exclusion, shame and guilt to become a joyful worshipper. In a sense she is an early recipient of Jesus' messianic promise in Luke 4 to proclaim good news, liberate prisoners and set the oppressed free. In the light of this story we can say that *God is in the business of transforming sinners into lovers.* Our calling as Christians today, then, is to try to see people in the same light.

b. The woman's great love commended (44–47)

Jesus now turns *towards the woman* (44), explicitly including her in the conversation that follows. He asks Simon a further question, *Do you see this woman?* (44). In the light of the discussion above, this can be taken literally, metaphorically and ironically! For, so far, Simon has not really seen her at all. Now Jesus forces him to consider her actions one by one, replaying the events in turn and using the same verbs (wet, wipe, kiss, pour). In doing so Simon is confronted not only by what she has done but why she acted the way she did. Even more uncomfortably, Jesus compares Simon's actions unfavourably to hers at each point:

> *I came into your house. You did not give me any water for my feet, but she wet my feet with her tears and wiped them with her hair. You did not give me a kiss, but this woman, from the time I entered, has not stopped kissing my feet. You did not put oil on my head, but she has poured perfume on my feet.* (44b–46)

---

[18] See <www.christiantoday.com/article/how-racial-division-has-held-back-the-uk-church/88062.htm>, accessed 12 April 2018.

Jesus' purpose is not to shame Simon, but to commend the woman and, in true kingdom-of-God style, to invert his assumptions about what attitudes and behaviour are pleasing to God. It is unlikely that Simon was discourteous regarding the lack of water, kiss and oil. As noted the conversation is respectful but he has not extended any hospitality beyond the minimum.[19] This is in stark contrast to the woman's costly sacrifice and deep respect for Jesus. Verse 47 forms a climax of the whole narrative and links back to the parable: *Therefore, I tell you, her many sins have been forgiven – as her great love has shown* (47a). Her great love, in other words, flows from God's great forgiveness. Her life has been transformed by her encounter with Jesus the liberator. She exemplifies attitudes of a disciple – humility, gratitude, service and love – all characteristics lacking in the Pharisee. We can only imagine what she thought as she listened to these words of praise from Jesus! To have a public reputation as a sinner presumably meant that she had endured the personal and social consequences for some considerable time. Jesus' affirmation must have felt like fresh water being poured on the parched ground of her heart. We can imagine his words being gratefully soaked up, giving her new life, a new status and new purpose. *But whoever has been forgiven little loves little* (47b) is not so much talking directly of Simon, but is a general statement indicating that absent or minimal love for God is an indication that the person has probably never experienced his transforming forgiveness in the first place.

c. Faith and forgiveness (48–50)

The story closes with Jesus speaking to the woman directly for the first time, a significant point easily overlooked. So far she has been talked *about*; now she is talked *to* – and in the most positive way imaginable. Jesus reinforces what he has just said about her to Simon. His words must have been the most wonderful that she had ever heard, *Your sins are forgiven* (48). The perfect tense assures her – and others listening – that her forgiveness is a 'done deal'. Her actions, and the motives behind them, at the dinner are thus affirmed by Jesus as legitimate and admirable (this further weakens the idea that her behaviour was shamelessly sexual). This authoritative public declaration of her new identity as a *forgiven* sinner was likely crucial for her future reintegration into society. It also, echoing the story of the paralysed man in Luke 5,[20] causes the onlookers to ask a

---

[19] Marshall, *Gospel of Luke*, p. 311.
[20] There the Pharisees and teachers of the law ask, 'Who is this fellow who speaks blasphemy? Who can forgive sins but God alone?' (5:21).

Christological question, *Who is this who even forgives sins?* (49). If Simon had earlier doubted that Jesus was a prophet, here the stakes are raised infinitely higher. Probably in response to the other guests' query, Jesus encourages the woman one last time with words of blessing, *Your faith has saved you; go in peace* (50).[21] In contrast to those doubting or rejecting Jesus, her response of faith in seeking him out and casting herself in supplication and reverence at his feet has saved her. She is now reconciled to God and can go forward fully assured of that liberating truth.

4. Do you see this woman?

This is not only a beautiful and touching story; it carries profound truths concerning what constitutes authentic Christian faith (and what does not). The woman has no name, she leaves behind not one spoken word and she is not commemorated in subsequent church history, yet she has much to teach us today. Luke presents her as an exemplary model of how to respond to Jesus in contrast to Simon. Jesus' question to Simon *Do you see this woman?* (44) therefore applies to us as well. We would do well to learn from someone who stands out in the New Testament as the person of whom Jesus speaks most highly and whom he defends at length. The story has at least three things to teach us.

a. Discipleship, love and gender

First, it would be remiss not to comment on the contextually significant point of the woman's gender. In a highly patriarchal Jewish culture a significant part of Simon's hostile reaction would have been due to Jesus' apparent disregard of what type of *woman* was touching him. Women had secondary status: they could not appear as witnesses in legal cases, were not educated in the Torah and could not teach men.[22] Yet Luke's story reverses all expectations. Jesus deliberately confronts assumptions of a male-dominated culture in holding up the woman as one of the greatest models of Christian discipleship in the New Testament. She, not the male Pharisee expert in the Torah, is to be emulated and learnt from. It is neither gender, nor status, nor past life that matter to Jesus, but faith and great love. This is consistent with Luke's affirmation of women

---

[21] See Luke 8:48 for a virtually identical assurance and blessing to another woman.

[22] For further discussion see Darrell Bock, *A Theology of Luke and Acts: God's Promised Program, Realized for All Nations*, BTNT (Grand Rapids: Zondervan, 2012), pp. 343–358.

throughout Luke–Acts.[23] The later outpouring of the Spirit, and his gifts, is given to males and females, Jews and Gentiles alike. Again this was radical then and remains radical today. Christianity does not have, despite what some prominent evangelical Christian leaders say, 'a masculine feel'.[24] Any such notion is incompatible with Jesus' words and actions in this story. Men have much to learn from women and women from men. Both genders have a common calling of loving and serving their Lord in humility and gratitude.

b. Faith and love detached

Second, the negative side of the story is about where faith and love are detached. Simon 'fails' where she 'succeeds', primarily in his lack of love. His superficial civility to Jesus contrasts painfully with the woman's great love. His self-perceived lack of a need of forgiveness closes him off from responding in faith.

Simon's encounter with Jesus needs to be taken to heart by any committed Christian. It is all too easy to ascribe to all the 'right' doctrines but live a life largely devoid of love for God and compassion for others. This separation between faith and love can take different forms. Some evangelicals tend to lionize celebrity leaders and preachers who build global 'brands'; but a preoccupation with giftedness, status, power, technology, efficiency and influence can marginalize the very virtues Jesus clearly values most – love, gratitude and humility. Others, of a more conservative bent, can see themselves as 'guardians of the gospel' yet defend it in a judgmental, arrogant and divisive spirit. A bright student can 'ace' every exam and appear excellently qualified for Christian ministry, yet cause untold damage to the church through pride and pastoral carelessness. Theologically, while a complex story, Christians have been deeply impacted by the Enlightenment. One consequence is the idea that 'faith' can be reduced to abstract doctrines that circumscribe theological orthodoxy. For example, as evangelicals we are very fond of statements of faith that attempt to describe the core doctrines of Christianity – I have been involved in drafting more than one. But even if they faithfully summarize biblical doctrines, they remain, at best, only partial descriptions of what it means to 'be Christian'. At

---

[23] It is significant that the following verses in 8:1–3 reveal that Jesus himself is supported by a group of women. Bock concludes about Luke–Acts that 'the role of women is particularly affirmed in terms of being community participants'. Ibid., p. 358.
[24] A proposal advanced by John Piper in 2012. See <www.desiringgod.org/messages/the-frank-and-manly-mr-ryle-the-value-of-a-masculine-ministry>, accessed 12 April 2018.

worst, they give a false impression that just assenting to their claims makes someone a Christian. To 'be Christian' is not just belief; it is, like the woman, to be transformed to be a lover of God who *gives her wholehearted allegiance to Jesus the king*. Such a transformation will also open the believer up to 'see' other sinners with compassion and grace.

Simon's separation of faith and love also provides a warning of how *not* to do mission. His outright hostility to a 'sinner' closes his eyes to the woman's obvious distress and condemns her from ever knowing that God could be gracious towards her. Jesus' approach could not be more different. The message of the whole story is that forgiveness, salvation and blessing are open to *anyone* regardless of previous status. This was a radical truth at a dinner table in Galilee, and it is radical now. Whatever her past sin, it did not define her for ever. He welcomes her hesitant approach and even her physical touch. He accepts her love and gives her hope. While not ignoring her past sin, he assures her publicly that she has a new status and blesses her. He, in other words, *loves* her. Christlike Christian mission needs to hold together such love with a willingness to talk honestly about sin, faith and forgiveness.

c. Faith and love combined

Third, faith and love summarize what Jesus finds so commendable in the woman. At the core of her faith is her humble yet courageous seeking after Jesus and her subsequent *experience* of his unexpectedly extravagant forgiveness. She is deeply aware of all that he has done for her. Faith expresses itself in love, and she demonstrates the depth of her 'great love', devotion and thankfulness in anointing and reverently kissing his feet. In her powerlessness, self-giving and humility she models not only what discipleship looks like in a kingdom where 'the first shall be last and the last shall be first'[25] and to be the greatest is to serve[26] but also foreshadows the shape of Jesus' life and ministry itself.[27]

For Christians today she is an inspiring example of how love is the only real 'hard' evidence of genuine faith. If you and I claim to have faith in Jesus, if we have had any experience of God's grace and forgiveness, then the 'proof' will be seen in lives of joyful love, worship and devotion to God. The greater our love the greater our

[25] E.g. Matt. 20:16 and parallels.
[26] E.g. Mark 9:35 and parallels.
[27] In John 13:1–17 Jesus, out of love (v. 1), washes the disciples' feet to demonstrate the nature of Christian service. In Phil. 2:1–11 Christian discipleship is to be patterned on Jesus' humility and self-giving mission.

awareness of the depth of God's forgiveness. The woman is a wonderful example of how a Christian is simply a sinner who has, by God's forgiveness, been transformed into a lover. Forgiveness is definitive (*Your sins are forgiven*), but being a lover is a lifelong adventure of faith. Reading this story, then, is perhaps a good time to do a 'love-audit' on our own lives: humbly to confess our sins, to seek afresh God's grace, to articulate all the blessings generously given to us in Christ, and to worship him anew in humble adoration and service.

John 15:9–17
13. Remain in my love

The idea that love is something that can be commanded seems strange, and perhaps even outrageous, to our modern ears. Is not authentic love instinctive and beyond the cold dictates of reason? Is it not practically a force 'outside' ourselves, over which we have little control, a power that sweeps us up in its embrace but may, just as suddenly, release us from its grip? Is not love conditioned in some way by the object of our love – perhaps a person's beauty or personality or intelligence? Does not the discriminating nature of such love make nonsense of a command to love one another indiscriminately? What if the other person is not loveable? Can love really be reduced to an act of obedience? And who, anyway, could possibly have the arrogance to issue a command to love?

These are some questions raised by our text in John 15:9–17. It opens with an imperative to *remain in my love* (9) and closes with another, *This is my command: love each other* (17). The verb and noun for 'love' (*agapaō* and *agapē*) occur nine times in total in verses 9–17. As discussed in chapter 7, John is the New Testament's pre-eminent author on love. The text itself forms part of Jesus' farewell discourse that spans chapters 13–17 and I have chosen it as the focus of this chapter for three reasons. First, in a section on love in the life and teaching of Jesus, it would be a major oversight not to discuss John's unique contribution. Second, a text from within the farewell discourse is particularly appropriate since, as Victor Furnish says, 'The Johannine commandments to "love one another" are at the very center of the moral and spiritual legacy which is presented in the Farewell Discourse.'[1] Third, verses 9–17 contain a threefold framework of love: the love of the Father for the Son, the Son's love

---

[1] Victor Furnish, *The Love Command of the New Testament* (London: SCM, 1973), p. 135.

for his disciples, and the disciples' love for one another as the means of remaining in Jesus' love. Apart from providing a useful inbuilt framework for a three-point sermon (!), this echoes wider themes in the Gospel of John as a whole and is therefore an excellent 'way in' to understanding the crucial place of love in the apostle's theology.

Verses 9–17 follow on from Jesus' final 'I am' saying in John's Gospel in which he introduces the metaphor of himself as the vine, the Father as the gardener (or keeper of the vineyard) and the disciples as the branches (1–8). A key theme running throughout 1–17 (and John in general) is that of 'remaining' or 'abiding' (*menō*), a word that appears eleven times in these verses alone. In verses 1–8 the emphasis is on *abide in me*, which appears five times. The vine is the life force, and it is only by remaining connected to it that the disciples will bear fruit (2, 4–5, 8). Such fruit-bearing brings glory to the Father and is 'hard evidence' that they are Jesus' disciples (8). Fruitless branches are barren because they have not remained connected to the vine. Just as in a vineyard, unproductive branches are thrown away and wither, later to be used as firewood (6). The implication is clear: authentic discipleship is seen in tangible ways (fruit). Fruitlessness is a sign that someone is not a disciple of Jesus.[2]

Verses 1–8 do not define what fruit means or how someone remains in the vine. These are the issues to which Jesus turns in verses 9–17. There is a striking shift in language here. Love is not mentioned in verses 1–8 but saturates verses 9–17. This ought to alert us to how love lies at the heart of abiding. Verse 9 encapsulates the 'three loves' present within verses 9–17 and I am going to take it as a key verse by which to structure our exposition: *As the Father has loved me, so have I loved you. Now remain in my love* (9).

1. 'As the Father has loved me': divine love

The Father's love for the Son is the fundamental source of all love that follows. Jesus' love for his disciples is rooted in and patterned on his Father's prior love for him. The disciples' task, in turn, is to remain in Jesus' love.[3] How the Father loves Jesus is not spelt out

[2] It is worth noting that in 'every instance when Israel in its historical life is depicted in the OT as a vine or vineyard, the nation is set under the judgement of God for its corruption'. George R. Beasley-Murray, *John*, WBC, vol. 36 (Waco: Word, 1987), p. 272. The wider theological implication here is that Jesus represents the true vine in contrast to OT Israel's failure to bear fruit. All who abide in him and bear fruit represent faithful Israel, a renewed people of God.

[3] For texts in John on the love of the Father for the Son see 3:35; 5:20; 10:17; 15:9; 17:23, 26. For texts on Jesus' love for his disciples see 13:1, 34; 14:21; 15:9, 12; 17:26. For commands to disciples to love one another see 13:34–35; 14:15, 21; 15:10, 12, 17. There are also commands to love the Son in 14:14, 21, 23; 16:27.

here, but hints are given throughout the Gospel. In 3:35 'The Father loves the Son and has placed everything in his hands.' In chapter 5 'the Father loves the Son and shows him all he does'.[4] Later the Son's self-giving obedience in laying down his life is a reason the Father loves the Son (10:17). In all three texts the love of the Father for the Son is expressed by continuous tenses indicating its ever-present reality. In John 17, during Jesus' great intercessory prayer to the Father for his disciples, he prays for their unity so that 'the world will know that you sent me and have loved them even as you have loved me'.[5] In 17:26 Jesus describes his entire mission in terms of making known the Father's love to his disciples: 'in order that the love you have for me may be in them and that I myself may be in them'. Returning to 15:9–17, it is made crystal clear that Jesus' obedience is intrinsic to his abiding in his Father's love: *just as I have kept my Father's commands and remain in his love* (10b).

Taken together these texts give a marvellous picture of how the Father and Son's unity within a dynamic personal relationship of love is extended to embrace all disciples of Jesus. Divine love is *prior* to any human love. In the light of this, we may say that for John it is only in God himself that we see what love truly is. The origin of love is God and God alone. For John, the great, basic and glorious truth about God is that love forms the core of his identity and basis for action in the world.[6] This is immeasurably good news for disciples both then and now. God will always act for good: all that he does flows out of his loving character. This is seen most supremely in the sending of the Son in the first place: 'For God so loved the world that he gave his one and only Son, so that whoever believes in him shall not perish but have eternal life.'[7]

This demonstration of the Father's love leads to joy! Just as Jesus experiences joy in his obedient keeping of his Father's commands, so disciples can together know Jesus' joy for themselves and that joy will be brimming over or *complete* (*plēroō*, 11). It is by *experiencing* God's love in his Son that disciples are welcomed into a transformed relationship of love with God and with one another.[8] In other words, the fact that God invites us to *participate* in his divine love through spiritual union (as branches) with his Son (the vine) should lead us to praise him together out of mutual overflowing love. Being a

---

[4] John 5:20.
[5] John 17:23.
[6] See chapter 7.
[7] John 3:16.
[8] The relationship of the Spirit to Father and Son is not in focus in John 15 but is a major theme within the Gospel and particularly within the farewell discourse.

Christian is a matter of the heart as well as of the head, of an experience of God's love as well as understanding it in our minds.

2. 'So I have loved you': friendship-love

The second love-related theme running through our text is the love that the Son has shown for his disciples (9, 12). The past tense is significant. In verse 9 Jesus has loved them as the Father has loved him. In verse 12 the disciples are to love one another *as I have loved you*. What form this love takes is unpacked in verse 13: *Greater love has no one than this: to lay down one's life for one's friends*. Clearly John, writing retrospectively, is referring to the cross here. But before we get there, to appreciate fully what Jesus is saying here we need to pause to consider the significance of the word 'friend' (*philos*).

Philos had deep resonances in the ancient world that a modern reader, for whom a 'friend' may be an acquaintance on Facebook whom he has never met in person, will tend to miss! For example, in Aristotle, friendship is the supreme form of human love, above any other types of relationship, whether sexual or with siblings, parents or children. This is because friendship-love (what he called perfect *philia*) is interested in the other for that person's own sake, treating the other virtually as a second self. Such friendship-love is admirable and ethical because it is essentially disinterested in the self.[9] For such love to flourish the two friends need to be 'good' by which Aristotle meant that they share an excellence of character (virtue) and an understanding of the best way to live life.[10] Aristotle is fantastically politically incorrect by today's standards in not believing that a man could have friendship-love with a woman since female virtue could never match that of a man! Nor did he hesitate to say a friend should be dropped if a gap in virtue developed between the two sides.

In contrast to Aristotle's Greek emphasis on equality, much Roman thought about friendship tended to see it functioning within hierarchical relationships of patrons and their clients. Friendship was not dependent on equality: patrons were called clients' friends and clients were friends of their patron.[11] Such friendship was also conditional: woven within it were a network of obligations and expectations that, if broken, would jeopardize the relationship.

[9] For excellent discussion of love in Aristotle see Simon May, *Love: A History* (London: Yale University Press, 2011), pp. 56–68.

[10] Ibid., p. 60.

[11] Craig Keener, *The Gospel of John: A Commentary*, vol. 2 (Peabody: Hendrickson, 2003), p. 1008.

It is impossible to know for sure how much Greek and Roman philosophies of friendship lie in the background of John 15; but given John's context of probably writing within a Graeco-Roman culture in Ephesus, it is fair to assume some relevance. Likely of more direct significance for John as a Jew is the Old Testament. There two figures stand out. In Genesis Abraham is chosen and taken into God's confidence (Gen. 15; 18:17–19) and is later described as a friend of God (Isa. 41:8; 1 Chr. 20:7; as well as in early Jewish writings like Jubilees 19.9). Perhaps Abraham's believing obedience is in mind in verse 14 when Jesus says, *You are my friends if you do what I command* (*entellō*). Moses too could be in view. We considered in chapter 1 his remarkable dialogue with God in Exodus 32 – 34, during which he is called a friend of God (33:11) and on which basis he dares to request a personal revelation of God's glory. He, more than anyone in the long story of the Old Testament, is allowed access to God's intentions (echoing John 15:15b, where disciples are allowed to know their master's business: *everything that I learned from my Father I have made known to you*).

However, John 15:13 talks not only about friendship, but about *dying* for one's friends. This concept was also known outside early Christianity. Keener writes that 'Courageous, heroic, and honorable death was an ancient Mediterranean virtue.'[12] He gives examples of the Jewish historian Josephus's describing those who died nobly for their nation or for fame and how the Greek world similarly admired those who laid down their lives for friend or nation. Epicurus, who highly valued friendship, is recorded as saying that a wise person would perhaps die on a friend's behalf but that such action was rare. Thus Keener argues that, while there are a variety of perspectives on friendship in the ancient world, both Romans and Greeks would 'readily grasp' the Christian concept of Jesus' dying on others' behalf, even if they were unfamiliar with the idea of Old Testament atonement.[13]

If friendship-love in John 15 shows both continuity and discontinuity with ideas of friendship in the Old Testament and the Graeco-Roman world, where does this leave us in applying John 15 for today? At least four connections can be made. The first three highlight the glorious and unique nature of Jesus' teaching on friendship-love, while the fourth sees some continuity with how the responsibilities of friendship were understood in the ancient world.

First, and most importantly, Jesus' self-giving death for his friends explodes any previous notions of friendship-love. Jesus' comment

[12] Ibid., p. 1005.
[13] Ibid.

that he *no longer* (15) calls them servants indicates a decisive new moment in salvation history. It was unheard of in Greek or Roman thought, or in the Old Testament, for God's Son, the eternal Word made flesh (John 1:1), to give up his own life for his friends. Such love is shocking in scope and immeasurable in generosity. The theologian Jürgen Moltmann captures something of the scandal of such love in the arresting title of his famous book *The Crucified God*.[14] Much earlier another German, Martin Luther, talked about *theologia crucis* (theology of the cross) as being the place where God is truly known as he reveals himself to us in infinite grace and love. This, most emphatically, is *not* a love of equals: a greater *disparity* of status, virtue and power is impossible to imagine. If depth of love is somehow proportionate to that which is given up for the good of others, then the cross represents the greatest act of love in all of history.

Second, the consequence of Jesus' self-giving love is that a disciple's status changes from being a 'slave' (*doulos*) to a 'friend': *I no longer call you servants, because a servant does not know his master's business. Instead, I have called you friends* (*philos*, 15a). This is important because under Jewish law a slave could not inherit his master's goods unless the latter's will freed the former. As Keener says, 'There would be no point in Jesus promising to share his words or goods with the disciples unless they were his friends and not slaves.'[15] Jesus' gracious designation of a new identity to his disciples opens them up to receive *everything that I learned from my Father* (15b). Particularly in mind here is knowledge – friends share their lives in contrast to a slave simply being told what to do. Father and Son hold nothing back in their blessing of disciples! It is worth taking time to try to absorb the personal implications of this astonishing verse. If you are a Christian, you are a beloved friend of Jesus with all that that entails. Like Abraham and Moses, believers are welcomed to know God personally.[16]

Third, being chosen as a friend of God is, unlike Greek ideas of being good or Roman patron-client relationships, not dependent on one's prior virtue or status. *You did not choose me, but I chose you and appointed you* (16a).[17] This is wonderfully liberating news of God's grace in action; it is given freely, not dependent on the recipient's

---

[14] Jürgen Moltmann, *The Crucified God: The Cross as the Foundation and Criticism of Christian Theology*, tr. R. A. Wilson and J. Bowden (London: SCM, 1974).

[15] Keener, *John*, p. 1013.

[16] See John 16:13–15 for how the Spirit of truth continues to make known the revelation of the Father and Jesus to disciples.

[17] In John Jesus talks about the chosenness of his disciples in several places: 6:70; 13:18; 15:16, 19.

worth. If it were dependent, then no one would ever be able to experience the blessings of love, joy and friendship with God described in verses 9–17. Whoever you are and whatever you have done does not determine your 'qualifications' to be called a friend by Jesus. It is Jesus who takes the initiative in embracing disciples as his friends.

Fourth, there is no innate contradiction between graciously being granted a new identity as a beloved friend of God and an expectation of reciprocal obedience. That the disciples are *appointed* (*tithēmi*, 16) indicates being chosen for a purpose – so that they *might go and bear fruit – fruit that will last* (16). In this sense there is some continuity with aspects of Greek and Roman views of friendship. A friendship is conditional in that the relationship needs to be maintained by both parties. What that looks like in practice for a disciple is the third theme of our text to which we now turn.

3. 'Remain in my love': obedient love

a. The paradoxical nature of Christian love

Promises and imperatives are peppered throughout verses 9–17: *Now remain in my love* (9); *If you keep my commands, you will remain in my love* (10); *My command is this: love each other* (12); *You are my friends if you do what I command* (14); *This is my command: love each other* (17). They do not sit in isolation within the Gospel but echo other such language, perhaps most famously the foot-washing scene in John 13 and its closing words 'A new command I give you: love one another. As I have loved you, so you must love one another.'[18]

There is a paradox at work here, one that feels profoundly counterintuitive for us contemporary Westerners who prize liberty, equality, and free choice as prerequisites for authentic love to exist. Disciples are no longer slaves but friends, yet that relationship takes the form of faithful *submission* to authoritative commands. This new status also seems to be *dependent* on obedience (14). To abide in Jesus does not mean 'some inert mystical fusion with him, but of [disciples] "following," "serving," and "obeying" him as the Son "obeys" the Father'.[19] Disciples are loved by Jesus, yet that love is clearly *conditional* on following orders (9–10) and on their loving one another (12, 17).

What is going on here? At the heart of the paradox is how modern love is understood as incompatible with certain ideas that Jesus

[18] John 13:34. See also John 14:15, 21.
[19] Furnish, *Love Command*, p. 145.

seems to have no problem whatsoever making intrinsic to love. Four words capture this tension: *authority, inequality, obedience* and *conditionality*. Throughout the Gospel and particularly in the farewell discourse, Jesus assumes an *authority* unparalleled in Judaism. Jesus is the eternal *Logos* who has become flesh (1:1, 14). There is therefore a profound 'ontological *inequality*' between the Son and his disciples. It is not by accident that the Gospel reaches its climax with Thomas's cry of worship, 'My Lord and my God!',[20] and John's concluding purpose statement that his Gospel is 'written that you may believe that Jesus is the Messiah, the Son of God, and that by believing you may have life in his name'.[21] As Richard Bauckham puts it, 'the relationship of Jesus the Son to his Father is integral to the definition of who the one true God is'.[22]

It is because of who Jesus is that the only appropriate response for his disciples is *obedience* to his commands. Yet the wonder of our text is that this is not obedience inspired by fear of a tyrannical deity, but out of love and friendship with the 'crucified God' who freely gives his life for his friends. Keener is helpful here:

> Friendship means not freedom to disobey but an intimate relationship that continues to recognize distinctions in authority . . . By obeying, [disciples] continue to make themselves more open recipients of God's love, 'abiding' and persevering in ever deeper intimacy with God.[23]

Yet love is also the *condition* for remaining in Jesus. Both remaining in Jesus and being his friends are dependent on obedience to his commands (10a, 14), and keeping Jesus' commands means loving one another (12).[24] Therefore, without love for one another disciples will not remain in Jesus' love. We need to beware of being conformed to the thinking of the world about love at this point. One of the great unquestionable beliefs of our modern age is that true love is unconditional[25] and that God's love is no different. At the risk of sounding heretical, this is at best a half-truth. At worst, it leads to an unbiblical lack of concern about the necessity of a transformed life for someone who claims to be a follower of Jesus. This can be

[20] John 20:28.
[21] John 20:31.
[22] Richard Bauckham, 'Monotheism and Christology in the Gospel of John', in Richard N. Longenecker (ed.), *Contours of Christology in the New Testament* (Grand Rapids: Eerdmans, 2005), pp. 148–166; see p. 165.
[23] Keener, *John*, p. 1015.
[24] Such language is also pervasive in 1–3 John. E.g. 1 John 2:3, 5; 5:3. The latter reads, 'In fact, this is love for God: to keep his commands . . .'.
[25] See the introduction to this book for more discussion.

conscious (God will forgive me for what I am about to do because he loves me) or unconscious (what I do does not really matter since God's love is so overwhelming in comparison). Divine love is *unconditioned* (it does not depend on any prior quality), but not *unconditional* (it does demand a reciprocal response). Jesus' commands in John 15:9–17 could not be clearer – disciples are already friends, but the quality of their relationship with him depends on obedience. This raises at least two questions we will deal with in turn.

(i) Can God's love be withdrawn?
This question brings us right into the heart of differences between Calvinists and Arminians and whether Christians can 'lose' their salvation.[26] Obviously this is an old and complex theological debate that we are not going to resolve here! But some brief comments are worth making in relation to the message of love. One is that this sort of abstract theological question about a theoretical possibility of 'What will God do if I do X?' is foreign to the thought of the New Testament. The real question there is 'What is the will of God?' This is Jesus' main concern in John 15. He wants the disciples to love one another as he has loved them. The metaphors of the vine in verses 1–8, living water (4:10), the bread of life (6:35) and 'I am the resurrection and the life'[27] are all making a simple point: Jesus himself is the source of eternal life. Not to be 'in' him is not to have life. In this sense, to try to press the metaphor of the vine as talking about the destiny of individual branches is to ask questions that the text is simply not addressing.

This said, however, we must not downplay the force of Jesus' teaching here. In John 15, as elsewhere in the Gospels, in Paul and other authors of the New Testament there is never a hint that 'faith and works' can be separated. In John, to believe[28] and abide in Jesus is to live a fruitful life of love. One cannot exist without the other. Just as a disciple experiences the Father's love in and through the Son (9), so she will love her fellow disciples (12, 17). The disciple who keeps Jesus' commands is the disciple who loves Jesus.[29] Gary Burge puts it this way: the disciples' appointment to bear fruit 'is

---

[26] I put 'lose' in inverted commas because words tend to be loaded with significance in this debate. An Arminian would likely replace 'lose' with 'throw away'. In other words, it is not an accidental misplacement of faith but deliberate conscious apostasy that results in losing salvation. A Calvinist might say that someone who does this was never a Christian in the first place since salvation cannot be lost.

[27] John 11:25.

[28] What it means to 'believe' (*pisteuō*) in Jesus is a central focus of John's Gospel.

[29] See John 14:21, 23–24.

not a mechanical productivity of fruit. The disciple steps into a relationship of love with both Jesus (15:9) and the Father (15:10), out of which a transformed life, a fruit bearing life, will flow.'[30] In this sense, love is the fruit of remaining in Jesus (15:8). Love for others is therefore an indispensable sign of being loved by God and loving God. Therefore Jesus' commands for his disciples to love one another must not be read as implicitly to suggest that our love is an optional supplement to God's prior love for us. No! Rather, love is an essential sign of being in relationship with God, who in himself exists in love: Father, Son and Spirit.[31]

(ii) What does it mean to love as Jesus has loved us?

A second searching question now needs to be addressed: What does it mean for disciples to love one another as Jesus has loved them (12b)? The answer is at once obvious and very difficult. The nub of Jesus' unique challenge is not so much the call to love one another (which is intrinsic to Old Testament faith), but *the standard of love entailed by loving as he loves*. We have already discussed how this takes the form of laying down his life for his friends. Those who follow the Messiah are therefore commanded to do likewise (15:13–14). Jesus has already given his disciples a memorable (and shocking to Peter at least) picture of what self-giving love looks like in practice through his enacted parable of foot-washing (13:1–17).[32] Its application is straightforward: 'Now that I, your Lord and Teacher, have washed your feet, you also should wash one another's feet. I have set you an example that you should do as I have done for you.'[33] Being a disciple is to accept a call to sacrificial love of others. That such a call is costly is captured by Peter's enthusiastic but tragically naive promise 'Lord, why can't I follow you now? I will lay down my life for you'[34] and Jesus' devastating reply (13:38). John's repeated emphasis on interdiscipleship love is set within a context of communal tensions.[35] Then, just as now, to *understand* Jesus' command to lay down our lives for others is much easier than *doing* it in practice. As Francis Moloney says, '*Words* about love can come easily enough; *lives* that demonstrate love are harder to come by.'[36] But Jesus' teaching is uncompromising: loving one another is

[30] Gary M. Burge, *John*, NIVAC (Grand Rapids: Zondervan, 2000), p. 418.

[31] John 14:15 captures this dynamic of love between Father, Son and Spirit.

[32] See 13:1 for how John emphasizes how the foot-washing is a demonstration of love.

[33] John 13:14–15.

[34] John 13:37.

[35] For more discussion of these tensions see chapter 7 on 1 John.

[36] Francis J. Moloney, *Love in the Gospel of John: An Exegetical, Theological and Literary Study* (Grand Rapids: Baker Academic, 2012), p. 210. Emphasis original.

the only duty laid out as a commandment for believers in the entire Gospel of John (13:34; 15:12).[37] It is here that 'the rubber hits the road' in terms of authentic *Christian* community.

4. Concluding applications: love from the 'inside out'

It is time to draw the three threads of love within these verses together. Some see John's theology of love as narrow, representing a 'shift from a love that is actively concerned about all the others now to a love that is primarily directed towards the inner circle of a particular Christian church'.[38] While John's focus is internal, this downplays the structure of love within the Gospel. Love in John works from the 'inside out'. As we have seen, it begins with the Father's love for the Son. Out of love for the world, the Father sends the Son so that all who believe in him may have eternal life. In love the Son obeys the Father and gives his life for his disciples, who now have the status of beloved friends. That transforming experience embraces them within the relationship of love and unity that already exists between Father and Son and demands that they be one with each other. Love for one another is a natural outgrowth (fruit) of being loved by Jesus and the defining mark of being a disciple. Such loving communities are to show God's love to the world. The 'inside-to-out' movement is what love is all about – it cannot be kept to itself: 'By this everyone will know that you are my disciples, if you love one another.'[39]

Let us focus on the 'inside' aspect for a moment and then the 'outside'. As part of writing this book – in an admittedly unscientific ad hoc survey! – I asked Christians about their experience of the love of God. While some spoke with joy about the subject, these were in the minority. Many did not believe that they are worthy of being loved by God. Some said they knew the theory but were not sure God's love was real. Probably the majority said they were simply too busy to think much about it – the subtext being that love is somehow a secondary 'bonus' to the real business of getting things done. Duty and work, it seems, trump love. So an important question to ask is, 'Where am I in this spectrum of experience?' If we realize that there is something missing, we can do something about it. These verses proclaim that God exists in a relationship of love, in himself and with his people. His love is extravagant and immeasurable. It is unconditioned on who we are or what we have done. It surpasses

[37] Keener, *John*, p. 924.
[38] Werner G. Jeanrond, *A Theology of Love* (London: T&T Clark, 2010), p. 37.
[39] John 13:35.

any other form of love imaginable. It gives Christians a new status as friends of God himself. These are glorious truths that we need to reflect upon, believe and take deep into our minds and hearts. Why not take time to study this passage, praise God, rejoice, be thankful, pray, write and sing with others in church of the love of God and what it means to you to be loved by God himself?

Now let us turn to the 'outer' other-focused dimension of love in John 15. An individual experience of love in John is not an end in itself. It is in and through radical communities of love that God's love is to be made known in the world.[40] Now this all sounds wonderful, but the profound challenge here is the non-negotiable and indiscriminate nature of Jesus' command to love one another. It is relatively easy to love people like ourselves, but loving as Jesus loves means loving and serving fellow believers even when they let us down. This is where Christian love is far more demanding and difficult than that which walks away from challenging people and situations. I have been a Christian long enough to have no illusions about how toxic relationships are not the preserve of 'the world'. Personality conflict, narcissism, pride, misunderstanding, bad teaching, criticism, thoughtlessness, unforgiveness, blame, misuse of authority, manipulation and bitterness are common within any group of people working together, including Christian organizations and churches. Frequently, division follows with people on both sides feeling justified that the other was at fault. In the light of John 15:9–17 such an outcome is a disaster and needs to be seen as such. However, division is often swept under the carpet and not talked about, or a church split is even presented as a 'growth opportunity'! You and I can take responsibility only for ourselves in such a situation of conflict. If we take Jesus' words seriously, it will mean first reflecting honestly *on our own part* in relational failure and 'owning' our own sin. Second, it may well mean repenting of our actions and attitudes. A third step requires the courage to take the initiative to seek forgiveness and reconciliation from those we may have wronged. It is only through such difficult and costly love that the God-given unity of the church will be maintained.[41]

It is to such inside-out love that Jesus calls you and me. And it is perhaps only through such authentic communities that our Western world, with its insatiable thirst for love amid transient relationships, loneliness and encroaching technological isolation, can taste and see God's love embodied. This is a breathtaking and humbling calling

[40] The 'world' (*kosmos*) in John is always a very negative term for that which opposes the good work of God.
[41] I am not talking here of dangerous or mentally or physically abusive situations that someone needs to escape for his or her own well-being.

in which the quality of relationships within the church take centre stage. They witness to the joyful reality of God's friendship-love expressed through the Son's laying down of his life at the cross and invite others into that transforming experience.

Part 4
The church as a community of love

1 Corinthians 12:31 – 13:13
14. The searing searchlight of love

1. A modern reading of 1 Corinthians 13

Paul's 'hymn to love'[1] is one of the most celebrated passages in the New Testament, if not the entire Bible. Its simple beauty graces innumerable weddings each year, often regardless of the religious beliefs of the couple in question. Such popularity is understandable. After all, do not the apostle's words capture love's universal appeal and attractive power? Who can possibly resist such a poetic description of love as *the* essential ingredient of a flourishing life (1–3), combined with a compelling portrait of what love looks like in practice (4–7)? Such love is, *in itself*, eternal and embodies the highest form of human experience (8–13). Love is therefore to be revelled in and pursued as that which gives our lives significance beyond ourselves. It elevates us to a higher plane of existence amid all the messiness of life and somehow lives on after our death.[2] Love, in this reading of 1 Corinthians 13, becomes a type of eschatological hope which is why it is also often read at funerals.[3] In death what survives of us is love. So understood, it becomes a redemptive force, liberating us from lower-order ambitions, temporary failures and apparently meaningless tragedies to give us a glorious picture of an eternally significant life.

This modern reading of Paul reflects what Simon May calls the 'divinisation of human love'.[4] Human love, in a sense, becomes a

---

[1] A term used by Kenneth E. Bailey, *Paul Through Mediterranean Eyes: Cultural Studies in 1 Corinthians* (London: SPCK, 2011), pp. 349–385.

[2] For further discussion of the shape of contemporary love see the introduction.

[3] Perhaps most famously by Prime Minister Tony Blair in an emotional performance at the funeral of Princess Diana in Westminster Abbey in 1997, <www.youtube.com/watch?v=NsZKQkVED_I>, accessed 4 June 2018.

[4] Simon May, *Love: A History* (London: Yale University Press, 2011), p. 5.

'religion'. The absence of the word 'God' from verses 1–13 reinforces this tendency: God disappears and love is worshipped in his place.

Yet to read 1 Corinthians 13 as an inspirational meditation on the abstract idea of love is to rip it out of its context within Paul's first letter to the Corinthian church. Far from being a warm and comforting text, verses 1–13 are more like a searing searchlight, their pure white rays relentlessly exposing the Corinthians' (and our) failures to love. This is why I have found this chapter to be the most difficult chapter in this book to write. No one likes to have dark hidden areas of their life laid bare. Paul's eloquent words are indeed inspiring, but they simultaneously cut like a scalpel through our often shrivelled, petty and self-centred love lives. Paul pens these words in the context of a church riven by division, sexual immorality, false theology and misplaced pride around their practice of spiritual gifts; particularly tongues. Given this background, 1–13 is not so much a hymn in praise of love per se as a call for followers of Jesus to embrace the difficult discipline of love. Such love is a long way from sentimentalism; as we will see, it requires humility and costly choices to walk in *the most excellent way* (12:31).

2. Love gone missing (13:1–3)

In the military AWOL means to be 'absent without leave' – a soldier is not where he is meant to be when duty calls. The penalties can be severe because the entire purpose of being in an army is to be under command and ready to go into action whenever required. If AWOL, the soldier has effectively negated *everything* he has been trained for. In verses 1–3 Paul describes a Christian life where love has 'gone AWOL'. The apostle's basic assumption is clear: *love is the essential mark of being a Christian*, without it *anything* a believer says or does is of *no value at all*. Without love the entire 'point' of being a Christian is negated. Neither is it that love is the 'solution' to Corinthian factionalism, nor is he comparing the superior way of love to an inferior pursuit of gifts: his point is that even good gifts are worthless without love. As Gordon Fee comments, it is not 'love versus gifts' but 'love as the essential context for gifts' (and indeed all Christian behaviour).[5]

Six examples of 'love gone AWOL' are given within three verses, each verse forming a distinct point in the apostle's argument. The examples link to what most impresses the Corinthians, Paul's rhetoric intentionally challenging their priorities and behaviour. His

[5] Gordon Fee, *The First Epistle to the Corinthians*, NICNT (Grand Rapids: Eerdmans, 1987), p. 625.

words should do the same for us today. The apostle's switch to the first person singular is significant. He is including himself in his words of warning. *No one, no matter how gifted, is exempt from the necessity of love.*

a. Without love I am meaningless noise (1)

Paul's first example focuses on speech; specifically the gift of tongues: *If I speak in the tongues of men or of angels.* Speech is a major theme within the letter, impressive rhetoric an indicator of wisdom within a Greek context. Earlier Paul acknowledges he did not meet their high expectations with his lack of eloquent, persuasive and wise words (2:1–4). The Corinthians also valued tongues as the most desirable gift of the Spirit. A likely interpretation is therefore to see *tongues of men* as referring to impressive human speech and tongues of *angels* talking of Spirit-inspired tongues. The Corinthians are satisfied that they were performing well in both[6] and Paul's aim is to puncture their misplaced confidence. Paul can thank God that 'I speak in tongues more than all of you,'[7] but even such Spirit-inspired speech is mere clamour if not accompanied by love. What exactly the image *a resounding gong or a clanging cymbal* (1) refers to has generated quite a few creative theories,[8] but it is probably best to take it simply as a reference to loud, meaningless noise. Imagine music you do not like, in a language you do not know, turned up to full volume! To paraphrase Macbeth, Paul's point can be put in almost existential terms: 'Without love I am full of sound and fury, signifying nothing.' To connect this sobering word of warning to our world, its focus should give pause to all who prize impressive speech. However many compliments received about life-changing preaching, however many devoted followers on Twitter, however many books sold or articles written, however popular a blog, however much students hang on our every word, however persuasive our evangelism, however many apologetic debates won, and however many fans rhapsodize about our poetry – all is just mere babble without love. Love's searing searchlight probes all

---

[6] Fee thinks it more likely that Paul is just describing speaking in tongues in two different ways. Ibid., p. 630.

[7] 1 Cor. 14:18.

[8] Prior sees a link to Corinthian Greek mystery-cult worship. David Prior, *The Message of 1 Corinthians*, 2nd edn (Leicester: Inter-Varsity Press, 1993), p. 227. Bailey 'hears' the hammering of soft brass in the market, *Paul*, pp. 360–361; and, after reviewing several other theories, Garland concludes that Paul's verbs suggest 'a clamorous noise' and that those who speak in tongues without love are 'no more than a bunch of loud clangers', David E. Garland, *1 Corinthians*, BECNT (Grand Rapids: Baker Academic, 2003), pp. 611–613.

Christians to reflect not only on what we say, but whether love shapes the words coming from our lips, pens and keyboards.

b. Without love I am nothing (2)

Three more examples of 'love gone AWOL' appear in verse 2, all concerning spiritual gifting. As with verse 1, the hyperbolic argument is structured along the lines of *even if I have extraordinary capacity X and have not love, I am negated*. If equating spiritual status with the presence of tongues is one mistake, linking it to the presence of potent gifts of the Spirit like prophecy, knowledge and faith is another.[9] Prophecy for Paul is to be valued most highly since it builds up the whole community (14:1–25). Knowledge and faith are very much Corinthian temptations.[10] One is an extraordinary ability to 'understand' (*eidō*) *all mysteries and all knowledge* (*gnōsis*). *Gnōsis* was a prized Corinthian possession (1:5; 8:1). Another is *a faith that can move mountains*, referring to a special gift of faith (12:9) that has powerful consequences.[11] The image goes back to Jesus (Matt. 17:20; 21:21; Mark 11:22). In other words, Paul is inviting the Corinthians to imagine a scenario where their spiritual ambitions are fulfilled beyond their wildest dreams. Note the threefold repetition: *all* mysteries, *all* knowledge, *all* faith.[12] The image is of someone who is given a revelation of hidden mysteries enabling her to know the very mind of God. No fuller experience of the *charismata* is possible to conceive. All this makes Paul's conclusion all the more stunning: without love *I am nothing*. This is a stronger personal negation than in verse 1. Even a Christian's knowledge and personal experience of God's power is meaningless without love. In other words, 'Spiritual gifts minus love equals zero.'[13] Paul is not writing in terms of modern psychology, but his *I am nothing* penetrates deep into issues of personal identity. In effect, he is saying that love alone is the path to being.

c. Without love, I gain nothing (3)

Paul adds a third rung to his ladder of examples, that of extreme self-denial. Illustration five, *If I give all I possess to the poor,*

[9] Paul lists all three of these gifts in 12:8–10 as examples of the diversity of the gifts of the Spirit beyond an unhelpful narrow focus on tongues.

[10] The Corinthian error was to think that they had 'arrived' in terms of tongues, wisdom and knowledge. Fee, *Corinthians*, p. 630.

[11] Ibid., p. 593.

[12] The NIV translators chose to drop the third 'all' linked to 'faith'.

[13] Garland, *1 Corinthians*, p. 614.

literally has a sense of feeding others (*psōmizō*, 'to feed' or 'dole out'). A concern for the poor permeates Paul's thinking (e.g. Gal. 2:10) and had a profound impact on his ministry. Often overlooked is the financial cost he bore in becoming an apostle to the Gentiles.[14] A rift between rich and poor was one of the many serious problems within the Corinthian church and Paul had earlier exercised every tool at his disposal (theological argument, judgment, apostolic authority) to change their divisive behaviour around the Lord's Supper (11:17–34). At the close of the letter he urges the Corinthians to give to their brothers and sisters in Jerusalem in keeping with their income (1 Cor. 16:1–2). Here he gives them an exaggerated picture of extreme Christian giving: *If I give all I possess to the poor*. Nothing is held back in meeting the needs of others. The image brings to mind two contrasting stories in Mark: Jesus' encounter with the rich young man who could not bring himself to give in this way (Mark 10:17–31) and the poor widow who did. Her gift of two copper coins prompted this response from Jesus:

> Calling his disciples to him, Jesus said, 'Truly I tell you, this poor widow has put more into the treasury than all the others. They all gave out of their wealth; but she, out of her poverty, put in everything – all she had to live on.'[15]

But Paul's teaching adds a troubling caveat to Jesus' positive assessment of the widow. Imagine if she gave out of some selfish ulterior motive (perhaps wanting to outdo her poor neighbour's single copper coin!), then even her costly sacrifice would gain her *nothing*. The same goes for giving today. Evidence is hard to assess, but let us suppose that many committed Christians give away about 10% of their income. This is probably a generous estimate, but the exact figure is not crucial. In comparison, someone giving away all they possess becomes a radical act of almost unimaginable generosity. Yet Paul says that even such giving has *no* spiritual value if not done out of love. This is a hard teaching! Its extreme edge only dramatizes the apostle's point: while Christianity cannot be reduced to love, such is its importance that even extraordinarily sacrificial behaviour is worthless without it.

Paul's argument becomes even more demanding in his sixth and final example: *If I . . . give over my body to hardship that I may*

---

[14] A point that Bruce Longenecker makes in *Remember the Poor: Paul, Poverty and the Greco-Roman World* (Grand Rapids: Eerdmans, 2010).
[15] Mark 12:43–44.

boast, but do not have love, I gain nothing. There is considerable debate about a textual variant here and whether *that I may boast* should be translated along the lines of 'to be burned'. Both are possible, with *that I may boast* the most likely.[16] To 'boast' in Paul often has a positive sense of confidence before God's future judgment in the light of faithful service beyond the call of duty (e.g. 1 Cor. 1:29–31; 9:15–16; cf. Rom. 5:2–3; 2 Cor. 1:14). But Paul's point is clear, however the word is translated. To give his body physically to hardship is the costliest and most personal form of self-giving there is. In doing so he is following the example of his crucified Lord. Elsewhere Paul talks about such suffering as a privilege (Phil. 1:30) and, of course, his life did end in arrest, trial, deportation to Rome and eventual execution. But even such ultimate self-sacrifice, if not done in love, would have gained him *nothing*. Love is the defining mark of authentic Christianity.

Discussion of these opening three verses has already brought us a long way from modern warm sentimentalism about the all-embracing redemptive power of love. But what is love? What does it look like in practice? These are the questions to which Paul now turns.

3. Love in action: fifteen descriptions (13:4–7)

a. Love as a choice

In the theological college where I work guest speakers are regularly invited to speak to students and staff. One such visit was by a psychotherapist, who addressed the issue of conflict. She outlined the broad dynamics of two opposing responses to hurt caused by injustice or the harmful actions of another, summarized in Figure 2.[17]

There is much we could discuss here, but the main point is how the 'movement towards hate' or the 'movement towards love' is a *choice*. We cannot control what others do, but we can take responsibility for how we respond when hurt. This is much easier said than done. 'Hurt' can range from a bruised ego to damage done by systematic sexual or physical abuse. The diagram is neither suggesting that deep injustice and pain are resolved by adherence

---

[16] Bailey, *Paul*, p. 363; Leon Morris, *Testaments of Love: A Study of Love in the Bible* (Grand Rapids: Eerdmans, 1981), p. 244; Fee, *Corinthians*, p. 634. Contra Garland, *1 Corinthians*, pp. 614–615.

[17] With thanks to Joanie Reilly for the ideas represented in this diagram. Used with permission.

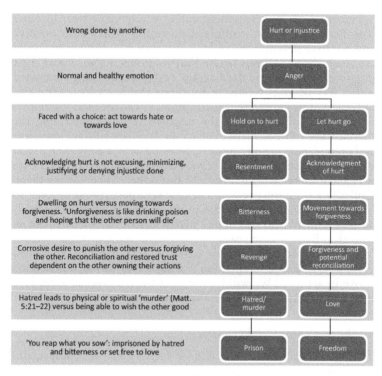

Figure 2: The choices of love

to some neat formula, nor does it minimize pain caused or how forgiveness is often a long and difficult journey. But it does capture a critical truth about love – it is *a choice worked out within all the messy realities of human relationships.* The 'movement towards hate' chooses to dwell negatively on the past and results in a life dominated by past injustice. We end up imprisoned and isolated, consumed by bitterness and a desire for revenge. In contrast, a 'movement towards love' acknowledges the full depth of the injustice done, but then acts to 'let it go', refusing to let the past dictate the future. This is essentially what forgiveness is: an act of the will that releases the *forgiver* from the negative control of what the other has done. It may or may not result in reconciliation; that depends on the other person and therefore cannot be guaranteed. Forgiveness sets us free from the past, and enables us to look beyond our own histories of injustice to the needs and struggles of others.

I mention this modern understanding of a choice between love and hate because of how strongly it correlates with Paul's positive and negative descriptions of love in verses 4–7. Fifteen examples are given, seven positives (split into two groups 4a, 6b–7) and eight negatives (4b–6a). As in the diagram, two paths are being contrasted – the 'way of love' versus its antithesis that leads to resentment, bitterness, division and self-justification. Given the mess the church is in, it is hard not to see the negative verbs as describing the Corinthians' self-destructive behaviour. It is they who are impatient and unkind, envying one another, boasting in themselves and proud of their own achievements. They are divided, insisting on their own way and even rejoicing in evil (5:1). But rather than condemn them, Paul offers an alternative vision of God's purpose for his people – to live in love. Another important point of correlation is how love is an action. In all fifteen examples love is described by a *verb*, not an adjective. Each is in the present continuous tense giving a sense of 'actions and attitudes which have become habitual, ingrained gradually by constant repetition'.[18] This is why this section is titled 'Love in action'.[19] We will look first at the positives of what love looks like in practice and then the negatives.

b. The way of love: eight positives

The opening couplet, *Love is patient, love is kind* (4a), encapsulates two aspects of love's response to others' actions, one passive and one active. Patience has been well described as 'long-tempered' – as opposed to being defensive or easily provoked.[20] It does not rush to retaliation, but exercises self-control in trying circumstances – whether suffering (Rom. 12:12; Col. 1:11) or the hurtful actions of others. It describes someone with the capacity to endure injustice, refusing to react and thus be controlled by others. Overall, the image is of putting aside 'my rights' for the long-term good of the other. *Love is kind* (*chrēsteuetai*) is better translated as 'love shows kindness'. It has an active sense of showing compassionate concern for someone else's well-being. A kind person is able not only to empathize with the struggles of others but comes alongside to lighten their load. It suggests a thoughtful, caring person who takes time to help others.

---

[18] Prior, *1 Corinthians*, pp. 229–230.
[19] Many English translations give the impression that the universal nature of love is being described 'timelessly' (e.g. *love is patient, love is kind*). Anthony C. Thiselton, *The First Epistle to the Corinthians*, NIGTC (Grand Rapids: Eerdmans, 2000), p. 1046.
[20] Morris, *Testaments of Love*, pp. 244–245.

While not explicit, these descriptions of 'love in action' describe God's own actions and attitudes that I have been unpacking in much of this book. In Exodus 34:6 it is the Lord who is a 'compassionate and gracious God, slow to anger, abounding in love and faithfulness, maintaining love to thousands, and forgiving wickedness, rebellion and sin'. In Hosea God is the lover who patiently and generously woos back his unfaithful bride. In Romans God's love is demonstrated by Christ's dying for us (5:6–8), an act of kindness intended to lead to repentance and restoration (Rom. 2:4; 11:22). In Ephesians it is out of his great love that God shows mercy and grace, giving believers a eschatological hope based on his 'kindness' (*chrēstotēs*) to us in Christ Jesus (2:4–7). The calling for the Corinthians is to show the sort of patient and kind love to one another as God has shown to them. The calling for us today is no different.

The next positive, love *rejoices with the truth* (6b), comes after a series of negative descriptions of what love is not. It sits in contrast to *Love does not delight in evil* (6a, discussed below). The sense is that love 'joyfully celebrates' or 'acclaims' truth.[21] This sounds lovely but what does it mean? Thiselton is particularly insightful here. In context 'truth' does not so much refer to doctrine as to relationship. It delights in a good report of others rather than taking satisfaction in their failure. But more than this, love has no desire to use 'truth' as a tool of self-interest. If postmodernism has taught us anything, it is a healthy scepticism around how 'truth-claims' can mask power interests of the self and of organizations. But love has no such hidden agenda: it is genuinely disinterested in the self and disengaged from a quest for power. This sets love free to seek truth honestly without concern for its impact on ourselves. Practically this means that 'love does not use manipulative devices and subtexts to protect itself from truth or the truth. It is honest and open, not defensive, for it has placed the good of the other above the good of the self.'[22]

Such love exposes our mixed motivations and selfish agendas, of which we may hardly even be aware. For example, in Christian ministry there is huge temptation, and often good reason, to hide the truth rather than rejoice in it. Pastors, churches and organizations have vested interests in presenting an image of success, growth and dynamism to an outside world of friends, peers, funders, supporters and book-buyers. The more powerful a denomination, the 'bigger' the ministry or the 'higher' the status of a famous pastor, the more money and power is at stake and all the more reason to suppress

---

[21] Thiselton, *First Epistle*, p. 1055.
[22] Ibid., p. 1056.

unwelcome truth. Sadly we have seen this process played out again and again right across the Christian church.[23] Paul gets to the heart of such manipulative public relations – it is not only unreal; it is unloving, putting the self before the interests of others.

The next four positives are each accompanied by an *all things* (*panta*). In the famous words of the AV, love 'Beareth all things, believeth all things, hopeth all things, endureth all things'; and in the NIVUK, *It always protects, always trusts, always hopes, always perseveres* (7). While perfectly fair translations they have two potential weaknesses. First, they tend to mask Paul's joyful exultation in the *unlimited nature of love*. For this reason Thiselton prefers the REB rendering 'There is nothing love cannot face; there is no limit to its faith, its hope, its endurance.'[24] Second, the traditional translation can open up a fundamental misunderstanding about the nature of Christian love. Is Paul saying that love is little more than a fatalistic determination to keep going in the face of injustices and hardship with little concern to change the world? This echoes Nietzsche's critique of Christianity as world-denying: embracing selflessness, humility and weakness instead of life itself.[25] Similarly Michel Foucault saw Christianity as conformist 'docility' and Freud as wishful thinking that 'believes all things' in order to 'endure all things'.[26] But such caricatures of life-denying 'docility' are a long way from Paul's theology of love! Together these four verbs picture love as a limitless, creative and transforming force empowering Christians to face whatever obstacles they encounter.[27] The first and fourth (*stegō*, 'to endure'; and *hypomenō*, 'to persevere') differ little and likely relate to present circumstances. The second and third (*pisteuō*, 'to trust'; and *elpizō*, 'to hope') probably look to the future and reappear in verses 8–13 in tandem with love. Overall, such present- and future-orientated love faces life head-on with strength and hope. Nothing compares to or can overcome it.

---

[23] As I write this in late 2018, two examples of failing to 'rejoice in the truth' are in the news. One is a Church of England independent review of a 2010 internal investigation into how the Church handled allegations of abuse. The review concluded that negative aspects were downplayed in order to protect the reputational character of the Church. A second is how the leadership team and entire elder board of the globally significant Willow Creek Community Church in Chicago resigned after systematically dismissing allegations by a number of women against Bill Hybels when he was Senior Pastor.

[24] Thiselton, *First Epistle*, p. 1056. His own translation is 'Love never tires of support, never loses faith, never exhausts hope, never gives up.'

[25] May, *Love: A History*, p. 192.

[26] Thiselton, *First Epistle*, p. 1057.

[27] Ibid.

Along these lines, one of the most famous sermons of recent years was that of Michael Curry, Presiding Bishop of the Episcopal Church USA, at the Royal Wedding of Prince Harry and Meghan Markle in May 2018. It was listened to by about two billion people and produced a huge media reaction and much debate among Christians globally.[28] His theme was 'There's power in love', but it was not a divinization of human love. His overall message was that love originates in the triune God, not us, and that love is therefore the most potent force in the world. 'Love is the only way. There's power in love. Don't underestimate it. Don't even oversentimentalize it. There's power, there's power in love.' In this Curry is at one with Paul.

c. The way of 'unlove': seven negatives

Sandwiched between the two sets of positives, are eight negative descriptions of what love does not do. It often is easier to define something by what it is not and that is what Paul does here. We know 'unlove' when we see it. Sadly much of Paul's list describes the Corinthians all too well. Just as it should have been a 'reality check' for them, so we should read this list self-critically today. How do these verbs describe my life and my church? What can I do if some 'hit too close to home'?

Few things are less attractive and more destructive to community than *envy* (4). The Greek (*zēloi*) has a sense of 'being filled' or 'burning' with envy. In 3:3 Paul has told the Corinthians that the fact that 'there is jealousy and quarrelling among you' is a sign of their lack of the Spirit (3:1–3). Envy is obsessed with the self rather than happily helping others to flourish. In terms of the body imagery of chapter 12, rather than working cooperatively for the good of the whole, envy works competitively, destroying the unity of the body in the process.

Love *does not boast* (4) continues a critique of self-centredness. The verb suggests ingrained self-promotion, trying to impress others, perhaps particularly by outstanding oratory that was so important to the Corinthians.[29] Motives for boasting can flow from insecurity (we need affirmation and respect to feel good about ourselves) or from narcissism (we genuinely think we are superior to others). Whatever its source, boasting only seeks admiration for the self, not others. Paul's teaching gains fresh significance in a culture shaped by social media, where we present carefully edited

---

[28] See <www.youtube.com/watch?v=5gonlKodrmk>, accessed 21 June 2018.
[29] Garland, *1 Corinthians*, p. 618.

215

'best versions' of ourselves to the world, competing for attention alongside innumerable others. Boasting is also a particular temptation for leaders, whose role naturally puts them in front of a listening (and captive!) audience.

The verb *proud* (*physioō*, 'to inflate', 4) could be translated 'arrogant' or 'puffed up'. It is unique to Paul and six of its seven occurrences in the NT are located in 1 Corinthians. He has already talked of the incompatibility of love and being puffed up with knowledge (8:1). Reiterating his point here suggests that arrogance is a particularly Corinthian trait. They thought they had 'arrived' in terms of wisdom (3:18), gifts (tongues), knowledge (8:2) and being spiritual (14:37). Arrogance has nothing to learn from others: 'I' have all the answers. It pictures people so wrapped up in themselves that they have no capacity to listen to, learn from or bless others. Such arrogance behaves as it likes, so it is unsurprising that the same verb is used by Paul to describe the Corinthians' pride about a man sleeping with his father's wife (5:2).

That love does *not dishonour others* (5) suggests some sort of shameful or improper behaviour. There has been quite a bit of such activity going on in Corinthians. The same verb describes a man acting improperly towards his betrothed (7:36), but similar behaviour shows itself in women somehow acting in a dishonourable way in worship (11:5) and the rich dishonouring the poor at the Lord's Supper (11:22). We could paraphrase Paul here to say, 'You are free to act as you wish, but do not use your freedom to disrespect others. Such behaviour is unloving.' As Westerners living within a culture of unrestrained individual freedom where 'anything goes' (within the law) we need to listen carefully to Paul's words. Love cannot be legislated for, but it can be evaluated. What impact does acting out our 'rights' and desires have on others? Does it respect or disrespect those around us?

The next example, love is *not self-seeking* (5; lit. *love does not seek its own*), encapsulates Paul's overriding point within his series of eight negatives. Love, by definition, does not pursue its own advantage. Earlier Paul tells the Corinthians that 'no one should seek their own good, but the good of others.'[30] The self is not the centre of love's universe. Love finds its fulfilment in seeking the benefit of others. This is the paradox at the heart of following a crucified Messiah, who gave himself freely for others. It is by losing our lives that we find them. It is in service that we are set free. It is the last who will be first and the first who will be last. It is in dying that we find life. However, this paradox can easily be caricatured (as it was

[30] 1 Cor. 10:24.

by Nietzsche, discussed earlier) or misunderstood. In terms of psychological health, 'not self-seeking' means neither having low self-esteem nor desperately trying to please others and destroying yourself in the process. The latter is well described in Cloud and Townsend's influential book *Boundaries*.[31] In it they describe Sherrie, a harried and unhappy people-pleaser. Motivated by fear, unable to say 'No' and thinking that Christian discipleship means suppressing her own humanity, she finds herself isolated, confused, guilty and depressed. The rest of the book unpacks how healthy boundaries enable us to love others well, not by controlling or 'rescuing' them, but by living in the freedom of knowing what we can and should take responsibility for and where we should not try to do this. It closes by revisiting Sherrie, her life transformed by setting healthy boundaries with her husband, son and work colleagues. Such boundary setting is not 'self-seeking' but the opposite: it puts selfish hidden agendas aside and pursues honesty, transparency and accountability in relationships for the good of all involved.

That love is *not easily angered* (5) is the opposite side of the coin to *Love is patient* (4). It is not constantly irritable, rushing to judgment. Such actions are another form of selfishness: being unwilling to think the best of another and setting the self up as 'judge, jury and executioner'.

The seventh example, love *keeps no record of wrongs* (5), combines memory and mathematics. The image is of 'leaving the past in the past', not continually dredging up someone's previous mistakes in the present. Taking us back to the diagram, rather than be controlled by the past, the way of love lets it go. This is another way of talking about forgiveness. Acknowledgment of past injustices is important, but love does not store up resentments, nurse grievances and dream of revenge. Rather it chooses the path of freedom and opens the door to reconciliation. This is what Miroslav Volf calls 'remembering rightly'. He writes:

> Being in God frees our lives from the tyranny the unalterable past exercises with the iron fist of time's irreversibility. God does not take away our past; God gives it back to us – fragments gathered, stories reconfigured, selves truly redeemed, people forever reconciled.[32]

[31] Henry Cloud and John Townsend, *Boundaries: When to Say Yes, When to Say No, to Take Control of Your Life* (Grand Rapids: Zondervan, 1992).

[32] Miroslav Volf, *The End of Memory: Remembering Rightly in a Violent World* (Grand Rapids: Eerdmans, 2006), p. 202. Cited in Bailey, *Paul*, p. 173.

This combination of not counting wrongs and of reconciliation reoccurs in 2 Corinthians 5:19a: 'God was reconciling the world to himself in Christ, not counting people's sins against them'. If this is the way God acts towards us, how much more are the Corinthians, and Christians today, to take the risk of showing such love to those who wrong us?

The final thing that love does not do is *delight in evil* (6a). This statement sits in contrast to 6b (love *rejoices with the truth*). Again the immediate context in Corinth is probably in mind. They have been rejoicing in various kinds of wrongdoing. Such an attitude is closely linked to arrogance, where 'I' am beyond anyone's judgment. But in a wider sense love takes no pleasure in injustice, violence, the failures of others or other forms of evil. Today, in a globalized digital world, multiple evils are ours to access at the touch of a few keys. No amount of regulation can stop us exploring dark thrills they may offer if we wish to do so. *Paul's 'defence' against evil is love.* Throughout church history many Christians have found such a 'strategy' naive at best and foolish at worst. They have 'protected' the church against evil through fear, threats, punishment and even tyranny. Not only do such responses not work; they betray a lack of faith in the transforming power of love. Authentic Christian love will delight in all that pleases God, turning from evil and rejoicing in truth.

4. The supremacy of love (13:8–13)

As we have seen, embedded within Paul's magnificent description of 'love in action' has been an implicit critique of Corinthian attitudes and practices. He now explicitly addresses their distorted priorities by comparing love and the charismata. *Love never fails* (8) links verses 1–7 with 8–13. Not only is love limitless (7); it is indestructible, eternal and without end (8).[33] The switch of emphasis to what is temporary or permanent is key to interpreting these verses. The Corinthians were prizing gifts like prophecy, tongues and knowledge. Yet such charismata are but temporary gifts given for a season. In the future *prophecies . . . will cease, tongues . . . will be stilled* and *knowledge . . . will pass away* (8). Verses 9 and 10 simply reiterate this point for knowledge and prophecy. In verses 11–12 it is as if the charismata are gifts given to a child, who when grown has no more use for childish things. The gifts are good in themselves, but are now no longer necessary. *When I became a man*

---

[33] The Greek is literally 'love never falls', most likely meaning never ceases to exist or is never overcome.

(11) is an eschatological image. In other words, it is a picture of the new creation come, when God will 'be all in all'[34] – a theme in chapter 15 in which the apostle rejoices at length. In the present *we see only a reflection as in a mirror*, but in the new creation *we shall see face to face* (12). The person in 'view' here is God: now we know him indirectly, just as the bronze mirrors of Corinthian craftsmen partially captured someone's reflection. In the future we will know him *fully* even as we are now *fully known* (12).

Verse 13 brings Paul's argument of 8–12 to a close, and forms the climax to the whole chapter: *And now these three remain: faith, hope and love. But the greatest of these is love.* Yet the meaning of this statement is not immediately obvious. Why the sudden appearance of faith and hope in a comparison of love with prophecy, knowledge and tongues? And how is love greater than faith and hope?[35] The answer lies in *And now these three remain.* It is in the present (*now*) that *faith, hope* and *love* 'exist' (*menō*, 'to remain' or 'abide'). Together they capture what it is to be a Christian in the present age, awaiting the new creation. 'Faith' (*pistis*) is in Christ, in whom there is forgiveness and new life. Christians are people of 'hope' (*elpsis*), journeying to a future destination where they will see God 'face to face'. Love is the *greatest* of the three because it alone exists within *both* the present and the future ages. Faith and hope will 'end' when the new creation comes; love continues for ever.[36]

From this perspective, Paul's argument is compelling. The gifts are not, as the Corinthians tended to assume, the definitive sign of spiritual 'progress' in the present. They are for now, but love is for now *and* the future: it is without limit in its power and duration. Everything else, gifts, and even faith and hope, pale in comparison. What will the new creation be like? Paul's answer lies in verses 4–7 – a place of dynamic, creative and joyful other-centred relationships, where love flourishes to its fullest unimaginable extent and where all that opposes it (4b–6a) has ceased to exist. A place, in other words, of love unleashed from all that holds it back in the present age – envy, boasting, pride, dishonour, self-seeking, unreasonable anger, unforgiveness and a perverse delight in evil – and where God's people are finally perfected to love as he loves. Love in the 'here and

---

[34] 1 Cor. 15:28.

[35] There are various interpretations of this verse. For detailed discussion see Thiselton, *First Epistle*, pp. 1071–1074; and Roy E. Ciampa and Brian S. Rosner, *The First Letter to the Corinthians*, PNTC (Nottingham: Apollos, 2010), pp. 651–666.

[36] Ben Witherington, *Conflict and Community in Corinth: A Socio-Rhetorical Commentary on 1 and 2 Corinthians* (Grand Rapids: Eerdmans, 1995), p. 272. An alternative view is to see faith, hope and love as all continuing, although perfected, into the new creation. Love is the greatest in that it reflects the character of God himself. Ciampa and Rosner, *First Letter*, p. 665.

now' is therefore neither merely a human ideal to be pursued in the absence of God, nor is it only how 'nicely' Christians should behave. Rather it is a foretaste of our destiny in the presence of the God of love himself. This is why, in the next verse, Paul exhorts the Corinthians to 'pursue love',[37] and later encourages them to 'Do everything in love.'[38]

He would surely tell us to do the same today.

[37] 1 Cor. 14:1, ESVUK.
[38] 1 Cor. 16:14.

Galatians 5:1–23
15. The liberating power of love

1. Galatians as a letter of pastoral concern

What is church for? Why be part of a community at all? What is the overall goal of Christian ministry? James Thompson, a Pauline scholar, has studied Paul's answers to these sorts of questions. He concludes that, for Paul, '*ministry is participation in God's work of transforming the community until it is "blameless" at the coming of Christ*'.[1] Galatians is an excellent example of Paul's pastoral priorities in action, and love plays a pivotal role in his argument. As an apostle who planted the church, he has brought them, by God's grace in Christ, into the story of God's people. Formerly pagans, they had experienced the power of the Spirit (3:2–5), justification by faith (3:7–9) and adoption as God's children (3:26–29; 4:4–7). But these experiences were the *beginning*, not the end, of new life in Christ. Paul's long-term vision is to see them shaped into the image of their Lord, Jesus Christ.[2] We see this concern emerging repeatedly throughout a letter full of passionate concern for their spiritual well-being and anger at those who are leading them into confusion.[3]

Love is mentioned five times and each occurrence is significant (2:20; 5:6; 5:13 [twice]; 5:22). In 2:20 love is described in terms of 'the Son of God, who loved me and gave himself for me'. Love is a major theme in chapter 5, as the apostle switches to moral exhortation in the final section of his letter. These texts will be the focus

---

[1] James W. Thompson, *Pastoral Ministry According to Paul: A Biblical Vision* (Grand Rapids: Baker Academic, 2006), pp. 19–20. Emphasis original.
[2] Ibid., pp. 24–28.
[3] Paul's anger at the Judaizers, who are persuading the Galatians to submit themselves to the law, is fierce and unrelenting: see 4:17; 5:8, 10, 12; 6:12–13.

of my exposition in the rest of this chapter.[4] Each example refers to the Christlike self-giving love of 2:20 that the Galatians are to display for one another. Therefore love in Galatians should be understood within Paul's broader desire to see transformation into the likeness of Christ among his converts. Nowhere is this clearer than 4:19–20: 'My dear children, for whom I am again in the pains of childbirth until Christ is formed in you, how I wish I could be with you now and change my tone, because I am perplexed about you!'

The precise content of the false teaching and Paul's response to it has become an area of vast debate that I can only touch on here.[5] A key point to note is that Paul the pastor is perplexed not only about the Galatians being misled by a false gospel (1:6) but about how that teaching is negatively impacting their spiritual progress. They had 'begun' with faith in Christ and the gift of the Spirit (3:1–2), but now Paul asks in exasperation, 'Are you so foolish? After beginning by means of the Spirit, are you now trying to finish by means of the flesh [*sarx*]?'[6]

Paul's concern for the Galatians' welfare is not theoretical. His language is uncompromising: their future is under real threat (4:11; 5:1, 4). He asks, in exasperation, *You were running a good race. Who cut in on you to keep you from obeying the truth?* (5:7). The 'race' that the Galatians are now running is an ugly one, marked by slavery (4:9–10, 21–31; 5:1), broken relationships with Paul (4:16) and with one another: *If you bite and devour each other, watch out or you will be destroyed by each other* (5:15). At the heart of their regression is misplaced trust. Rather than continuing with faith and the Spirit, they have foolishly been persuaded that obedience to the Mosaic law – including circumcision and all the markers of Jewish identity – is the means of Christian moral progress. Paul is incandescent. The law had a good purpose within salvation history (3:15 – 4:7), but it cannot empower for moral transformation: 'For if a law had been given that could impart life, then righteousness would certainly have come by the law.'[7] Only faith in Christ and the associated gift of the Spirit leads to life. To trust in the law is to choose a way antithetical to the Spirit – the way of the flesh (5:13a).

The flesh in this sense is like a spiritual realm, opposed to the Spirit. Formerly they were enslaved to those 'who by nature are

---

[4] For exegesis and exposition of the letter as a whole see e.g. John R. W. Stott, *The Message of Galatians*, BST (Leicester: Inter-Varsity Press, 1992).

[5] I refer to the New Perspective on Paul. A helpful introduction is James K. Beilby and Paul R. Eddy (eds.), *Justification: Five Views* (London: SPCK, 2012).

[6] Gal. 3:3.

[7] Gal. 3:21.

not gods'.[8] The irony is that now, despite the fact that they 'are known by God', they are 'turning back to those weak and miserable forces'.[9] Paul asks rhetorically, 'Do you wish to be enslaved by them all over again?'[10] Their retreat to slavery is therefore not a return to the worship of false gods, but to an embrace of the Mosaic law. This is a stunning thing for a Jewish teacher to say! Paul is equating Gentile worship of false gods with obedience to the law in that *both* represent a life of slavery. But slavery to what? The answer seems to be to the 'weak and miserable forces' of 4:9, also called the 'elemental spiritual forces [*stoicheia*] of the world'.[11] It is difficult to be sure of the precise nature of these cosmic forces since Paul does not define them,[12] but the more important point is what they do. Bruce Longenecker captures their destructive impact:

> Powerful yet strangely indeterminate forces, the *stoicheia* play a role in creating precisely the opposite of what we see in the loving unification of distinct groups of people 'in Christ' (Gal. 3:26–29); that is, the *stoicheia* are those forces that make use of differentiation and distinction in order to promote relationships of discord within (what Paul calls) 'this present evil age' (1:4).[13]

A life under the law, slavery and the flesh has loveless 'results': *The acts of the flesh are obvious: sexual immorality, impurity and debauchery; idolatry and witchcraft; hatred, discord, jealousy, fits of rage, selfish ambition, dissensions, factions and envy; drunkenness, orgies, and the like. I warn you, as I did before, that those who live like this will not inherit the kingdom of God* (5:19–21). If the Galatians pursue this course, only judgment awaits: 'Do not be deceived: God cannot be mocked. A man reaps what he sows. Whoever sows to please their flesh, from the flesh will reap destruction'.[14] In complete contrast, a life of freedom in the Spirit results in good fruit (5:22–23). In other words, it cements across

---

[8] Gal. 4:8.

[9] Gal. 4:9.

[10] Ibid.

[11] Gal. 4:3.

[12] In Paul there are various powers at work opposed to God, including Satan, sin and death. In Ephesians Christians struggle against rulers, authorities, powers of this dark world and spiritual forces of evil (6:12).

[13] Bruce W. Longenecker, 'Faith, Works and Worship: Torah Observance in Paul's Theological Perspective', in Scot McKnight and Joe Modica (eds.), *The Apostle Paul and the Christian Life: Missional and Ecclesial Implications of the New Perspective* (Grand Rapids: Baker, 2016), pp. 47–70; see p. 59.

[14] Gal. 6:7–8a.

deep religious, social and gender differences the unity that already exists for those who are one 'in Christ' through faith.[15]

To summarize, what we have in Galatians is a spiritual battle being played out between two forces: life in the Spirit versus life in the flesh. The arena is the moral character of the community. This means that love, for Paul, is far more than the quality of a relationship between two individuals: it is the principal evidence that the Spirit is at work, enabling transformation into the image of Jesus. We will now turn to specific texts to examine the importance of love in more detail. Three themes emerge and will be discussed in turn: the primacy of love, love and freedom, and the Spirit and love.

2. The only thing that counts (5:6)

One of the most theologically significant verses in the entire letter is 5:6, *For in Christ Jesus neither circumcision nor uncircumcision has any value. The only thing that counts is faith expressing itself through love*.[16] It makes a scandalous claim. Circumcision was the mark of covenant membership; to dismiss it as spiritually irrelevant is to negate the unique status of Israel as God's chosen people, identified by their obedience to the Torah. In Christ such boundaries are transcended. Uncircumcised Gentiles now share the same way 'in' to God's covenant promises to Abraham: faith in Christ:

> So in Christ Jesus you are all children of God through faith, for all of you who were baptized into Christ have clothed yourselves with Christ. There is neither Jew nor Gentile, neither slave nor free, nor is there male and female, for you are all one in Christ Jesus. If you belong to Christ, then you are Abraham's seed, and heirs according to the promise.[17]

We should not miss the significance of Paul's Christocentric language. Believers, of whatever hue, are 'in Christ', are 'all children of God', are 'baptized into Christ', 'clothed' with Christ and 'belong to Christ'. This is language of spiritual union and new identity. 'In Christ' they become one with each other. Old identities do not cease to exist but are drastically relativized. Their primary identity is now

---

[15] Gal. 3:28.

[16] Scot McKnight notes that 5:5–6 is a masterful summary of the entire letter. 'Here we find (1) faith (2) the Spirit of God (3) justification (4) future hope (5) love, and (6) the polemics against circumcision.' *Galatians*, NIVAC (Grand Rapids: Zondervan, 1995), p. 251.

[17] Gal. 3:26–29.

as brothers and sisters, children of God, whom, through the Spirit, they can now call 'Abba, Father.'[18]

Within this new identity *faith expressing itself through love* has pride of place as *The only thing that counts* (5.6). This is an extraordinary statement. Oliver O'Donovan puts it this way:

> Love is not *a* principle on which we may act, one principle among others; it is not the most *important* of all principles; it is not even the *sole* principle. It is the architectonic structure of all principles, unifying the moral law and giving it coherence.[19]

Love for one another overcomes the deepest divisions of the ancient world; it is the defining characteristic of the new covenant community. The literal sense of 5:6 is *faith working* [*energeō*, 'to be at work in'] *through love*. This sort of 'power' language reminds us that the underlying issue in Galatians is two conflicting sources of power.[20] It is faith that leads to a dynamic relationship with God, empowered by his Spirit and evidenced in a life of practical action for the good of others. 'For Paul, the corporate life of the Christian community is to be the social embodiment of the self-giving and loving Christ.'[21]

We need to pause here to consider some implications of what has just been said. Love is no peripheral doctrine, as if faith is 'core' and love is a hoped-for, but secondary, outcome. Faith in Christ expresses itself in love: 'the phrase is almost a single concept, faith-through-love, love-energized-faith'.[22] Christians acting in unloving ways (like the Galatians) nullifies the whole purpose of being in Christ. If this is the case, we dare not overlook unloving attitudes and actions within our own lives and within the church. Paul certainly did not. In effect, they represent a spiritual crisis that he diagnosed and addressed with heartfelt passion. A form of self-righteousness (trusting in our own works rather than faith) has been seen, by many Christians for a very long time, as the 'big danger' being addressed in Galatians. But I wonder if understandable, but intense, concentration on doctrinal issues in the letter has, ironically,

---

[18] Gal. 4:6.

[19] Oliver O'Donovan, 'Flesh and Spirit', in Mark W. Elliott, Scott J. Hafemann, N. T. Wright and John Frederick (eds.), *Galatians and Christian Theology: Justification, the Gospel, and Ethics in Paul's Letter* (Grand Rapids: Baker Academic, 2014), pp. 271–284; see p. 280. Emphases original.

[20] James D. G. Dunn, *The Epistle to the Galatians*, BNTC (London: A&C Black, 1993), p. 271.

[21] Bruce W. Longenecker, *The Triumph of Abraham's God: The Transformation of Identity in Galatians* (Edinburgh: T&T Clark, 1998), p. 72.

[22] Dunn, *Galatians*, p. 272.

tended to marginalize Paul's main pastoral reason for writing. After all, you cannot get much more important than *the only thing that counts*. Ever since Luther, Galatians has been a touchstone for defending the wonderful doctrine of justification by faith. But should not the apostle's zeal for moral transformation mean that we are just as scandalized by the oxymoron of 'loveless Christianity' as by threats to an apostolic understanding of justification? Should it not mean that we are inspired to address, for example, bitterness, unforgiveness, divisiveness, selfishness with every fibre of our beings for the glory of God and the integrity of the gospel?

3. Freed to love (5:1, 13–14)

Our second theme is how love, in Galatians, is intimately connected to freedom. An initial point to make is that Christian freedom has multiple facets and is broader than love, but love is an indispensable component of Christian freedom. Verses 5:1 and 13–14 are significant. In the first, Paul proclaims freedom to be the goal of Christ's saving work (5:1a). Freedom is then explicitly linked with love and fulfilment of the law in verses 13–14. In these verses we see how Christian freedom is both freedom *from* and freedom *for*. Let us discuss each in turn.

a. Freedom from

The double emphasis on freedom in verse 1 is important: *It is for freedom that Christ has set us free.* Paul is not saying when or how they were set free but rejoices in the fact of freedom for all Christians. His point is well caught in the words of the African-American spiritual quoted by Martin Luther King in his 'I Have a Dream' speech: 'Free at last, free at last. I thank God I'm free at last!' Given such wonderful liberation, the apostle pleads for them to stand firm in it. In this sense, Paul's theology of freedom has a polemical edge; it is forged in contrast to 'freely' choosing once again to being *burdened . . . by a yoke of slavery* (5:1b). The yoke was a familiar image for the law among Jewish teachers.[23] Such a decision is, for Paul, incomprehensible foolishness with sobering consequences (5:2–4). In verse 13a freedom is from a different, but closely related, form of bondage – the flesh: *You, my brothers and sisters, were called to be free. But do not use your freedom to indulge the flesh.* I have

---

[23] Although seeing it as a 'yoke of slavery' would have been anathema within Judaism. For Paul, Gentile believers would effectively be enslaved if compelled to submit to the Mosaic law.

discussed earlier what the flesh represents; save to say here that it is the antithesis of a life of freedom in the Spirit. For the Galatians it took the form of taking on the Mosaic law. But it could be any attempt to live without the Spirit. To choose the flesh is to go backwards spiritually, resulting in a powerless life of sin, disunity and alienation from Christ.

There is a paradox at work here. It is very likely that the Judaizers were telling the Galatians that a life without the Mosaic law would lead to self-indulgence and a loss of holiness.[24] Paul's gospel of Christian freedom appeared to be too ill-defined. Yet the irony is that if the Galatians choose to use their God-given freedom to live to the law/flesh, their freedom destroys itself. They end up living as if they were never liberated in the first place.

As Christians in the West today we face a dizzying amount of personal freedom within a culture that proclaims daily that the route to happiness is to indulge the self. And the tragic reality is that, out of a mixture of all sorts of motives, we can, and do, freely make such enslaving decisions. They take innumerable forms – whether around sex, power, money, status, a need for acceptance, or other drivers. Such freedom can be scary. So an opposite response, reacting against the spectre of untrammelled liberation, is legalism. We define, legislate for and circumscribe detailed rules for 'spiritual' behaviour in an attempt to control the enslaving desires of the self.

In contrast to both these approaches, the 'genius' of God's gospel revealed to Paul (1:11–12) is that it represents a completely different 'answer' to the 'problem' of human freedom and how to live a virtuous life. Freedom is combined with community, slavery, love and the Spirit in a unique, unexpected and inspiring way. It is to this positive vision of what freedom is *for* that we now turn.

b. Freedom for

Quite simply, for the Christian, freedom is not to be used for the self, but for the good of others. Unpacking this a bit more, the surprising paradox of the Christian life is that liberation is found in obedience to Paul's command to *serve one another humbly in love* (13b). *Serve* (*douleuō*) is literally 'be a slave'. Love is the all-embracing context in which service to one another is enacted. The NRSVA captures the sense well: *but through love become slaves to one another*. The irony is palpable here. Throughout the letter Paul has warned *against* the danger of slavery; now he *commands* it. The 'another' reminds us of the intrinsically corporate nature of love.

[24] McKnight, *Galatians*, pp. 262–265.

Love needs others to exist! By definition it is other-focused. But more than this, a diverse community like that in Galatians (3:28) will survive only if held together by love. Without love it has no future (5:15). This pastoral concern is why love is front and centre in Paul's exhortations in chapter 5. In contrast to their destructive misuse of freedom, 'Love is the service *of* freedom *to* freedom, an engagement in community for the sake of each other.'[25]

In verse 14 the apostle introduces a decisive – and radical – argument in support of the primacy of love and that simultaneously relativizes the importance of the law that had so captured the Galatians' imagination: *For the entire law is fulfilled in keeping this one command: 'Love your neighbour as yourself'* (14). This is both a historical and a theological claim. Within the history of salvation, love is the climactic fulfilment of the law.[26] In other words, the Galatians need to recognize that the law was never an end in itself. As the law itself says, God's 'goal' for his people is love. But, while the law had a useful function, it had no power to 'produce' love. As I will discuss in a moment, now that Christ and the age of the Spirit have come, the temporary function of the law has come to an end – love 'originates' elsewhere. Love of neighbour, not Torah obedience (like circumcision) 'keeps' the law. This is why Paul can later say 'Carry each other's burdens, and in this way you will fulfil the law of Christ.'[27] In effect, the law is redefined as finding its true purpose in relationships of love and mutual service within a community of believers 'whose lives are being transformed by the Spirit in conformity to the character of Christ'.[28]

If Paul's glorious account of Christian freedom turned the Galatians' ideas of the Christian life upside down, it should do the same today for us, if for different reasons. Western culture has a narrative of freedom very different from that of Paul. While it cannot be reduced to one strand,[29] the story of the free individual is the thread that holds the storyline together. It is inseparable from the rise of modern capitalism, a force that now pervades pretty well every aspect of modern life. Daniel Bell has identified two (among others) key ways capitalism views human nature: 'the individual' and 'free to choose'. In terms of the former, we live in a culture that revolves

[25] O'Donovan, 'Flesh and Spirit', p. 279. Emphases original.

[26] The specific command of Lev. 19:18 is quoted. In this, Paul is echoing Jesus (see chapter 11). Paul's omission of the Shema (love for God) is likely due to his focus on the necessity of love for one another.

[27] Gal. 6:2.

[28] Longenecker, *Triumph of Abraham's God*, p. 83.

[29] Freedom can take individual, social, artistic, psychological and political forms. McKnight has a more detailed discussion of different facets of Western freedom than we have space for here. See *Galatians*, pp. 253–261.

around meeting the desires of the autonomous individual. As self-made beings, we are independent 'entrepreneurs of ourselves . . . in a sense we all become "small business owners," and the small business that we are about is the production of our self'.[30] Consequently, all we have is ours – our bodies, our successes, our possessions – and we are free to do with them as we wish. *We are under no one else's authority.* We 'neither owe nor properly expect anything from others beyond that to which each individual voluntarily commits'.[31] In regard to the latter, capitalist freedom fosters a world of endless choice, whether sexual, career, brands, travel, experiences or identity. *What* is chosen is not as significant as the *right* to choose unhindered from interference from others imposing their will on me. There is, therefore, *no meaning beyond individual freedom* as long as there is a market for that choice. It is freedom for freedom's sake.

A deeper conflict with Paul is hard to imagine. Christians are not sovereign individuals, but are responsible to others within a diverse community of faith. We are not our own gods, but belong to God. This world and all it offers is not the only thing that counts: faith expressing itself in love is what matters. We are not set free in order to live for ourselves, but to love one another as Jesus loved us. Freedom is not an end in itself: we are liberated in Christ so as to be conformed to his likeness. For Christians, to live according to capitalism's false values is to imitate the Galatians' retreat to 'weak and miserable forces'[32] that enslave rather than liberate.

Paul's words also speak right into contemporary church relationships. Basically, he tells the Galatians that love is all that can hold the church together; without it they will destroy one another (5:13–15). The same applies to any church today. I assume your church is much like mine, which is made up of a diverse range of people, many with little in common with one another. There are differences of personality, social standing, age, education, ethnicity, gender, marital status, wealth, employment status, national identity and so on. There is no reason for such people voluntarily to embrace the demands of community apart from their common faith in Christ. Without love any group like this will rip itself apart as individuals pursue their own agendas. Much church division can be dressed up as issues of theological principle, but more often it is a failure to submit our opinions to the difficult demands of listening to and working with others. In contrast, the types of actions characteristic

---

[30] Daniel M. Bell, *The Economy of Desire: Christianity and Capitalism in a Postmodern World* (Grand Rapids: Baker Academic, 2012), p. 96.

[31] Ibid., p. 97.

[32] Gal. 4:9.

of a healthy church are described in 6:1–5: gentle restoration (6:1), carrying one another's burdens (6:2), humility (6:3), lack of competition (6:4) and generous sharing (6:5). There are few things more beautiful than to be part of a community that is practising such practical love.

4. The Spirit, love and the passions (16–26)

The third theme of our text is the Spirit and love: 'Where does love come from? How do we change? How do we live a life pleasing to God?' Paul's urgent plea in Galatians is to convince them that it is only the Spirit, not the law or flesh, that empowers moral transformation in the believer.[33] Two verses talk about passions and desires: *So I say, live by the Spirit, and you will not gratify the desires* [epithymia, 'desire'] *of the flesh* (16); and *Those who belong to Christ Jesus have crucified the flesh with its passions* [pathēma, 'passion'] *and desires* (24). In the ancient world the passions were seen as obstacles to an ethical life, with Greeks turning to education and Jews to the Torah as the means to overcome their malign impact.[34] Given this context, the Judaizers have likely been teaching that the law is the means by which the passions can be overcome. So, for Paul to say that uncontrolled *desires of the flesh* (16) lead to destructive *acts of the flesh* (19–21) is not unexpected. What is revolutionary is his rejection of the Torah as a solution to the problem of the flesh and its desires. Such desires, for Paul, represent a deeper problem. Behind them lie 'self-centredness, self-interestedness, self-indulgence, self-aggrandisement' – in short, a 'demeanour of unhealthy self-referentiality' that 'stands in complete disparity with the self-giving love of Christ'.[35] The law cannot free people from themselves: 'all those who obey God in Christ can do so only because of divine empowerment enjoyed by all those who have been united to Christ by the Spirit'.[36] So Paul's answer to the question 'Where does love come from?' is 'The Spirit.' A consequence of living by the Spirit or keeping in step with the Spirit is *fruit* (22). It is no accident that first in the list of the Spirit's fruit is *love* (22). Its location almost certainly is due to its foundational character (5:6, 13) and its centrality in

---

[33] This theme is prominent elsewhere, particularly in Rom. 8:1–16.

[34] James W. Thompson, *Moral Formation According to Paul: The Context and Coherence of Pauline Ethics* (Grand Rapids: Baker Academic, 2011), pp. 136–141.

[35] Longenecker, *Triumph of Abraham's God*, p. 73.

[36] Timothy G. Gombis, 'Participation in the New Creation People of God in Christ by the Spirit', in Scot McKnight and Joe Modica (eds.), *The Apostle Paul and the Christian Life: Missional and Ecclesial Implications of the New Perspective* (Grand Rapids: Baker, 2016), pp. 103–124; see p. 124.

Paul's ethics (Rom. 13:8–10; 1 Cor. 13; Col. 3:12, 'And over all these virtues put on love, which binds them all together in perfect unity'). It is fruit of the Spirit, with love leading the way, that *alone* provides the solution to the problem of Galatian divisiveness:

> This quality of self-giving love seems, to Paul's mind, to be . . . an eschatological quality reproduced in the lives of those united with Christ by means of the Spirit of Christ. It is little wonder then, that it appears first in the list, since Paul considered it to be the fundamental characteristic of Christ's own life and imagined it to be the context out of which all other Spirit-generated character- istics arise.[37]

But how does this transformation work? What is the dynamic between the believer and the Spirit in which fruit, including love, can flourish? It seems that within the spiritual battle between flesh and Spirit those who belong to the new age have moral choices to make. Just as they are to choose freedom, not slavery (5:1), so Christians are to choose the Spirit, not the flesh (16, 24–26). This is not a form of do-it-yourself holiness: Paul's whole point is humanity is *incapable* of overcoming the flesh without divine help. But that help is now freely available. Paul's argument throughout verses 16–23 confidently presupposes that those in Christ can and should win the battle through the Spirit (16, 18, 23). The result is 'an astonishingly assured vision of the Christian life as freedom from sin, death and the flesh'.[38] As Western individualists we can all too easily assume this is our 'private war'. But this misses the overwhelmingly corporate and relational nature of the Christian life. As we have seen, the Spirit brings believers into a whole new set of relationships – both 'in Christ' and united to one another within a new family identity as children of God. The Christian journey is never solitary – we walk in the Spirit, encouraging each other along the way to have a faith that is working through love.

5. Conclusion: love as a 'weapon' within a cosmic battle

We began by asking what is the overall objective of pastoral ministry? What is church all about? What gives shape and purpose to the Christian life? Galatians provides rich answers with profound

---

[37] Longenecker, *Triumph of Abraham's God*, p. 71.

[38] Patrick Mitchel, 'The New Perspective and the Christian Life: *Solus Spiritus*', in Scot McKnight and Joe Modica (eds.), *The Apostle Paul and the Christian Life: Missional and Ecclesial Implications of the New Perspective* (Grand Rapids: Baker, 2016), p. 98.

implications for our lives today. It tells a story of liberation, open to anyone through faith in Christ. Justified, adopted and empowered by the Spirit, a Christian is equipped with her brothers and sisters to participate in a spiritual battle against destructive forces that seek to spoil God's good work of redeeming his world through Christ. At the heart of this battle is love (5:6). Paradoxically, within the new age of the Spirit, love is the prime 'weapon' by which the flesh, division, enslaving desires and cosmic powers opposed to God are overcome. Such love is a foretaste of God's future in the present. It is in self-giving love that we are set free from ourselves to become like our Lord Jesus Christ, fulfilling the purpose of the law in the process. Bruce Longenecker puts it succinctly:

> To us, the word love might sound like emotional sentimentality; bearing burdens might sound like a pastoral nicety; becoming slaves to one another might sound like a metaphorical platitude. For Paul, however, these were part of the arsenal in a cosmic battle against dysfunctional forces that collude to corrupt and corrode a world that God is reclaiming through Christ, to his praise and glory.[39]

If this is the case, then the *primary* goal of all pastoral ministry and church work should be to pray for, teach and model vibrant communities of love witnessing to the grace of God in Christ. We may even say that the final aim of all evangelism, preaching, mission, pastoral care and teaching is Christlike love. We dare not begin anywhere else. Love is the glue that holds the church together. Sacrificial love is costly and difficult, but is to be embraced in the light of eschatological hope: 'Let us not become weary in doing good, for at the proper time we will reap a harvest if we do not give up.'[40] While Christian love, if it is to be authentic, is primarily embodied within the church community, it is not confined there: 'Therefore, as we have opportunity, let us do good to all people, especially to those who belong to the family of believers.'[41] Love in this perspective is also the motive for Christian mission and social action in the world.

---

[39] Longenecker, 'Faith, Works and Worship', p. 62.
[40] Gal. 6:9.
[41] Gal. 6:10.

Ephesians 5:21–33
16. Subversive love: Christian marriage

To talk about marriage in the West today is to enter a minefield. Buried just under the cultural surface are numerous explosive questions. One, primarily among some Christians, is 'How does marriage work?' What 'roles' do the husband and wife have according to the Bible? Perhaps the most politically volatile in wider society is 'Who is marriage for?' One answer is 'Everybody, regardless of gender or sexual orientation.'[1] Another, quite different, reply is 'Why bother with marriage at all?' In the UK marriage is on the decline. Legalization of civil partnerships for heterosexual as well as homosexual couples has broadened choice for partners wishing to formalize their relationship. For those who do 'take the plunge', four in ten marriages end in divorce. It is a risky, expensive and outdated practice with patriarchal overtones that calls for hard-headed premarital agreements rather than naive protestations of love.[2]

Why begin here? Well, as we turn to one of the most significant texts about love and marriage in the New Testament, it is important to bear two things in mind. First, all theology is contextual. How 'the Bible speaks today' into contemporary debates about love

---

[1] As the century progresses, it is likely that marriage will be further widened to include other alternatives such as polyamorous relationships. E.g. Carrie Jenkins argues that love needs to be redefined to where 'the love of a polyamorous triad is seen as valuable as the love of a monogamous couple'. Why she limits her argument to a triad is unclear. Carrie Jenkins, 'How a Hackneyed Romantic Ideal Is Used to Stigmatise Polyamory', *AEON Magazine*, <www.aeon.co/ideas/how-a-hackneyed-romantic-ideal-is-used-to-stigmatise-polyamory>, accessed 12 October 2018.

[2] In this vein, journalist Sonia Sodha muses that 'Maybe it wouldn't be such a bad thing if, when someone got down on one knee, the next thing uttered wasn't "yes" or "no", but "what type of proposal are you making me?"' 'There's love, you'll say, but is there any real point in getting married these days?' *Guardian*, 6 October 2018, <www.theguardian.com/commentisfree/2018/oct/06/theres-love-youll-say-but-is-there-any-point-in-getting-married-these-days>, accessed 12 October 2018.

and marriage will sound quite different from how it did so when Ephesian Christians first read Paul's words within their Graeco-Roman culture. *To hear well what it says today, we will need to do the hard work of listening to what it meant then.* Second, modern controversies remind us that beliefs and practices around love, marriage and the family are inherently public and political. As we will see, they were even more so in Paul's day. Given this fact, the main argument of this chapter will be that the apostle's teaching on love and marriage in Ephesians 5 represents a *radically countercultural form of Christian discipleship*. If this is the case, then what such 'countercultural dissent' looks like for Christian love and marriage today is a question that also lies before us.

1. Context

a. Walking in love and not as the Gentiles walk

To appreciate fully Paul's teaching on love and marriage in Ephesians, verses 5:21–33 need to be read within their context within the overall flow of the epistle.[3] Believers have been 'included in Christ' and 'marked ... with a seal, the promised Holy Spirit'.[4] They now share in God's unlimited power through which Christ has been raised victorious (1:19–23). Formerly held captive by such powers (2:1–3), God, out of his 'great love' has made believers 'alive with Christ' and seated them 'in the heavenly realms in Christ Jesus'.[5] Astonishingly, this new status is available to Jewish and Gentile believers, who form a new humanity (2:15), a holy temple, 'a dwelling in which God lives by his Spirit'.[6]

Two key phrases in the letter are 'to walk' (*peripateō*) and 'in love' (*en agapē*),[7] which appear together at important junctures in Paul's argument in chapters 4–5. In 4:1–2 all the Ephesians are exhorted to 'walk in a manner worthy of the calling to which you have been called ... bearing with one another in love' (*en agapē*, ESVUK). Such a life stands in stark contradistinction to the surrounding Graeco-Roman culture (a theme particularly running through 4:14 – 5:14). Believers are to put off of their 'old self' and put on their 'new self'.[8] This involves no longer walking 'as the

---

[3] See chapter 9, where general background questions regarding Ephesians are discussed in more detail.
[4] Eph. 1:13.
[5] Eph. 2:4–6.
[6] Eph. 2:21–22.
[7] *En agapē* appears in 1:4; 3:17; 4:2, 15–16; 5:2.
[8] Eph. 4:22, 24.

Gentiles do'[9] in the futility of their minds, hardness of heart, impure living and subsequent separation from God (4:17–19). In contrast, believers are urged to 'walk in love [*en agapē*] as Christ loved [*ēgapēsen*] us and gave himself up for us, a fragrant offering and sacrifice to God'.[10] *This verse acts as a purpose statement for all the ethical commands that follow in 5:3 – 6:9.* Holy living (5:3–7), living as 'children of light' (5:8–14) and walking wisely (5:15 – 6:9) *are all illustrations of a way of life marked by love.* In other words, these are general commands for all believers as, filled by the Spirit (5:18), they model their lives on the self-giving love of Christ. To live this way is inevitably to come into conflict with the values, attitudes and ethics of the Graeco-Roman world. Nowhere is this more sharply apparent than in the final explanatory clause of what being filled with the Spirit looks like: *Submit to one another out of reverence for Christ* (5:21).[11] This is very probably why, immediately after stating this command, the apostle turns his attention to what such a radical calling looks like for believers within the day-to-day political and social world that they inhabit – that of the Graeco-Roman household.

b. Subverting the household code

Household codes appear elsewhere in the New Testament[12] and were familiar features of ethical discussion in the ancient world that was structured around themes of honour/shame, patronage and kinship.[13] The household was the basic unit of Roman life, giving structure to religious, social, political and economic beliefs.[14] As such it was more like a small business with various categories of people in hierarchical relationships associated with it. By law the

[9] Eph. 4:17, ESVUK.

[10] Eph. 5:2, ESVUK.

[11] Vv. 18–23 form one sentence in Greek, with a single subject ('You' – the Ephesians) and single verb in the form of an imperative ('be filled with the Spirit') followed by four present participial clauses in 19–23 describing what such filling looks like. The fourth clause concerns mutual submission out of reverence for Christ and instructions to wives to submit to their husbands.

[12] Household codes are also found in Col. 3:18 – 4:1; 1 Tim. 2:8–15; 6:1–10; Titus 2:1–10; 1 Peter 2:18 – 3:7.

[13] While uncertain, the most likely background for NT codes is the Hellenistic concept of household management, with which Paul would have been familiar. For an overview see Harold W. Hoehner, *Ephesians: An Exegetical Commentary* (Grand Rapids: Baker, 2002), pp. 720–729. For analysis of the Graeco-Roman world see David deSilva, *Honor, Patronage, Kinship & Purity: Unlocking New Testament Culture* (Downers Grove: IVP Academic, 2000).

[14] Timothy G. Gombis, 'A Radically New Humanity: The Function of the *Haustafel* in Ephesians', *JETS* 48 (2005), pp. 317–330; see p. 320.

man was the *paterfamilias*, the ruler of the household (patron). A woman would typically be married by eighteen, entering the household not out of love but primarily to bear children and maintain the family line, ideally through sons.[15] Husband and wife were not equal partners: he was the patron, she the inferior client. He had power, wealth, authority and honour; she received her identity, social standing and any property from him. He received honour from fulfilling public responsibilities of provider and patron. She was expected to reciprocate by being a mother of his offspring and returning to him respect, loyalty, obedience and chastity.[16] Slaves did hard work and had no legal rights at all: they were under the absolute rule of the *paterfamilias*. All of this is so far removed from our modern idea of a private residence for a nuclear family of autonomous individuals that we need great care not to read the text anachronistically.

The Ephesian household code has several distinct characteristics. An important point is how, at significant junctures, it departs from typical features of ancient codes:

1 As standard, instructions are given to three sets of pairs: wives–husbands, children–parents and slaves–masters.
2 However, in each case the 'weaker' or powerless person in the relationship is addressed first (e.g. wives, 22–24). This is unusual. Normally only those in positions of authority were addressed.[17] The 'weaker' partners were assumed simply to fulfil their proper function.
3 In each case wives, children and slaves are all assumed to have autonomy. While commanded to submit (wives, 22, 24) or obey (children, slaves), they are persuaded to do so by a theological argument. This is in stark contrast to Greek literature, where the 'lesser' partner was often denigrated.[18] Women, for example, were seen as inferior to men in every respect and slaves obviously required no persuasion to obey!
4 Things start to become seriously subversive when we consider the basis for submission. Wives are to submit to their husbands *as to the Lord* (22), with similar instructions to children (6:1) and slaves (6:5–8). To put this differently, a Christian wife is primarily responsible to Jesus, not to her husband. This is a significant

---

[15] Gordon Fee, 'The Cultural Context of Ephesians 5:18–6:9', *Priscilla Papers* 16.1 (winter 2002), pp. 3–8; see p. 3.
[16] Cynthia Long Westfall, *Paul and Gender: Reclaiming the Apostle's Vision for Men and Women in Christ* (Grand Rapids: Baker Academic, 2016), pp. 21–22.
[17] Hoehner, *Ephesians*, p. 724.
[18] Ibid., pp. 724–725.

relativization of the absolute power of the patron. It puts all six categories of people within the household code on a level footing. Their identity and role is no longer defined by the hierarchical assumptions of Graeco-Roman culture, but by their common identity as disciples of the Lord. There are strong parallels here to the radical social and political implications of Galatians 3:28: 'There is neither Jew nor Gentile, neither slave nor free, nor is there male and female, for you are all one in Christ Jesus.'

5 But the truly revolutionary aspect of Paul's household code emerges from what is said to the husband. While the 'dominant' partner in each pairing is given a theological basis for how they are to act in regard to the 'weaker' partner, husbands are clearly the apostle's main target. Four times as many words are addressed to the man as to the wife. In the other two relationships the emphasis is the reverse – twice as much is said to the 'weaker' partner. 'This in itself suggests that the crucial matter for Paul is with what Christ has done to the first relationship.'[19] We shall concentrate on the nature of that transformed relationship below because it is to the husband that Paul has most to say about love.

This all suggests that Paul is doing something new and unexpected with the household code. Just how radical his instructions to women and men are will become more apparent the closer we look.

2. Submission subverted

Verse 21 states, *Submit to one another out of reverence for Christ.* Submission is a socially and politically loaded term today. It tends to carry a sense of inferiority for the 'weaker' party and a potential abuse of power for the dominant party. This negative perception makes it difficult for us to appreciate how it was understood in Paul's day. The verb *hypotassō* literally means 'the ordering of something under something else' and when used in the passive voice (as it is here) it denotes a voluntary submission of one person to another.[20] This fits with the immediate context of submission being an act consistent with being filled with the Spirit. In the wider context such 'other-centred' mutual submission stands out against the cunning, craftiness, deceitful scheming, impurity and greed of the Gentiles (4:14–17). In contrast to such self-centred agendas mutual submission springs from a common 'fear' (*phobos*) or

---

[19] Fee, 'Cultural Context', p. 4.
[20] Frank Thielman, *Ephesians*, BECNT (Grand Rapids: Baker Academic, 2010), p. 372.

reverence for Christ. All believers are united in Christ and therefore share a common goal. Ephesians 4:15–16 describes this dynamic beautifully:

> Instead, speaking the truth in love [*en agapē*], we will grow to become in every respect the mature body of him who is the head, that is, Christ. From him the whole body, joined and held together by every supporting ligament, grows and builds itself up in love [*en agapē*], as each part does its work.

Submission is a profoundly *Christian* concept and forms a notable theme within the New Testament. It defines all relationships between Christians. 'Submission was so important for New Testament writers because it described the self-giving love, humility and willingness to die that are demanded of all Christians.'[21] Mutual submission is consistent with Paul's frequent use of 'one another' language throughout Ephesians. There is no hint of one 'side' being required to obey the other here: the sense is a proper ordering of relationships depending on the context in which people find themselves.

Thielman[22] notes how such a radical inversion of authority is consistent with Paul's teaching about himself as a slave to all (1 Cor. 9:19) and believers under his care ('serve one another humbly in love'[23]). To this should surely be added the teaching of Jesus himself. Christians belong to an 'upside-down kingdom' where 'the first shall be last and the last shall be first'.[24] They follow a crucified Lord who taught that 'whoever wants to be first must be your slave, just as the Son of Man did not come to be served but to serve, and give his life a ransom for many'.[25] To be a disciple of Jesus is to accept a call to sacrificial love and service of others. The motive for mutual submission is deep reverence for the Lord and a subsequent heartfelt desire to follow his example. This is why the theological basis for obedience given to every one of the six categories within the Ephesian household code is their allegiance to Christ. 'Within each pair of relationships mentioned there is, in fact, a third partner, Christ himself . . . His presence will encourage the household to relate in humility, service, patience, forgiveness and love to one another.'[26] This 'Christianizing' subversion of Graeco-Roman

---

[21] Klyne Snodgrass, *Ephesians*, NIVAC (Grand Rapids: Zondervan, 1996), p. 292.
[22] Thielman, *Ephesians*, p. 373.
[23] Gal. 5:13. See chapter 15.
[24] Matt. 20:16 and parallels.
[25] Matt. 20:25–28 and parallels.
[26] Derek Tidball and Dianne Tidball, *The Message of Women: Creation, Grace and Gender*, BST (Nottingham: Inter-Varsity Press, 2012), p. 239.

household codes that were predicated on hierarchical power relationships is truly revolutionary.

Two comments are needed before we move on. First, verse 21 and the wider theology of Christian submission just discussed, makes it clear that in verses 25–33 husbands are not somehow 'exempt' from submission. Submission is a Christian calling not just a wifely one! Attempts to 'drive a wedge' between verses 21 and 22 do not work.[27] As we noted earlier, verses 18–23 form one long uninterrupted sentence in Greek. Indeed verse 22 is so intricately connected to 21 that it does not even contain the verb to submit; it literally reads, *Wives, to your own husbands as to the Lord.* Another version of this approach is to argue that *Submit to one another* (21) means, in effect, 'let each of you be subordinate to the one he or she should be subordinate to'.[28] But the verse itself gives no hint that submission is so narrowly restricted. Verse 21 is significant *because it confronts Graeco-Roman assumptions around authority and submission.* Howard Marshall puts it this way:

> What Paul is doing, then, is to teach the need for a concern for one another's interest and for a mutual submission in the church which provides a new context for the one-sided submission that was expected within certain relationships at the time. He is doing something new, even startling, with the language here.[29]

Second, it is undeniable that the Ephesian household code calls wives to submit and children and slaves to obey – husbands, parents and masters are not commanded to do either. There is a clear connection, in other words, between submission and fulfilling appropriate roles within the authority structures of the time. The critical question for how 'the Bible speaks today' on this issue, then, becomes whether Paul intends to lay down timeless 'gender roles' within marriage. 'Complementarians' argue he does, seeing in Paul a softened form of hierarchy in that wives and husbands are equal in status but have different God-given gender-based 'roles', his that of 'headship' authority within the relationship, hers that of

---

[27] One example is in my now battered 1980 NIV edition that inserted, without justification, a heading 'Wives and Husbands' after verse 21, detaching it from what follows.

[28] Stephen B. Clark, *Men and Women in Christ: An Examination of the Roles of Men and Women in Light of Scripture and the Social Sciences* (Ann Arbor: Servant, 1980), p. 76, n. 4. Cited in Hoehner, *Ephesians*, p. 717.

[29] Howard Marshall, 'Mutual Love and Submission in Marriage: Colossians 3:18–19 and Ephesians 5:21–33', in R. W. Pierce, R. M. Groothuis and G. D. Fee (eds.), *Discovering Biblical Equality: Complementarity Without Hierarchy* (Downers Grove: InterVarsity Press; Leicester: Apollos, 2005), p. 197.

submission.[30] Such a reading is unconvincing exegetically: it is to read *into* the text something that is not there (eisegesis) rather than drawing meaning within the text out of it (exegesis). The discussion below will unpack how Paul engages with Graeco-Roman expectations around hierarchical gender roles but that is a very different thing from mandating those structures in perpetuity.[31] His real concern in our text is to instruct believers, by employing theological arguments, to be *authentic followers of Jesus in whatever social role they find themselves*. His focus is not on wives – that they are to submit would have been uncontroversial within the culture's patronage system – but on husbands. As we will see, what he says there dramatically challenges male patronage and power and redefines the status and value of his wife at the same time. It is therefore profoundly ironic that much traditional interpretation of this passage goes into great detail about male 'headship' and female submission;[32] yet Paul's priorities are elsewhere: to elevate the status of wives and radically redefine the power and authority of husbands within 'God's new society' of the church.[33]

3. The basis of submission: instructions to wives (22–24)

We come now to probably the most famous, and perhaps notorious, verses in Ephesians. The wife's submission is an integral aspect of Christian discipleship (*to the Lord*, 22; and *as the church submits to Christ*, 24). It is given voluntarily rather than coerced. Verse 24 makes clear that her submission encompasses *everything* – there is no area of life to which it does not apply. Yet, as discussed above, her submission cannot be detached from the previous verse commanding mutual submission. This immediately qualifies Graeco-Roman notions of female submission. Paul's language also carefully avoids using the verb 'to obey' (*hypakouō*) that is applied to children

---

[30] E.g. Clinton E. Arnold proposes and applies a complementarian reading of Eph. 5:21–33. *Ephesians*, ZECNT (Grand Rapids: Zondervan, 2010), pp. 363–410. Tim Keller probably represents a typical moderate 'complementarian' description of marriage. Tim Keller with Kathy Keller, *The Meaning of Marriage: Facing the Complexities of Commitment with the Wisdom of God* (London: Hodder & Stoughton; New York: Dutton, 2011).

[31] Craig S. Keener, *Paul, Women and Wives: Marriage and Women's Ministry in the Letters of Paul* (Peabody: Hendrickson, 1992), p. 211.

[32] Probably the best traditional interpretation of this passage is John R. W. Stott, *The Message of Ephesians: God's New Society*, BST (Leicester: Inter-Varsity Press, 1984), pp. 213–236. It is telling, however, that his conclusion consists of five points addressed to *wives* as to why they should submit rather than addressing husbands (Paul's priority).

[33] This is John Stott's term for the church as described in Ephesians.

and slaves.[34] There is no hint that her submission means obedience or that she is in some sort of inferior role. Rather, she is freely and humbly to serve her husband in love.

It is the *theological basis* for her submission that is the greatest cause of debate today. *For the husband is the head of the wife as Christ is the head of the church, his body, of which he is the Saviour* (23). Snodgrass comments that this is 'surely one of the most abused and debated texts in the New Testament'.[35] Certainly it is a fact that for much of church history Christian interpreters of selected biblical texts like this one[36] have concluded that women *are* inferior to men. Chrysostom declares that men have 'pre-eminence in every way'.[37] Aquinas asserts that woman is naturally subject to man because 'in man the discretion of reason predominates'.[38] Commenting on Genesis, Luther concludes that the female sex is inferior to the male sex; because of Eve's deception and sin, all women are now subject to men.[39] Because the woman was created second, Calvin argues that women should be subject to men, who have 'superior authority and status'.[40] Charles Hodge proclaims that man's supremacy enables and entitles him to command: 'This superiority of the man ... is taught in Scripture, founded in nature and proved by all experience.'[41]

Most modern scholars within the evangelical world, whether 'complementarian' or 'egalitarian', are keen to distance themselves from such past voices.[42] Much, of course, depends on what is meant by the husband being *head [kephalē] of the wife* (23).[43] I do not have space here to replay what is a complex and long-running debate[44]

[34] 1 Peter 3:1–6 is the one example within NT household codes where the verbs 'to submit' and 'to obey' are linked.

[35] Snodgrass, *Ephesians*, p. 294.

[36] Gen. 1 – 3, 1 Cor. 11:3, 14:34–35, Eph. 5:23 and 1 Tim. 2:8–11 are probably the most influential in this respect.

[37] Chrysostom, *Homily 9 on 1 Timothy*. Cited in Kevin Giles, 'A Critique of the "Novel" Contemporary Interpretation of 1 Timothy 2:9–15 Given in the Book, *Women in the Church*. Part 1', *EvQ* 72.2 (2000), pp. 151–167.

[38] Aquinas, *Summa Theologica*, I, Q.92.

[39] Luther, *Commentary on Genesis*, Gen. 3:1. Cited in Giles, 'Critique', pp. 151–167.

[40] Calvin, 1 *Timothy* Commentary, p. 217. Cited in Giles, 'Critique', pp. 151–167.

[41] Charles Hodge, *Commentary on the Epistle to the Ephesians* (Grand Rapids: Banner of Truth, 1964), p. 312. Cited in Giles, 'A Critique', pp. 151–167.

[42] Modern 'complementarians' do not stand in continuity with church history here. It is a novel argument to say women are equal in status and gifting with men and yet selected leadership roles in church and family are open only to men.

[43] Christ is talked of as 'head' three times in Ephesians: 1:22; 4:15–16; 5:23.

[44] For a review of various views see A. F. Johnson, 'A Review of the Scholarly Debate on the Meaning of "Head" (*Kephalē*) in Paul's Writings', *ATJ* (2009), pp. 35–57. Anthony C. Thiselton also has an extensive discussion of *kephalē*, in *The First Epistle to the Corinthians*, NIGTC (Grand Rapids: Eerdmans, 2000), pp. 812–823.

except to offer a proposal for a way forward. Biblical images (like *kephalē*) 'work' through allusion and metaphor rather than precisely worded definitions. As such they can carry various meanings. There probably is some notion of authority connected to *kephalē*. Its use in closely related texts like 1:22 and Colossians 2:10 talks of the subjection of all things under Christ. Such an image suggests his authority over all other powers. However, 'head' can also communicate a sense of prominence in terms of honour and visibility, in keeping with the role of the *paterfamilias* in Graeco-Roman culture.[45] Others have proposed that 'source' or 'origin of life' captures how Paul uses 'head' here and elsewhere.[46] But the critical issue is *how* Paul intends the image of 'head' to function within his pastoral instructions. Therefore, *kephalē* should be interpreted primarily by its context within the letter.

Looking more closely, we see how 'head', like 'submission', is also being reimagined by Paul. A husband's 'headship' is to be modelled on *how* Christ acts as head of his body, the church. Where readers in the ancient world might have expected the sentence to end along the lines 'of which he is the ruler', it surprisingly closes with *of which he is the Saviour* (23). This link of *head* and *Saviour* defines 'headship'. Rather than power, honour, status and authority, normally associated with the patron, Christlike 'headship' is synonymous with sacrificial voluntary self-giving love for the good of others. Such 'headship' is primarily about other-focused relationship. It brings us back to 5:2 and how it shapes all that follows. 'The marital love between husbands and wives . . . further demonstrates what it means for the audience to "walk" as children beloved by God and Christ within the dynamic realm of being "in love" (5:1–2).'[47]

'Head', in this framework, is the one with authority and power (husband/Christ) acting in a way that fosters love with his body (wife/church). It is to read into the text, and to disrupt the focus of Paul's argument, to see her submission rooted in the 'order of creation' or the essential natures of masculinity and femininity. Verse 23 makes best sense within the context of the Graeco-Roman patronage system.[48] As it is from Christ, as 'head', that all benefits are experienced by the church, so it is in the husband–wife relationship. The church's/wife's response in each case is gratitude, honour and submission. It is, in other words, an *analogy* through which Paul

[45] Tidball and Tidball, *Message of Women*, pp. 212–213.
[46] E.g. Westfall, *Paul and Gender*, pp. 75–105.
[47] John Paul Heil, *Ephesians: Empowerment to Walk in Love for the Unity of All in Christ* (Atlanta: SBL, 2007), p. 254.
[48] Westfall, *Paul and Gender*, p. 101.

draws 'a comparison between the benefits that the church receives from Christ and the tangible benefits that a wife receives from her husband'.[49] The analogy illustrates the deeply subversive character of relationships within the new creation community. In the following verses the subversive nature of such 'walking in love' reaches its climax in Paul's extended instructions to husbands. As noted earlier, the men are the main target of his teaching. Quite astonishingly, as we will see, *it becomes the husband's task to give his wife the same status and treatment as the male* paterfamilias.

4. Graeco-Roman husbanding turned upside down

The fact that the apostle tells husbands to love their wives four times in nine verses[50] should alert us to how love is at the core of what he wants the husbands to grapple with and do! In typical Pauline fashion such commands are given Christ-centred theological foundations. Three arguments are given and we will look at each in turn.

a. Love as Christ loved the church (25–27)

Verse 25 explicitly echoes the command of 5:2: Jesus' self-giving love is the model for Christian husbands to *love your wives, just as Christ loved the church and gave himself up for her* (25). For the husband to love his wife self-sacrificially was virtually unheard of in Paul's world. This new obligation for a Christian husband turns Graeco-Roman understanding of male patronage on its head. But not only this; he is commanded to treat his wife as he has been treated by his own head (Christ): *to make her holy, cleansing her by the washing with water through the word, and to present her to himself as a radiant church, without stain or wrinkle or any other blemish, but holy and blameless* (26–27). Westfall brings out how Paul's imagery in verses 26–27 is a radical study of reverse expectations regarding the husband's role. Just as Christ's love for the church is exemplified in metaphors of sanctification, 'which is described in terms of domestic chores normally performed by women: giving a bath, providing clothing, and doing laundry (including spot removal and ironing)', so

> through use of analogy and metaphor, Paul has told the husband to follow Christ by serving his wife's needs; this is a brilliant

---

[49] Ibid., p. 22.
[50] Three commands and one explanatory comment: 5:25, 28 (twice), 33.

description of servanthood, how the first may be last, and how one may love one's neighbour as oneself when one is an authority in the world's power structures.[51]

The overall result is that

> In effect, Paul flips the patron metaphor of being the wife's head (protector and source of life). Instead of expecting or demanding client reciprocity (submission), the head supplies low class domestic service to the body that is ordinarily expected from women or slaves. The head nurtures (as a mother/nurse cares for a baby), feeds and cares for its own body. In effect, Paul has told husbands to wash their wives' feet and much more.[52]

That the person with power and status follows Christ through humble service fits the text, Paul's wider pastoral concerns within Ephesians for love and unity, is fully consistent with the apostle's Christologically shaped love ethic and resonates with the teaching of Jesus himself.[53] It does not amount to a complete overthrow of first-century patriarchy: Paul is working *within* his Graeco-Roman cultural context, and the husband is still a patron. But it does so redefine those cultural norms in terms of mutual love and service as to have far-reaching social and political implications. In effect, the wife's submission and the husband's love become indistinguishable in practice, a point John Stott made many years ago:

> What does it mean to 'submit'? It is to give oneself up to somebody. What does it mean to 'love'? It is to give oneself up for somebody, as Christ 'gave himself up' for the church. Thus 'submission' and 'love' are two aspects of the very same thing, namely of that selfless self-giving which is the foundation of an enduring and growing marriage.[54]

b. He who loves his wife loves himself (28–29, 33)

Christ's love for the church continues to be applied to husbands' love for their wives in verses 28–33. A second theological reason is drawn out of the image of Christ/husband as head: that in loving their wives husbands are loving their own bodies (28–29, 33). Again there are radical implications for a Christian understanding of

---

[51] Westfall, *Paul and Gender*, p. 94.
[52] Ibid., pp. 165–166.
[53] Matt. 7:12 and parallels.
[54] Stott, *Message of Ephesians*, p. 235.

gender relations compared to that of the Graeco-Roman world. Just as Christ is head and the church is his body (29b), so the husband is head and the wife is his body (28–29a). Just as Christ loves, feeds and cares for his body the church, so the husband is to love and care for his wife. We should not miss how these domestic tasks of cooking and serving were considered women's work.[55] Roles are again subverted. It is the husband who is now providing food and nurture for his wife. It is almost as though she has become the patron/male in the metaphor, he the client/female! Paul closes his argument with a probable reference to Jesus' summary of the law and the prophets: *each one of you also must love his wife as he loves himself* (33).[56] The apostle's point is unambiguous: *husbands should treat their wives as they themselves, as patrons in the ancient world with all their male privileges, would expect to be treated.* Within Paul's vision for God's new society such love is to be as natural as loving yourself. It would not have been so in the world into which he wrote and represents, Westfall argues, a new 'Golden Rule in gender relationships.'[57] It also, we should not miss, dramatically alters women's status, as they are loved and served as a male *paterfamilias* would expect to be treated.

c. One flesh (30–32)

But the apostle is not finished yet. In typical Pauline fashion he goes to Scripture to illustrate and support his teaching, in this case Genesis 2:24: *For this reason a man will leave his father and mother and be united to his wife, and the two will become one flesh* (31). Again the implications are subversive. The image of one flesh 'breaks down the Graeco-Roman philosophy about hierarchy and the separation between the genders in favour of an organic unity and biological interdependency'.[58] Husband and wife are joined together in mutual service and love. It is a metaphor of sexual union symbolizing the unity of 'head' and 'body' joined as one. It is *this* apostolic vision that transcends all transient human cultures in whichever context they find themselves. We can say this because it parallels how all believers are joined in the one body of Christ, the church (30, 32). Such unity is a *profound mystery* (32) for Paul: all believers are blessed with all the benefits of Christ their head by being united within his body. The 'one flesh' of creation is combined

---

[55] Westfall, *Paul and Gender*, pp. 56–59, 94.
[56] Mark 12:31, citing Lev. 19:18.
[57] Westfall, *Paul and Gender*, p. 95.
[58] Ibid., p. 94.

with Christ's personal love for his church to give a new quality to marriage[59] and particularly new challenges for Christian husbands.

5. Conclusions: countercultural love and marriage today

We have argued that Paul so subverts cultural assumptions of hierarchical order that relationships between husbands and wives are reconfigured to a point where 'In the final analysis, submission and *agapē* love are synonymous.'[60] But what does a countercultural Christian marriage, consistent with Paul's teaching to the Ephesians, look like in our modern world? Christians today also live and work in a culture 'ordered' by very different beliefs and values from that of Paul's vision of the church. As the West moves further into post-Christendom, the gap between Christian and Western understanding of love and marriage is becoming wider and deeper. Many of these changes are beyond the scope of our text. We would need a much broader discussion of the New Testament's teaching on love, sex and marriage to say anything about (for example) our culture's abhorrence of celibacy and rapid embrace of same-sex marriage, queer theory and fluid understandings of sexual orientation.[61] In Ephesians the apostle simply speaks about heterosexual Christian marriage. We can, however, draw out where his main concerns address our contemporary culture. They do in at least three places: in the distinct *character* of Christian love, in the *corporate* nature of Christian marriage and in unique *challenges* for Christian husbands.

a. The distinct character of Christian love

Paul would surely call Christian couples today to relationships ordered by a different ethic than that of Western culture, 'ordered' as it is by individualism, an unrealistic obsession with sex and romantic love, a contractual approach to relationships, a subsequent divorce culture and deep-seated fears of giving up autonomy to another. Given this background it is hardly a surprise that marriage makes less and less sense in today's world. In contrast, an authentically Christian marriage will be marked by partners giving of themselves generously to the other, with Jesus as their head and Lord. To 'walk in love' is to take steps of faith that the present and future belong to God and that life is about pleasing him (5:10).

---

[59] Hoehner, *Ephesians*, p. 782.

[60] Snodgrass, *Ephesians*, p. 296.

[61] For a useful resource see Thomas A. Noble, Sarah K. Whittle and Philip Johnston (eds.), *Marriage, Family and Relationships: Biblical, Doctrinal and Contemporary Perspectives* (London: Apollos, 2017).

Such love-filled relationships speak of a different type of order, one 'created in the community of the new creation by mutual love, mutual submission, mutual deference and by giving up the will to power'.[62] Miroslav Volf describes the paradoxical nature of this alternative order:

> To give less than you expect to receive is selfishness, no matter how warm your heart feels in the other's presence. To give as much as you receive is to be fair. But to love is to give more than you hope to receive. Is love a raw deal? From the point of view of contractual relations it is. But love has its own rewards. Remember that Jesus said it is more blessed to give than to receive. The return I get when I practice self-giving love is not more to me, but more to us – more to the beauty of our common love.[63]

Obviously this is an ideal: fallible human beings will stumble and fall. But a Christ-centred marriage will be one where repentance, forgiveness, covenant commitment and realism about ourselves will sustain a relationship through the joys, disappointments, griefs and everyday sins of married life. It speaks of God's future world breaking into the present, each partner empowered and filled with the Spirit, yet also called, like their Lord, to a constant dying to the self in the hope of final redemption (Eph. 1:7, 14; 4:30). In this sense, Christian marriage is a form of co-discipleship, where husband and wife call each other in love to costly Christlikeness. They know each other like no one else does. It is in marriage that our true selves are laid bare and they are far from pretty. This means that the other person will never reach our idealistic notions of 'perfect love', nor will we match theirs. This is the idea behind 'Hauerwas's Law', which says, 'You always marry the wrong person'![64] Such realism about our limitations means that both husbands and wives have a unique responsibility and ability to speak the truth in love and so help their partner grow to maturity in Christ (4:15). Mutual submission includes listening to, and acting on, such constructive criticism!

b. The corporate nature of Christian marriage

A dominant assumption of Western society is that mutual love is the primary criterion for the recognition of sexual relationships. Love,

---

[62] Tidball and Tidball, *Message of Women*, p. 248.

[63] Miroslav Volf, *Against the Tide: Love in a Time of Petty Dreams and Persisting Enmities* (Grand Rapids: Eerdmans, 2010), p. 54.

[64] Stanley Hauerwas, 'Sex and Politics: Bertrand Russell and "Human Sexuality"', *CC* (19 April 1978), pp. 417–422.

sex and the option of marriage all belong to the private domain of the individual lovers, regardless of gender. A good example of this shift is the enormous cultural momentum that has gathered behind same-sex marriage. Western governments, by-and-large, are declaring themselves agnostic as to the gender of a couple/parents and their marital status. Gender is irrelevant compared to love when it comes to a political ordering of sexual relationships. My point is not to get side-tracked into a debate about same-sex marriage, but to illustrate how deeply assumptions about love being private are now rooted within political liberalism. This seems so obvious that to question it is to risk ridicule, incredulity and even possible court action.

It is vital for Christians to understand that the issues here are much deeper than mere disagreement over who can get married. Where Ephesians 5 clashes head-on with Western culture is how Christian marriage is *not a private relationship* in which love, happiness, fulfilment and relationship are enjoyed. Paul simply talks about marriage as an *example* of where previously existing Christlike love is to be worked out. The primary 'location' for love is not the 'nuclear family' but the community of the church. The word 'church' (*ekklēsia*) appears six times within 5:23–32, and 29b–30 describes Christ's (motherly) care for all believers since they *are members of his body* (30). The origin of love is not the lone individual, but the 'great love' of God in Christ[65] that creates a community of beloved believers (5:1) tasked with loving one another across deep cultural, ethnic, gender and socio-economic divisions. It is within this diverse community that we learn how to love, and some then take that learning into marriage. In other words, *Christian love is overwhelmingly ecclesiological*. Stanley Hauerwas explains it this way:

> The church makes possible a context where people love one another. Love is not *necessary* to marriage, and the only reason why Christians love one another – even in marriage – is because Christians are obligated to love one another. Love is a characteristic of the church, not the family *per se*. You don't learn about the kind of love that Christians are called to in the family and then apply it to the church. You learn about that kind of love from the church and then try to find out how it may be applied in the family.[66]

[65] Eph. 2:4.
[66] Stanley Hauerwas and David Bourns, 'Marriage and the Family: An Open Dialogue Between Stanley Hauerwas and David Bourns', *QRT* 56.3 (January 1984), pp. 4–24; see p. 23. Emphasis original.

This relativization of the importance of married love gives space for the community to embrace singleness as an equally, if not even higher, calling than marriage.[67] Marriage is not a necessity for Christians, but a vocation. It is never an end in itself and it is certainly not the 'promised land' where all our needs for intimacy and love are met. Those who are married are not to enclose themselves within a cocoon of the self-sufficient modern family. They belong first and foremost to the Lord and therefore their brothers and sisters whom they are commanded to love (4:2; 5:2). They need the community of the church to help sustain them in their vocation of marriage. The church needs Christian marriages to be porous, welcoming others within the community, whether married or single, into relationship for the good of the community. One couple comes to my mind as I write this who have opened up their home to me and numerous others, over many years, with generosity and love. I hope you can think of similar examples. An outward-looking marriage that serves others is a powerful witness to the transforming love of God.

c. Modern challenges to Christian husbands

Paul's instructions to husbands are breathtaking. The apostle challenges established power structures and gives a beautiful picture of Christian marriage that perfectly fits Jesus' upside-down teaching of life within the kingdom of God. Husbands are to give themselves up without reservation for their wives' flourishing. Like Christ, power and privilege are to be set aside in favour of self-giving love. To love his wife as his own body he is to honour her like he, the *paterfamilias*, enjoyed honour by default. Similarly to be *one flesh* (31) pictures her sharing his identity and status. The whole tone of Paul's teaching is to give husbands a radically new vision of marriage in which their wives are of equal worth within the body of Christ. With this new vision comes new responsibilities. The primary one is obedience. Husbands are commanded four times to love their wives. Paul, of course, has earlier written in 1 Corinthians defining what love is (and is not) so it is perfectly reasonable to assume a similar meaning for love in Ephesians.[68] A husband then and now has a choice to love. He is not to seek anything for himself, but rejoices in the blessing of the other even at cost to his 'rights'. He is not to seek to control or subjugate her for his own benefit but liberates his wife to be fully herself. That love is kind points to

---

[67] Historically, celibacy was the preferred option within the church. For further discussion see chapter 5.

[68] See chapter 14 for discussion of 1 Cor. 13.

husbands showing patience, care and empathy to their wives, a picture reinforced by the images of washing, feeding and caring in Ephesians 5. Such behaviour goes well beyond the hierarchical and legal relationship of patron/husband and client/wife. Modern relationship studies have shown that kindness 'glues couples together' and is the 'most important predictor of satisfaction and stability in a marriage. Kindness makes each partner feel cared for, understood, and validated – feel loved.'[69] Nothing will thwart his relentless commitment to his wife's good. That he is to love her as himself means that if she is dishonoured in some way he is to protect her and seek for her the same benefits that he enjoys as a man. On this theme, Westfall comments:

> The analogy between Christ and the husband should lead men to share authority, status, power, and resources, and bring freedom that is comparable to what their head, Jesus Christ, provided for them and intends for the rest of his body. Men should love women and treat them literally like themselves, not just as they imagine they would want to be treated if they were women.[70]

What, we can only wonder, would be the impact on innumerable Christian marriages if husbands obeyed Paul's teaching here? If you are a husband reading this, why not prayerfully consider what this text is commanding you to do?

On a wider scale, Snodgrass argues that 'Since the text places greater responsibility on the privileged person . . . Christian men ought to be particularly concerned to seek justice for women.'[71] If the picture for women in the ancient world was overall a grim one of oppression and exploitation,[72] the picture can hardly be said to be much better globally today. Movements like #MeToo, however imperfect, have only pulled back the cover on countless injustices and abuses perpetrated by men against women within Western society.[73] Other studies paint an even blacker portrait of global gender-based violence which is linked to beliefs that women are of lesser value than men. Elaine Storkey writes:

[69] Emily Esfahani Smith, 'Masters of Love', *Atlantic* (12 June 2014), <www.theatlantic.com/health/archive/2014/06/happily-ever-after/372573/>, accessed 1 November 2018.

[70] Westfall, *Paul and Gender*, p. 95.

[71] Snodgrass, *Ephesians*, p. 316.

[72] Stott, *Message of Ephesians*, pp. 224–225.

[73] See <www.en.wikipedia.org/wiki/Me_Too_movement>, accessed 31 October 2018.

Today, gender discrimination operates in different practices in diverse cultures, much of it taking a sexual nature. Selective abortion, female genital mutilation, enforced marriage, honour killings, sex-trafficking, prostitution, sexual assault and rape as a weapon of war are all aspects of the way women's bodies become targeted for abuse.[74]

Her phrase 'women's bodies' brings to mind Paul's instruction to husbands to love their wife's body as their own body. The scale of injustice against women can seem overwhelming, but at the very least Paul's words call those in leadership within the church (most likely men) humbly to come alongside women to speak and act for justice, to counter abuse, protect the vulnerable and bring misuse of power to account. It also reinforces how Paul's inspiring theology of marriage is no academic debate, but can be a matter of life and death. It remains as radically countercultural today as it was in Ephesus nearly two thousand years ago.

[74] Elaine Storkey, 'Shadows Across Gender Relations', in Noble, Whittle and Johnston, *Marriage, Family and Relationships*, pp. 237–255; see p. 238.

1 Timothy 6:2b–10
17. Love gone wrong: money

Misdirected love

Who am I? By what values or story should I live? What or whom do I live for? What do I hope for? Some of us may think about these sorts of questions more than others, but, I suggest, pretty well all of us, whether consciously or unconsciously, answer them in some way.[1] Our answers are seen tangibly in the choices we make, the desires we pursue, the relationships we forge and in the hopes that shape us. In short, what we love – what we are most deeply committed to – will be revealed in how we act in the world. This is a theme that has surfaced from time to time throughout this book and was brilliantly captured by Augustine over 1,500 years ago – we are first and foremost lovers.[2] Therefore, perhaps the most revealing spiritual question to be asked is not 'What do you believe?' but 'What do you love?'

But, as we have seen, Augustine was only rearticulating a profound biblical theme: we are lovers created to find fulfilment, purpose and happiness in rightly directed love. The Bible's persistent concentration on the importance of how and what we love is why, I suggest, it has so much to say about greed.[3] For greed is nothing but a distorted or misdirected form of love, what the Bible calls 'idolatry'. Ephesians 5:5 is a good example: 'For of this you can be sure: no immoral, impure or greedy person – such a person is an idolater –

---

[1] I realize this is a broad statement that assumes a certain mental capacity that may not be the case for young children or adults with profound learning disabilities.

[2] See introduction and chapter 10 for further discussion of Augustine and love.

[3] In the NT several Greek words are used for greed. One is *pleonexia* (greediness), in Mark 7:22; Luke 12:15; Rom. 1:29; Eph. 4:19; 5:3; Col. 3:5; 1 Thess. 2:5; 2 Peter 2:3, 14. Another is *aischrokerdēs* (greedy), in 1 Tim. 3:8; Titus 1:7. A third is *pleonektēs* (greedy), in 1 Cor. 5:10, 11; 1 Cor. 6:10; Eph. 5:5.

has any inheritance in the kingdom of Christ and of God.' [4] Greed can take many forms – for food, status, sex, power and pleasure for example. Our focus in this chapter is one form of greed – the love of money.

The Bible has more to say about money than pretty well any other ethical issue.[5] Not all of it is negative by any means. In the Old Testament wealth can be a sign of reward for faithfulness and hard work. In the New Testament it can be a source for meeting human needs.[6] However, in both Testaments there are severe warnings about the seductive power of money that intensify in the New Testament.[7] Jesus' warnings are stark. His language of 'heart' and 'love' highlight how our relationship with money reveals where our allegiance lies: 'Do not store up for yourselves treasures on earth . . . But store up for yourselves treasures in heaven . . . For where your treasure is, there your heart will be also'[8]; 'No one can serve two masters. Either you will hate the one and love the other, or you will be devoted to the one and despise the other. You cannot serve both God and Money'[9]; 'Life does not consist of an abundance of possessions' and judgment awaits 'whoever stores up things for themselves but is not rich towards God'.[10] Serving money is a form of *discontent*, an unsatiated lust for more that drives us to pursue the object of our desire in the hope that, once obtained, we will be satisfied. James is similarly blunt. The whole book can be read as a warning about the spiritual dangers of the transient attractions of wealth (Jas 1:10–11). Riches can delude believers to attributing more worth to the wealthy (2:1–12). Covetous desires for more in order to 'spend what you get on your pleasures'[11] leads to destructive competition ('fights and quarrels'[12]). Such behaviour is adulterous, characteristic of those who are friends with the world and enemies of God (4:4). Those who have hoarded wealth, used it unjustly and 'lived on earth in luxury and self-indulgence'[13] should 'weep and

---

[4] Col. 3:5 is similar.

[5] For overview and discussion of the biblical material see Craig R. Blomberg, *Neither Poverty Nor Riches: A Biblical Theology of Possessions* (Leicester: Apollos, 1999); Ben Witherington, *Jesus and Money: A Guide for Times of Financial Crisis* (Grand Rapids: Brazos, 2010); Walter Brueggemann, *Money and Possessions* (Louisville: Westminster John Knox, 2016).

[6] Witherington, *Jesus and Money*, pp. 13–15.

[7] Ibid., p. 15.

[8] Matt. 6:19–21; cf. Luke 12:22–32.

[9] Matt. 6:24.

[10] Luke 12:15, 21.

[11] Jas 4:3.

[12] Jas 4:1.

[13] Jas 5:5.

wail because of the misery that is coming on you'.[14] These should be sobering words for all Christians and especially so for those of us who live amid the unparalleled wealth of the twenty-first-century West. We will consider below what it means to be a faithful follower of Jesus in a consumer culture structured around an organized form of dissatisfaction that fosters desires for more. We will do so through the lens of Paul's famous words about love and money in 1 Timothy 6, and so it is to that text that we now turn.[15]

2. The love of money is a root of all kinds of evil (6:2b–10)

Our interest is in 6:6–10, and particularly the connections between *the love of money* (10), *harmful desires* (9) and *contentment* (6). But we begin with brief discussion of false teachers and verses 2b–5 since they help set the context and introduce the issue of how the desire for financial gain can corrupt Christian ministry.

a. Godliness as a means of financial gain (6:2b–5)

Paul is writing from Macedonia to Timothy in Ephesus, charging him to combat 'false teaching' (*heterodidaskaleō*, 1:3; 6:3) and hold on to true faith (1:19). The content of such heterodox teaching is not easy to pinpoint. It has departed from the goal of God's work, which is 'love' (*agapē*, 1:5a), and is resulting in 'controversial speculations' (1:4), 'myths and endless genealogies' (1:3) and 'meaningless talk' (1:6). Its proponents 'do not know what they are talking about' (1:7). In chapter 4 the false teachers, fulfilling the Spirit's warning that in 'later times' (4:1) some would abandon the faith, have 'cauterized' their consciences and have become 'hypocritical liars' (4:2). The result is an anti-worldly dualism that denies the goodness of creation and therefore forbids good things like marriage and eating certain foods (4:3).

Verse 6:2b marks a transition where Paul, beginning to draw his letter to a close, returns to the destructive behaviour of the false teachers. Many commentators have drawn attention to how the structure of the apostle's polemic follows familiar patterns of ancient rhetoric, where the moral failures of one's opponents are linked to base motives.[16] *These are the things you are to teach and insist on* (6:2b) probably refers to all the apostle's previous instructions. The

---

[14] Jas 5:1.
[15] Debates about the authorship of the Pastoral Epistles are beyond my remit here. It will be assumed that Paul is the author.
[16] E.g. Luke Timothy Johnston, *Letters to Paul's Delegates: 1 Timothy, 2 Timothy, Titus* (Harrisburg: Trinity Press International, 1996), p. 196.

false teachers have gone astray theologically and ethically. They have rejected *the sound [hygiainō,* 'to be healthy'] *instruction of our Lord Jesus Christ and to godly [kat' eusebeian] teaching* (6:3). In other words, they have abandoned the truth of the gospel, which originates in Jesus Christ.[17] By doing so, once again, they show their ignorance and arrogance. The 'fruit' of such beliefs and attitudes is serious damage to the church and to themselves. In the church there is an unhealthy (*noseō,* 'to be sick') interest in controversies and quarrels *that result in envy, strife, malicious talk, evil suspicions and constant friction between people of corrupt mind* (6:4–5a). In terms of the teachers themselves Paul's analysis is devastating. Their 'sickness' has resulted in debased thinking. Ironically for people motivated by money (to be discussed in a moment) they *have been robbed of the truth* (6:5). All in all, their 'relish for profitless argument is positively pathological'.[18]

The final symptom of their apostasy is that *they think that godliness is a means to financial gain* (6:5). How godliness is being manipulated for selfish profit is not explained, but we can make an educated guess from the rest of the letter and wider evidence of the socio-economic make-up of the early Christian communities. Witherington notes that 'it is not true that the Christian movement was only populated by the poor and in fact the indications are that those of higher status played a disproportionately large role compared to their actual numbers in Pauline churches'.[19] For example, a few verses later Paul has words of instruction about the rich within the church (6:17). Earlier we learn that some were slave owners (6:2) and also that Paul was aware that some women were adorning themselves with elaborate hairstyles, gold, pearls and expensive clothes (2:9). Some younger widows even had the luxury of idleness and had become busybodies (5:13), while other widows in real need were not being looked after by their relatives, who were failing to fulfil their responsibilities to their family and to God (5:4, 8, 16). All this indicates that there were a significant minority of wealthy believers within the Ephesian church and associated tensions were developing as a result of attitudes and behaviour of at least some within this group. This is not dissimilar to tensions within the church in Corinth, where the rich were not waiting for the poor

---

[17] Gordon D. Fee, *1 and 2 Timothy, Titus,* NIBC (Peabody: Hendrickson; Carlisle: Paternoster, 1995), p. 141.

[18] John R. W. Stott, *The Message of 1 Timothy and Titus,* BST (Leicester: Inter-Varsity Press, 1996), p. 147.

[19] Ben Witherington, *A Socio-Rhetorical Commentary on Titus, 1–2 Timothy and 1–3 John,* Letters and Homilies for Hellenized Christians, vol. 1 (Nottingham: Apollos; Grand Rapids: IVP Academic, 2006), p. 282.

at the Lord's Supper (1 Cor. 11:17–34) and I have already commented on James's robust criticism of any partiality towards the rich. The false teachers' selfish motives contrast starkly with those required for church leaders listed earlier in the letter (3:2–12) and particularly that they be 'not quarrelsome, not a lover of money'.[20] Witherington suggests that 6:5 describes 'a contentious situation with men vying for religious position and power, exacerbated by false teachers who think that godliness is a means of financial gain'.[21]

Sadly the problem of leaders using a distorted form of Christianity to enrich themselves sounds all too familiar to our modern ears. The prosperity gospel is now a global phenomenon, extending its reach from North America,[22] all over the West and especially in the rapidly expanding churches of the Global South.[23] Also called 'dominion theology', 'faith gospel' or 'health and wealth gospel', it promises prosperity as a fruit of faith. It is defined as follows:

> God has met all the needs of human beings in the suffering and death of Christ and every Christian should now share the victory of Christ over sin, sickness and poverty. A believer has a right to the blessings of health and wealth won by Christ and he/she can obtain these blessings merely by a positive confession of faith.[24]

At its crassest it results in statements like this from Georgia-based pastor Creflo A. Dollar: 'I own two Rolls-Royces and didn't pay a dime for them. Why? Because while I'm pursuing the Lord those cars are pursuing me.'[25] The evangelical Lausanne Movement's Theology Working Group has issued 'A Statement on the Prosperity Gospel' coming out of consultations in Africa. In it they state:

> We recognize that Prosperity Teaching flourishes in contexts of terrible poverty, and that for many people, it presents their only

---

[20] 1 Tim. 3:3.

[21] Ibid., pp. 284–285.

[22] For analysis of the prosperity gospel in America see Kate Bowler, *Blessed: A History of the American Prosperity Gospel* (Oxford: Oxford University Press, 2013).

[23] For discussion of the African story see Lovemore Togarasei, 'The Pentecostal Gospel of Prosperity in African Contexts of Poverty: An Appraisal', *Exchange* 40 (2011), pp. 336–350.

[24] Paul Gifford, *African Christianity: Its Public Role* (London: Hurst, 1998), p. 33. Cited in Togarasei, 'Pentecostal Gospel', p. 337.

[25] Bowler, *Blessed*, p. 17. In 2015 Dollar launched a failed attempt to raise $65 million to buy a G650 Gulfstream private jet. He said, 'If I want to believe God for a $65-million-dollar plane, you can't stop me, you can't stop me from dreaming,' <https://www.huffpost.com/entry/creflo-dollar-jet_n_7129548>, accessed 18 November 2018.

hope . . . We acknowledge and confess that in many situations the Church has lost its prophetic voice in the public arena. *However, we do not believe that Prosperity Teaching provides a helpful or biblical response to the poverty of the people among whom it flourishes. It vastly enriches those who preach it, but leaves multitudes no better off than before, with the added burden of disappointed hopes.*[26]

Yet it would be too easy to decry the extravagant excesses of famous prosperity teachers and fail to look closer to home – to our own motives for involvement in church life and ministry. We do not know, but it is perfectly possible that the false teachers started off with healthy intentions and became 'sick', seduced by the attractive lure of money. These verses should prompt us to check our own motives, that they flow from a love of God and service of others rather than our own gain. Certainly, while Christian workers are to be paid a fair wage (1 Tim. 5:18), there should be no 'career path' in Christian ministry with leaders 'naturally progressing' to bigger churches and salaries.

b. Godliness and contentment versus love of money (6–10)

It is into this disorderly mess of greed, ambition and twisted desires that verses 6–10 speak simple but radical words about godliness and contentment. The apostle's argument can be divided into two points. They reflect how he is writing polemically. On the one hand, he is articulating a positive vision of the Christian life as one of trust in the provision of God. On the other hand, he is also battling against false teachers whose lives and ministries have been destroyed by the pursuit of wealth. Two mutually opposing ways of life are in view: one brings happiness, the other misery. We will look at each in turn.

(i) Godly contentment (6:6–8)

Paul's word about *contentment* (*autarkeia*, 6) echoes that of Philippians 4:11–13 – that there is *great gain* in combining *godliness* (*eusebeia*) and contentment. The irony is clearly deliberate: the *great gain* (6) is not material or financial, but spiritual. The apostle would also have been well aware that *autarkeia* was an important idea within Cynic and Stoic philosophy concerning possessions.[27] It

[26] See <www.lausanne.org/content/a-statement-on-the-prosperity-gospel (16/01/10)>, accessed 1 December 2018. Emphasis original.

[27] I. H. Marshall, in collaboration with Philip H. Towner, *A Critical and Exegetical Commentary on the Pastoral Epistles*, ICC (Edinburgh: T&T Clark, 1999), pp. 644–645.

carries the sense of 'self-sufficiency' or independence, 'emphasizing the willingness to be satisfied with what one has, rather than having that craving disease that always seeks more'.[28] In this context it is a perfect word to use, but now adapted within a Christian framework.[29] It speaks to how contentment flows from finding sufficiency in God alone and not from looking elsewhere – particularly to money and all it supposedly promises. Verses 7 and 8 illustrate the point in the form of a proverbial couplet, which again would have been well-known ideas in the ancient world – both Jewish and Greek.[30] The first – *For we brought nothing into the world, and we can take nothing out of it* (7) – has the sense that there is no reason to pursue possessions between entry and exit. Marshall rightly observes that, by itself, the proverb does not prove that we should be content with little in the interim. Rather, it is making a general point 'about temporality against eternity and the relative values of each'.[31] Or, to put it differently, what we possess in this world does not define us. Money and possessions neither enable existence to begin with, nor are they of value in death; so there is no point in greedy pursuit of them during life. The second proverb – *But if we have food and clothing, we will be content with that* (8) – commends a simple lifestyle, satisfied with the essentials of life. Such contentment is liberating because it frees us from the tyranny of 'more' – endlessly pursuing what we do not have, and looking for something that cannot be found! This proverb also has strong parallels with the teaching of Jesus that I discussed earlier (Matt. 6:25–34; Luke 12:22–32). Greed is the antithesis of contentment. Godliness, in contrast, *is its own gain* and leads to contentment with 'enough'.

(ii) Love of money (6:9–10)

Paul now returns to the false teachers one last time, contrasting their lives and motives with that of godly contentment. While written for a context in Ephesus long ago, his words continue to resonate down through the centuries since they speak to all *who want to get rich* (9). His diagnosis is damning and should give any Christian serious pause about the spiritual dangers associated with wealth.

Verse 9 graphically pictures the grievous consequences of greed. Wanting more is a *temptation and a trap*. The two belong together in that money (the *temptation*) draws its prey (*those who want to*

---

[28] Johnston, *Letters to Paul's Delegates*, p. 200.

[29] OT wisdom is also a likely background source. Job 1:21 states, 'Naked I came from my mother's womb, and naked I shall depart.'

[30] Marshall and Towner, *Pastoral Epistles*, p. 646.

[31] Ibid.

get rich) into a *trap*. There they are effectively imprisoned by their *many foolish and harmful desires* (*epithymias*).[32] These desires *plunge people into ruin and destruction*. The picture is of being overwhelmed or sinking without hope. The point is how something powerfully attractive (money) not only fails to deliver on its alluring promise but ensnares those who are drawn to it. This is why the desire for more is *foolish* (*anoētos*) or 'senseless' – it is self-destructive. Given this dreadful diagnosis, Gordon Fee justifiably asks, from a Christian perspective, 'Why would anyone want to get rich?'[33]

Some point out that in this verse wealth in itself is not wrong, but the desire for it is.[34] The warning is primarily to false teachers, those who want to get rich, not to wealthy congregational members.[35] While technically correct, this qualification can all too easily weaken the urgency of Paul's warning. Those who are rich will inevitably be motivated by a desire to stay rich! At the end of a detailed discussion of the Bible's teaching on wealth Jonathan Bonk concludes, 'It is clear that Christianity was never designed to make people comfortably at ease with wealth and power.'[36] Fee's question is one all Christians need to grapple with – both those who are dissatisfied with what they have and those who already have much. As Stanley Hauerwas says, 'Scripture is clear. If you are a Christian who is wealthy or desires to have wealth, you have a problem. Yet in our day greed is seldom identified as a major problem for Christians.'[37] As discussed above, the consistent witness of the New Testament is that riches are laden with spiritual danger and ought to be viewed with great caution.

We come now to verse 10, one of the most (mis)quoted verses in the New Testament. Within the argument, it functions as a concluding explanation of verse 9, applied to the false teachers. Its first sentence unpacks why the love of money is so harmful. The second refers to the false teachers as a factual example of love gone wrong.

Paul again quotes a proverbial saying that would have been familiar to Jews and Greeks, *the love of money is a root of all kinds*

---

[32] The conflict between such harmful desires and Christian living surfaces regularly in Paul. For further discussion of how such desires are overcome through life in the Spirit see chapter 15.

[33] Fee, *1 and 2 Timothy*, p. 143.

[34] E.g. Walter L. Liefeld, *1 & 2 Timothy, Titus*, NIVAC (Grand Rapids: Zondervan, 1999), p. 204.

[35] Witherington, *1–2 Timothy*, p. 287, n. 454.

[36] Jonathan Bonk, *Missions and Money: Affluence as a Missionary Problem Revisited*, American Society of Missiology Series 15 (Maryknoll: Orbis, 2006), p. 156.

[37] Stanley Hauerwas, 'More or, a Taxonomy of Greed', in *Working with Words: On Learning to Speak Christian* (London: SCM, 2011), p. 128.

of evil (10).[38] The NIVUK is right here. It is not, as commonly misunderstood, that 'money is the root of all evil'. The text is not saying money itself is spiritually toxic, it has the *love of money (philargyria)* in view. Nor is it claiming that the love of money lies behind every evil. However, these clarifications do little to blunt the force of the apostle's warning. As verse 9 has indicated, *the love of money* leads to multiple ruinous consequences. *Philargyria* appears only here in the New Testament.[39] It has a sense of avarice or covetousness, describing a dissatisfied, discontented person lusting after more and willing to pursue wealth no matter what the cost. Tragically, this is exactly what the false teachers have chosen to do. *Eager [oregō, 'to crave' or 'strive for'] for money* they have *wandered from the faith.* Riches have become their idol, leading to apostasy. Money has replaced God as the ground of their being and source of their identity. Witherington's words are apt:

> if we love things like money and use people to get them, then we have exactly reversed the way God intends us to operate. Things are not capable of love or carrying on a love relationship with a human being. It is in the end a form of idolatry, and of trying to find our life, support and sufficiency in something other than God.[40]

In giving themselves wholeheartedly to money they *pierced themselves with many griefs*. The imagery is graphic: their sick love has led them to be like people who have accidentally impaled themselves, causing no end of anguish. Fee puts it well: 'they have "sold out" the gospel . . . they had come to love money and it did them in'.[41]

These are strong words. But in writing them Paul echoes Jesus and James in particular.[42] This fact should make us ask what is so dangerous about wealth? The answer lies in what money can *do*. Essentially, *money is power*. It has a unique capacity to effect tangible change in the world. It apparently offers us many tempting things: freedom from worry, security, access to the best health care, independence, status, choice, pleasure, respect, self-esteem and success, to name a few. In sum, money promises us the possibility of

[38] I. H. Marshall lists numerous parallels in ancient philosophers. *Pastoral Epistles*, p. 652, n. 55.

[39] *Philargyroi* (lovers of money) occurs in 2 Timothy's description of the terrible times of the last days when 'People will be lovers of themselves, lovers of money . . . without love . . . brutal, not lovers of the good' (2 Tim. 3:1–3). The only other appearance of *philargyroi* in the NT is in Luke 16:14, describing the Pharisees.

[40] Witherington, *1–2 Timothy*, p. 289.

[41] Fee, *1 and 2 Timothy*, p. 146.

[42] Blomberg, *Neither Poverty Nor Riches*, p. 212.

fulfilling our deepest longings. Words like *want* (9), *desires* (9), *love* (10) and *eager* (10) reinforce how the issue is one of the *heart* – what we love motivates us at a fundamental level. This is why the Bible talks of money and possessions as 'seductions that lead to idolatry. The Bible attests that money and possessions are not inanimate objects. They are rather forces of desire that evoke lust and "love" in a way that compels devotion and eventually servitude.'[43]

With good reason journalists and detectives know that to 'follow the money' will most often lead to the motive of a corrupt deal or ruthless crime. Love of money lies behind most of the great evils of our world. At a relational level it leads to things like jealousy, theft, arrogance, lying and murder. On a wider scale, environmental destruction, global financial crashes, the pornography industry, drug empires, prostitution, scandals in food production, bribery, violence, spiralling global debt, cyber-crime, embezzlement, exploitation of the poor, match-fixing scandals, property speculation, the explosive growth of online gambling, pharmaceutical companies deliberately selling addictive opioids, modern slavery and people trafficking, exorbitant rents, zero-hours contracts, political corruption, secret data-harvesting by multinationals, flouting of health and safety regulations, and the arms industry making vast profits at the expense of countless lives – are all driven by an avaricious desire for money.

This is why Christians today, who are called to love God not mammon, are to have a critically detached relationship with money. In this vein, writing about money and possessions in the Pastoral Epistles, Walter Brueggemann argues:

> It takes no imagination to see that the same pressures are now upon the church in a market-propelled society. Resistance and alternatives to the ideology of money that propels our society is as urgent now in the church as it was then.[44]

In the next section it will be argued that contemporary Western consumerism parallels Paul's diagnosis of the 'sick love' of the false teachers in Ephesus. In the light of this, a concluding section will explore how Christians today can practise 'godly contentment' (6:6) within a culture where 'enough' is never enough. There are no simple answers, but try we must if we are to hear how the Bible speaks today about how to 'dethrone Mammon'.[45]

---

[43] Brueggemann, *Money and Possessions*, p. 8.

[44] Ibid., p. 246.

[45] This is a reference to the Archbishop of Canterbury Justin Welby's very helpful Lent Book, *Dethroning Mammon: Making Money Serve Grace* (London: Bloomsbury, 2017).

3. 'Sick love' today: consumerism as manufactured discontent

The 'theology' of modern consumerism embodies a 'gospel' (story of good news) profoundly at odds with the gospel of Jesus Christ. Or, in Brueggemann's words, 'the claims of the Bible amount to a deep critique' of the economic assumptions of our society.[46] This is a big claim that needs explanation. It would be all too easy at this point to get lost in detailed theological assessment of the beliefs inherent within Western free-market consumerism. Many examples of such works exist,[47] but we will limit ourselves to some everyday examples of how modern consumerism targets the heart and depends on creating insatiable desires for more. To do so we will visit a large shopping centre or mall in the company of James K. A. Smith.[48] He invites us to see the mall as a place of worship: a place communicating a vision of a very different kingdom that wants to 'grab hold of our *kardia*' and wants 'nothing less than our love'.[49] It has, he suggests, four elements.

The first is, *I'm broken, therefore I shop*. This refers to how consumerism bombards us with visions of perfection (icons of physical beauty, success, sexiness, relationships) that implicitly *condemns* us imperfect consumers. This is a consumerist version of 'sin'. Its purpose is to 'impress upon us a deep sense of lack'[50] as we wander around the mall and unconsciously take in condemnatory messages. It generates a *need*, which would otherwise not be felt, to assuage that lack by buying material goods. In other words, consumerism depends on the 'organised creation of dissatisfaction'.[51] Such a system *requires discontentment* in order to thrive and

---

[46] Brueggemann, *Money and Possessions*, pp. 10–11.

[47] Some examples are Craig Bartholomew and Thorsten Moritz, *Christ and Consumerism: A Critical Analysis of the Spirit of the Age* (Carlisle: Paternoster, 2000); Vincent J. Millar, *Consuming Religion: Christian Faith and Practice in a Consumer Culture* (London: Continuum, 2003); William T. Cavanaugh, *Being Consumed: Economics and Christian Desire* (Grand Rapids: Eerdmans, 2008); Laura Hartmann, *The Christian Consumer: Living Faithfully in a Fragile World* (Oxford: Oxford University Press, 2011); Daniel M. Bell, *The Economy of Desire: Christianity and Capitalism in a Postmodern World* (Grand Rapids: Baker Academic, 2012); Kevin Hargaden, *Theological Ethics in a Neoliberal Age: Confronting the Christian Problem with Wealth* (Eugene: Cascade, 2018).

[48] James K. A. Smith, *Desiring the Kingdom: Worship, Worldview and Cultural Formation*, Cultural Liturgies, vol. 1 (Grand Rapids: Baker Academic, 2009), pp. 93–103. This idea is not unique to Smith, but he is exceptionally good at drawing out the theology at work in the apparently mundane act of shopping.

[49] Ibid., p. 93.

[50] Ibid., p. 97.

[51] This phrase derives from Charles Kettering (1876–1958), inventor and head of research at General Motors.

prosper: 'no matter how much we have, it is not enough'.[52] 'Better' is *nearly* within reach *if only* I can possess X, Y or Z by spending money. Thus we love money for the apparent 'salvation' that it offers. Theologian Daniel Bell describes the dysfunction of the system this way: 'The problem that drives the entire economic enterprise is rooted in the unquenchable, infinite nature of human desire.'[53]

Second, within the mall we *shop with others*. But this is no grace-filled community of equals. It is, rather, a *competitive* environment where we not only evaluate ourselves against consumerist ideals, but judge others against them as well. Smith gives a couple of examples with which most of us will be able to identify. As a male acquaintance approaches,

> we may catch ourselves looking him up and down, noting clothes that seem to be from Old Navy rather than Abercrombie & Fitch (and from last season at that!); he's got a big clunky cell phone that's about two years old;[54] his tastes in music seem a bit dull and dated; and he's from a part of town that we wouldn't walk through at night. Or while we are sitting at the Starbucks in the food court, we might find that our eyes are constantly darting to watch the other girls and women passing by. In just the blink of an eye, we find that we've sized them up from top to bottom; noticed their hair and sandals; wordlessly scorned their garish make-up and chubby ankles; or silently admired, even craved, their D&G sunglasses or their naturally wavy hair.[55]

Such relentless comparison results in either self-congratulation (I'm better than X) or demoralization (I do not measure up). People are reduced to objects to be assessed – 'a war of all with all'.[56]

Smith's third strand of consumerist ideology is *I shop (and shop and shop), therefore I am*. By this play on René Descartes, Smith means that shopping holds out a quasi-theology of 'redemption'. A goal of shopping is to acquire goods to *heal* our problems – whether our bodies, our skin, our clothes, our image or our self-esteem. A good example of this endless pursuit of 'redemption' is apparent

---

[52] Peter Block, Walter Brueggemann and John McKnight, *An Other Kingdom: Departing the Consumer Culture* (Hoboken: Wiley, 2016), p. 2.

[53] Bell, *Economy of Desire*, pp. 102–103.

[54] A colleague tells me that some children at a local secondary school deliberately throw their 'old' iPhones at a wall so that their parents will replace them with the latest version!

[55] Smith, *Desiring the Kingdom*, p. 98.

[56] Ibid., p. 99.

in what theologian Werner Jeanrond calls the Western 'cult of the body':

> Fasting, painful sporting activities, beauty operations, all sorts of medicines and remedies are recommended in order to reach a higher level of control over the body. A new and perfect body is longed for – a kind of secular object of salvation. The desire for the perfect body seems to have replaced the desire for the perfect soul in many quarters of Western society. This fight against the present and imperfect body and for the new and perfect body can, of course, never end. Asceticism, once the hallmark of religious aspirations, has made a comeback in the secular cult of the body. This cult of the body has seemingly reached eschatological proportions. Moreover, this desire for perfect bodies has become an inexhaustible source of wealth generation for those market forces that have offered their mediating remedies to meet this desire, fully conscious of the fact that this desire can never be stilled. Love cannot be made through the production of perfect bodies.[57]

As Jeanrond hints, behind consumerism's glossy façade is the unacknowledged secret that its redemptive powers are illusory. There may be a thrill of purchasing a desired object or experience, but it soon fades. The problem with shiny holiday brochures populated with perfect happy families is that when we go on holiday, we bring ourselves with us! False hopes of redemption lock us into a cycle not only of acquisition but of restless consumption. *Lasting contentment cannot be bought.*

Smith's fourth strand of consumer ideology is *Don't ask, don't tell*. This refers to how the globally unsustainable costs of Western consumerism's vision of 'the good life' are carefully hidden from consumers. The myth that contentment and happiness are attainable to all at minimal cost must be maintained. The reality is quite the reverse.[58]

Discontent. Greed. Competition. Motivated by financial gain. A misplaced trust in the redemptive promises of wealth. Being trapped in a cycle of self-destructive behaviour driven by a lust for more. Pursuing, without restraint, money and all it has to offer. Such is the nature of Western consumer culture. Parallels between it and the beliefs and behaviour of the false teachers in 1 Timothy are startling.

---

[57] Werner G. Jeanrond, *A Theology of Love* (London: T&T Clark, 2010), p. 12.
[58] The very success of the Western 'way of life' in creating endless desire for more is destroying the planet and is inextricably linked to systemic injustice.

If Paul's response is contentment and simplicity (6:6–8), what does it look like for Western Christians to practise such virtues today?

4. De-idolizing money through rightly directed love

It would be possible, and not without value, at this point to segue into discussion of what a suitably simple lifestyle looks like for disciples of Jesus today. Any theology needs to be earthed in real life. But to jump prematurely into 'Ten practical steps to beat consumerism' would, ironically, be a pragmatic and consumerist move that would deal only with symptoms rather than the underlying 'sickness'. Note how Paul refrains from giving detailed instructions to Timothy on money management to pass on to Christians in Ephesus. Rather he 'goes for the heart' in diagnosing that *misdirected love lies at the core of the false teachers' apostasy* (6:10). As we see from his closing charge to Timothy (6:11–19), Paul's 'solution' to greed is rightly directed trust.[59] Together with 6:6–8 these verses paint an alternative theological vision to the love of money that answers each of the four questions asked at the beginning of this chapter. We will look at each in turn to conclude this discussion.

To the first question of identity – 'Who am I?' – the answer is a man or woman of God (6:11).[60] Contrary to the idolatry of greed, believers are not autonomous consumers condemned to lives of endless discontent in which redemption is never quite attainable.

To the second question of 'By what values or story should I live?', Christians have been given *eternal life* (6:12) by the God *who gives life to everything* (6:13). This immeasurable gift means that they are to *flee* (6:11) from 'sick love' characterized by greed, dissatisfaction and selfishness and are to *pursue righteousness, godliness, faith, love, endurance and gentleness* instead (6:11). In other words, believers are people who are being transformed from the 'inside out' by an experience of God's lavish generosity. The words of Daniel Bell capture this dynamic wonderfully well:

As we share Israel's election in Christ, we are set free from an economy whose circulation is ruled by scarcity, debt, retribution and finally death. In Christ, we share in the abundant life of the Immortal, which is not the solitude of self-sufficiency, but life lived as donation, as the ceaseless giving (and receiving) of the gift

[59] For concise exegetical discussion of 6:11–19 see Stott, *Message of 1 Timothy and Titus*, pp. 154–163.

[60] While Paul's words here address Timothy as a 'man of God', they are clearly applicable to all Christians and will be taken as such in the following discussion.

of love . . . We are freed from captivity to an economic order that would subject us to scarcity, competition, dominion, and debt, that would distort human desire into a proprietary and acquisitive power.[61]

A graphic example of how God's extravagant gift in Christ disempowers the lure of money appears in 6:17–18. Here Paul comments briefly on the responsibilities of rich Christians within the community.[62] Rather than derive their identity from wealth and so become arrogant or trust in the illusion of security offered by money (6:17a), they are *to put their hope in God, who richly provides us with everything for our enjoyment* (6:17b). Instead of keeping their riches to themselves, such Christians are *to do good, to be rich in good deeds, and to be generous and willing to share* (6:18). Such unrestrained giving reveals a heart set free from the love of money. This is why it is quite justifiable to argue that what we do with 'our' God-given money is probably the most significant indicator of Christian spirituality. A tight wallet indicates little or no experience of God's grace and possibly an idolatrous love of money (6:9–10). Open-handed giving is a way to de-idolize money. It demonstrates a concern for equality and justice that confronts the love of money head-on. Radical generosity undermines our temptation to root our identity and security in money. It is therefore effectively 'heretical' within a Western culture of scarcity and 'never enough'. We might even say that *sacrificial giving profanes all that money represents*, which is why such giving is so rare.[63]

In terms of the third question – 'What or whom do I live for?' – Timothy, and by extension all Christians, are not to fall for the trap of loving inanimate things like money and possessions that can never satisfy. Rather they are to give themselves completely to the only person worthy of wholehearted worship: *God, the blessed and only Ruler, the King of kings and Lord of lords, who alone is immortal and who lives in unapproachable light, whom no one has seen or can*

---

[61] Daniel M. Bell, *Divinations: Theopolitics in an Age of Terror* (Eugene: Cascade, 2017), pp. 71–72.

[62] There is quite a bit of wordplay on riches in these two verses. They include the adjective 'rich' (*plousios*, 17a), the noun 'riches' or 'wealth' (*ploutos*, 17b), the adverb 'richly' (*plousiōs*, 17c) and the verb 'to be rich' (*plouteō*, 18a). Stott, *Message of 1 Timothy and Titus*, p. 160.

[63] E.g. Barna published research in 2013 indicating that while evangelicals were the most generous religious group in the USA, only about 12% gave 10% of their gross income away. (The average giving among evangelicals is likely closer to 3–5%.) Dave Kinnaman of Barna noted that giving generally is viewed as a luxury, to be done when affordable. See <www.barna.com/research/american-donor-trends/>, accessed 15 December 2018.

see (6:15–16). Rightly directed worship takes our focus off the self and on to God and serving him first (6:13–14). Worship subverts greed. Hauerwas again: 'The alternative to a world of greed is a people capable of participating through worship in the love of the Father for the Son through the Spirit.'[64]

The final question, 'What do I hope for?', probes what kinds of desires drive our choices. Love of money is symptomatic of a life driven by the physical 'this-worldly' power of all that money can buy. *This is why modern consumerism is relentlessly non-eschatological.* It has no 'bigger story' or *telos* (end) than 'this life'. In fact, it is effectively disinterested in questions of purpose or morality; what matters is what sells in meeting (often artificially created) market demand. Like the desires of the false teachers (6:9), such distorted short-term priorities are self-destructive.[65] Christian hope puts such misshapen desires in the shade. As C. S. Lewis put it so memorably many years ago, they are mere shadows of the real:

> Our Lord finds our desires not too strong, but too weak. We are half-hearted creatures, fooling around with drink and sex and ambition when infinite joy is offered us, like an ignorant child who wants to go on making mud pies in a slum because he cannot imagine what is meant by the offer of a holiday at the sea. We are far too easily pleased.[66]

Instead of this pathetic image, Christianity's vision of eschatological hope is to revolutionize how disciples live in the present. The power of money should be disarmed by hope, resulting in Christians living lives of radical simplicity and contentment (6:6–8). Thus Timothy is to take *hold of the eternal life* to which he has been called (6:12) and remain faithful *until the appearing of our Lord Jesus Christ* (6:14). As discussed earlier, those with money are to hold to it lightly, use it to bless others and *put their hope in God*, not in wealth (6:17–18). Echoing Jesus, Paul concludes that by generosity and good deeds

---

[64] Hauerwas, 'More', p. 138.

[65] Alan Storkey writes that 'Perhaps 20% to 50% of what we now produce has little or no real value to humanity. We'd often be better off without cigarettes, alcohol, fast food, weapons, drugs, media dross, technically fast but slow on the road cars, advertising, cosmetics, sugar drinks, security systems, lotteries, and many other things which sell. Rather than being goods, they are bads, indifferents or mere rubbish, and our degraded values merely make us poorer.' 'Postmodernism Is Consumption', in Craig Bartholomew and Thorsten Moritz (eds.), *Christ and Consumerism: A Critical Analysis of the Spirit of the Age* (Carlisle: Paternoster, 2000), p. 103.

[66] C. S. Lewis, *The Weight of Glory and Other Addresses* (New York: HarperOne, 2001), p. 25.

such believers *will lay up treasure for themselves as a firm foundation for the coming age, so that they may take hold of the life that is truly life* (6:19).

This is a vision worth 'investing' in. Godliness with contentment is, indeed, great gain.

Conclusion
A vision for human flourishing

1. Three strands of love

The aim of this book has been to hear how the Bible speaks today about the magnificent theme of love. Each chapter, in this sense, is a stand-alone exposition. If you have arrived here after working your way through each one, congratulations! If, like me, you often turn to a conclusion first, you will get a taste here of some theological themes and questions that have materialized over the last seventeen chapters or so.

First, however, allow me a general comment on the overwhelming impression with which I am left at the end of this study. In the preliminary pages of this book Ben Witherington remarks on the rarity of biblical studies of love. Thomas Jay Oord notes the same strange lack within much Christian theology.[1] More will be said below, but it has become clear that love defines the nature of God and gives shape to the entire biblical narrative. The immeasureable depth of divine love is revealed at the cross, and love is the 'goal' of the redemptive work of the triune God among his people. Love is therefore the true measure of all Christian spirituality and theology. If this book helps, even a little, to put love back where it belongs at the centre of Christian teaching, preaching and experience, then it will have more than done its job.

Three strands of love wind their way through the Old and New Testaments and now is a good time to reflect on each. The first, divine love, is the core thread around which the other two are entwined. They are human love for God ('vertical love') and human love for one another ('horizontal love'). This image of a threefold

[1] Thomas Jay Oord, *The Nature of Love: A Theology* (St Louis: Chalice, 2010), pp. 4–13. Oord also proposes some reasons here for the neglect of love within much Christian theology.

cord may help in picturing how each strand is distinct but also intimately related to the others.

2. God the lover

a. Divine love in the Old Testament

The great good news of the Hebrew Scriptures is that the one true God, the source of all that exists, is a God who *abounds in love*. The Old Testament is the *particular* story of God's unbreakable covenant love for his people Israel, but one that is not an end in itself. In this sense, divine love is *selective* – God will have mercy and compassion on whom he wills (Exod. 33:19) – but behind such electing love is reconciling love for all creation. There is a paradox here that runs through the whole Bible. Scripture's focus is on God's love for his chosen people, yet it is through that narrow lens that the blessing of divine love is refracted outwards towards all. In the Old Testament, few places is this more beautifully described than in Deuteronomy 10:12–22.[2] God's impartial love embraces the weak, marginalized and vulnerable, including those within Israel *and* those who are foreigners and slaves.

God's love is also *unconditioned* in that it is not dependent on the merit or faithfulness of the beloved. Covenant love is worked out in and through all the vagaries and failures of human history. God's extraordinary long-suffering love takes the form of a relentless commitment to his people in the face of rebellion and sin. We have looked at a selection of texts in part 1 that touch on this theme, but examples could be multiplied. Again and again the redemptive story of Israel is *utterly dependent* on God's faithfulness to his promise. Without divine love quite simply there would be no covenant, no Old or New Testament, no good news and no hope of a better world.

All that God does is loving. In Exodus 32 – 34 Yahweh's *ḥesed* love is steadfast, demonstrating his kindness and graciousness. Divine love leads to *deepened relationship* with his people. However, this is anything but 'like-for-like' love. There is a chasm between divine and human love. God is utterly other, unknowable, glorious and all-powerful. This immeasurable *disparity* of loves means that the only appropriate human response to God's love is fear and obedience. Israel are to submit wholeheartedly to their God (this is a point to which we will return below).

This means, regardless of popular assumptions about love, *God's love is not unconditional*. It demands a response of fidelity and trust.

---

[2] See chapter 2.

At least two implications follow, which sit paradoxically alongside one another. One is that *love cannot be forced*, even by God. Hosea is an extraordinary illustration of God's self-chosen vulnerability in loving Israel: they freely choose to pursue other gods. Yahweh responds by tenderly wooing them back at significant cost to himself. Here is divine love as zealous passion for a restored relationship with his estranged bride. Israel's obedience to God is to emerge out of repentance and their rediscovery of the depth of God's love. Yet, at the same time, human love for God is also *commanded* (Deut. 6:4–5). We return to this tension between free response and divine command below.

As discussed at several points in this book, however uncomfortable it may make us moderns, *God is a lover but also a just judge*. The Bible sees no incompatibility between divine love and judgment. 'The divine hostility, or wrath of God, has always been an aspect of his love. It is not separate from God's love, it is not opposite to God's love, it is not something in God that has to be overcome.'[3] God's beloved people are not exempt from such judgment. Yet God is slow to anger. Throughout the Old Testament, divine judgment is graciously forestalled while prophetic warnings appeal for repentance. But ultimately judgment does fall. For God not to resist, and ultimately overcome, the terrible sins that disfigure his world would be a failure of both divine love and divine justice.

These comments on judgment bring us to a final point about divine love in the Old Testament: the deep connection between God's *love and forgiveness*. No relationship can survive on justice alone: forgiveness is essential for a relationship to thrive. The wondrous thing about God's covenant love is that it is the 'innocent' party who takes the initiative to forgive. Such love opens up new possibilities of reconciliation. Out of death comes life, out of judgment comes hope. For example, in Exodus divine forgiveness leads to a covenant renewal (Exod. 34:1–4). In Hosea it offers a picture of a relationship reborn, flourishing in a promised land of blessing (Hos. 2:14–23).

b. Divine love in the New Testament

It should be no surprise that there is significant continuity in how the New Testament talks of God's love.[4] The 'story of Jesus'

---

[3] Fleming Rutledge, *The Crucifixion: Understanding the Death of Jesus Christ* (Grand Rapids: Eerdmans, 2015), p. 323.

[4] This is contrary to Anders Nygren, who drew a sharp, and unconvincing, contrast between Jewish love functioning within the law versus Christian love set free from law. *Agape and Eros: The Christian Idea of Love*, tr. Philip S. Watson (Chicago: University of Chicago Press, 1982 [1930–36]), p. 251.

completes the 'the story of Israel'. In other words, God's relentless covenant love reaches its promised climax with the arrival of the Messiah. In the Synoptic Gospels Jesus reaffirms the double-love command – to love God and neighbour is to fulfil the law – but speaks rarely of God's love as such. One example is that his command for his disciples to love their enemies is rooted in God's own kindness and mercy to the ungrateful and wicked (Luke 6:35–36).[5] It is in a wider sense that God's abounding love is central within the preaching and ministry of Jesus concerning the kingdom of God – in his welcoming love of sinners, in his healing of the sick and in his confrontation with evil in the power of God's Spirit.

It is when we begin to look more closely at how the identity, mission and death of Jesus has been understood by the writers of the New Testament that their unique perspectives on divine love comes into sharper focus (part 2 of this book). Jesus is on practically every page of the New Testament and all the evidence points to how God's covenant love is *reinterpreted* in the light of the dramatic events recounted in the Gospels. To use theological language, radical innovations in Christology (Jesus' identity) have a major impact on soteriology (salvation). Brief illustrations from the texts discussed in part 2 will help flesh out this claim.

For Mark, the Messiah is God's beloved Son in whom is embodied the presence and rule of God.[6] In his prologue we glimpse the Father's delight in and love for his Son. It points to something that is worked out more fully in the rest of the New Testament, that God in himself is a triune community of self-giving love: Father, Son and Spirit working in harmony to effect salvation. The glorious, transcendent God chooses to work within history (immanence) to establish his kingdom on earth through the incarnation and mission of his Son.

For John, quite simply, 'God is love'.[7] While implied in the Old Testament and throughout the New, no one else explicitly connects God's essence with love. But John is no eccentric radical. To equate God and love is to say, with the rest of the Bible, that *all* God does is loving. It also highlights the *disparity* between divine and human love: God loves the hostile, fallen world. For John, again as elsewhere in the Bible, this extraordinary love is revealed in what God *does*. There is no mystery here: he tells us plainly what God's love looks like in practice – the sending of his one and only Son into the world. That such love is *unconditioned* (does not depend on human qualities) is evident in that God first loved us, not that we

[5] See chapter 11.
[6] See chapter 6.
[7] 1 John 4:8, 16.

loved God. It creates a *new community* of those loved by God to whom John writes. That divine love continues, as in the Old Testament, to be *conditional* is everywhere in John. Those who love God are to obey his commands. But where John (and Paul as we will see in a moment) really begins to 'innovate' is the deep connection he makes between divine love and the cross of Christ. *Divine love reaches its zenith in the Son's atoning death*. Divine love for John – and the rest of the New Testament authors – is cruciform.

While Paul does not use Johannine language, equating God with love, he echoes John in interpreting Jesus' death for us as the supreme demonstration of divine love. Again it is God's *unconditioned* love that takes the initiative to restore *relationship* – leading to justification and reconciliation and being made alive in Christ. In the background in John, but foregrounded in Paul, is a scandalous *widening* of divine love beyond the boundaries of Israel. Crucially for Paul this is not his own innovation. God's original promise to Abraham is interpreted by the apostle as *always* having had the Gentiles in mind. Paul is only explaining a divine mystery that had, up until Christ, been hidden.[8]

Both John and Paul, in distinct ways, root divine love in Christology. God's love develops far beyond any previous understanding in that it is *God himself*, the incarnate Son, the Word made flesh, who gives his life freely for us on the cross and is subsequently vindicated as the risen Lord. John's language is striking – Jesus is uniquely loved by his Father – but Paul's Christology is just as 'high'.[9] It is this truly revolutionary development in the theology of love that, more than any other factor, lies behind Christianity's *discontinuity* with other religions including Judaism. Larry Hurtado comments that, in comparison with pagan thought,

> [t]he notion that there is one true and transcendent God, and that this God loves the world/humanity, may have become subsequently so much a familiar notion . . . that we cannot easily realize how utterly strange, even ridiculous, it was in the Roman era . . . the emphasis on God's love and the appeal for an answering 'love-ethic' characterizing Christian conduct comprise something distinctive. We simply do not know of any other Roman-era religious group in which love played this important role in discourse or behavioural teaching.[10]

[8] E.g. Rom. 16:25; 1 Cor. 2:7; 4:1; Eph. 1:9; 3:4, 9; 6:19; Col. 1:26; 4:3; 1 Tim. 3:16.

[9] See Gordon Fee, *Pauline Christology: An Exegetical-Theological Study* (Peabody: Hendrickson, 2007).

[10] Larry W. Hurtado, *A Destroyer of the Gods: Early Christian Distinctiveness in the Roman World* (Waco: Baylor, 2016), pp. 64–65.

Similarly in regard to the Old Testament and Jewish thought:

> In comparison with the devotional pattern that was typical of ancient Jewish tradition, the early Christian movement was identifiable and distinguishable particularly by the extraordinary reverence typically given also to Jesus along with God.[11]

So radical is this development that Christianity effectively represents a new kind of 'religion' that worships Jesus alongside the Father. God's love is cruciform: it is a defining mark of Christian faith that it is *God incarnate* on the cross, his body broken and his blood shed for us because of his immeasurable love.

3. Human love for God

a. Obedience, experience, trust and worship

Four words come to mind regarding how the Bible talks of human love for God: *obedience, worship, experience* and *trust*. All four run continuously throughout Scripture, but, as with divine love, undergo significant development in the New Testament. It is impossible to separate them, so they will appear organically in the conversation below.

A tension has surfaced regularly during our discussion, namely that human love for God is commanded.[12] Examples throughout Scripture are innumerable but by far the most important is the Shema. In the New Testament, an example is John, where Jesus tells his disciples that they will remain in his love if they keep his commands, just as he has remained in his Father's love by keeping his commands (15:10).

However, various objections come to mind. Logically, if love is a free response, how can it also be commanded? Theologically, what does it suggest about someone with infinite power commanding those with finite power to love him? Is God some sort of insecure tyrant? Pastorally, does not such a command lead to relational repression? For instance, are believers to love God regardless of dreadful circumstances that he either allows to happen or foreordains? Can love be questioned? Ethically, does such a love command not open the door to a type of Nuremberg defence: 'An order is an order'? Whatever God commands must be done even if it appears to put love for God before our fellow humans, including

---

[11] Ibid., p. 66.
[12] See esp. chapters 2–4 and 13.

those we love – think of Abraham with his knife raised in obedient faith over his son Isaac. Is this not the sort of love that leads to Inquisitions and Jihads, where innocent victims pay the price for the faithful's blind love for their God?

It is easier to ask such questions than to answer them! They open up issues that would take a further book to address and have occupied Christian theologians and philosophers for centuries.[13] However, we can say this: while human love for God throughout the Bible takes the form of utter commitment, such allegiance is not blind. Beside me on a metal filing cabinet is a fridge magnet with the words 'Give thanks to the LORD, for he is good.'[14] This is just one example of how Scripture insists, in myriad ways, that God is worthy of our love: in him is no evil at all. The witness of both Testaments is that God is *unlike* all other gods. His electing love is unbreakable, passionate, forgiving and orientated to his people's blessing. The vast disparity between divine and human love does not negate the reality that human love for God, while commanded, is *love*. He is not to be loved with our eyes closed and fingers crossed. He is to be loved wholeheartedly because he alone is worthy of such *worship*. Psalm 33 is one example:

> Sing joyfully to the LORD, you righteous;
> it is fitting for the upright to praise him.
> Praise the LORD with the harp;
> make music to him on the ten-stringed lyre.
> Sing to him a new song;
> play skilfully, and shout for joy.
>
> For the word of the LORD is right and true;
> he is faithful in all he does.
> The LORD loves righteousness and justice;
> the earth is full of his unfailing love.[15]

Worship embodies a complete orientation of life. It takes the form, we may say, of devotion and praxis. It is inspired by God's prior love and forgiveness (Hos. 1 – 3; Deut. 10:12–22; 1 John 4:7–10; Rom. 5:1–11; Eph. 2:1–10; Luke 7:36–50; John 15:9–17). It leads to lives shaped by humility, gratitude and obedience. We should not be afraid to admit a profound paradox here: the command to love God with heart, soul and strength is to say that 'You will find

---

[13] See Werner G. Jeanrond, *A Theology of Love* (London: T&T Clark, 2010), for a tour through the theological history of Christian love.
[14] Ps. 136:1.
[15] Ps. 33:1–5.

freedom in submitting yourself completely to God's will.' Such absolute commitment is, at the same time, a voluntary act.

Where New Testament worship departs from Jewish understanding is in how Jesus is given the same sort of utter commitment and wholehearted love as God in the Old Testament. Two examples appear in this book but it is a pervasive theme throughout the New Testament.[16] Nowhere is gratitude for forgiveness more beautifully expressed than in the woman's exemplary 'great love' for Jesus in Luke 7. Elsewhere Jesus makes the astonishing demand that disciples love him above every loyalty, even family. To be a disciple within the kingdom of God is to lose your life.[17]

All of this is a very long way indeed from a sugar-coated discipleship that promises nothing but blessings, unconditional love, affirmation and self-fulfilment, which disfigures so much of contemporary Christianity. Such 'cheap love' is symptomatic of a Western culture in which love has been detached from its biblical moorings and overloaded with unrealistic expectations. The reasons behind love's exaltation are well described by the husband–wife team of German sociologists Ulrich Beck and Elisabeth Beck-Gernsheim:

> Love is glorified largely because it represents a sort of refuge in the chilly environment of our affluent, impersonal, uncertain society, stripped of its traditions and scarred by all kinds of risk ... weighed down by expectations and frustrations, 'love' is the new centre round which our detraditionalised life revolves.[18]

Simon May's incisive analysis lists the burdens love now carries:

> the more individualistic we become the more we expect love to be a secular journey for the soul, a final source of meaning and freedom, a supreme standard of value, a key to the problem of identity, a solace in the face of rootlessness, a desire for the worldly and simultaneously a desire to transcend it, a redemption from suffering, and, a promise of eternity. Or all of these at once.[19]

But Christian love cannot be had without cost. As we have seen throughout this book, love is difficult, not easy: it requires repentance

[16] Bruce W. Longenecker, *Contours of Christology in the New Testament* (Grand Rapids: Eerdmans, 2005).

[17] See chapter 10.

[18] Ulrich Beck and Elisabeth Beck-Gernsheim, *The Normal Chaos of Love*, tr. Mark Ritter and Jane Wiebel (Cambridge: Polity, 1995), pp. 2–3.

[19] Simon May, *Love: A History* (London: Yale University Press, 2011), p. 239.

and humility, a faith dependent on God's grace and the empowering presence of his Spirit. Love takes time to develop, it is a hard-won virtue that develops over time as the result of moral choices to walk with the Spirit and live a life in the world shaped by the story of the gospel.

From start to finish the Bible is a story of relationship, encounter and human *experience* of God. Human love for God is therefore anything but abstract theory. Again this is a major biblical theme that previous chapters have touched on along the way. Yahweh's remarkable dialogues with Moses lead to the dramatic scene of his being allowed to see and experience something of God's fearsome presence. Love for God in the Shema is far more than mere obedience: it embraces all of our humanity – heart, soul and strength – and impacts every aspect of daily life. Similarly later in Deuteronomy 10 the people of Israel need to circumcise their hearts and turn in repentance to God so that they can love him heart and soul. In Hosea Israel experiences the unmerited forgiving and tender love of God. These are only flavours of Old Testament experience of God but they reveal the profound depth of encounter between God and his people, the nature of which continues into the New Testament. One subject our texts in part 1 did not overlap with was the Spirit. While present throughout the Old Testament, the Spirit generally is given to particular people for particular tasks. It is here where New Testament *discontinuity* of believers' experience of love of God becomes most pronounced. For example, in 1 John to know God is to love. John does not explain how this works in detail, but the Spirit is integral to his theology.[20] It is in Paul in whom believers' experience of the Spirit takes centre stage.[21] God's forgiveness in Christ needs to be appropriated in faith through the Spirit. In doing so, believers *experience* God as never before as his love is 'poured out into our hearts through the Holy Spirit'.[22] The gift of the Spirit leads to adoption, as God's beloved children can even call him '*Abba,* Father'.[23] Even Moses' powerful encounters with Yahweh cannot compare with such unfettered access to God's loving presence. Nothing in all creation can separate a believer 'from the love of God that is Christ Jesus our Lord'.[24]

Human love for God is, at heart, *trust.* This, at root, was Abraham's test (and we should note that his hand was stayed and an

[20] E.g. 1 John 3:24.
[21] A classic text is Gordon Fee, *God's Empowering Presence: The Holy Spirit in the Letters of Paul* (Peabody: Hendrickson, 1994).
[22] Rom. 5:5.
[23] Gal. 4:6.
[24] Rom. 8:39; cf. Eph. 3:16–19.

alternative sacrifice provided by God). It was lack of trust that led to Israel's great apostasy in the Sinai desert (Exod. 32 – 34). In Deuteronomy 6 Israel are told to be careful not to forget the Lord as they encounter temptations of wealth, worship (idolatry) and worry (that God would fail them in times of need). Hosea begins with a dramatic picture of betrayal and shattered trust. This, in microcosm, is the challenge of the Old Testament story. Despite God's *ḥesed* love, his people's unfaithfulness eventually leads to the catastrophe of exile. A New Testament example of distorted love is love of money (1 Tim. 6).[25] The 'dynamics' of the destructive power of idolatry remain the same throughout Scripture. This is why Augustine's insight that we are lovers and the definitive spiritual question as to what or whom we will love has been so useful in this book. The 'task' of believers is to 'love rightly' by giving themselves fully to their Lord above all other loyalties. Such rightly ordered love leads to a life of human flourishing.

The bond between love and trust brings us back to our earlier question about loving God in the midst of pain and suffering. Is it, as Simon May argues, that 'loving demands unreserved submission to the laws of the ultimately inscrutable loved one'?[26] By this he means that a real relationship with God, who is the source of our being, requires 'stubborn acceptance and offers no predictable or calculable benefits'.[27] Job is May's prime example. At the heart of a genuine love-relationship with God is a willingness to receive good or bad from his hand (Job 2:10). No answer to the question 'Why suffering?' is given by God or should be sought. Rather trust in, and love for, God means submitting to his will in the face of suffering. While May, I think, overplays God's unknowability, he is on to something profoundly important. In both Testaments there are no guarantees of quid pro quo blessings in loving God. Christians follow a crucified Messiah. Discipleship means death to self and a willingness to die physically. Loving enemies brings no guarantee that they will love back.[28] In Paul suffering is to be expected, even if it will not have the last word because of God's love in Christ and the eschatological hope of his victory.

b. Does love of God deny our humanity?

A final question remains concerning human love for God: does it deny our humanity? This is important to discuss, even if briefly,

[25] See chapter 17.
[26] May, *Love: A History*, p. 31.
[27] Ibid., p. 32.
[28] See chapter 11.

because it represents a significant objection to Christianity – most famously expressed by Nietzsche. He despised Christian love because rather than affirming life and all it offers, he saw it as a form of escapism that exalts selflessness and humility while fostering guilt and weakness.[29] As May summarizes it, 'The result is to set us against ourselves. We are incited to hate what is real – our own nature and the world of change and adversity in which it is located – and to love what is unreal.'[30] Thus, ironically, for Nietzsche *hatred* of nature, of life and of ourselves is what drives 'the religion of love'. It must be said that for some strands of anti-worldly Christian spirituality, particularly around the body, sex and pleasure, he has a point.[31] But Nietzsche's negative description of Christian love is simply unrecognizable from the dynamic, courageous and challenging calling of love within the New Testament. It is with consideration of the wonderful good news of God's agenda for his people as a community of love that we will close this book.

4. Love in community: a vision of a flourishing life

Earlier we talked about how, today, it is Christians who are often seen as the opponents of love.[32] Within post-Christendom generally the Christian church faces a crisis of credibility, 'out on its own', now the prop of a supportive wider culture has been removed. This reality poses a deep challenge for the mission of the church, but is one that should be welcomed. The only 'strategy' the church has is renewal from within – to *be* a compelling testimony to the power and beauty of love, which overflows into the world. We can tinker all we like with externals like vision and mission statements, new programmes and ministries, attractive facilities, good-quality coffee, charismatic leaders, excellence in preaching, precise theological orthodoxy and so on, but unless churches are attractive communities of compelling love reflecting the self-giving character of our triune God, we are wasting our time. Our calling as disciples of Jesus is to be known for scandalous and unpredictable love, a love that loves for love's sake rather than for any other agenda. Love is the 'evidence'

---

[29] Friedrich Nietzsche, *Beyond Good and Evil*, *Ecce Homo* and *On the Genealogy of Morals* in *The Basic Writings of Nietzsche*, tr. W. Kaufman (New York: Modern Library, 1967), discussed in May, *Love: A History*, pp. 190–198.

[30] May, *Love: A History*, p. 191.

[31] See chapter 5 for discussion of the negative legacy of Augustine's theology of sex and the body.

[32] See the introduction.

that the Christian faith truly 'works' and leads to a life of human flourishing.[33]

Love for others in both Testaments shares the same theological foundation, the imitation of God – a point that has surfaced at various points in parts 1 to 4. It is as they imitate God that God's people will reflect his beauty to the rest of the world. However, as with the previous two strands of love in the Bible, we see both continuity and discontinuity in the story of 'horizontal love'.

'Love your neighbour as yourself'[34] summarizes how Israel was to be a community of justice. That justice was even to overflow beyond the boundaries of Israel: 'The foreigner residing among you must be treated as your native-born. Love them as yourself, for you were foreigners in Egypt. I am the LORD your God.'[35] As discussed earlier, this command to love the foreigner is reiterated in Deuteronomy but with the additional rationale that Israel is to love this way because Yahweh 'defends the cause of the fatherless and the widow, and loves the foreigner'.[36] In the New Testament we see this same pattern of divine imitation but with a revolutionary new perspective because neighbour-love is comprehensively reimagined in the light of the life, teaching and death of Jesus Christ.

That transition begins with the radical teaching of Jesus himself: discipleship within the kingdom of God means loving enemies. The parable of the good Samaritan is effectively neighbour-love redefined as enemy-love. While based on the imitation of God – they are to show mercy because their Father is merciful (Luke 6:36) – such love is unprecedented. The authority for such new teaching rests entirely with Jesus: he claims absolute allegiance, even to death.[37] Disciples are now to imitate him as they imitate God. As discussed in chapter 11, it is a historical fact that, as followers of a crucified and non-violent Messiah, the first Christians were deeply committed to a life of non-violence within the world.

In John's Gospel there is a fascinating and beautiful cycle of imitation going on, but it now has a profoundly Christ-centred character: the Father loves the Son; the Son loves the disciples as he has been loved by the Father; the disciples love one another as they have been loved by Jesus.[38] Similarly in John's first letter love

---

[33] For more discussion of Christianity as a 'flourishing life' see Miroslav Volf and Matthew Croasmun, *For the Life of the World: Theology That Makes a Difference* (Grand Rapids: Brazos, 2019).

[34] Lev. 19:18.

[35] Lev. 19:34.

[36] Deut. 10:18–19.

[37] See chapter 10.

[38] John 15:9–17.

takes concrete expression of being like Jesus in the world.[39] Belief and behaviour are inextricably linked: to know God is to love one's brothers and sisters in a Christlike way.[40] In Jesus' great prayer for believers in John 17 it is through such love that the outside world will experience the love of the Father: 'Then the world will know that you sent me and have loved them even as you have loved me.'[41]

Turning to Paul, it will suffice to give just a flavour of how his theology of neighbour-love is transformed in the light of Christ. Recall how his overriding concern as a missionary pastor was for the moral transformation of communities under his care as they awaited the coming of Christ.[42] At the heart of that transformation was an experience of God through faith in Christ and the empowering gift of the Spirit. As a result, membership of the covenant community is thrown wide open. Only love can hold such communities together and Paul expounds a breathtaking and innovative theology of neighbour-love in his letters to these new churches.

Chapter 14 examined how 1 Corinthians 13 describes human love that imitates that of God. No text in the New Testament testifies more eloquently to the deeply humanizing power of Christian love. Contrary to Nietzsche and all who see love as 'weak', here is tough love in action and it is *good*. Christian love is not mystical, nor passive docility; nor is it a pragmatic strategy to attain a goal: it is a way of life that imitates God's character and actions in the world, and in doing so is a foretaste of the world to come.

In Galatians it is horrifying to some that the covenant community could now include Torah-free Gentiles. Boundaries of religion, socio-economic status and gender are relativized (Gal. 3:28; cf. Col. 3:11). Neighbour-love is now based theologically on believers' union in Christ through the Spirit and their common experience of God as *Abba*. It is love that is the defining characteristic of this subversive community within the ancient world. Such love completes God's original covenant with Abraham and fulfils the law. It is forgiving relationships of mutual love that are powerful evidence of the presence of the Spirit and a foretaste of God's future. Again, as in John, while the overriding focus is love within the community of the church, love is not to be kept to itself but is to be shared practically with all people (Gal. 6:10).[43]

---

[39] 1 John 4:17.

[40] 1 John 4:20–21.

[41] John 17:23; cf. 13:35.

[42] See esp. chapter 15.

[43] Elsewhere in Paul love is the motive for his apostolic ministry of reconciliation that tries to persuade others of the gospel of Christ (2 Cor. 5:14).

In Ephesians Christocentric neighbour-love takes an even more dominant role: as beloved children within a diverse community believers are to be 'imitators of God' and are to 'walk in love, as Christ loved us and gave himself up for us'.[44] God's love creates a community of love and unity that implicitly undermines the social, political, cultural and gender hierarchies of the ancient world. In doing so it speaks beautifully of God's grace and the transforming power of the Spirit.[45] As we discussed in chapter 16, this is the context in which Christian marriage is reimagined – husbands in particular are to imitate Christ in setting aside power and status in favour of self-giving love. Marriage is not a private arrangement between two individuals; rather it is a covenant between two Christians who belong within the community of the church. It is also here that we need the whole Bible. Despite the negative legacy of Augustine and others concerning the body and love, Pauline teaching on marriage in no way negates the beautiful and physically affirming teaching on mutual love, sex and desire within the Song of Songs.[46]

All of this is to emphasize how the overwhelming emphasis in the New Testament is that the community of the people of God are to *embody* love. Love is the way of Jesus, and his disciples are to follow his lead. It is in loving one another that spiritual battles are fought – paradoxically love is God's prime 'weapon' in that war.[47] It is in and through love that the church is to become the attractive 'better place' that God has called us to be on behalf of the world.[48] In doing so she points to the 'better place' to come – when God's kingdom comes in all its glory and when 'we shall see face to face'.[49]

Now perhaps this sounds as if Christian love involves a turning in on itself with its back to the world? Is it not the church's primary vocation to be outward focused? Someone stating this objection might say:

Of course, the church should have her own house in order relationally and be busy teaching and proclaiming the gospel. If we do not, we will lack credibility. Yes, we await a final consummation of the kingdom and cannot create heaven on earth

---

[44] Eph. 5:1–2, ESVUK.

[45] See chapter 9.

[46] See chapter 5.

[47] See esp. chapter 15 for love within a battle with the flesh, desires and cosmic powers.

[48] John C. Nugent, *Endangered Gospel: How Fixing the World Is Killing the Church* (Eugene: Cascade, 2016).

[49] 1 Cor. 13:12.

ourselves. But has not the kingdom already arrived with Jesus? Is not the mission of the church to join in with God in helping to transform our local communities and even nations while working for political and social justice? Is not the calling of the church to hold power to account? Should we not be caring for God's good creation, especially since we face an impending ecological crisis?

I admit I have huge sympathy with this view, but writing this book has only confirmed its shortcomings, particularly its weak ecclesiology. Each chapter has reinforced for me how 'horizontal love' in the Bible concerns the spiritual flourishing of the community of the people of God as they imitate their God. *There is virtually no focus, Old Testament or New, on transforming the world outside the covenant community.* Love for God and one another is to be the defining focus of the people of God throughout the Bible. For example, John Barclay argues that what is remarkable is just how *insignificant* the Roman Empire is in the thinking of Paul.[50] Or, as McKnight argues, the church is to be an 'alternative politic' to the politics of the world by being 'a witness to the world of a new worship, a new law, a new king, a new social order, a new peace, a new justice, a new economics, and a new way of life'.[51] In other words, *the primary task of the church is to be the church* – to be a foretaste of God's kingdom come in the present and to invite others into it. This is God's 'mission strategy' for the world and therefore it should be ours. This is not, as is frequently misunderstood, a programme for a type of monastic retreat into religious communities detached from the world: 'A church that does not exist for the world does not exist as the church.'[52] It is as churches live up to their God-given vocation that their inner dynamic of love will 'overflow' into their local communities – this is the 'inside-out' sort of love that I discussed in chapter 13.[53]

Perhaps this all sounds light years away from your experience of church. Maybe you despair at times of what seems like an unbridgeable gap between the New Testament's high theology of love and reality on the ground. If so, it is worth bearing in mind that

[50] John Barclay, *Pauline Churches and Diaspora Jews* (Grand Rapids: Eerdmans, 2016; first published in Tübingen by Mohr Siebeck, 2011), pp. 363–388. See also Scot McKnight and Joe Modica (eds.), *Jesus Is Lord, Caesar Is Not: Evaluating Empire in New Testament Studies* (Downers Grove: IVP Academic, 2013).

[51] Scot McKnight, *Kingdom Conspiracy: Returning to the Radical Mission of the Local Church* (Grand Rapids: Brazos, 2014), p. 101.

[52] Nugent, *Endangered Gospel*, p. 204.

[53] John 15:9–17. See Nugent, *Endangered Gospel*, pp. 166–191, and McKnight, *Kingdom Conspiracy*, pp. 111–118, for more extensive discussion of what this looks like in practice.

Paul and John's magnificent teaching on love developed within situations of relational conflict, heresy, immorality, identity conflict and greed.[54] It is *because* of our human fallibility that we need to understand, teach and practise the New Testament's glorious vision of love, and it is my prayer that this book will be of help in that task. It is not our job to imitate the world; it is our joy, rather, to imitate the triune God of love: Father, Son and Holy Spirit. The theology of love is redrawn in the light of the Son, sent by the Father in the power of the Spirit. It is our privilege and gift to have been drawn into that relationship of love. As a consequence, love is our motive to preach and teach that gospel while demonstrating its tangible power in deep relationship with others through the transforming work of the Spirit, whose fruit is love.

More personally, no one else can 'walk in love' for us. John's words 'Let us love' invite each of us to put our lives under 'the searing searchlight of love'. Am I willing to obey Jesus' command to love? Humbly to die to myself? To forgive? To treat lack of love as scandalous? To be a person of unity and reconciliation? Not to destroy relationships through greed but foster them through generosity? To bear others' burdens? To care for those in need? And to love across the deep divisions of race, gender, status and power that characterize our modern world? Practising such faith, Paul would say, is 'the only thing that counts'.[55]

---

[54] In mind here are Galatians, Romans, 1 Corinthians, Ephesians and 1 Timothy.
[55] Gal. 5:6.

Study Guide

HOW TO USE THIS STUDY GUIDE

The aim of this study guide is to help you get to the heart of what Patrick has written and challenge you to apply what you learn to your own life. The questions have been designed for use by individuals or by small groups of Christians meeting, perhaps for an hour or two each week, to study, discuss and pray together. When used by a group with limited time, the leader should decide beforehand which questions are most appropriate for the group to discuss during the meeting and which should perhaps be left for group members to work through by themselves or in smaller groups during the week.

PREVIEW. Use the guide, along with the contents pages, chapter and section headings, as a map to become familiar with what you are about to read, your 'journey' through the book.

READ. Look up the Bible passages as well as the text.

ANSWER. As you read look for the answers to the questions in the guide.

DISCUSS. Even if you are studying on your own try to find another person to share your thoughts with.

REVIEW. Use the guide as a tool to remind you what you have learned. The best way of retaining what you learn is to write it down in a notebook or journal.

APPLY. Translate what you have learned into your attitudes and actions, considering your relationship with God, your personal life, your family life, your working life, your church life, your role as a citizen and your world-view.

Introduction: What is love? (pp. 1–13)

1 What diagnosis of love is presented by James K. A. Smith (pp. 1–2)?
2 How does love reveal itself according to Thomas Jay Oord and what are the implications (pp. 2–4)?

3 In what five ways is 'love' understood in the twenty-first century and what critique can we offer (pp. 4–9)?
4 What two compelling reasons demonstrate the need to reflect clearly and biblically about love (pp. 9–11)?
5 How does the author explore the theme of love and how significant is it for theology (pp. 11–13)?

PART 1. LOVE IN THE OLD TESTAMENT

Exodus 34:6–7
1. Abounding in love, punishing the guilty
(pp. 17–29)

1 What details indicate the seriousness of the people's actions in the golden calf incident (pp. 17–19)?

'Israel are now rewriting history and changing their allegiance in the process. The past is being refashioned, as it often still is today, to fit the agendas of the present' (p. 18).

---

2 What three themes in the conversations between God and Moses are highlighted as relevant to the question of God's love and judgment (pp. 20–21)?
3 How is the essential nature of Israel's God revealed to Moses (pp. 21–22)?
4 What is the meaning of *ḥesed* and how is it reflected in 1 John 4:8 (pp. 22–23)?
5 How are we to understand the apparent injustice of later generations being punished for the sins of their forebears (p. 23)?
6 Why is the widespread belief that the Hebrew Bible is all about vengeance and 'an eye for an eye' unfounded (pp. 23–24)?
7 What would have been the consequences of justice without love (pp. 24–25)?
8 Why is Exodus 33 – 34 relevant for Christians today (pp. 25–26)?
9 How does 'Love is God' work out in practice and why is it false teaching (pp. 26–28)?
10 What does Moses' experience tell us about God and what is the 'astonishing' claim made by Paul in the New Testament (pp. 28–29)?

Deuteronomy 10:12–22
2. God's love for the outsider (pp. 30–41)

1 What are the causes, scale and consequences of the current refugee problem (pp. 30–31)?
2 How is Deuteronomy structured and what are the five obligations in 10:12–13 (pp. 31–32)?

'Love is core to the five obligations and, given its prominence in the book as a whole, it is possible to see the other four as practical outworkings of what it means for Israel to love their God' (p. 32).

---

3 How are verses 14–16 and 17–19 creatively structured in parallel (p. 33)?
4 In what way are verses 14 and 17 powerful reminders (pp. 33–34)?
5 Where does the focus move in verses 15 and 17b–18 and what questions does it raise (pp. 34–36)?
6 'Verse 16 takes aim at Israel's hearts and necks . . .' What is meant by this (p. 37)?
7 What is not, and what is, the motive for Christian love in the world today (p. 38)?
8 How are the themes of love and justice reiterated throughout Scripture (pp. 38–40)?
9 In what way has hard-edged capitalist culture influenced the church in the West (pp. 40–41)?

Hosea 1 – 3
3. God the betrayed, yet persistent, lover (pp. 42–55)

1 What is the 'stunning image of God that we are confronted with in Hosea' and what is the significance of the Hebrew word *'āhab* (pp. 42–43)?
2 What is the historical and literary setting of Hosea 1 – 3 (pp. 43–44)?
3 Why is Hosea 'a mysterious book' and what options have been suggested for the relationships it describes (pp. 44–45)?
4 How do the names given to Hosea's children contribute to the 'gathering sense of doom' and why is the outcome unexpected (pp. 45–47)?
5 What two themes dominate Hosea's message to Israel and how are they developed in chapter 2 (pp. 47–50)?

6 How are the themes of chapters 1 and 2 developed in chapter 3 (p. 51)?

7 What does God's 'extraordinary campaign' reveal and how is that portrayal reflected in the New Testament (pp. 51–53)?

8 What is meant by 'cheap grace' and in what way does the message of Hosea exclude that concept (pp. 53–54)?

9 What are the two challenges Hosea poses for Christian love today (pp. 54–55)?

Deuteronomy 6:4–25
4. Love the Lord your God (pp. 56–65)

1 What is the Shema and what options are there for translating it (pp. 56–57)?

'Such is our obsession with love, it is not too much to say that it is a modern idol – something we pursue with all of our being. Yet in Hosea, love is obedience to God; it is corporate rather than individualistic, it is not about self-fulfilment but disciplined faithfulness' (p. 55).

---

2 What is meant by three-dimensional listening and what is cognitive learning (p. 57)?

3 In what three ways may we understand the oneness of God (pp. 57–58)?

4 What is meant by affective listening (p. 58)?

5 How should the *command* to love be understood (pp. 58–60)?

6 What three warnings are given in verses 10–19 (pp. 60–61)?

7 In what sense can loving God be said to be behavioural (pp. 61–62)?

8 How does Perry Shaw's approach to theological education tie in with holistic love in practice (pp. 62–63)?

9 What five lessons from the Shema can we apply today (pp. 63–65)?

Song of Songs 4 – 5
5. Erotic love (pp. 66–82)

1 What do the writings of Joy Davidman and C. S. Lewis reveal about erotic love (pp. 66–67)?

2 Why is the Song of Songs important for a study on love in the Bible and what challenges does its exegesis present (pp. 67–71)?

3 What mistakes are to be avoided in interpreting the Song of Songs (pp. 70–71)?

4 What metaphors are used in the 'adoring male gaze' and how should we understand them (pp. 71–74)?

'The day-to-day destructive impact of the male gaze on women is probably impossible to overestimate – especially if you are a man. It is the driving force behind the pornographic revolution of our Internet age – there would not be pornography without 'market demand'. But there is such a thing as a 'rightly directed' male gaze and it is described here in verses 1–7' (p. 72).

---

5 How does the 2012 Report prepared for the NSPCC under-line the contemporary relevance of the Song of Songs (pp. 74–75)?

6 Why does Garrett suggest that 4:16 – 5:1 is the structural centre-piece of the whole book (pp. 75–76)?

7 How should we understand the detail of the way the woman describes her lover (pp. 76–78)?

8 In what six ways should the Song of Songs shape our thinking today (pp. 78–82)?

Interlude (pp. 83–87)

1 Why was it for good reason that Marcion was declared a heretic (p. 83)?

2 In a biblical theology of love what does the 'outer circle' represent (pp. 83–84)?

3 What is the 'second circle' (p. 84)?

4 What is the redemptive work which constitutes the 'third circle' (pp. 84–85)?

5 What is the 'fourth, inner circle' and in what way is it connected to the outer circle (pp. 85–86)?

6 What is the Septuagint and how significant is its usage of the words *agapē*, *agapaō* and *phileō* (p. 86)?

7 How does the New Testament differ in its words for love and why do we need to be cautious about conclusions based on linguistic usage (pp. 86–87)?

PART 2. THE LOVE OF GOD REVEALED IN THE MISSION AND DEATH OF JESUS CHRIST

Mark 1:1–15
6. 'You are my Son, whom I love' (pp. 91–103)

1 In what way had Israel's dreams faded in the period before the coming of Jesus and how had they responded (p. 91)?
2 What is meant by all the Gospels doing 'retrospective theology' (p. 92)?
3 What three concerns are evident from the very beginning of Mark's Gospel (pp. 92–93)?
4 What role does John the Baptist play in Mark's introduction to Jesus (pp. 93–94)?
5 What questions are raised by Mark's introduction and how does he answer them (pp. 94–95)?
6 What is the significance of Jesus' baptism and in what two ways did Jesus receive divine affirmation (pp. 95–96)?
7 What is the Old Testament background to Jesus' sonship and how does Mark move us beyond it (pp. 96–98)?
8 Which Old Testament allusions throw light on the Father's love and delight and what are the implications for our understanding of the triune God of love (pp. 99–101)?
9 What is the tension running through the prologue of Mark and why is it good news (pp. 101–103)?

1 John 4:7–10
7. God is love (pp. 104–118)

1 How far do you identify with the situation described here (p. 104)?
2 Why is 1 John 4:7–14 an impossible text to ignore (pp. 105–106)?
3 What are the clues within 1 John that help explain his emphasis on love and how do they apply to the church today (pp. 106–108)?

'Imagining that we hold the power to control spiritual renewal makes hearing what God has to say to us almost impossible and repentance unnecessary. It precludes space for critical self-reflection in how we might be deeply compromised in our love lives – our love of the world and all it offers' (p. 108).

---

4 What is significant about (a) John's use of *agapōmen* and (b) the description *God is love* (p. 109)?
5 'The vertical shapes the horizontal.' What does this mean (pp. 109–110)?
6 How does the sending of Jesus reveal the 'bigger' story of God (pp. 110–111)?
7 What is meant by the 'dialectical tension between exaltation and humility' in Johannine love (pp. 111–113)?
8 In what ways does Johannine love come into conflict with post-Enlightenment secular popular culture (pp. 113–114)?
9 How should we understand the word *hilasmos* and what are its implications (pp. 114–116)?
10 What seven conclusions can we draw from John's exposition of love (pp. 116–118)?

Romans 5:1–11
8. Love and justification (pp. 119–131)

1 Do you think of Paul primarily as an 'apostle of love' (pp. 119–120)?
2 How is the context within which Romans was written reflected in its objectives (pp. 120–121)?
3 What framework does Paul use at this stage of his argument (pp. 121–122)?
4 What are the three dimensions of God's justifying love (pp. 122–123)?

'What is astonishing is how Paul clearly understands Jesus to be not only the Son of God in the sense of being God's chosen kingly Messiah and descendant of David but also the pre-existing eternal Son, sent by his Father into the world and whose resurrection reveals his true identity' (p. 124).

---

5 Why is Christology inseparable from justification and how does Paul highlight it (pp. 123–124)?
6 What is the significance of the terms *Christ*, *Son* and *Lord* (pp. 124–125)?
7 In what two ways is God's love experienced in the present (pp. 125–127)?
8 How does the future hope expressed by Paul differ from human positive thinking (pp. 127–128)?
9 What does it mean in practical terms to be called to a life of love (pp. 128–129)?

10 How can God's love be reconciled with suffering (pp. 129–130)?
11 Why is it important to retain the reality of divine judgment (pp. 130–131)?

Ephesians 2:1–10
9. God's great love (pp. 132–145)

1 What is reflective practice and how is it illustrated in Paul the pastor (pp. 132–133)?
2 What evidence is there that love forms the central and overall purpose of Ephesians (pp. 133–134)?
3 How do you respond to 'the gospel of self-esteem on steroids' (pp. 134–135)?
4 How does Paul diagnose the human condition in verses 1–3 (pp. 135–137)?
5 With what two associated ideas does Paul explore the nature and scope of God's immeasurable love (pp. 137–138)?
6 What four important dimensions of this passage shed light on the love of God (pp. 138–140)?
7 How should we evaluate the contributions of Luther, Yancey, Barclay and Bonhoeffer (pp. 140–141)?
8 What does it mean to 'walk in love' and how is this priority emphasized throughout Ephesians (pp. 141–144)?
9 What five applications can be drawn from this chapter (pp. 144–145)?

PART 3. LOVE IN THE LIFE AND TEACHING OF JESUS

Matthew 10:34–39
10. The cost of love (pp. 149–160)

1 How do you respond to the questions at the head of this chapter (p. 149)?
2 What three interrelated themes form the broader context of Matthew 10:34–39 (pp. 149–151)?
3 Why is the mission of Jesus couched in such troubling imagery (pp. 151–153)?
4 Why does Jesus choose familial love as a foil for his demands (p. 153)?

'Many people today imagine Jesus as a man preaching a message of universal love and inclusion. While this idea may appeal to our modern notions of tolerance, it has little to do with the Jesus of the New Testament' (p. 152).

5 What does it mean to love Jesus before family and what cultural assumptions does it challenge (pp. 154–156)?
6 What did taking up the cross mean when Jesus first spoke these words and what does it mean for us today (pp. 157–158)?
7 How should we understand the key word *psychē* in these verses (p. 158)?
8 What four insights into the nature of love are contained in Augustine's theology (pp. 159–160)?

Luke 6:27–36; 10:25–37
11. Enemy love (pp. 161–176)

1 How do we define an enemy and in what two ways is it natural to react (pp. 161–162)?
2 How does Luke set the context for Jesus' teaching on loving your enemies (pp. 162–164)?
3 In what way is 'kingdom life' characterized by upside-down values (pp. 163–164)?
4 How are verses 27–36 structured (p. 164)?
5 In what way is Jesus' command more radical than Lev. 19:18 and 10:19 and what three exhortations to practical action does he add (pp. 164–165)?

'The heart of the Sermon is a call to action – of what followers are to do as they navigate a hostile world populated with enemies. The overriding emphasis is that a disciple's love for others should be disarming and disconcerting, subverting normal expectations of love and pointing puzzled enemies to the eschatological future blessings of the kingdom of God' (p. 164).

6 What four challenging illustrations are found in verses 29–30 (pp. 165–166)?
7 What is distinctive about the 'Golden Rule' and how does Jesus illustrate it (pp. 166–167)?
8 Which of the seven suggested applications of Jesus' command resonate most with you (p. 167)?

9 How do verses 35–36 summarize and reiterate earlier themes (p. 168)?
10 How does the parable of the Good Samaritan illustrate Jesus' teaching in the Sermon on the Plain (pp. 168–170)?
11 What are the implications of Jesus' teaching for the church (pp. 170–172)?
12 What are the implications of Jesus' teaching for Christian non-violence (pp. 172–175)?
13 What are the implications of Jesus' teaching for the hope of divine justice and the nature of love itself (pp. 175–176)?

Luke 7:36–50
12. A woman's great love (pp. 177–188)

1 On what grounds should we regard the woman in Luke's account as different from the one in Matthew 26, Mark 14 and John 12 (pp. 177–178)?
2 What sort of occasion is being described and how should we interpret the woman's motives (pp. 178–179)?
3 How have her actions been interpreted and what misinterpretations should be avoided (pp. 179–180)?
4 What does Simon's reaction reveal about him (p. 181)?
5 What two things was Jesus teaching Simon through his parable (pp. 181–183)?
6 What impact should these lessons have on our lives as individuals and as the church today (pp. 182–183)?
7 What was Jesus' purpose in contrasting Simon's conduct with that of the woman (pp. 183–184)?
8 What is the 'significant point easily overlooked' in this account (pp. 184–185)?
9 What are the three things (at least) which the story has to teach us (pp. 185–188)?

John 15:9–17
13. Remain in my love (pp. 189–201)

1 What questions are raised by John 15:9–17 and for what three reasons has the author chosen it (pp. 189–190)?
2 What is the relationship between verses 1–8 and verses 9–17 (p. 190)?
3 How is the Father's love for Jesus illustrated in John's Gospel (pp. 190–192)?

'Divine love is prior to any human love. In the light of this, we may say that for John it is only in God himself that we see what love truly is. The origin of love is God and God alone. For John, the great, basic and glorious truth about God is that love forms the core of his identity and basis for action in the world' (p. 191).

4 What light does the Graeco-Roman culture in Ephesus throw on our understanding of *philos* (pp. 192–193)?
5 Which Old Testament characters are likely to have influenced John's concept of friendship (p. 193)?
6 In what four ways can we apply John 15 today, taking into account its meaning in the ancient world (pp. 193–195)?
7 What is the paradox at the heart of Christian love and what four words capture its tension (pp. 195–197)?
8 How does Jesus' teaching here relate to 'abstract theological' questions about salvation, faith and works (pp. 197–198)?
9 In what way does Jesus' teaching go beyond the Old Testament command to love (pp. 198–199)?
10 What is meant by love from the 'inside out' (p. 199)?
11 How would you respond to the author's ad hoc survey (pp. 199–200)?
12 What three steps should we take in situations of conflict (pp. 200–201)?

PART 4. THE CHURCH AS A COMMUNITY OF LOVE

1 Corinthians 12:31 – 13:13
14. The searing searchlight of love (pp. 205–220)

1 Why is it illegitimate to idealize the abstract idea of love on the basis of 1 Corinthians 13 (pp. 205–206)?
2 Why has Paul chosen his six examples of 'love gone AWOL' (pp. 206–207)?

'However many compliments received about life-changing preaching, however many devoted followers on Twitter, however many books sold or articles written, however popular a blog, however much students hang on our every word, however persuasive our evangelism, however many apologetic debates won, and however many fans rhapsodize about our poetry – all is just mere babble without love' (p. 207).

3 What is the focus of Paul's first example (pp. 207–208)?
4 What is the focus of Paul's next three examples in verse 2 (p. 208)?
5 What is the focus of Paul's fifth example and how do the two stories from Mark reinforce it (pp. 208–209)?
6 Why is Paul's sixth example even more demanding (pp. 209–210)?
7 What critical truth is captured in the Figure 2 diagram (pp. 210–211)?
8 What are the eight positives in Paul's description of the way of love (pp. 211–215)?
9 What are the seven negatives in Paul's description of the way of 'unlove' (pp. 215–218)?
10 What switch of emphasis is key to interpreting verses 8–13 (pp. 218–220)?

Galatians 5:1–23
15. The liberating power of love (pp. 221–232)

1 Why was Paul so concerned for the welfare of the Galatians (pp. 221–222)?
2 What should we understand by the flesh [*sarx*] and the elemental spiritual forces of the world [*stoicheia*] (pp. 222–224)?
3 Why is 5:6 'a scandalous claim' and how does Paul justify it (pp. 224–226)?
4 What constitutes the captivity from which Christ has set us free (pp. 226–227)?
5 What are the positive outcomes of Christian freedom and how do they conflict with the narrative of Western culture today (pp. 227–230)?
6 How does Paul answer the question, 'Where does love come from?' – both negatively and positively (pp. 230–231)?
7 What are the implications of Christian love for our lives today (pp. 231–232)?

Ephesians 5:21–33
16. Subversive love: Christian marriage (pp. 233–251)

1 What two things is it important to bear in mind when exploring love and marriage (pp. 233–234)?
2 What is the context of Ephesians 5:21–33 within the overall flow of the epistle (pp. 234–235)?
3 What relationships within contemporary Roman households were reflected in household codes (pp. 235–236)?

4 What five characteristics distinguish the Ephesian household code (pp. 236–237)?

'*Submission is a profoundly* Christian *concept and forms a notable theme within the New Testament. It defines all relationships between Christians . . . There is no hint of one "side" being required to obey the other here: the sense is a proper ordering of relationships depending on the context in which people find themselves*' (p. 238).

---

5 What evidence is there that submission defines all relationships between Christians (pp. 237–239)?
6 Is Paul laying down timeless 'gender roles' within marriage in this passage (pp. 239–240)?
7 How has male headship been interpreted historically and why is a fresh approach needed (pp. 240–243)?
8 What three arguments does Paul use in his instructions to husbands (pp. 243–246)?
9 What are the distinctive features of Christian love within marriage (pp. 246–247)?
10 What are the implications of recognizing love as ecclesiological rather than personal (pp. 247–249)?
11 What is the particular responsibility of Christian husbands within marriage (pp. 249–251)?

1 Timothy 6:2b–10
17. Love gone wrong: money (pp. 252–268)

1 What does the Bible have to say about money (pp. 252–254)?
2 How does the description of false teachers set the context for teaching about money (pp. 254–255)?
3 What evidence do we have of wealth and its influence within the early church and in the church today (pp. 255–257)?
4 What are the positive benefits of godly contentment (pp. 257–258)?
5 What are the spiritual dangers associated with wealth (pp. 258–259)?
6 What is the connection between love of money and idolatry (pp. 259–260)?
7 'Essentially, *money is power*.' What results from the abuse of that power (pp. 260–261)?
8 What are the four elements of James K. A. Smith's critique of modern consumerism (pp. 262–264)?

9 What are the four questions asked at the beginning of this chapter and how are they answered in Paul's closing charge to Timothy (pp. 265–268)?

Conclusion
A vision for human flourishing (pp. 269–284)

1 What are the three strands of love in the Bible and how do they relate to one another (pp. 269–270)?
2 What is meant by describing God's love as selective, unconditioned but not unconditional, just and forgiving (pp. 270–271)?
3 In what ways does the New Testament continue and complete the Old Testament picture (pp. 271–274)?
4 Can the paradox of love as a free response and yet obedience to a command be resolved (pp. 274–275)?
5 Can the paradox of worship as an absolute commitment and yet a voluntary act be resolved (pp. 275–277)?
6 Which aspect of experiencing God's love in the New Testament goes beyond the Old Testament (p. 277)?
7 How is the bond between love and trust illustrated in Old and New Testaments (pp. 277–278)?
8 Is Nietzsche's criticism of Christian love valid (pp. 278–279)?
9 What is the theological foundation of love for others in both Testaments and how is it developed (pp. 279–282)?
10 How would you answer the criticism that Christian love involves a turning in on itself with its back to the world (pp. 282–284)?

The Bible Speaks Today: Old Testament series

The Bible Speaks Today: New Testament series

The Message of the Sermon on the Mount (Matthew 5 – 7)
Christian counter-culture
John Stott

The Message of Matthew
The kingdom of heaven
Michael Green

The Message of Mark
The mystery of faith
Donald English

The Message of Luke
The Saviour of the world
Michael Wilcock

The Message of John
Here is your King!
Bruce Milne

The Message of Acts
To the ends of the earth
John Stott

The Message of Romans
God's good news for the world
John Stott

The Message of 1 Corinthians
Life in the local church
David Prior

The Message of 2 Corinthians
Power in weakness
Paul Barnett

The Message of Galatians
Only one way
John Stott

The Message of Ephesians
God's new society
John Stott

The Message of Philippians
Jesus our Joy
Alec Motyer

The Message of Colossians and Philemon
Fullness and freedom
Dick Lucas

The Message of Thessalonians
Preparing for the coming King
John Stott

The Message of 1 Timothy and Titus
The life of the local church
John Stott

The Message of 2 Timothy
Guard the gospel
John Stott

The Message of Hebrews
Christ above all
Raymond Brown

The Message of James
The tests of faith
Alec Motyer

The Message of 1 Peter
The way of the cross
Edmund Clowney

The Message of 2 Peter and Jude
The promise of his coming
Dick Lucas and Christopher Green

The Message of John's Letters
Living in the love of God
David Jackman

The Message of Revelation
I saw heaven opened
Michael Wilcock

The Bible Speaks Today: Bible Themes series

The Message of the Living God
His glory, his people, his world
Peter Lewis

The Message of the Resurrection
Christ is risen!
Paul Beasley-Murray

The Message of the Cross
Wisdom unsearchable, love indestructible
Derek Tidball

The Message of Salvation
By God's grace, for God's glory
Philip Graham Ryken

The Message of Creation
Encountering the Lord of the universe
David Wilkinson

The Message of Heaven and Hell
Grace and destiny
Bruce Milne

The Message of Mission
The glory of Christ in all time and space
Howard Peskett and Vinoth Ramachandra

The Message of Prayer
Approaching the throne of grace
Tim Chester

The Message of the Trinity
Life in God
Brian Edgar

The Message of Evil and Suffering
Light into darkness
Peter Hicks

The Message of the Holy Spirit
The Spirit of encounter
Keith Warrington

The Message of Holiness
Restoring God's masterpiece
Derek Tidball

The Message of Sonship
At home in God's household
Trevor Burke

The Message of the Word of God
The glory of God made known
Tim Meadowcroft

The Message of Women
Creation, grace and gender
Derek and Dianne Tidball

The Message of the Church
Assemble the people before me
Chris Green

The Message of the Person of Christ
The Word made flesh
Robert Letham

The Message of Worship
Celebrating the glory of God in the whole of life
John Risbridger

The Message of Spiritual Warfare
The Lord is a warrior; the Lord is his name
Keith Ferdinando

The Message of Discipleship
Authentic followers of Jesus in today's world
Peter Morden

The Message of Love
The only thing that counts
Patrick Mitchel

Printed and bound by CPI Group (UK) Ltd, Croydon, CR0 4YY

13/04/2025

14656471-0002